THE
FACELESS
VILLAIN

A COLLECTION OF THE EERIEST
UNSOLVED MURDERS
OF THE 20TH CENTURY

VOLUME THREE

Jenny Ashford

Photo by Thomas Luisier

Table of Contents

Introduction

When I first started working on *The Faceless Villain* series, way back in late 2016, I had no idea how much it would take over my life, and how each of the hundreds of names of the murder victims I wrote about would be indelibly etched into my psyche.

I've always been fascinated by true crime, as I'm sure most of the readers of this series are, but I sometimes struggle with the moral ambiguity of it all, as I believe I mentioned in the introduction of *Volume One*. You definitely have to have a certain type of mindset to find these types of cases entertaining, for lack of a better word, but I would argue that what I and most other true crime junkies find so fascinating is not necessarily the grisly details of the crimes themselves—though those are a draw; I'm not going to lie—but rather the opportunity to use our capacity for deductive reasoning to try and solve the crimes ourselves.

As a matter of fact, writing these three books has really given me a new appreciation for law enforcement and other individuals who investigate these crimes, and has also inspired me to get more involved in amateur sleuthing, in the hopes of one day being able to help bring at least one family peace, and perhaps also bring a murderer to justice.

Just as in the first two volumes of this series, I used a somewhat stringent but also idiosyncratic method for curating the cases included herein. As before, I tended to leave out political assassinations and mob hits, unless the case was too well known to omit, or otherwise had aspects that made it particularly interesting or mysterious. I also didn't include cases with few details reported; state databases, I discovered, are depressingly filled with unsolved homicides, but some of them merited only a sentence or two of description, for whatever reason, and these I opted to exclude from the narrative.

This time around, I did feature a few disappearances, if they were believed to be linked to other murders in a series (for example, the Highway of Tears or the Texas Killing Fields slayings), and in a similar situation I also talked about a few connected homicides that were actually solved. I also focused on a few cases where the killer was almost certainly known, but died before being brought to justice. As in the first and second volumes, I stuck with a mostly chronological narrative, though I skipped ahead at times if clarity seemed to warrant it.

I want to thank each and every one of you for coming along on this three-year journey with me through the twentieth century, and I hope you enjoy this final installment. I'm planning to tackle some more true crime for my future projects, as it has become a greater and greater obsession over the past few years as I wrote and researched this series.

Be well, and keep trying to solve the unsolvable.

1980

The town of Montverde, less than forty miles from downtown Orlando in central Florida, was home to less than four-hundred residents in 1980, and was bordered by Lake Apopka on one side and vast stretches of scenic orange groves on the other. It was also the kind of place where everyone knew their neighbors, and no one locked their doors at night. This small-town utopia, however, would be irrevocably scarred in the spring of that fateful year.

Georgia Jane Crews was a pretty, blonde twelve-year-old who was active in her local Methodist church, enjoyed sewing her own clothes, and was a big fan of country music legend Kenny Rogers. In fact, on the late afternoon of April 8th, 1980, Georgia was planning to go to her best friend's house to watch her idol in the TV movie *The Gambler,* and thought she might also drop into the Stop & Go convenience store along the way to pick up a few snacks.

Earlier that afternoon, her parents Linda and Mike, who were commercial fishermen, had gone to nearby Lake Florence to lay out their catfish lines. They had taken their fifteen-year-old son Charles along with them, but sixteen-year-old Tony had stayed back at the Crews' Highland Avenue home with his little sister Georgia. At around five-thirty p.m., Tony and a friend were listening to records in the house when Georgia told them she was heading out. The girl was accompanied by her faithful and much beloved bulldog, Tiger.

More than an hour went by. The friend that Georgia was supposed to be visiting claimed she never turned up. Tony Crews began to worry, and discovered that his sister hadn't been seen at the convenience store either. When the rest of the Crews family returned from their work, everyone began scouring the neighborhood for the missing girl, but ominously, all they found was Tiger, who sat resolutely at a crossroads near the Crews home and refused to budge. There was also a trail of child-size footprints that meandered partway up an adjacent dirt road before stopping abruptly.

The tiny, close-knit community was sent into a panic, as not only had a sweet, innocent young girl completely vanished, but no one in town had seen a single suspicious thing. Had a stranger been responsible for taking Georgia, they reasoned, then surely this individual would have stood out, been noticed; this did not seem to be this case. This led many residents to the uncomfortable conclusion that the kidnapper may have been one of their own. Over the subsequent days, more than half of Montverde's population rallied all of their attention and resources into searching for Georgia.

On April 10th, two days after the child's disappearance, the phone rang at the Crews household. A male voice on the other end of the line said flatly, "Hello...you know that girl that you're looking for...yeah, the twelve-year-old... yeah, she's dead." Both Georgia's grandmother and the wife of the town marshal received similar phone calls, but none of them was able to be traced.

Despite these horrifying messages, the Crews family was still holding out some hope that Georgia would be found alive. But less than a week later, their hopes would be cruelly dashed.

On April 16th, an unnamed family was taking a popular shortcut from their apartment complex to the back of a K-Mart store in Casselberry, approximately twenty-five miles away from where Georgia had gone missing. Upon noticing a foul odor, the family followed their noses and soon came across a set of woefully decomposed remains, lying face up in a patch of bushes.

The victim was clad in jeans and a tank top and wore no shoes: a perfect description of Georgia's outfit on the night she vanished. A comparison of x-rays—which revealed a distinctive bone spur that Georgia had suffered from— confirmed the identification, though the Crews family was spared the agony of seeing the body, as it was no longer recognizable as Georgia. Subsequent checks of dental records and a much later DNA comparison left no doubt of the dead girl's identity.

An autopsy determined that Georgia had not been sexually assaulted, and that the cause of her death was a single stab wound in her lower back. There was no other evidence at the scene that could point to the killer, though investigators were fairly certain that he had indeed been a local, as the townsfolk feared. The fact that Georgia's footprints in the road had simply stopped without signs of struggle near her home was a good indication that someone had come along and picked her up in a vehicle, and this someone was perhaps a person she knew and had no reason to fear.

It would be nearly five months before any new developments in the case emerged, and even then, the outcome would remain frustratingly murky.

****

But in the meantime, on the other side of the Atlantic Ocean and about a month after the death of Georgia Crews, twenty-two-year-old university student Jessie Earl was elated to have finished her exams, and was looking forward to taking a little break. A second-year graphics student at Eastbourne College of Art and Design in Sussex, England, Jessie lived alone in a small bedsit, but on Wednesday, May 14th, she called her parents from a seaside phone booth and told them she'd be coming to London on Friday to visit them, and to stay over the weekend.

Friday evening passed with no word from Jessie, though at first her parents simply thought she had missed the last train and would turn up the next morning. But when Saturday afternoon came and went with no sign of their daughter, John and Valerie Earl became extremely concerned. That evening, Valerie decided to take a train down to Eastbourne herself, to see what might have gone wrong.

When she arrived, Jessie's landlady let Valerie into the flat, and upon entering, Valerie noted that the place looked eerily as though Jessie had simply stepped out for a moment. A partly eaten dish of chicken and rice was left out on the bedside table, the windows and curtains were open, and Jessie's purse lay untouched in the middle of the neatly-made bed. Of Jessie herself, however, there was absolutely no sign.

A survey of friends and neighbors confirmed that Jessie had been seen at various points on Thursday, presumably going about her normal business. In fact, another tenant in the building, Ivy Selby, stated that she had spoken to Jessie that day, and that Jessie had been headed out to her doctor's office to drop off a note to refill her asthma prescription. This note was discovered at the doctor's office, but the prescription had never been picked up. It was believed that Jessie had returned to her home after this errand, for the clothes Ivy had said Jessie was wearing were later found in her flat. But no sightings of Jessie Earl were reported after Thursday afternoon. It seemed as though she had simply walked out the front door of her apartment and dropped off the face of the Earth.

Her parents would exist in a sort of agonizing limbo for the ensuing nine years before they discovered what had ultimately become of her.

****

Less than two weeks after Jessie Earl disappeared in England, another woman would vanish without trace in California, under unsettling circumstances which still haunt the public imagination right up until the present day.

Thirty-two-year-old Dorothy Jane Scott was a quiet, deeply religious woman, a single mother who lived in Stanton, California with her aunt and her four-year-old son Shawn. Her ex-husband had moved to Missouri some time before, and to help support herself and her child, Dorothy had taken a job as a secretary for a pair of psychedelic head shops in Anaheim, one of which had previously been owned by her father. She was in the habit of leaving Shawn in the care of her parents in Anaheim while she worked, sometimes until fairly late into the evening.

For several months prior to her going missing, Dorothy had been receiving a series of frightening phone calls from a man whose voice she thought she recognized, but could not quite place. This individual was evidently obsessed with her, alternating between declaring his undying love for her and threatening her life. He was also clearly stalking her very closely, particularly when she was at work, as he often told her details of what she had been wearing or doing on any particular day.

On one occasion, this unidentified male demanded that Dorothy go outside because he had left something for her. When she followed his instructions, she found a dead rose lying on the windshield of her car. And on an even more terrifying day, the caller explicitly told Dorothy that he was planning to "cut you up into bits so no one will ever find you." Dorothy, understandably rattled, began taking karate classes, and even looked into purchasing a handgun, though she was reluctant to keep the weapon in the house around her young son.

Despite dealing with this campaign of harassment, Dorothy was trying to live as normal a life as she could manage. On May 28th, 1980, she followed her usual routine, dropping Shawn off at his grandparents' house, then continuing on to work. There was an employee meeting that night, and Dorothy attended, along with several of her coworkers.

However, at around nine p.m., Dorothy couldn't help but notice that another employee at the meeting, Conrad Bostron, wasn't looking all that well. He had an inflamed red rash on his arm, and appeared pale and ill. She offered to drive him to the emergency room at nearby UC Irvine Medical Center, and Conrad agreed. Another coworker, Pam Head, told them she would come along to help out.

On the way to the hospital, Dorothy stopped at her parents' house to check on Shawn and tell them what was going on. While there, she also took off the black scarf she had been wearing and replaced it with a red one. After that, the three of them continued on to the emergency room in Dorothy's car.

Pam and Dorothy sat in the hospital waiting room chatting for a couple of hours while Conrad was being seen to. It turned out that the rash on Conrad's arm had come from a black widow spider bite, and he was treated and given a prescription before being discharged at around eleven p.m.

Because Conrad was still feeling under the weather, Dorothy said that she would go out to the parking lot alone and bring the car around to the entrance to pick them up. Pam and Conrad went to the pharmacy to pick up the prescription as Dorothy made a quick trip to the ladies' room and then stepped out into the night.

Conrad and Pam were finished with their business at the pharmacy after only a few minutes, and went to the entrance to wait for Dorothy to bring the car around. After a brief time passed and the car did not appear, the pair went outside to the sidewalk and looked out into the hospital's parking lot.

It was then that Pam and Conrad saw Dorothy's white 1973 station wagon barrelling toward them, its headlights whiting out their vision so that they were unable to determine who was driving. They waved frantically to signal the car to stop, but it blew right past them and took a hard right turn out of the parking lot before speeding off into the darkness.

Confused, Pam and Conrad waited at the hospital for a further two hours, surmising that perhaps Dorothy had some kind of emergency with her son and had to get back to her parents' house to tend to him. Finally, though, they realized that something was drastically wrong, and went back into the building, where Pam phoned Dorothy's parents to ask if they had seen her. They had not. Pam then called the police to report Dorothy Scott missing.

At around four-thirty a.m., police discovered Dorothy's vehicle ablaze in an alley about ten miles away from the medical center. No evidence of Dorothy or her alleged kidnapper was found at the scene.

A week passed with no hint of Dorothy's fate. Then, on Wednesday, June 4th, the phone rang at the Anaheim home of Dorothy's parents, Jacob and Vera. When Vera answered the phone, the male caller asked if she was related to Dorothy Scott. Vera confirmed this, and then the man said brusquely, "I've got her," and hung up.

Similar phone calls would plague the Scotts nearly every Wednesday afternoon for years. Sometimes the caller would state that he had Dorothy, other times he would say that he had killed her. In like fashion, after the *Orange County Register* newspaper ran a story about the disappearance in their June 12th issue, the man called their offices as well. Not only did this individual have details about the case that were not then known to the public—for example, that Conrad had been treated for a spider bite and that Dorothy had stopped to change out her black scarf for a red one—but he had no qualms about telling the managing editor, "I killed Dorothy Scott. She was my love. I caught her cheating with another man. She denied having someone else. I killed her."

Though police were certain that the caller had indeed kidnapped and possibly murdered Dorothy, a few of his statements were questionable. He claimed, for instance, that Dorothy had phoned him from the hospital on the night she vanished. Coworker Pam Head insisted that this was impossible, as Dorothy had been at her side all evening, and at no point had she excused herself to use the pay phone. The only time Dorothy had been out of her sight, Pam said, was when she went into the rest room prior to walking out to the parking lot.

The caller's further statement that Dorothy had been "cheating with another man" was also contradicted by Dorothy's parents and coworkers, who told authorities that Dorothy had not been dating anyone seriously, and in fact rarely dated at all, as she was focused on work and caring for her son.

The mysterious phone calls, as well as the uncertainty surrounding Dorothy Scott's whereabouts, would continue for the following four years.

****

As the summer of 1980 wore on, a young woman would go missing from her hometown of Nashua, New Hampshire and later turn up dead in the deserts of Arizona. Though she remained unidentified for decades, referred to as Pima County Jane Doe or "Flower Girl," she was finally given her rightful name in the summer of 2015: Brenda Gerow.

In 1980, Brenda was twenty years old and working two jobs: as a clerk in a convenience store, and as a bartender at a biker joint in Massachusetts. At the time, she was dating a twenty-six-year-old man by the name of John Kalhauser, known as Jack to his friends.

At some time in July of 1980, Brenda told her family that she and Jack were either moving away together or going away on a trip, though it is unclear if she told them where they were going specifically, or when they would be returning. According to her parents, Brenda did keep in contact with them for several months following her departure, and her brother later confirmed that she had called him from New Mexico approximately two to three weeks after she left. At one stage she even told her family that she would be coming back home soon. It was a promise that she would ultimately be prevented from keeping.

When months had passed with no word from their daughter, Brenda's parents tried to report her as a missing person, but police seemed less than helpful, informing the Gerows that Brenda was an adult and was perfectly within her rights to take off around the country without telling her family where she was.

It would be nine months before a body was found, and even then, the Gerows had no idea it belonged to Brenda until well into the twenty-first century.

****

Miles to the south, only a few short days after Brenda Gerow left home, the Dumois family was heading out for a vacation from their residence in Tampa to a rented cottage on Anna Maria Island, a beautiful seven-mile stretch of land off the west coast of Florida. Dr. Juan Dumois, a pediatrician, was accompanied by his wife Maria and the couple's four children, and the family was planning a relaxing, two-week holiday full of sunbathing, boating, and fishing.

This latter activity, in fact, was the order of the day on Friday, August 1st. At approximately nine a.m., Dr. Dumois, his brother-in-law Raymond Barrows, and two of the Dumois children—thirteen-year-old Eric and nine-year-old Mark—loaded up their boat and headed for the Kingfish Boat Ramp. Maria and the other two children—nineteen-year-old Juan III and sixteen-year-old Anna—stayed behind at the cottage.

The fishing in the Gulf of Mexico was apparently very good that day, and the group returned to the ramp late that afternoon with a cooler full of fish. Dr. Dumois hitched the boat to the back of his 1977 Oldsmobile Vista Cruiser, and began the short drive back to the vacation house.

Moments later, though, a man pushing a bicycle emerged from a copse of trees near the boat ramp and flagged the car down. This individual was lean and well-muscled, standing about six feet tall, with blue eyes, a cleft chin, and thick brown hair combed back off his forehead. He appeared to be in his late twenties or early thirties, and reportedly spoke with what was possibly a New England accent.

When Dr. Dumois asked what he wanted, the man replied that he had hurt his ankle while riding his bike, and would appreciate a ride to the condominium complex around the corner. Dr. Dumois affably agreed, even helping the man load the ten-speed into the boat. The stranger then climbed into the back seat of the Oldsmobile next to Eric and Mark.

Then, as Dr. Dumois began driving once again, the hitchhiker pulled out a gun and began shooting.

Raymond Barrows was shot first, then the killer targeted each boy with a bullet to the head. Dr. Dumois was subsequently shot twice in the head at close range before the stranger grabbed the wheel of the vehicle and steered the car off the road into the grass. The killer then exited the car, retrieved his bike from the boat, and rode off toward the parking lot of a nearby supermarket.

As it turned out, the entire sequence of events had been spotted by a witness, Robert Matzke, a retired Air Force lieutenant colonel who had been in the front yard of his condominium and had seen the Oldsmobile coming to a halt. He was unaware that anyone had been shot, but thought the car had perhaps been in an accident. He told his wife Mary to call the police and report the incident, then got in his own vehicle and set off after the man on the bicycle.

Evidently, Robert pulled up alongside the stranger, at which point the man again produced a .22 and shot Robert in the back of the head, causing his vehicle to veer off and hit a parked car in the supermarket lot. A woman who had been in the grocery store believed she had witnessed another car crash, and reported it to police at a little past five p.m. Though like Robert Matzke, she did not realize that anyone had been shot, she was able to tell police that the man on the bicycle had loaded it into the back of a tan Ford with a black top driven by another individual, and that this vehicle had then sped away with both men inside.

Another witness to the event was island resident and amateur photographer John Toth. As he was leaving the TV repair shop he owned on the island, he spotted Dr. Dumois's vehicle swerving off the highway onto the roadside, and saw the killer emerge from the car. Just as in all the other cases, John was also unaware that he had just witnessed a shooting, but was intrigued enough to start photographing the scene with the camera he always had close to hand. Though the photographs he produced did capture an image of the murderer, unfortunately John had, in his haste, forgotten to turn on the auto focus, and the pictures were far too blurry to identify the individual in question.

Though Raymond Barrows would ultimately survive his injuries, Dr. Dumois, his two sons, and Robert Matzke would all die as a result of the shooting. And because the crimes were initially reported to authorities as two separate automobile accidents, arriving officers did not realize they were investigating a murder scene, and not only failed to secure the area, but allowed numerous volunteers to assist in extricating the victims from their cars. Adding insult to injury, the Oldsmobile had also happened to come to a stop near a sprinkler, which drenched the vehicle with water and wiped away valuable evidence.

Despite a massive search of the island and the nearby mainland, no trace of the killer or the getaway car was ever found. Detectives struggled to come up with a motive for the apparently random attack, investigating leads pertaining to Dr. Dumois's escape from Castro's Cuba in 1960; possible links to the Mafia or the drug trade; and speculations that a disgruntled parent of one of his juvenile patients had perhaps murdered him for reasons of retributive justice. It was also hypothesized that Raymond Barrows could have been the actual target of the execution, engendered by a hit man hired by a cocaine cartel. None of these avenues of inquiry yielded any progress, however.

Two main suspects were briefly considered in the wake of the quadruple homicide. One of these was Richard Lee Whitley, a native of Chicago who had been picked up in Tampa shortly after the Kingfish Boat Ramp murders and was wanted by the FBI in conjunction with a homicide that had taken place in Falls Church, Virginia. The other was William Peter Kuhlman, who had recently been acquitted of the murder of a Bradenton, Florida woman that was undertaken with a .22 caliber handgun. Both men were eventually cleared of suspicion.

The case fell into an uneasy obscurity not long afterward, and remains unresolved nearly forty years later.

****

In September of 1980, in another part of Florida, there was a seeming break in the case of Georgia Crews, the twelve-year-old girl who had gone missing from her Montverde home back in April and had turned up dead only days later.

An inmate at an Iowa prison by the name of Albert Lara, serving time for the May 1980 murder of fifteen-year-old Jill Annette Peters, confessed to Lake County Sheriff Malcolm McCall that he was also guilty of killing Georgia Crews. Detectives eagerly took his statement, which read, in part, "...I drove down a couple miles or so and pulled over where a bunch of trees were and kind of hid my car and...threw her in the back of the...trunk or whatever. Then I drove on, found some trees, sat there and drank some beer, thought a while, and then I took her out of the trunk and put her in the back seat. I guess I commenced to rape her or something. She started struggling. She got away. I grabbed her, and at the time, my right hand found an object, an ice pick or a screwdriver or something, and I stabbed her on her lower back..."

A deeper delve into Lara's movements at the time Georgia was slain seemed to suggest that he was in central Florida at the time, but that was the only convincing piece of circumstantial evidence that could be confirmed pertaining to Lara's guilt. Throwing doubt upon the whole sad affair was the fact that Lara's statement contradicted certain details of the murder scene, and the further knowledge that Lara had a troubling history of confessing to various violent crimes around the country that there was no way he could have perpetrated. Indeed, in the particular case of Georgia Crews, investigators suspected that Lara was simply copping to her murder so that he would be moved from his decrepit Iowa prison cell to what he hoped would be slightly more agreeable accommodations in Florida.

Given these uncertainties, Lara was dismissed as a suspect later in 1980, and was likewise cleared after a 1994 reexamination of the case. Opinion is divided on whether Lara remains the most likely suspect, but so far, his guilt has never been able to be conclusively proven.

The investigation stood fallow until 2013, when a new push to solve the cold case uncovered a clue that had been dismissed or unnoticed the first time around. In the files, detectives came upon a photograph of a cross necklace that had been found either on or near Georgia's body at the site where she had been dumped. The Crews family insisted that this necklace did not belong to Georgia; she did indeed wear a cross, they stated, but it was a small gold one that had been a gift from her grandmother. The particular cross found with the girls' remains was a larger pendant made of silver, and appeared to have been hand crafted out of machine or motorcycle parts.

Authorities released photos of the odd piece of jewelry to the public in the hopes of stirring up fresh leads, but as of this writing, no further progress on the murder of Georgia Crews has been made.

****

Autumn of 1980 began to fall, and out in the American West, two brothers were driving along a dirt road in Henderson, Nevada. It was about nine-thirty p.m. on the evening of Sunday, October 5th.

Suddenly, one of the brothers, off-duty police officer John Williams, spotted something strange lying in the scrub off State Road 146. The men pulled over and got out of their truck, and upon closer inspection, realized that the object they had seen was the nude body of a young girl, lying face down and seemingly posed on the ground.

The victim had been dispatched with appalling violence. It appeared that she had been punched repeatedly in the face, so hard that one of her bottom teeth had been knocked out. She had also been bludgeoned several times in the back of the head with what the coroner believed was likely a framing or roofing hammer. And as a grim *coup de grace*, her killer had also stabbed her seven times in the lower back with some unknown, two-pronged implement.

There was no evidence of sexual assault, but whoever had murdered the girl had washed the body, and left a scrap of a yellowish-orange shower curtain nearby, suggesting that the victim had been slain at a house or motel room in some other location and subsequently dumped along the roadside. A post-mortem estimated that she had been dead for less than twenty-four hours before her remains were discovered.

A description of the young woman was duly released to the public. She was thought to be somewhere between fourteen and twenty-five years old, but most likely around seventeen or eighteen. She was white, stood five-feet-two-inches tall, and weighed about one-hundred-three pounds. She had light brown, shoulder-length hair, and eyes that were variously described as blue, hazel, or possibly green.

In addition, she had several fillings, a notable gap between her upper right central and lateral incisors, and impacted wisdom teeth. She had also undergone a dental procedure known as suturing to straighten one of her teeth, leading investigators to believe that she came from a relatively affluent background, as the procedure was expensive and purely cosmetic.

Further, her ears were pierced, and she wore silver nail polish. She also sported a fresh, amateur tattoo of the letter S, etched in blue ink on the inside of her right forearm. It is unclear whether she drew the tattoo herself or whether it was administered by someone else, possibly her killer.

Detectives naturally commenced a far-reaching probe to identify the victim as well as bring her murderer to justice. But despite all their efforts, the girl remained nameless, and to this day is still known only as Arroyo Grande Jane Doe. John Williams, the man who found her remains, paid for her headstone, and still visits her burial site regularly with his wife.

The body of Arroyo County Jane Doe has been exhumed four times as of this writing, and fingerprints, facial reconstructions, and a DNA profile are all on record. The case was officially reopened in June of 2015, but so far, her identity and that of her killer remain a mystery.

****

Nearly a month after the unidentified murder victim turned up in Nevada, yet another young woman would be found dead, this time more than thirteen-hundred miles away in Texas. She would share the tragic distinction of remaining anonymous right up until the present day.

It was a little past nine p.m. on the night of November 1st, 1980, when a truck driver making his way past the Sam Houston National Forest near Huntsville, Texas saw the nude body of a young girl lying about six yards off the shoulder of Interstate Highway 45.

The victim was a white female aged somewhere between fourteen and eighteen years old, standing around five-foot-six and weighing approximately one-hundred-five to one-hundred-twenty pounds. She had light, reddish-brown hair cut to shoulder length, hazel eyes, and appeared well-nourished and in excellent health, leading detectives to believe that she came from a middle- to upper-middle-class family that took exceptional care of her.

Unique characteristics included an inverted right nipple, and a vertical scar near her right eyebrow. Her fingernails were unpainted, but her toenails bore pink polish, and though her clothes were never found, a pair of red and brown sandals that the girl had reportedly been carrying with her was found at the scene. She also wore a distinctive blue or brown glass pendant on a thin gold chain around her neck.

Just as in the case of Arroyo County Jane Doe, this victim had endured an unimaginable ordeal before her death. She had been viciously raped and sodomized with some unknown blunt object, and scraps of her pantyhose and underwear were found lodged in her vagina. She had also been brutally beaten about the face and body, and her right shoulder bore a deep bite mark. The coroner believed that the girl had been killed by ligature strangulation, perhaps with her own pantyhose. He also reported that she had only been dead for about six hours when her remains were discovered.

After authorities released a description of the victim—dubbed Walker County Jane Doe—to the public, a few witnesses came forward who claimed to have seen the girl in the hours before her death. Two employees of the Hitch 'n' Post Truck Stop and the manager of a Gulf gas station all told police that they had seen a girl matching Walker County Jane Doe's description on October 31st, the day before her body was found. They independently reported that the girl had been wearing a scruffy yellow top, jeans, and a white knit sweater, and carried a pair of red and brown sandals in her hand.

The gas station manager further informed investigators that the girl had gotten out of a blue 1973 or 1974 Chevy Caprice and had then come into the station and asked him for directions to the Ellis Prison Farm. Afterwards, the girl left the station on foot and started making her way north.

Later that same day, a waitress at the truck stop said that the girl had asked her for directions to the prison farm as well, and told police that she had drawn the girl a map. The waitress stated that the girl spoke of a friend that she was meeting at the prison farm, and told the waitress that she was nineteen years old, which the waitress did not believe, suspecting that the girl was possibly a runaway. During the course of the conversation, the waitress claimed that the girl said she came from either Aransas Pass or Rockport, Texas, though inquiries in both locations yielded no clues as to the mysterious girl's identity. Likewise, an examination of inmates at the Ellis Prison Farm failed to shake loose any relevant information.

The body of Walker County Jane Doe was exhumed in 1999, at which time a DNA sample was obtained. The case was reopened in November of 2015, but so far, no positive developments have been reported, though a handful of theories about the girl and her killer have been swirling since then.

One of the most persistent emerged only a month after the case was reopened, and posits that Walker County Jane Doe is actually a runaway from Corpus Christi, Texas by the name of Cathleen or Kathleen. This possible lead stemmed from a brother and sister who, while looking through old photographs from their childhood, discovered a picture of themselves and a girl they had met at a motel in Beeville, Texas in the summer of 1980. They recalled that this girl was living in the motel with an unknown couple at the time, that she closely matched the description of Walker County Jane Doe, and that she had allegedly told them that she wanted to go meet a friend of hers who was incarcerated at Sugarland Prison. As of this writing, this link remains intriguing but unsubstantiated.

It has also been hypothesized that Walker County Jane Doe was slain by the same perpetrator who murdered the unidentified victim known as Orange Socks in Georgetown, Texas in October of 1979 (a case discussed in volume two of this work). And just as in that case, serial killer Henry Lee Lucas has been put forward as a person of interest, though authorities claim that the bite mark found on Walker County Jane Doe's shoulder does not match Lucas's dental records.

There is further speculation that Walker County Jane Doe could have been the victim of an unknown serial killer who is believed to have murdered at least three other women in 1980 and dumped all of their bodies along Interstate 45.

Thus far, detectives have eliminated sixteen missing persons as inconsistent with the case of Walker County Jane Doe, but they remain hopeful that the victim will one day have her identity restored and her murderer caught and punished.

****

Before 1980 came to a close, a troubled young girl in Kalamazoo, Michigan would disappear without trace, and though her body would be found only a month into the new year, she would remain unidentified for decades, known only as Bossier Doe until authorities in 2015 finally matched her with her true identity: Carol Ann Cole.

Carol was seventeen years old in 1980, and had something of a dysfunctional family life. Her parents had divorced some time before, and Carol and her sister Jeanie had gone to Kalamazoo to live with their grandmother. By all accounts, Carol had also been having trouble with drugs, and in 1979, traveled to San Antonio, Texas to live with her mother and begin attending rehab meetings at the Palmer Drug Abuse Program.

Though Carol had left her sister and grandmother behind in Michigan, she was fairly diligent about writing them letters and keeping them apprised of her movements by phone. That was why, in late December of 1980, Carol's grandmother became worried after she hadn't heard from Carol in quite a while. She managed to discover that Carol had left the drug program and gone to live with friends in Shreveport, Louisiana, but these friends claimed that Carol had left to go to a party sometime in December and had never come back.

There was also some evidence to suggest that Carol may have spent some time at another facility subsequently, the New Bethany School for Girls in Arcadia, Louisiana. Photographs taken at the facility appear to show a girl that closely resembles Carol Cole, and it has been hypothesized that the clothes Carol was wearing when her body was later found were consistent with dress codes put in place by the school.

Whatever the truth of the matter, though, it would be at least four weeks before her remains turned up, and almost four decades before she was definitively identified as Carol.

1981

> Harris County Does

> Carol Ann Cole

> Brenda Gerow

> The Keddie Murders

> Marcia King: Buckskin Girl

> Raymond Nels Nelson

> Ken McElroy

> Vishal Mehrotra

> The Nude in the Nettles

> The Highway of Tears

> Dana Bradley

Shortly into the new year, on January 12th, 1981, a dog sniffing around a privately-owned, wooded area near Houston, Texas discovered the partially buried and decomposed bodies of two probable teenagers who remain unidentified to this day.

The victims had apparently been murdered about two months previously, and the amount of time that had passed since their deaths meant that their faces were unrecognizable. The female, thought to be white, Native American, or a mixture thereof, was aged anywhere from fifteen to twenty-five years old, stood between five-foot-four and five-foot-nine, had long, reddish-brown hair pulled back in a ponytail, and a noticeable gap between her front teeth. She wore no clothing, though a bloody towel and a pair of green jogging shorts were discovered near the body. The cause of death was believed to be strangulation; it did not appear that she had been sexually assaulted.

The male victim, likely her companion, was possibly white, aged between fifteen and thirty, and around the same height as the female. He had brown eyes, and wavy brown hair that extended nearly to his shoulders. He also had prominent eyebrows and evidence of a former injury in the region of his upper vertebrae. Like the female, he had excellent dental health, but unlike her, he had been bound and gagged before being beaten to death, leading some to speculate that he had been the target of the killer's attack, and that the female had possibly been murdered simply to eliminate a witness.

Fingerprints, facial reconstructions, and DNA samples are on file for both victims—known as the Harris County Does—but as of this writing, no one has come forward to claim them, though more than a dozen individual missing persons have been ruled out as possible identities.

Incidentally, the exact location where the bodies were discovered—about one-hundred yards off Wallisville Road in Houston—was nearly the exact same spot where the remains of fifteen-year-old murder victim Michelle Garvey would be found in July of 1982. Michelle had run away from home about a month prior to her body being recovered, and it is believed that she may be yet another casualty of the so-called Texas Killing Fields murders, a discussion of which began in volume two of this work and will continue in the present volume. Michelle was raped and strangled, and her body remained unidentified until

2014, when a DNA sample taken from the remains in 2011 was finally matched to the DNA of the victim's brother.

****

Sixteen days after the Harris County Does were unearthed in Texas, another unidentified homicide victim was found in Louisiana, though in this latter case, the identity of the slain teenage girl would eventually be established.

On January 28th, 1981, a man named John Chesson was out hunting with his son when the pair reportedly came across the degraded remains of a young woman. The victim was determined to be a white female between fifteen and twenty-one years old, of average height and weight, with shoulder-length blonde hair. It appeared that she had painted her fingernails and forcibly removed the braces from her teeth not long before her death. She was clad in a white, long-sleeved shirt with colored stripes, jeans, and a beige hooded sweater. Oddly, her size-seven shoes had several names written on them, including Resha, David, and Michael Brisco.

An autopsy revealed that she had been stabbed to death approximately one to two months previously; the knife thought to be the murder weapon was discovered in the dirt near her body. As the victim carried no identification and did not seem to match any known missing persons, she was given the name Bossier Doe, after Bossier Parish, where she had been found.

Shortly after the discovery, serial killer and known exaggerator Henry Lee Lucas confessed to killing the unknown victim, just as he had in the previous murders of Orange Socks and Caledonia Jane Doe (who would later be identified as sixteen-year-old Tammy Jo Alexander; both cases were discussed in the previous volume of this work). Skeptical authorities almost immediately dismissed his admission, as it was known that Lucas was in Florida when Bossier Doe had been murdered.

The case thenceforth went cold, and many years passed. Then, in 2015, a follower of a Facebook group concerning the Bossier Doe case happened to cross-reference the photo reconstruction of the victim with a photo of a known missing person from a Craigslist ad: seventeen-year-old Carol Ann Cole, who had vanished sometime in December of 1980 after allegedly leaving a house in Shreveport, Louisiana. DNA tests conducted later that year confirmed that Bossier Doe was indeed Carol Cole, and the remains were eventually sent back to Michigan to be buried by the girl's family.

Though there are no solid suspects in the murder of Carol Ann Cole, there is an intriguing person of interest in the form of John Chesson, the man who stumbled across the body and reported his discovery to police. Chesson's daughter, Frances Aucoin, told police that she believed her father had taken the hunting trip specifically to "find" the remains and thus allay suspicion from himself, and further claimed that she had seen a girl resembling Carol Cole in the company of her father after he reportedly picked her up hitchhiking.

Frances also alleged that her father was abusive, and indeed, John Chesson was later convicted of murdering his mother-in-law in 1997, and is currently serving a life sentence for the crime.

John Chesson's son, who was present when his father found Carol Cole's body, committed suicide in 2008.

****

April 3rd of 1981 would bring a grim resolution to two missing-persons cases that had baffled police since the mid-1970s (and were outlined in volume two of this work). The bodies of twelve-year-old Brooks Bracewell and four-teen-year-old Georgia Geer, who had last been seen at the U-Totem convenience store in Dickinson, Texas in September of 1974, were discovered in a ditch in Alvin, Texas. The girls were the latest in a long list of victims dumped in the so-called Texas Killing Fields, a list that had by no means reached its end.

****

Days later, another hunting trip would uncover a troubling mystery, this time in the Arizona desert.

On April 8th, hunters driving along Interstate 10 in Tucson spotted a denim jacket hanging from a tree just along the road. They stopped to investigate, and thereafter happened upon the decomposed body of a young woman, clad in jeans, brown shoes, and a dark blue blouse with a floral design and red, puffy sleeves.

The victim, unidentified at the time, was thought to be around five-foot-two and one-hundred-five pounds, with long, light-colored hair and a white spot on one of her upper front teeth. A post-mortem examination determined that she had been sexually assaulted and then murdered by ligature strangulation, approximately two days before her remains were found. It was also assumed, from the presence of numerous scratches on her skin, that she had been running through a wooded area shortly before her death, presumably in an attempt to escape her killer.

Fingerprints were later taken, but matched no missing persons on file. Because the distinctive blouse she was wearing led some investigators to surmise that she had been working at a nearby county fair, photos of the clothing, as well as a rudimentary sketch of the woman's face, were released to the public, but no leads emerged from this avenue of inquiry either. For a time, it was even theorized that she was possibly a victim of Golden State Killer Joseph DeAngelo, who at that time was still unidentified.

It would be late 2014 before a definitive break in the case would occur. In that year, authorities were looking into a link between the unknown victim and a photograph they had found in the possession of a man named John Kalhauser back in 1995. Kalhauser had been arrested for assault, and the photograph—of a young woman holding a bouquet of flowers in an area of what appeared to be Massachusetts—was confiscated during a search of his home, though the suspect refused to identify the subject of the picture.

The woman in the photograph was later noticed to bear a striking resemblance to the reconstruction of the victim found in the Arizona desert in April of 1981, then known as Pima County Jane Doe. After releasing the photo to the public and then contacting the family of twenty-year-old Brenda Gerow, who had moved away from Massachusetts in the summer of 1980 with then-boyfriend John Kalhauser, a definitive identification of the murdered woman was finally made and confirmed through DNA in 2015.

Because the photograph of Brenda was found in Kalhauser's home and had been taken between 1979 and 1981, and because Kalhauser was the last known individual to have seen Brenda alive, investigators quickly considered him a person of interest in her murder. Adding to their suspicion was the fact that Kalhauser was, in 1999, convicted of the 1995 murder of his wife Diane Van Reeth; had formerly been convicted of yet another homicide—that of Paul Chapman in 1974—and indicted for an attempted murder in 1979, though he jumped bail shortly after this indictment and lived under an assumed name for a time. He remains in prison in Massachusetts at this writing on a second-degree murder charge stemming from the disappearance and presumed murder of his wife.

Though other candidates for Brenda Gerow's killer were considered—including an unknown man who Brenda reportedly left a nightclub with—most investigators are leaning heavily toward the theory that John Kalhauser murdered his one-time girlfriend and dumped her body in the desert. But as no solid evidence of his guilt has yet been uncovered, her death remains officially unresolved.

****

Only days after the body of Brenda Gerow turned up in Arizona, an unbelievably horrific quadruple homicide occurred in a remote cabin in the Sierra Nevada Mountains of California. The case, enshrined into true crime history as the Keddie Murders, still resonates throughout the tight-knit communities of Plumas County, more than thirty years after the event.

Thirty-six-year-old Glenna Sharp, more commonly known as Sue, was originally from Connecticut, but in late 1980, she left her husband James, and subsequently moved with their five children—fifteen-year-old Johnny, fourteen-year-old Sheila, twelve-year-old Tina, ten-year-old Rick, and five-year-old Greg—to cabin twenty-eight at the Keddie Resort in northern California. Sue chose this location in particular because it was quite close to where her brother Don lived, and now that she was a single mother, she felt better knowing that family was only a short drive away.

The Sharps had lived in Keddie for only a few months, but all of the children had developed friendships with other kids who lived in neighboring cabins. In fact, on April 11th, Sheila was planning to stay overnight with the Seabolt family in cabin twenty-seven, while Johnny was spending the day with a school friend of his, seventeen-year-old Dana Wingate. The boys had been wandering around downtown earlier in the afternoon, and later in the evening, reportedly hitchhiked back to Quincy, California, where they were spotted at a party.

Sue was at home in cabin twenty-eight with her two youngest boys and their friend, twelve-year-old Justin Smartt, who lived two cabins over. Tina, who had been watching TV at the Seabolts' place next door, came home at a little before ten p.m., only an hour or so after her older sister Sheila had gone there to sleep over. Johnny and Dana arrived back at the cabin shortly afterward and went to hang out in Johnny's basement bedroom.

At some point later on that night or early the following morning, another individual or individuals with murderous intent entered the cabin through the back door.

At approximately seven-forty-five a.m. on the morning of April 12th, Sheila walked back to cabin twenty-eight, opened the front door, and seconds later went racing back to the neighbors' place, screaming that there were three dead people in her house.

The Seabolts called the police, and then they and Sheila went back to the cabin to get Rick, Greg, and Justin out of the house via a back window, so that they would not have to go through the living room and see the carnage the killer (or killers) had left behind. For whatever reason, the murderer had left the three boys unharmed, and at first, authorities believed that all three of them had slept through the entire event.

When investigators arrived and combed the scene, they found a crime as grisly as it was unexplained. All three victims had been bound with surgical tape and electrical wire, all had blunt force trauma to the back of their heads that was consistent with blows from a hammer, and both Sue and Johnny had their throats slashed. Dana Wingate, despite having the same head injuries as the other two victims, had been manually strangled.

Sue Sharp had also been gagged by a bandanna and her own underwear, which had been taped over her mouth. She further bore several additional stab wounds in her chest, as well as an imprint from the butt of a Daisy BB gun on the side of her head. Though she was found naked from the waist down, there was no evidence of sexual assault. It also appeared as though the killer had moved her body into a less exposed position and partially covered it with a sheet and a yellow blanket.

The walls and floor of the living room were copiously splattered with blood. Though detectives suspected that two different hammers were used in the commission of the homicide, only one was recovered from the scene. Additionally, a steak knife was found near the bodies, the blade of which was bent nearly in half from the force the killer had exerted while stabbing his victims. A second knife was found in a trash can behind the Keddie general store a short time later.

No sign of forced entry was apparent, though a single unidentified fingerprint was discovered on the handrail of the back steps. All the lights in the cabin were found to be off, and all the curtains were drawn; the phone had also been left off the hook. A survey of the neighbors established that no one seemed to have heard anything unusual, save for one couple who thought they heard a sound like muffled screaming at approximately one-thirty a.m., but dismissed it after they could not determine where it was coming from.

When officers spoke to the three children who had been in the cabin at the time of the murders, Justin Smartt attempted numerous times to tell them that twelve-year-old Tina Sharp was missing, but this fact apparently did not sink in until several hours had gone by. Sheila also informed the authorities that Tina's shoes and jacket had vanished from the cabin as well. When the reality of Tina's disappearance was finally noted, the FBI and the Department of Justice became involved in the case and organized a grid search.

Interestingly, even though Justin first claimed to have slept through the incident, he later told authorities that he dreamed details of it, and when placed under hypnosis by a child psychologist, actually admitted that he had seen the crime occur. He stated that two men had been in the house talking to Sue, and that a violent argument broke out when Johnny and Dana arrived home, after which the men had taken Tina out the back door before coming back in and proceeding to kill the others. From Justin's recollections, investigators produced sketches of the alleged perpetrators, one of whom was clean-shaven with short, dark blond hair, the other of whom had long, greasy black hair and a mustache; both the men were in their late twenties and wore gold-framed glasses.

Law enforcement wasted little time in tracking down suspects in the brutal and apparently random crime. One individual who had abruptly left Keddie shortly after the murders was picked up in Oregon and questioned, but released after passing a polygraph. Perhaps one of the most promising persons of interest, though, was someone even closer to home.

Justin's father Marty Smartt, who lived in cabin twenty-six with his wife Marilyn and their son, drew the attention of authorities when he began providing several "helpful" clues in the case that gave detectives the distinct impression that he was seeking to allay suspicion from himself. He told them, for example, that he had lost a claw hammer very similar to the one police believed had been used in the murder. Further, his wife Marilyn said she had found Tina's bloody jacket in the basement of the Smartt home and had turned it into police, though investigators claim to have no record of this.

Marilyn, in fact, was quite certain that Marty and his friend, John "Bo" Boubede, had been responsible for the multiple murder at cabin twenty-eight. She stated that she had dropped the two men off at the Backdoor Bar at around eleven p.m., and that they had specifically wanted

Sue Sharp to come along with them. Marilyn allegedly told them that Sue would not want to go, and called her to ask, at which point Sue reportedly declined the invitation.

Marilyn told police that when she left them at the bar and went back to the Smartt home to sleep, Marty and Bo were angry about Sue's refusal. Other witnesses in the bar also claimed that the men had been behaving belligerently. Marilyn further alleged that she had awakened at around two a.m. on April 12th and witnessed Marty and Bo burning some unknown item in the wood stove.

Not only that, but Marilyn left Marty on the day following the murders, maintaining that he was abusive. In fact, she further declared that Sue had long been encouraging her to divorce Marty, and cited this "interference" in the Smartt marriage as a motive for Marty to kill Sue.

Not long after the murders, Marty moved to Reno, Nevada, and sent Marilyn a letter that supposedly contained the statement, "I've paid the price of your love and now I've bought it with four people's lives." Though Marilyn could not recall ever receiving this letter, it was eventually recovered in the case files, though it had been overlooked at the time of the active investigation.

A therapist in Reno also later came forward and stated that Marty had confessed to him that he had killed Sue and Tina, but would not admit to killing Johnny or Dana.

Despite Marilyn's conviction that her husband was one of the killers, Sheriff Doug Thomas cleared him after he passed a polygraph; Bo Boubede was likewise polygraphed and dismissed, in spite of his purported Chicago mob ties.

The case stagnated thereafter, with neither solid suspects nor Tina's whereabouts emerging. It would, in fact, be three long years before Tina's ultimate fate would be discovered, and decades after that before any new leads would bubble to the surface.

****

Later that same month, in the American Midwest, yet another young woman would be found dead along the side of a highway and remain unidentified for years to come.

The date was April 24th, 1981, and farmer Greg Bridenbaugh was driving along Greenlee Road near the city of Troy, Ohio, when he saw what appeared to be an incongruous piece of clothing in the dirt just off the shoulder. Upon stopping his vehicle and examining the scene more closely, he was shocked to discover the remains of a redheaded girl curled into a fetal position and lying in a ditch.

The victim was fully dressed, but wore no shoes or socks. The fact that the bottoms of her feet were clean indicated that she had been killed elsewhere and then dumped along the road, which was only five miles from the busy Interstate 75. An autopsy determined that the girl had probably only been dead for a few hours before her remains were found.

She was thought to be in her late teens to early twenties, stood around five-foot-five, and weighed approximately one-hundred-twenty-five pounds. She had light brown eyes, freckles, a sun-tinged complexion, and a small, pointed nose. Her red hair was braided in two plaits on either side of her face, and bound with blue rubber bands. She was clad in a pair of Wrangler jeans, a brown and orange sweater, and a very distinctive, fringed deerskin poncho that appeared handmade and was lined with purple fabric. It was this striking garment which had first alerted Greg Bridenbaugh to her presence, and it also gave her the name by which she was known until her identity was restored nearly four decades later: Buckskin Girl.

The coroner found no evidence of sexual assault, though the victim had clearly been beaten severely around the head and neck, and had suffered a lacerated liver. The cause of death was determined to be strangulation.

Authorities at first surmised that the young woman had been a runaway, as they were quickly able to determine that she was not from Ohio. Though there had been at least one unknown serial killer prowling the particular area where her body was discovered—a killer who purportedly went by the CB handle "Dr. No" and exclusively targeted exotic dancers and sex workers—Buckskin Girl did not seem to fit this profile, and had not been raped like the other victims of this elusive perpetrator.

Fingerprints and a facial reconstruction were duly produced, but years passed with no progress toward identifying the woman or her likely killer. Then, in 2016, analysis of particles on the victim's clothing indicated strongly that the girl had been wandering around the country for some time prior to her death, making stops in the northeast as well as Fort Worth, Texas and southern Oklahoma.

And in 2018, after the victim's DNA was analyzed by the DNA Doe Project, the young woman was definitively identified as twenty-one-year-old Marcia King, who had last made contact with friends and relatives in late 1980, in Little Rock, Arkansas. After her name was made public, witnesses came forward and claimed to have seen her in Louisville, Kentucky approximately two weeks before she was found murdered.

Though Marcia had never been officially reported missing, as her family simply believed she was traveling the United States and living her own life, her mother had never ceased looking for her, and had deliberately remained in the same house and kept the same phone number, in case her daughter should decide to return. Sadly, Marcia had only been alive for a few months following her departure from home.

Beginning in 1991, investigators attempted to establish a link between the death of Marcia King and the serial killer who was preying on sex workers in Ohio, but though some aspects of the crimes were similar—the fact that the victims had all been beaten and strangled, for example, and had some pieces of clothing and jewelry taken by the killer—other attributes did not seem to jibe, such as the fact that Marcia had not been sexually assaulted, was very clean and well-groomed, and had been simply left in a ditch as opposed to being wrapped in a sleeping bag and kept refrigerated for a time, as at least one of the serial killer's other victims had been. The theory was also put forth that a different serial killer, one who had perpetrated a series known as the Redhead Murders, might be responsible, but this line of inquiry was also eventually ruled out.

The possibility remains that Marcia was hitchhiking around the country and ran into the wrong person, or alternately was killed by an individual she was involved in a romantic relationship with. Though the King family was grateful to finally be able to lay their daughter to rest, the question of who murdered her still remains an open wound.

****

It was the first day of June 1981, and politics in Washington DC was chugging along in its usual way, until a grisly find in an apartment near Catholic University would set tongues wagging in the capitol.

Raymond Nels Nelson was the son of Swedish immigrants, a fiercely intelligent and irreverent figure who had served in the Navy before working his way up the ranks at *The Providence Journal and Evening Bulletin* in Rhode Island. He later parlayed his talents as a reporter into a political career, managing the Senatorial campaign of Claiborne Pell, who would be elected against all odds and would go on to help create the well-known Pell Grant, which provided tuition aid to lower-income college students. After leaving Pell's service, Raymond Nelson would go on to join the Senate Committee on Rules and Administration.

Raymond was well regarded professionally, though his personal life was a bit more complicated. He was an alcoholic, and could sometimes be difficult to get along with. He was married and had three children, but in 1976 came out as gay, after which he left the Rhode Island home he had shared with his family and moved to Washington DC. However, he maintained a close relationship with his children, and remained legally married to his wife.

On June 1st, though, it became apparent that someone was keen to silence Raymond Nels Nelson, for whatever reason. Police were summoned to his Quincy Street abode on that day, only to find that the erstwhile reporter and Senate staffer had been beaten to death with his own typewriter. The floor surrounding the remains was strewn with old magazines and newspapers.

Suspiciously, authorities allowed a Senate staffer into the apartment to claim some so-called "sensitive" documents from amid Raymond's belongings, though it is still unknown what these documents contained. Further, Raymond's children, who had been with their father the night before his murder, were never interviewed by police, and worse still, investigators themselves later admitted that the entire crime scene had been staged, though they did not elaborate as to why, or to whose benefit the ruse was undertaken.

The murder seems to have fallen into a shadowy obscurity since that time, and no new leads have been forthcoming. Whether the death of Raymond Nels Nelson was related to his political connections, his homosexuality, or some other cause is still a frustrating enigma, and his family has been left with no sense of closure or justice for the past thirty-eight years.

****

Back in the Midwest later that summer, an extraordinary case would make headlines around the United

States, a crime that would explore the uncomfortably gray area between the arguable breakdown of the rule of law and the conspiratorial actions of an alleged group of fed-up vigilantes.

Residents of the tiny town of Skidmore, Missouri had, in 1981, been under siege for more than twenty years, the long-suffering victims of a one-man criminal onslaught going by the name of Ken Rex McElroy. He had been born to migrant farm workers, and had only reached the tender age of fifteen years before he clearly decided that tormenting the innocent was to be his sole mission in life. Starting out as a petty thief and cattle rustler, Ken soon graduated to stalking, arson, assault, and statutory rape.

He was also a notorious womanizer, having fathered at least ten children by different mothers, and in fact was still married to his third wife when he met the girl who would become his fourth and final: twelve-year-old Trena McCloud. Two years after meeting Ken, fourteen-year-old Trena was pregnant, had dropped out of school, and had gone to live with Ken and his wife Alice, who he subsequently divorced in order to marry Trena, all the better to avoid a statutory rape charge.

Shortly after Trena's child was born, though, she and Alice joined forces and fled McElroy's home, going to stay with relatives. But Ken found them in record time, and forced them back into his clutches. He then burned down the home of Trena's parents, and shot their dog dead.

Despite the numerous accusations levied against Ken McElroy—including allegedly shooting a farmer named Romaine Henry, threatening the biological child of a foster family who briefly took in Trena and her baby, and myriad other crimes large and small—no charges ever seemed to stick, likely because Ken was known to intimidate witnesses into silence, sometimes sitting outside their homes with his pickup truck every day for weeks at a stretch, and making sure the townsfolk got a good look at the guns he was always waving around.

In mid-1980, though, it finally seemed that the so-called "town bully" might be getting some comeuppance at last. At around that time, one of his daughters was reportedly caught stealing candy from a Skidmore grocery store, and was thereafter confronted by a clerk named Evelyn Sumy. Just following this incident, Ken McElroy began stalking the owners of the store, seventy-year-old Ernest "Bo" Bowencamp and his wife, and in July, actually shot the elderly grocer in the neck with a shotgun as the old man waited on the loading dock behind the store.

Bo survived his injuries, but it seemed that this crime was the straw that broke the camel's back. Ken was arrested, and was shockingly not able to wriggle his way out of charges this time around, though to residents' dismay, he was only handed a two-year sentence.

And even worse was to come, for the judge then released Ken on bond pending the appeal of his conviction. Ken seemingly delighted in rubbing salt in the wound, striding into the D&G Tavern after his release, carrying a rifle and openly threatening to finish off Bo Bowencamp.

The town of Skidmore had had just about enough of Ken Rex McElroy. Because the stunt with the rifle was a violation of Ken's bond, several townsfolk approached the sheriff deputy and told them they would testify against Ken at the anticipated hearing. Arrangements were made for these residents to receive a protective escort to the courthouse, but then Ken's attorney, Richard McFadin, was able to get the hearing postponed.

Skidmore inhabitants were livid. From their perspective, they had been cowering under threat from this man for decades, and it appeared that there was nothing that law enforcement could do to prevent him from running roughshod over the entire town and doing essentially whatever he liked. Even Ken's own lawyer admitted defending Ken from three or four felony charges every year, and getting him off scot-free.

A large number of the townsfolk held a secret meeting at the Legion Hall on the morning of July 10th, 1981, in order to decide what to do. Though the content of their discussions remain a mystery, some residents later reported that the best idea the county sheriff could offer was encouraging the angry citizens to form a neighborhood watch. In their opinion, though, this was not going to cut the mustard.

As the meeting took place in the center of town, an oblivious Ken McElroy was making his way to the D&G Tavern, accompanied by his wife Trena. They both sat drinking at the bar for a little while, and then Ken bought some beer to take home. His lawyer, perhaps sensing that something was in the air, had purportedly warned Ken to lay low for a while, but Ken was not a man to be told what to do.

Meanwhile, word of Ken's whereabouts reached the people at the meeting, and slowly, residents began trickling out of Legion Hall and toward the tavern, until the bar was nearly full. Before they had left the meeting, the sheriff had allegedly reiterated his suggestion about the neighborhood watch and discouraged anyone from confronting Ken. He then left town, perhaps to wash his hands of the event that he must have suspected was about to go down.

Ken and Trena, evidently not noticing the ominous buildup of citizens inside the bar, finished up their drinks and then headed out to the street, climbing into their pickup truck that was parked outside. Moments later, shots began ringing out.

Amid the hail of gunfire, Ken McElroy was shot twice, once in the head and once in the neck, though at least four other shots missed their mark. One of the bullets came from an 8mm Mauser, while the other issued from a .22 Magnum. It was believed that one of the shooters had been about halfway down the block, while the other had been somewhere behind the truck.

Despite the presence of between thirty and sixty people on the street when Ken was shot, no one called an ambulance, and when police questioned the witnesses, every single one of them said they hadn't seen a thing. In fact, the only person to identify one of the potential shooters was Trena, who had been seated next to her husband in the truck when he was shot, but was unharmed.

It appeared that the town of Skidmore had finally taken some form of revenge against the man who had terrorized them for years, and their tight lips ensured that no one would ever be indicted for the crime. Though Trena filed a wrongful-death lawsuit against the town in 1984, it was eventually settled out of court for less than twenty-thousand dollars, with no one willing to admit any guilt.

To this day, the residents have kept their secret, and the broad-daylight murder of forty-seven-year-old Ken McElroy remains unsolved.

****

Nineteen days after the town bully of Skidmore, Missouri was gunned down in his pickup truck in front of several dozen witnesses, a little boy in the United Kingdom would vanish off a crowded street and remain missing for nearly seven months.

July 29th, 1981 was a significant day in British history, as it was the wedding day of Prince Charles and Lady Diana Spencer, who would famously go on to become the much beloved Princess Di. London was thronged with spectators to the lavish event, and among the crowds was a small family known as the Mehrotras. Vishambar Mehrotra, a solicitor who would later become a magistrate, had immigrated to the UK from India in 1978, leaving his estranged wife behind, and he was accompanied on the move by his two children, one of which was an eight-year-old boy named Vishal.

Vishal, his father, sister, and nanny had watched the wedding procession as it wound its way through the London streets, and soon afterward began making their way back toward the East Putney tube station. Vishal was going to take the train home alone, while the rest of his family stayed in the city to do some shopping. The boy waved goodbye and headed off toward Carlton Drive. He was never seen alive again.

A massive search was undertaken, though at first, authorities were operating under the assumption that Vishal had set out of his own volition, perhaps in an attempt to return to India to see his mother. Days after he vanished, anonymous tips placing the child on a Chelsea-bound bus, or in the company of an unidentified middle-aged man in a khaki jacket and hat, kept police on their toes, but none of these nebulous leads panned out.

Vishal's fate would not be discovered until two months into the following year, and his gruesome death would dredge up uncomfortable rumors in the capital about the possibility of a secretive and murderous pedophile ring comprised of high-placed members of the British government.

****

Elsewhere in England a month later, a phone call came in to the offices of the Ripon police in North Yorkshire. It was approximately eight a.m. on the morning of August 28th, 1981.

"Near Scawton Moor House, you will find a decomposed body among the willow herbs," said the voice on the line. The officer who had taken the call, PC John Jeffries, attempted to get the caller to state his name and address, but the individual declined "for reasons of national security" and hung up the phone. The call had lasted less than one minute, and was not able to be traced.

When a constable local to the area arrived at the site the caller had specified, he found nothing amiss at first, but after an extensive search, eventually came across what appeared to be part of a human skull. At that point, he phoned for CID, and after detectives cut down some of the surrounding nettles and dug around a bit more, they were able to recover most of the rest of the remains.

Because of the state of decomposition, surrounding plant growth, and the fact that the lid off a cup of yogurt was found beneath the body that bore a sell-by date approximately two years earlier, authorities surmised that this must have been how long the victim had been there. Due to its concealed location, it was extremely unlikely that anyone would have found the remains by accident, despite the area being popular with picnickers. It was this fact that led police to initially assume that the caller who had reported the corpse was also possibly the killer.

The victim, dubbed "The Nude in the Nettles," was a woman of about thirty-five years old, standing five-foot-two and with dark brown hair, cut into a pageboy style. She wore no clothing and had no jewelry. At some point, she had given birth to two or three children, and didn't appear to have taken very good care of herself: most of her teeth were missing and had been replaced with a dental plate, and the few teeth that did remain were stained with tar, indicating the woman had been a heavy smoker. She also would have suffered from a bad back during her life, as one of the vertebrae in her neck was malformed. She had also fractured her right ankle at some stage in the past.

Though detectives never released a cause of death to the public, the case was treated as a homicide due to the situation in which the body had been found.

Investigators fanned out from the location of the victim's last resting place in an effort to identify her and clarify her last moments on earth. About a mile away from the dump site, a pair of underwear and a black evening gown were discovered hanging from a tree, though these articles were never able to be definitively linked to the Nude in the Nettles. Likewise, a lead concerning an escaped inmate from nearby Askham Grange women's prison also went nowhere, as the inmate was later found to be alive and well.

Though an intensive probe was also undertaken to identify the man who had initially called the body in to police, eventually it was determined that the caller was probably not the killer, simply because it seemed farfetched to presume that the murderer would have waited two years to report the crime. In addition, it was entirely possible that someone—perhaps someone in the military—could have come across the body and reported it anonymously because they did not wish to get involved.

One of the most persistent theories about what happened to the Nude in the Nettles is that she may have been a victim of infamous Yorkshire Ripper Peter Sutcliffe, who in 1981 was convicted of thirteen murders and seven attempted murders. Sutcliffe, a truck driver during the time of his killing spree, would have driven through the area where the body was found at around the time she was probably killed. Further, the Nude in the Nettles may very well have been a prostitute, like Sutcliffe's other victims were.

On the other hand, certain aspects of the crime scene in the Nettles case don't really adhere to Sutcliffe's modus operandi, and because the authorities have not released details of the woman's cause of death, it remains unclear if the method of murder matched those of the Yorkshire Ripper's other victims, though her skull did not appear to display the hammer blows that were a hallmark of many of Sutcliffe's other homicides. He was also disinclined to leave the bodies naked, and had a tendency to pose them, which was not consistent with the manner in which the Nude in the Nettles' remains were discovered.

The DNA profile of the victim was added to the UK's national database in 2013, but as of this writing, she remains unidentified.

****

Later that fall, two women would be found dead in British Columbia, Canada along the notorious Highway of Tears, a four-hundred-fifty-mile stretch of Highway 16 that has served as a horrifying dumping ground for multiple serial killers since at least 1970. Though some of the victims of the unsolved homicides—many of whom were indigenous women—were discussed in volume two of this work, and more will be discussed later on in this present volume, the location merits a brief mention here, even though in the cases of these two particular women, a perpetrator would eventually be tracked down.

At approximately one-thirty a.m. on October 10th, 1981, thirty-six-year-old Jean Mary Kovacs was seen gathering firewood near Purden Lake, at the intersection of Highway 16 and Old Cariboo Highway. She thereafter disappeared, and her body was discovered the following day in a ditch about twenty-five miles east of Prince George, British Columbia. She had been shot four times in the head with a .22 caliber firearm.

Just over a month later, thirteen-year-old Roswitha Fuchsbichler was visiting a friend, but vanished some time after two a.m. on the morning of November 14th, 1981 while attempting to hitchhike home. A week later, her remains were discovered in the woods north of Prince George. She had been stripped nude, beaten, and stabbed to death.

In both cases, a single culprit was ultimately found to be responsible: serial killer Edward Dennis Isaac, who confessed to both crimes, among others. In May of 1987, Isaac was convicted of manslaughter in the death of Roswitha Fuchsbichler, and sentenced to life in prison. He was subsequently charged with the murder of Jean Mary Kovacs in February of 1988.

Though two casualties of the Highway of Tears had obtained some rough kind of justice, many of the victims yet to come would get no such comfort, and the cursed stretch of road would continue to swallow up women and girls for many years to come.

****

On the opposite end of Canada, as 1981 was drawing to a close, another young girl would disappear while trying to thumb a lift.

Fourteen-year-old Dana Bradley had been hanging out at a friend's house in St. John's, Newfoundland on December 14th, but at around five p.m., decided she had better start heading toward home, as her mother was having a birthday celebration that night. Like many young people of the era, she had no qualms about hitching a ride, and according to witnesses, was picked up by a dark-haired male driving a 1973 to 1976 Plymouth Valiant, or possibly a Dodge Dart.

Four days later, on December 18th, a man out looking for a Christmas tree in the woods near Maddox Cove came upon Dana's battered remains. She had been sexually assaulted, and murdered by several blows to the head from an unknown blunt instrument. Some sources claim that the body was found posed as though for burial, and that the killer had tucked the girl's schoolbooks under her arm.

A man would confess to the homicide five years later, but his involvement is by no means certain, and the case grew ever more labyrinthine as the years wore on.

1982

> Valentine Sally

> Vishal Mehrotra

> Michelle Garvey

> Princess Doe

> The Highway of Tears

> The Cheerleader in the Trunk

> Rachael Runyan

> The Chicago Tylenol Murders

> Delta Dawn

> Sonya Green & Annette Lawrence

On February 14th, 1982, an officer from the Arizona Department of Public Safety was patrolling an area off westbound Interstate 40 near the town of Williams, when he came upon the body of a young woman lying beneath a cedar tree just twenty feet off the shoulder of the road. Because of the date on which the remains were found, she would later be dubbed Valentine Sally.

The victim was a white female somewhere between the ages of fifteen and twenty-four, but probably around seventeen. She stood about five-foot-four, weighed one-hundred-twenty pounds, had long, straight, strawberry-blonde hair and blue eyes. She was clad in a red and white striped sweater, and a pair of size nine, Seasons brand designer jeans with a handkerchief in the pocket. The belt loops of the jeans were also notably torn, as if her killer had utilized them to drag her to the dump site.

Sally's other distinguishing features included healed scars on her left foot and right thigh, and the fact that she had had partial root canal surgery on one of her molars approximately one week before her death, which was thought to have occurred about ten to fourteen days prior to her body being recovered. Though the state of decomposition meant that the cause of death was not certain, it was believed that she had been either strangled or suffocated, though it did not appear that she had been sexually assaulted.

The area where the victim's body lay was adjacent to a long incline that truckers often used to pull over to cool their brakes, suggesting that whoever had killed Sally had probably been driving a semi truck, which would not appear suspicious parked at that particular spot.

The victim's hands were too degraded to obtain fingerprints, but dental charts and later DNA were successfully extracted, and a facial reconstruction sketch was produced. Not long after the sketch went public, a waitress named Patty Wilkins at the Monte Carlo Truck Stop in Ash Fork, Arizona contacted authorities and told them that she had seen a girl matching Sally's description at the restaurant at around three or four a.m. on the morning of February 4th.

Patty further stated that Sally had been in the company of an older white male, aged about sixty-five and wearing a cowboy hat accented with peacock feathers, who gave the impression of being the girl's father or other relative. Sally—who according to the waitress appeared to be about seventeen and was strikingly beautiful—had complained about the pain in her tooth and had asked for aspirin, but hadn't wanted any food. Patty told police that the man with Sally seemed genuinely concerned about her welfare, and went on to say that the situation had not struck her as sinister, or even particularly unusual.

Though the eyewitness sightings as well as the distinctive detail of the root canal gave investigators hope that the victim would be quickly identified, this was sadly not to be the case. Two years would go by with no leads, until in 1984 it was believed that Valentine Sally had been matched to her rightful name. But the outcome of that particular avenue would be a heartbreaking one that has yet to see a satisfactory resolution.

****

Less than a fortnight later, back in England on Thursday, February 25th, a pair of men out hunting pigeons in a copse near Chichester happened upon a human skull and part of a rib cage. It didn't take long for the partial skeleton to be identified as eight-year-old Vishal Mehrotra, who had disappeared on his way to the Putney tube station back in late July of 1981. Since the remains were recovered more than thirty miles away from where the boy had last been seen, it seemed almost certain that he had been abducted and murdered.

No clothing was found alongside the body, which was thought to have been deposited at the dump site on or around July 29th, the same day that Vishal had gone missing.

Police fielded more tips from the public, including the sighting of a suspicious vehicle parked on the A272 near where the bones were found, but all of the clues led to nothing but dead ends. Easily the most ominous occurrence in the days following the discovery of Vishal's body, though, was the phone call received by the child's father Vishambar.

The voice on the other end of the line informed Visham-bar that his son's death was connected to a secret cabal of highly-placed pedophiles who operated out of a former hotel called the Elm Guest House in southwest London, a location less than a mile from where Vishal had vanished. According to the caller, several prominent figures in the British government were engaged in kidnapping and sexually molesting young boys there.

Vishambar recorded the strange phone call and took the recording to police, but investigators didn't seem to take it all that seriously, believing it was probably a crank. The fact that the lead was not sufficiently followed up on, however, would suggest to many later researchers into the case that the authorities were deliberately trying to cover up for the judges, politicians, police officers, royals, and pop stars though to be involved in the alleged pedophile ring.

It would take until 2012 before the accusations concerning Elm Guest House would be formally looked into; an investigation called Operation Fairbank was launched on the back of a list of purported pedophiles drawn up by Labour councilor Chris Fay. Later investigations—Operation Fernbridge in 2013 and Operation Midland in 2015—failed to find any evidence of wrongdoing at Elm Guest House, though, and notably, Chris Fay was later convicted of fraud. In 2016, all investigations into the charges were ceased, and apologies were issued to people whose names had appeared on the list. Despite this, many individuals still suspect a cover-up in several cases of missing and murdered boys in the area.

There was another suspect in the murder of Vishal Mehrotra who was not connected to the goings-on at the Elm Guest House, but was involved with a proven gang of pedophiles nonetheless. This was Sidney Cooke, a carnival worker also known by the nickname Hissing Sid, who between the decades of the 1960s and the 1980s used his fairground "Test Your Strength" attraction to lure young boys into his orbit, whereby he would then drug them and take them back to his accomplices to gang-rape, abuse, and sometimes kill.

Though he was ultimately convicted of two murders—those of fourteen-year-old Jason Swift and seven-year-old Mark Tildesley—Cooke admitted to a horrifying number of rapes of young boys, and was given two life sentences in 1999. It should be noted that in July of 1981, there were two fun-fairs operating very close to the area where Vishal had disappeared.

Another person of interest in the homicide was laborer Brian Field, who in 2001 was convicted of the 1968 rape and murder of fourteen-year-old Roy Tutill. Though Field was reportedly investigated in regards to the death of Vishal Mehrotra, there was insufficient evidence to charge him with the crime.

The kidnapping and murder of the eight-year-old remains open and unsolved as of 2019.

****

Early that summer, back in the United States, a red-haired teenage girl would climb out of her bedroom window in the middle of the night and turn up dead exactly one month later, though her body would remain unidentified for more than thirty years.

Michelle Garvey was, in 1982, living with her family in New London, Connecticut, but by all accounts was something of a troubled girl. She had run away from home a few times before, and was once later found at a relative's house.

But on June 1st—two days before her fifteenth birthday—Michelle decided to leave once again, perhaps to return to her native New Jersey, a destination she had mentioned on several occasions. It is believed that she snuck out of her window in the wee hours of the morning, and perhaps got a ride with someone passing by, or maybe a friend with whom she had planned the whole escapade.

At any rate, when her parents discovered her absence, they duly reported her missing, though decades would pass before they received any closure on what had ultimately become of their daughter.

On July 1st, however, a set of human remains was recovered in Baytown, Texas, incidentally in the exact same spot where the bodies of the Harris County Does had been found buried back in January of 1981.

This victim, unidentified at the time, was a white female believed to be between fifteen and twenty, standing around five-foot-one, with blue eyes, curly red hair, and a scar on one foot. She was clad in corduroy pants and a brown, long-sleeved shirt with embroidery on the pocket. Because the shirt was unbuttoned and no bra or shoes were discovered, investigators assumed that she had been sexually assaulted before being strangled to death.

It took many years before the victim could be matched with a known missing person, largely due to the distance between the site where the body was found and the location from which the girl had vanished. But in 2014, after some detective work by amateur investigators on the Websleuths Internet forum, it was revealed that the remains belonged to fifteen-year-old Michelle Garvey, who had run away from her home in Connecticut a month prior to the body being found. How she came to be murdered more than seventeen-hundred miles away in Texas was a puzzling conundrum, and for a time it was thought that her death might have been linked to the Texas Killing Fields murders which have been discussed throughout this series.

Most detectives working the case surmise that Michelle must have been attempting to hitchhike to some unknown location and got into a car with the wrong person at some point, but further than that, there have been no new developments in the case since Michelle's identification and her subsequent laying to rest by the Garvey family.

****

Later that July, another young woman would be found murdered many miles away in New Jersey, but unlike in the previous case of Michelle Garvey, this victim has yet to have her identity restored.

On July 15th, 1982, a worker named George Kise at the Cedar Ridge Cemetery in Blairstown spotted something strange in a ravine at the rear of the graveyard. Upon closer inspection, he found that it was the corpse of what appeared to be a teenage girl whose face was so badly beaten and mutilated that she was unrecognizable.

The victim, later given the appellation Princess Doe, was white, thought to be between fourteen and eighteen years old, standing around five-foot-two and weighing approximately one-hundred-five pounds. She had brown, shoulder-length hair, but her eye color could not be determined due to the extensive trauma to the face. The pathologist also noted that her two front teeth were noticeably darker than the others.

When discovered, Princess Doe was clad in a red, short-sleeved V-neck sweater and an ankle-length peasant skirt, though neither shoes nor undergarments were ever found. There was a gold cross necklace tangled in her hair, and oddly, her fingernails were painted red, but only on her right hand. She otherwise had no significant identifying marks.

The autopsy estimated that Princess Doe had been dead for between one to three weeks. Cause of death was blunt force trauma to the head, but as the body had lain outdoors for so long in the stifling heat and humidity of the summer, it was never conclusively proven whether she had been sexually assaulted, or whether there was any trace of drugs in her system. Due to the presence of defensive wounds on her hands and arms, it was assumed that she had fought back against her attacker.

In the years since her discovery, there have been several theories floating around as to who Princess Doe was and who might have killed her. One persistent hypothesis held that she was actually Diane Dye, a teenager from San Jose, California who had gone missing in late July of 1979. Some law enforcement officers were so certain that Princess Doe was Diane Dye that they announced it at a 2003 press conference. However, other officers, as well as the Dye family, never believed that Princess Doe was Diane, and indeed, a later DNA comparison ruled this identification out.

Various other investigators have put forward the possibilities that she may have been a runaway who had been working in Ocean City, Maryland under an assumed name, or perhaps that she was a truck-stop prostitute in the New Jersey area, though neither of these claims has been substantiated. From an isotopic analysis of her teeth and clothing, it appeared that the girl had spent some time in the Midwest or Northeast, and perhaps Arizona, though the most solidly-backed theory is that she was probably from Long Island, New York. Several witnesses came forward after photos of her clothing were released to the public and stated that they had seen clothing very similar to hers in a particular store in Long Island, and one woman even claimed to have seen Princess Doe alive in a shop across the street from the cemetery about two days before it was thought she was murdered.

As far as suspects go, the strongest as of this writing is Arthur Kinlaw, whose name came to the attention of detectives in 1999 after his wife Donna was arrested in California for attempted welfare fraud. Donna reportedly told police that Arthur had murdered two women in 1982, crimes for which he was later convicted. She also stated that he had murdered a prostitute earlier that year, and that in July, he had brought a teenage girl to their home, who was later killed in a cemetery. Donna could not provide enough details about this particular homicide to confirm that it was Princess Doe, however, and a sketch she later produced of the girl her husband had brought home did not resemble the sketch of the unknown victim. While Arthur remains a person of interest, there is not enough evidence to tie him to Princess Doe, and until she is definitively identified, establishing a link between killer and victim will be next to impossible.

The people of Blairstown chipped in and laid the young girl to rest six months after her body was found, under a headstone reading, "Missing From Home, Dead Among Strangers, Remembered By All."

****

As the summer went on, back in British Columbia, Canada, the Highway of Tears would claim another young life, though as in the previously mentioned cases, the familiar assailant would eventually be found and charged.

On August 16th, 1982, the body of fifteen-year-old Nina Marie Joseph was discovered in Freeman Park in Prince George. She had been stripped naked and stabbed multiple times before being strangled with a length of cord from her own jacket.

As in the earlier homicides of Jean Mary Kovacs and Roswitha Fuchsbichler from the autumn of 1981, serial killer Edward Dennis Isaac would eventually be convicted of manslaughter in connection with the murder of Nina Joseph; his sentence was handed out in June of 1986. Key to his capture in Nina's specific case was the fact that Issac's ex-girlfriend testified against him, claiming that she had helped him dispose of Nina's body.

Though Isaac was thought to be responsible for only these three murders, many other serial killers were still out there prowling the Highway of Tears, and more victims would come to light before the decade was out.

****

Just over a week later, on August 24th, a pair of hikers out looking for mushrooms in Gambrills State Park in Frederick, Maryland chanced across a steamer trunk, which was partially covered with leaves and sticks, but did not appear to have been deliberately concealed. What the hikers found inside the trunk sent them hightailing it out of the area to summon the police.

When authorities arrived, they processed the scene. The abandoned trunk contained the skeletal remains of a white female, thought to be between eighteen and twenty-five years old but possibly as old as forty-five, standing around five-foot-two to five-foot-six, and weighing between one-hundred and one-hundred-thirty pounds. She had medium-length, reddish-brown hair and extensive dental work—including several fillings, two crowns, and a root canal—which appeared as though they had been performed quite a long time in the past or perhaps by a student at a dental school. No clothing or jewelry was found with the body; the only other object recovered from the trunk was a dark-colored towel.

Due to the state of decomposition, neither the cause of death nor the time of the homicide could be determined. The pathologist estimated that the woman could have been dead for up to ten years, and that it was possible she could have been strangled, but this was by no means certain.

The victim had suffered from a back injury known as spondylolysis, and this fact, coupled with the significant wear on her pelvis, suggested that in life she had been a dancer, cheerleader, or gymnast, leading her to be dubbed by investigators, "The Cheerleader in the Trunk."

Unfortunately, her remains were far too degraded to obtain either fingerprints or DNA, though an updated sketch of her face was released to the public in 2012 in the hopes that someone would recognize her. As of this writing, though, her identity and that of the person who killed her are still a mystery.

****

Two days later and more than two-thousand miles away, a little girl would be abducted only a few feet from her home and be found dead weeks later. Her murder would become instrumental in the establishment of a more codified law enforcement response to missing children cases, and serve as the basis for the 1983 passage of the Missing Children's Act in the US Congress.

Three-year-old Rachael Runyan lived in the small, seemingly safe town of Sunset, Utah with her parents and her two brothers: five-year-old Justin, and eighteen-month-old Nate. The Runyans' house was situated adjacent to the playground of Doxey Elementary School, and was also very close to Mitchell Park, where the children often played.

It was shortly before noon on Thursday, August 26th, 1982, and the three children asked their mother Elaine if they could go to the school playground for a little while before they ate. Ordinarily, Elaine wouldn't have allowed them to go outside to play on their own, but the playground was only fifteen feet from the house, and Elaine could keep an eye on the children through the kitchen window as she prepared their lunch, so she told them it would be all right.

Approximately one hour later, Elaine called the kids back, but only Justin and Nate answered her summons, and they seemed terrified. They told their mother that a man had approached them and told them he would take them to the nearby grocery store and buy them bubble gum and ice cream. All three children had followed him part of the way to his car before thinking better of it, but when Justin and Nate expressed doubts about accompanying him, the man had suddenly snatched up the screaming Rachael, stuffed her into his vehicle, and taken off.

The boys described the kidnapper as an African-American male in his early thirties, standing about six feet tall with a fairly slim build. They said he had a handlebar mustache and hair cut in a short Afro, and had driven away in an older-model, blue four-door with wood paneling on the sides. Justin and Nate further stated that the man had been sitting in Mitchell Park drinking a cup of coffee and talking to various children before he ultimately abducted Rachael.

Authorities as well as the Runyan family wasted no time in beginning a desperate search for the child, going from house to house, distributing composite sketches of the perpetrator, and taking to the national media to ask for the public's help in finding little Rachael. A few leads did crop up in the wake of the investigation, but sadly, all led to dead ends.

The search would proceed at full tilt until the late afternoon of September 19th, when it would come to a tragic conclusion. A family out picnicking in the town of Mountain Green, approximately fifteen miles from Sunset, discovered what they initially believed was a doll partially floating in a stream. To their horror, they soon realized that they had actually stumbled across the nude, hog-tied, and horribly decomposed body of three-year-old Rachael Runyan.

Though cause of death could not be established due to the state of decomposition, the coroner surmised that the girl had perhaps been smothered. He was unable to reliably ascertain whether she had been raped, but given the fact that the child was found naked, it seemed a likely prospect.

Shortly after Rachael's remains were laid to rest, the US Congress passed the Missing Children's Act, which would establish a database of the descriptions, blood types, and fingerprints of missing children with the FBI, and further allow parents of missing children to access this database. The state of Utah also later put in place the Rachael Alert system to quickly inform the public of active child abduction cases and prioritize media announcements when kidnappings occurred. This system was in place until 2003, when it became subsumed under the nationwide AMBER Alert system.

In 1985, police looked into the possibility that a Satanic cult had perhaps been involved with the crime, after a bizarre message was found scrawled on the wall of a laundromat near where Rachael's body was found. It read: "Beware. I'm still at large. I killed the little Runyan girl! Remember beware!!!" The note was signed with an upside-down cross and the numbers 666. Though this avenue of inquiry was pursued, most investigators seem to have come to the conclusion that the message was written by a prankster.

The Rachael Runyan case was reopened in 2007, and though DNA tests were performed on a few items that had been found with Rachael's body, none yielded any solid leads. But the most promising person of interest in the case came to light in 2011, when a man was arrested in Pennsylvania for assaulting his girlfriend and abducting their five-year-old son, who was luckily found unharmed.

Upon investigating this individual, detectives determined that he had been living in Sunset, Utah at the time Rachael was murdered, that he closely resembled the composite sketch produced by the description given by Justin and Nate Runyan, and that he had a relative who owned a four-door blue car with wood paneling, very similar to the vehicle the kidnapper had been seen leaving the scene of the crime in. Police do not have sufficient evidence to charge this man with the murder, though he remains at the top of their suspect list.

Rachael's mother Elaine has gone on to become a tireless advocate for missing and abducted children. The park from which Rachael was taken was renamed in the child's honor in 2016, and in 2017, Utah established the Rachael Runyan Missing and Exploited Children's Day on August 26th in order to bring greater public attention to child safety issues.

****

As fall of 1982 began to descend, an alarming series of tragedies would begin to unfold in the suburban communities in and around Chicago, Illinois. The aftermath of the incident—which would leave seven people dead and an entire nation terrified and paranoid—would lead to sweeping changes in US law, as well as a significant alteration of the culture itself.

On September 29th, 1982, twelve-year-old Mary Kellerman woke up in her Elk Grove Village home with mild cold symptoms. Her parents gave her a single extra-strength Tylenol capsule, the type that contained acetaminophen. Less than an hour later, the little girl was dead.

About seven miles away, in the suburb of Arlington Heights, a twenty-seven-year-old postal worker named Adam Janus also passed away, from what at first was believed to be a sudden and massive heart attack. Upon hearing of the death, Adam's family members descended on his home to offer mutual support to one another. While gathered there, Adam's twenty-five-year-old brother Stanley and Stanley's nineteen-year-old wife Theresa both swallowed Tylenol capsules from the bottle in Adam's medicine cabinet. Stanley died later that afternoon, while Theresa lingered in the hospital for two days before also expiring.

The following few days would see three more suspicious deaths in the area: thirty-five-year-old Mary McFarland, thirty-five-year-old Paula Prince, and twenty-seven-year-old Mary Weiner. By this stage, September had given way to October, Adam Janus's cause of death had been found to be cyanide poisoning, and authorities were beginning to link all these mysterious crimes to bottles of extra-strength Tylenol.

Sure enough, once the capsules from all of the victims' households were tested, it became clear that someone was adulterating random packages of the over-the-counter medications with potassium cyanide. Thorough searches of retail locations selling the medicine in the Chicago area produced a further three bottles of poisoned capsules still available for purchase at local drug stores.

Police, as well as Johnson & Johnson—the manufacturers of Tylenol—reacted with admirable swiftness to the crisis, alerting the media, driving the streets with bullhorns, even going door to door in Chicago neighborhoods to get warnings out and confiscate bottles of the offending painkillers. Johnson & Johnson immediately issued a recall of the over thirty-one-million bottles of extra-strength Tylenol in US circulation, and instantly ceased all advertising of the product as well.

An investigation into the source of the tampering soon ruled out adulteration at the manufacturing level, since the tainted bottles had all been produced by different pharmaceutical factories. And because the deaths all occurred around the Chicago area, it was deduced that the killer was stealing or purchasing bottles of Tylenol from various retail outlets, tampering with the capsules, then sneaking them back onto store shelves. Indeed, security footage of victim Paula Prince in one of the affected stores showed an unidentified, bearded man following quite closely behind her as she shopped. Though detectives sought this man as a person of interest, they were never able to locate him.

One suspect who helpfully announced himself, however, was James William Lewis, who in October of 1982 sent a letter to Johnson & Johnson claiming responsibility for the poisonings and demanding a one-million-dollar ransom to cease his activities. But Lewis lived in New York City, not Chicago, and police were unable to find any further evidence linking him to the product tampering, though he was charged with extortion and ended up serving thirteen years in prison; he was released in 1995.

Another man named Roger Arnold was also investigated, and though he was cleared, the media frenzy that followed in the wake of his questioning would end up having tragic consequences. Arnold blamed an acquaintance of his, Marty Sinclair, for allegedly telling police that he kept potassium cyanide in his home, and in 1983 he decided to kill Sinclair for betraying him. Unfortunately, Arnold instead shot another individual who only resembled Sinclair: John Stanisha, who was completely uninvolved with the incident and didn't know either man. Arnold was later convicted of second-degree murder and served fifteen years. He died in 2008.

Other persons of interest included rampage poisoner and shooter Laurie Dann from Winnetka, Illinois, as well as notorious Unabomber Ted Kaczynski, but neither of these leads have so far borne any fruit.

In a heartbreaking coda to the case, several copycat incidents took place in the years following the original outbreak, including additional deaths in New York, Texas, and Washington State.

The panic and uncertainty surrounding the entire affair led to many notable changes in the United States, including a 1983 law making it a federal offense to tamper with consumer products. Johnson & Johnson and other large corporations also worked together with law enforcement to develop more stringent quality controls at the point of product manufacture, and most famously introduced much more tamper-resistant packaging, including foil induction seals and the replacement of the capsule drug format to the now-ubiquitous solid pill "caplet." Consumer experts have credited Johnson & Johnson's honest, immediate reaction to the tragedy and their willingness to work with law enforcement to improve product safety around the country for their almost unbelievable return to market dominance less than a year after the poisonings occurred.

The investigation into the Chicago Tylenol Murders was reopened in 2009, on the twenty-fifth anniversary of the event, and shortly afterward, original suspect and ransom letter writer James William Lewis willingly gave a DNA sample to the FBI, as did his wife. Federal agents also searched the Lewis home in Massachusetts, but have not released their findings to the public at this writing.

****

Miles to the south, on the fifth of December 1982, a trucker by the name of Ted Hammond was driving a route that took him through Moss Point, Mississippi when he noticed what appeared to be the body of a young woman floating in the Dog River (now known as the Escatawpa River). He called police, informing them that the woman was face down and wearing a blue plaid shirt.

Investigators arrived on the scene in short order, but could not find a woman's body where the trucker had specified. Broadening their search, however, uncovered something even more horrific: the remains of a little girl in the very same river, concealed by weeds around ten miles from the I-10 bridge.

The victim was white, and between one and two years old, with curly, strawberry-blonde hair and an indeterminate eye color thought to be blue or brown. She was dressed in a pink, checkered dress and a diaper, and appeared healthy and well-nourished, weighing around twenty-five pounds.

When the toddler was examined by pathologists, it was determined that she had been dead for approximately thirty-six to forty-eight hours prior to being found. It looked as though someone had attempted to smother the child before throwing her off the side of the bridge, but she was still alive when she hit the river; the presence of water in her lungs suggested that she had drowned.

After a description of the girl—dubbed Delta Dawn or Baby Jane—was released to the public, several witnesses came forward to state that, days earlier, they had spotted a barefoot young woman in a blue plaid shirt carrying a toddler along the side of the I-10. The witnesses further claimed that this woman was clearly agitated, and though a handful of them had apparently pulled over and asked if she needed help, she refused all offers.

The sightings of this mysterious woman—perhaps Delta Dawn's mother—led detectives to speculate that the woman had either attempted to smother her own child before throwing herself into the river to commit suicide, or alternately that a male perpetrator had picked up both the woman and the toddler and had murdered them both. Neither line of inquiry yielded anything close to a break in the case.

To date, the body of the unknown young woman has never been found, and Delta Dawn has still not been identified. Though DNA was successfully extracted from the child's remains in 2009, there have been no matches, and the case has been at a near standstill for the past ten years.

****

Just before Christmas of 1982, in Ohio, two murders would take place within a week of one another, with the bodies discovered in very close proximity. To this day, neither case has been resolved, and it is unknown whether the two crimes are related, though it seems quite likely.

On Wednesday, December 15th, fourteen-year-old Sonya Green left her East Cleveland home at a little past eight a.m. to go to school at Kirk Junior High. She evidently never made it there. Her body was found buried under a snow bank behind Severance Center the following day; she had been either strangled or asphyxiated.

Days later, on the 23rd, the remains of young teacher Annette Lawrence were found in the same spot, albeit in the trunk of her own car. Specific cause of death was unclear, though obviously a homicide.

Cleveland police renewed efforts to solve both cases in 2016, but no progress has been made since that time.

1983

> The Redhead Murders

> St. Louis Jane Doe

> Peter Ivers

> Janice Weston

> The Texas Killing Fields

> Donna Jean Awcock

On the day before Valentine's Day of 1983, a body was found alongside a West Virginia highway, and although law enforcement wasn't aware of it yet, the dead woman may have been the first discovered victim of a possible serial killer who seemed to target red-haired females.

An elderly couple was traveling along Route 250 in Littleton, West Virginia when they saw what appeared to be a nude mannequin just off the side of the road. They stopped their vehicle for a closer look, and realized instead that the naked corpse of a woman had been dumped just off the shoulder of the highway.

The victim was thought to be between thirty-five and forty-five years old, stood about five-foot-six, and weighed one-hundred-thirty-five pounds. She had reddish-auburn hair, and likely brown eyes, though the state of decomposition of the remains made her eye color difficult to determine. Other distinguishing marks included a Caesarean scar across her abdomen, and another small scar on one of her index fingers. A post-mortem determined that she had been dead for approximately two days.

Because there was snow on the ground but none on the body, and because there were signs of footprints in the frost, it was believed that the woman had been killed elsewhere and dumped there not long before the couple happened across her. The cause of death could not be verified with any certainty, though the pathologist surmised that she had been strangled or suffocated. She did not appear to have been sexually assaulted, and her excellent physical hygiene made detectives doubt that she was a transient or a prostitute.

The victim was never identified, and thus became known as Wetzel County Jane Doe. When information about her death was released to the public, a witness came forward and claimed they had seen the unknown woman in a bar in Wheeling, West Virginia not long before her body was found. Another witness reported seeing a middle-aged white male of average height and weight near the spot where the woman's body had been dumped. Police sought the man for questioning, but his identity was likewise never established.

It is still unclear whether Wetzel County Jane Doe was indeed the victim of the serial killer responsible for the so-called Redhead Murders that would take place throughout the 1980s across a vast swath of states, including, not only West Virginia, but also Pennsylvania, Kentucky, Tennessee, Arkansas, and Mississippi. This killer, sometimes referred to as the Bible Belt Strangler, seemed to target prostitutes or hitchhiking women and girls who had red or auburn hair, and is believed to have murdered between six and eleven victims, more of which will be discussed later on in this book.

****

A little over two weeks later, on February 28th in St. Louis, Missouri, two individuals broke into an abandoned Victorian house on Clemens Avenue, ostensibly to look for scrap metal. While they were in the basement of the dwelling, one of them decided to light a cigarette, and the glow from its tip suddenly illuminated a grisly scene.

Lying on the floor of the basement was the half-nude body of a young woman, situated on her stomach. She wore a bloody yellow sweater with long sleeves, though her pants and underwear were missing. Her hands were tied behind her back with red nylon cord.

Worst of all, the victim had been cleanly decapitated. Her head was nowhere to be seen.

When authorities arrived, they carefully turned the victim over and realized that she was much younger than they had initially estimated: perhaps only between eight and eleven years old. She was an African-American child, probably between four-foot-ten and five-foot-six. She had no unusual marks or scars, save for evidence that she might have suffered from a mild form of spina bifida. Her fingernails bore two coats of red polish.

During the autopsy, it was confirmed that she had been raped, and probably killed by strangulation before being beheaded with an extremely sharp carving knife. Because the basement was nearly free of blood, it was assumed that the girl had been murdered elsewhere and later left in the abandoned house, presumably around five days before she was discovered.

The investigation was stymied, of course, by the failure to find the girl's head; neither facial reconstruction nor dental records could be utilized to help identify the victim. To add insult to injury, police desperately sent the girl's sweater and the red cord that had bound her wrists to a psychic several years after the murder, but the evidence was subsequently lost in the mail and has never been recovered.

Unfortunately, the St. Louis Jane Doe—sometimes also referred to as Hope or Little Jane Doe—matched no area missing persons cases, and remains unknown to this day. Her body was exhumed in 2013 to obtain a DNA profile, and at that time an isotopic analysis of her bones was also performed. The results of that analysis seemed to suggest that the girl was probably a native of one of the states of the American southeast, though her origins could not be narrowed down any further.

While the child remains unidentified, a person of interest in the murder was eventually singled out: a man by the name of Vernon Brown, who had spent four years in prison after a 1973 conviction for molesting a twelve-year-old girl. He was later suspected of the murder of a nine-year-old named Kimberly Andrews, and in 1986 admitted to two more killings, those of nine-year-old Janet Perkins and nineteen-year-old Synetta Ford. Janet was bound and strangled with a rope, while Synetta was strangled with electrical cord and stabbed multiple times.

Though Vernon Brown never confessed to killing St. Louis Jane Doe, he was convicted of the other crimes, and was executed by lethal injection in 2005. The gruesome death of the little girl found beheaded in the basement of the Clemens Avenue Victorian has yet to be resolved.

****

In early March of 1983, within the hip, underground music and film scenes of Los Angeles, California, a murder would take place that snatched from the world a man whose name is mostly forgotten today, even though at the time he stood at the nexus of everything that was experimental and up-and-coming in the 1980s; a man so connected that his biographer Josh Frank linked him "to every major pop culture event of the last thirty years."

Peter Ivers was born in Chicago, but didn't live there long before moving to Arizona with his family, and then on to Boston. When he grew older, he studied classical languages at Harvard, but later found his passion and became a musician and songwriter, playing harmonica and singing, and releasing his first album in 1969. He also performed live as the opening act for The New York Dolls and Fleetwood Mac on separate occasions.

Despite the relatively low profile of his own work, Peter had many influential fans and friends, and was instrumental in many burgeoning entertainment scenes after moving to Los Angeles in the early 1970s. Most famously, in 1977, he wrote and sang "In Heaven (The Lady in the Radiator Song)" for David Lynch's debut film *Eraserhead*, and later was able, through his girlfriend Lucy Fisher, to arrange a screening of the movie for Francis Ford Coppola and Mel Brooks, who would go on to offer David Lynch the director's chair on *The Elephant Man*, a move that surely launched Lynch's long and esteemed career.

Peter was also closely allied with John Belushi, Harold Ramis, and other well-known LA comedians, and was involved with both *National Lampoon* and *Saturday Night Live*. He played harmonica with John Cale, and was called the greatest harmonica player alive by no less than Muddy Waters. He produced an EP by Swans' frontman Michael Gira, and later wrote songs for the Pointer Sisters and Diana Ross.

Perhaps his best-known credit today, however, was as host of the television program *New Wave Theatre*, which started its life on a local UHF station in Los Angeles before going national on the young USA Network as part of their *Night Flight* variety show. The program featured live performances by new wave and punk bands from the LA area, such as the Dead Kennedys, Fear, 45 Grave, The Circle Jerks, and The Angry Samoans, as well as interviews with the bands, skits, and weird interstitial video clips.

While Peter Ivers was the theatrical, sardonic face of *New Wave Theatre*, the show had been created by Canadian David Jove, who had reportedly spent the sixties hanging out with the Rolling Stones, calling himself Acid King Dave, and allegedly participating in the notorious Redlands drug bust of Mick Jagger and Keith Richards. He later went on to helm another alternative-music-based variety show called *The Top*, which also featured comedians such as Bill Murray, Dan Aykroyd, Chevy Chase, Andy Kaufman, and Rodney Dangerfield. David Jove's name would come up in a far more sinister capacity after the spring of 1983, however.

On March 3rd, Peter Ivers, then thirty-six years old, was found bludgeoned to death by a hammer in his Los Angeles loft. Police who arrived to investigate the homicide, for whatever reason, seemed rather cavalier about securing the crime scene, allowing Peter's friends and admirers to go through his apartment, contaminating any evidence that might have been present. Most infamously, *New Wave Theatre* creator David Jove was permitted to take the bloodied blankets off of Peter's bed, an act that fueled speculation later on that Jove had been the killer.

Indeed, many of Peter's friends still maintain that David Jove was the most likely suspect, due to his purportedly provocative and bullying behavior, with one acquaintance in particular comparing him to Charles Manson. Comedian Harold Ramis, also briefly a suspect before being cleared, admitted that of everyone in their circles, Jove was the only person he couldn't rule out in the murder.

On the other hand, others who knew Jove, including many LA musicians who had featured on his show, believed that he was innocent. David Jove passed away from pancreatic cancer in 2004, denying killing Peter until the very end.

Other theories had it that perhaps Peter Ivers was slain by someone targeting David Jove, or was perhaps just the unlucky victim of a random homicide perpetrated by someone looking for money or drugs. The neighborhood where he lived, it should be noted, was essentially Skid Row, populated by squatters and various lowlifes.

Not surprisingly, given the slapdash nature of the LAPD investigation, the murder of Peter Ivers very quickly went cold, and the name of this multi-talented man, who was at the hub of so much of the cultural vanguard of the era, slowly drifted into obscurity. When Josh Frank and Charlie Buckholtz wrote a biography of Peter in 2008, it prompted authorities to reopen the case, though missing and tainted evidence is still impeding the investigation to this day.

Harvard University established the Peter Ivers Visiting Artist Program shortly after his death, at the behest of his girlfriend Lucy Fisher.

****

Later on that fall, across the Atlantic Ocean, a wealthy, professional woman would be savagely beaten to death by the side of a road in England, and though many strange clues hint at an unusually intriguing mystery surrounding her slaying, it remains unresolved more than three decades later.

Thirty-six-year-old Janice Weston was a successful solicitor, a partner at a firm known as Charles Russell and Company, and aside from her generous salary was also quite well off due to a large inheritance left to her by an elderly associate. She lived in West London with her husband Tony, a property speculator.

On September 10th, 1983, a Saturday, Janice was reportedly at her office until sometime between four and five o'clock in the afternoon, after which she drove home to her flat and prepared a meal. Tony was away in Paris all weekend, showing a chateau to a pair of prospective buyers.

At some point before she had finished eating, Janice apparently needed to leave the flat, and she did so, abandoning half her dinner and a partially drunk glass of wine on the table. Oddly, she took an overnight bag with her, as well as a bottle of wine, half a loaf of bread, the manuscript of a book she was working on, and a small purse containing thirty-seven pounds in cash, but she left her larger handbag—which held her credit cards and identification—behind at home. She then headed out in her silver Alfa Romeo. Speculatively, she may have been heading to Clopton Hall, Northamptonshire, where she and her husband owned an investment property that they were in the process of refurbishing, though it is notable that the property was at the time unfinished and contained no furniture or amenities, other than a couple of sleeping bags.

The following morning, at approximately nine a.m., a cyclist on the northbound A1 discovered the body of Janet Weston, just half a mile south of the Brampton Hut roundabout. Janice was fully clothed, but her head and face had been bashed in with a car jack, which was recovered not far away. Her facial injuries were so severe that it took police three days to conclusively identify her. She also had numerous other defensive wounds, indicating that she had fought viciously against her attacker.

On September 15th, Janice's Alfa Romeo turned up abandoned in Regents Park, smeared with bloodstains but free of fingerprints. The location where the car had been discarded was only about three miles from the Weston residence.

As the homicide investigation proceeded, it was confirmed that Janice had likely stopped to change a flat tire very near to where her body had been found; she had purportedly picked up a spare tire from a shop in Kensington on the day before her death, and this tire had been fitted on the rear driver's side, though bizarrely, the original tire was never located. Investigators also discovered oil on Janice's fingers.

It was clear from the outset that robbery was probably not the motive, as Janice's purse, still containing cash, was found beneath the seat of the vehicle. A half-empty bottle of wine was also present, perhaps suggesting that someone else had been in the car with Janice, for she was reportedly adamant about not drinking and driving.

The moment Janice's husband Tony arrived home from his business trip in France, police picked him up and commenced grilling him for over fifty hours, though he had several witnesses, both clients and hotel employees, who placed him in Paris the entire weekend. He was subsequently released, though investigators could not rule out the possibility that he could have hired someone to kill his wife in his absence.

A close friend of Janice's named Sheila Surgeoner informed detectives, however, that Janice had sometimes been in the habit of picking up hitchhikers, and hypothesized that one such person may have done her in.

A few interesting leads bubbled to the surface in the days following Janice's death. As many as six witnesses came forward to claim that they had seen a man changing the tire on a silver Alfa Romeo by the side of the A1 sometime around midnight on Saturday. This individual was never identified.

Eerier still, a man who owned a tire store in Royston told police that shortly after Janice's body was discovered on September 11th, a man had come into the shop to purchase two license plates that were reportedly the same numbers as those from Janice's vehicle. This man was likewise never located, though descriptions of his clothing were similar to those worn by the person seen changing the tire on the side of the motorway.

Many theories have been put forward about the enigmatic case, most of them attempting to account for Janice's possible destination and her somewhat odd behavior before her disappearance. It seemed that she had left her flat in a hurry, perhaps to meet someone who eventually ended up killing her following an altercation. The brutality of the crime, the use of a weapon of convenience, and the fact that the body was not hidden tends to support the idea that the murder was not planned, and maybe undertaken by someone who knew the victim.

Since the murderer had obviously driven Janice's car away after the crime, it would seem that he had either been in the car with her or had approached her on foot. Whether this was the same man who was allegedly seen purchasing the license plates the next day is still unknown. And though the spot where she was found and her probable direction of travel indicated that she might have been going to the Clopton Hall property, this is by no means certain, though the keys to the house were found on her person.

Some researchers have suggested that the spare tire could have been the key to the whole mystery, as it may have contained drugs that either Janice or her husband Tony was attempting to smuggle. However, there is little evidence to support this hypothesis, and it seems unlikely that the wealthy Janice would get involved in drug smuggling when she was definitely not short of money.

The investigation into the murder of Janice Weston was reopened in 2018, but as of this writing, the puzzle has yet to be solved.

****

In October of 1983, the cursed parcel of land known as the Texas Killing Fields would swallow up yet another young woman, though her remains would not be found until the following year.

Twenty-three-year-old cocktail waitress Heide Villareal-Fye was, like earlier Killing Fields victims Brooks Bracewell and Georgia Geer, last seen leaving a convenience store, where she had gone to use a pay phone, though the store in this particular case was in League City, Texas. Heide disappeared on October 10th, and her whereabouts would be unknown until the spring of 1984.

****

Three days later, in London, Ontario, Canada, a young woman would be gruesomely murdered in a fashion reminiscent of some earlier crimes in the area, and the city's unofficial moniker of "the serial killer capital of the world" would get yet another possible point for accuracy.

Seventeen-year-old Donna Jean Awcock had been baby-sitting for a neighbor on the night of October 13th, 1983, but hadn't yet phoned home to tell her mother when she would be getting back. In fact, it seems that at around two-thirty a.m. on the morning of the 14th, Donna walked to a convenience store a couple of blocks away to purchase some cigarettes. She was never seen alive again.

On the following afternoon, police recovered her half-nude and badly bruised body from the banks of the Thames River near Fanshawe Dam. She had been raped and manually strangled.

Significantly, the killer had also left an orange plastic bag stuffed down the victim's throat, perhaps to prevent her from screaming. This detail was telling, as it tied in with a handful of other murders by the so-called "Tissue Slayer" that had taken place years earlier, specifically the killings of sixteen-year-old Jacqueline Dunleavy and nine-year-old Frankie Jensen, both of whom had been murdered in 1968 and found with pink facial tissues stuffed down their throats. A third victim, sixty-six-year-old Irene Gibbons, was slain in her home in the summer of 1975 in a somewhat similar manner. All three cases were discussed in the second volume of this work.

It remains possible that Donna may have been a victim of one of the serial killers operating around London, Ontario at the time, though her family has gone on record as stating that they believe the man who killed her had been stalking her for quite some time and moved west after the murder, never to be heard from again.

A new appeal for information in the case was made in late 2017, though no fresh leads have been forthcoming, and the fifty-thousand-dollar reward remains unclaimed.

****

The month of October had yet to draw to a close when the predator stalking the Texas Killing Fields seemed to strike again, though the victim in this instance has yet to be located.

Fourteen-year-old Sondra Ramber was last seen at her home in Santa Fe, Texas, but what happened to her after that was anyone's guess. When her parents returned to the house on the late afternoon of October 26th, they found the front door standing wide open, food cooking in the oven, and Sondra's coat and purse still in her room.

Authorities believe that her disappearance is likely linked to other Texas Killing Fields crimes, but as of this writing, no definitive connection has been made.

1984

- Valentine Sally
- The Texas Killing Fields
- The Kerry Babies Case
- The Keddie Murders
- Vernon County Jane Doe
- Catrine da Costa
- Dorothy Scott
- Margaret & Seana Tapp
- The Redhead Murders
- Christine Jessop
- Grégory Villemin
- Günther Stoll: The YOG'TZE Case
- Lisa Hession

In the first months of 1984, Lieutenant Jack Judd of the Coconino County Sheriff's Office in Arizona believed he might have hit upon a lead in the case of Valentine Sally, the unidentified young woman found near Interstate 40 on February 14th of 1982. While poring through the missing persons files, he discovered a record of a girl named Melody Cutlip, who had run away from her home in Florida back in 1980. Thinking that the teeth in the photo of Melody looked similar to the teeth of Valentine Sally, he sent the information off to an expert to see if there was a match.

Using a rather questionable method—that is, attempting to line up Valentine Sally's bite marks with an enlarged photograph of Melody Cutlip's teeth—odontologist Homer Campbell declared that the two young women were one and the same, and the sheriff's office proceeded to contact the Cutlip family in Florida to let them know that their daughter had been located dead in Arizona and would be shipped home for burial forthwith.

However, Melody's parents did not believe that Valentine Sally was their missing daughter, and declined to have the remains shipped to them. Consequently, Valentine Sally was buried in Arizona under a headstone paid for by Patty Wilkins, the truck stop waitress who had been one of the last people to see Sally alive. The grave marker bore two names: Sally Valentine, and Melody Cutlip.

But in a happy turn of events, Melody Cutlip turned up alive and well at her parents' Florida home in 1986. Though the family made numerous attempts to have Valentine Sally's gravestone scrubbed of their daughter's name, they were never successful in doing so, and in an eerie and tragic twist, Melody herself actually died twelve years later, in a 1998 car accident in Louisiana.

The identity of Valentine Sally, then, remains unknown.

****

On April 4th, 1984, in League City, Texas, a dog returned to its owner's home on Calder Road after a brief exploration of the neighborhood. The animal carried a human skull in its mouth.

Tracing the dog's movements back, the remainder of the body was discovered, and quickly identified as belonging to twenty-three-year-old Heide Villareal-Fye, last seen using a pay phone at a League City convenience store on October 10th, 1983. The victim had been beaten severely with some blunt, heavy object, resulting in broken ribs and a fractured skull that was most likely the cause of death.

The Texas Killing Fields, it seemed, had stolen another young life.

****

Ten days later and more than four-thousand miles away, the finding of a dead infant on an Irish beach would lead to a gross miscarriage of justice and a cultural sea-change in the country concerning women's rights, a long-standing fight that still continues to the present day.

It was April 14th, and a man jogging along White Strand beach in Cahirsiveen, County Kerry, Republic of Ireland happened upon the remains of a three-day-old baby in the sand. The child had been strangled, and stabbed more than two dozen times.

The Irish police, known commonly as the Gardaí, had no clue as to who the infant belonged to, or who might have murdered him. The ensuing inquiry, which to modern sensibilities seems like something more akin to a medieval witch hunt than a twentieth-century police investigation, saw detectives grilling thousands of women of child-bearing age from across the peninsula, trying to locate someone who might have just given birth, and asking probing questions about boyfriends, adultery, sexual histories, and whether the women knew anyone who had been hiding their pregnancy or had attempted to obtain an illegal abortion at some point in the recent past.

Soon enough, the Gardaí had found a candidate: a twenty-four-year-old woman named Joanne Hayes, who lived on a small farm in Abbeydorney, about fifty miles away from the beach where the murdered infant—dubbed Baby John—had been found.

Joanne seemed to tick all the boxes: she had been having an affair with a married man named Jeremiah Locke, which had come to an end a few months before. She had been pregnant and trying to conceal it from family and coworkers. And she had given birth to a child only one day before Baby John's remains were recovered.

Joanne was brought before the Gardaí and interrogated. The baby she had given birth to, she said, had died shortly after being born, and she had buried him secretly at the family farm. She had developed complications a few days after the birth, however, which had necessitated her visiting a hospital; the Gardaí had seen a record of this when they scoured the medical files of all the facilities in the area. She insisted that Baby John was not her child, and claimed she could prove it, if only they would dig at her family's farm and find the body of her own infant.

But after hours of alleged strong-arming and possible physical force exerted by the Gardaí, a confused and exhausted Joanne confessed to having killed Baby John. She would later maintain that the Gardaí had threatened her and her daughter Yvonne in order to get her to own up to the crime. In fact, after the interrogation, she rather quickly recanted her confession, charging that it had been coerced out of her.

Joanne was sent to a psychiatric hospital, where she was finally able to convince the authorities to search the farm where she lived. There they found the remains of a newborn infant, exactly where Joanne had claimed they would be, and what's more, the baby had type O blood, just like Joanne did. The child found on the beach had blood type A.

Though police grudgingly dropped the charges, it didn't stop them from still attempting to pin Baby John's murder on the hapless Joanne. They tried to account for the differing blood types by theorizing that Joanne had actually given birth to twins fathered by two different men, via the rare condition of heteropaternal superfecundation. Though this scenario was not impossible, it seemed far-fetched, given the circumstances.

Worse still, during the investigation, the authorities had few qualms about assassinating Joanne's character, exposing her private life to public scrutiny and excoriating her sexual morality. The Ireland of 1984, it must be stressed, was still very much under the patriarchal sway of the Catholic Church: abortion, long since unobtainable in practice, had been officially made illegal the year before. Contraception was only prescribed to married women, and then only sparingly. Even condoms required a prescription for purchase. Irish schools, with church-approved curriculum, did not teach any form of sex education. Even divorce was illegal up until 1996. The stigma surrounding out-of-wedlock births was so profound that it was not unusual at all for girls to die giving birth in hiding, or even going so far as dumping their newborns in rivers or quarries to keep from having to own up to the societal shame of being an unwed mother.

In this cultural atmosphere, then, it was not surprising that Joanne Hayes was vilified, though many Irish women sympathized with her plight and sent her yellow roses in support. The police who questioned Joanne were investigated, but later cleared of all charges that they had physically and psychologically coerced her into a false confession. Thirty-four years after the incident, they formally apologized, and in 2019, reportedly offered a monetary settlement to the Hayes family, though the sum apparently came with some strings attached: Joanne would not be allowed to take any further legal action against the Gardaí, would receive no written apology, and would be forbidden from discussing the case going forward. In addition, the State would admit to no liability in the matter. As of this writing, the Hayes family has not accepted these conditions and is considering legal action.

The murder inquiry into the death of Baby John was reopened in 2018, but so far has not been resolved.

****

Back in Plumas County, California, more than three years had passed since the grisly multiple murder at cabin twenty-eight in Keddie. In the interim, nothing of note had occurred in the investigation, but then came April 22nd, 1984.

A man out collecting bottles at a camp near Feather Falls stumbled across part of a human skull and jawbone lying in the dirt. Before the remains were identified, the sheriff's office of Butte County received an anonymous telephone call claiming that the bones belonged to twelve-year-old Tina Sharp, who had been missing since her mother, brother, and a family friend had been viciously slain in April of 1981.

Sure enough, later that summer, the remains were indeed confirmed as those of Tina Sharp. The spot where she had been found lay nearly one-hundred miles away from her family's cabin in Keddie. Discovered along with the body was a pair of Levi's jeans with one pocket missing, a child's blanket, a blue jacket, and an empty dispenser of surgical tape.

Suspects Marty Smartt and Bo Boubede had been cleared of the murders after passing polygraph tests, but new evidence later came to light that seemed to complicate the issue. At the time of the slayings, Marty had stated that he had lost or misplaced a hammer from his own cabin; this was significant because two hammers had been used to slaughter Glenna Sue Sharp and the other victims, and only one was recovered from the scene. In 2016, though, a hammer matching the description of the one Marty claimed to have lost was dredged from a pond near the Smartt's former cabin. Its location suggested to investigators that the weapon had been deliberately concealed there.

Bo Boubede died in 1988, and Marty Smartt in 2000; neither was ever charged in the Keddie murder case. In 2018, however, more new leads surfaced in the form of a DNA profile obtained from a piece of tape found at the crime scene. This profile, according to investigators, matches a living suspect, which would seem to rule out Marty Smartt and Bo Boubede, who are both deceased. No further announcements as to this suspect's identity have yet been made.

The ghastly quadruple murder at cabin twenty-eight has long been a topic of fascination with the American public, and has generated several documentaries, as well as supposedly being the loose inspiration for the 2008 horror film, *The Strangers*.

****

Later that spring, in the Midwest, another woman would be found murdered alongside a highway. On the night of May 4th, 1984, three teenagers driving along Old Line Road near Westby, Wisconsin happened upon a set of remains lying a short distance off the side of the road. The victim had been so savagely beaten about the head that her face was nearly unrecognizable, and both of her hands had been severed at the wrist and removed, presumably to make identifying her even more difficult.

The woman, eventually christened Vernon County Jane Doe, was white, and thought to be between fifty and sixty-five years old, with blue eyes and permed brown hair that was beginning to go gray at the temples. She stood about five-foot-five, weighed around one-hundred-fifty pounds, and wore dentures, which had been broken in the attack and were discovered lying near the body. A man's Seiko watch was also recovered not far away.

The cause of death was blunt force trauma to the head; the victim's eye socket and jaw had been shattered, and there was also a wound near her left ear, possibly the result of a stabbing. The coroner estimated that the victim had died between twenty-four and forty-eight hours prior to being found, and was likely bludgeoned elsewhere before being dumped at the side of the road.

Jane Doe was fully clothed, wearing a black dress with a blue and white paisley print, a light blue turtleneck, a multicolored coat with a pink and purple lining, a pair of nylons rolled down to her knees, and tan slip-on shoes. Some of the clothing appeared to have been handmade, though none of the articles contained brand tags of any sort, indicating that her killer had removed them, again to forestall identification.

After news of the discovery went public, two witnesses came forward and claimed they had seen a bright yellow compact car, possibly a Datsun, pulled over at the side of US Highway 14—approximately three miles from the dump site—at around nine-forty-five p.m. on May 4th. They further stated that they had seen a man walking around the car from the passenger side to the driver's side. A composite sketch was produced from the couple's description.

Police examined the site where the car had been seen, and found tire tracks indicating that someone had recently made a quick U-turn at the spot. Authorities theorized that the man had been intending to dump the body at this location, but was frightened off by the couple driving by, at which point he got back into the car, turned around, and sped off to discard the body elsewhere.

One promising lead in the case emerged in the form of an organized group of criminals who had been writing fraudulent checks from the account of a missing Amherst, Wisconsin woman. Though this woman had disappeared right around the same time as Vernon County Jane Doe was discovered dead, detectives suspected that the unknown murder victim was probably not a local.

The remains were exhumed in 2015 in order to update the facial reconstruction images and to obtain a DNA profile. The woman's clothing was also later sent for further forensic testing, which eventually confirmed that the victim had not been from Wisconsin, but had likely originated from somewhere in Arizona or New Mexico.

The fact that the assailant had made numerous attempts at disguising the woman's identity—by removing the victim's hands and cutting tags out of her clothing, for example—it seems probable that the perpetrator knew the victim and could be linked back to her. But as of 2019, investigators still have no inkling of who the woman is or who might have murdered her.

****

In June of 1984, a young woman would disappear from a Stockholm street and later turn up butchered, in a crime that would eventually go on to become Sweden's most notorious unsolved murder and the inspiration for Stieg Larsson's internationally best-selling book, *The Girl With the Dragon Tattoo*.

Twenty-eight-year-old Catrine da Costa, a prostitute and heroin addict, was a regular fixture on the Malmskillnadsgatan, the short stretch of road in the Stockholm city center where sex workers plied their trade. Catrine had been married once before and had a son, but had fallen on hard times.

On June 10th, she was seen getting out of a man's car, but thereafter seemed to vanish without a trace. Catrine's mother, who had maintained a very close relationship with her, became extremely concerned when she didn't hear from her daughter, and reported the disappearance to police.

There was no sign of her until July 18th, when pieces of her dismembered corpse were discovered in a garbage bag beneath an overpass in Solna, just north of the city center. More parts were recovered a few weeks later, though her head, internal organs, genitalia, and one breast remain missing. Though the victim was identified as Catrine da Costa through her fingerprints, a cause of death was never able to be determined.

Shortly after the body was found, a pathologist named Teet Härm came to the attention of investigating authorities. Härm was known to frequent prostitutes, and worked at a forensics lab at the Karolinska Institutet, a location almost exactly halfway between the sites where the two sets of body parts were found.

Not only that, but in 1982, Härm's wife Ann-Catherine was found hanging in the couple's home. Though the coroner ruled her death a suicide, police suspected Härm may have killed her, particularly because she had filed for divorce shortly before she died, and Härm had reacted with odd detachment to her passing. It was Ann-Catherine's father, in fact, who alerted detectives to consider Härm as a person of interest.

Further, rather eerily, the pathologist specialized professionally in cases of strangulation, and had written several papers on the subject, as well as aided the authorities in other homicide investigations where the victims had been strangled. Notably, a former supervisor of Härm's named Jovan Rajs was convinced that Härm was the killer, and stated as much to investigating officers.

A survey of the prostitutes of the Malmskillnadsgatan produced fifty positive identifications of Härm, and one woman even claimed that he had beaten her up during their encounter. A search of Härm's home turned up knives and violent pornography as well; the doctor was then arrested for the murder of Catrine da Costa.

Meanwhile, as all of the investigation surrounding Härm went on, another individual was also appearing on the police's radar. This was a former colleague of Härm's, a general practitioner by the name of Thomas Allgen. Not long after Catrine da Costa's remains were recovered, Allgen's wife Christina was in the process of divorcing him, on the grounds that he had sexually abused their two-year-old daughter. Though this claim was never conclusively proven, Christina would soon insist that the child made statements indicating that she had witnessed a woman being cut apart by her father and another man who looked like Härm. As Allgen and Härm were known to be acquainted, Allgen was subsequently arrested also.

Arguments presented at the trial of the two men included all of the aforementioned circumstantial evidence, as well as the statements of two owners of a photography shop in Stockholm who claimed that they had developed a set of photos in the summer of 1984 that appeared to depict a body cut into pieces; these photos were later picked up, they said, by a pair of men matching the descriptions of Härm and Allgen.

The doctors were initially convicted of murder in the case, though due to a technicality concerning unauthorized interviews with the media given by some of the jurors, the verdict was soon overturned. A public outcry ensued, and Härm and Allgen were later put back on trial.

At this second hearing, the men were acquitted of murder, especially as Catrine's cause of death had never been conclusively established, though the judge stated that he believed Härm and Allgen were at least guilty of cutting up Catrine's corpse. However, as desecration of a body was not a major offense and held a very brief statute of limitations, the suspects were released.

The verdict caused a massive controversy in Sweden, thathas never really been satisfactorily resolved. Though the doctors were deemed not guilty of the murder, a large portion of the public was of the opinion that they had gotten away with a horrific crime, and various campaigns by members of the press and others were later able to get both doctors' licenses to practice revoked.

Härm attempted suicide in 1985, and in later years, both he and Allgen tried to sue the state for defamation, and to recover the loss of income that had been incurred by their suspected involvement in the murder. To date, none of their legal actions has been successful, and it remains unknown whether they were, in fact, guilty of killing Catrine da Costa.

Interestingly, there was another suspect who was initially believed to be very promising, though police eventually dismissed him for reasons that are still a bit murky. Polish butcher Stanislaw Gonerka had been in a mental institution since 1974, after having been convicted of strangling and dismembering a woman whose body parts were later found discarded in several garbage bags. Gonerka had only been released from the hospital three months before Catrine was murdered, and was also recognized as a regular among the prostitutes of the Malmskillnadsgatan; he was thought, in fact, to have purchased Catrine's services specifically, as his name was found written in her diary.

Gonerka died in 1987, and though forensic evidence was obtained from his body in order to try to match it with physical evidence recovered from Catrine's remains, no definitive link could be made, and the case is still unsolved.

****

On August 6th, 1984, back in the United States, there was a tragic resolution to the disappearance of thirty-two-year-old Dorothy Jane Scott, who had been abducted from a hospital parking lot in Anaheim, California after taking a coworker to get treated for a spider bite on the evening of May 28th, 1980.

A set of partially burned human bones, lying right next to a dog's skeleton, was discovered by a construction worker just off of Santa Ana Canyon Road. Investigators surmised that the remains had been in the area for at least two years, as there had been a brush fire in 1982 that could have accounted for the scorching of the bones. A ladies' watch and a turquoise ring were also unearthed at the site, accessories identified as belonging to Dorothy Jane Scott. Dental records soon confirmed the identification.

Though cause of death could not be determined, Dorothy's watch had stopped at twelve-thirty a.m. on May 29th, 1980, indicating that the woman had been murdered shortly after her vehicle was seen speeding away from the UC Irvine Medical Center by her coworkers.

The main suspect in the homicide, the man who had allegedly been stalking Dorothy for some time before she vanished, had been phoning his victim's parents, as well as the local newspaper, for years following the disappearance. He had only stopped in April of 1984, after Dorothy's father Jacob had answered the phone, rather than her mother Vera.

However, not long after Dorothy's body was found, the calls began again, though just as before, the suspect never stayed on the line long enough for the calls to be traced. While authorities are all but certain that the caller is most likely Dorothy's killer, he has never been identified, and no arrests in the case have ever been made.

****

The following day, across the globe in Australia, there would be a shocking double murder in a Victoria suburb that remains one of the best-known unsolved homicides in the country.

Thirty-five-year-old nurse and law student Margaret Tapp was a beautiful and socially popular young woman, and apparently had no qualms about getting attention from married men. In fact, the home in Ferntree Gully that she shared with her nine-year-old daughter Seana had been purchased for her by a married doctor she had dated for some time. After the doctor's death in 1983, his widow had attempted to wrestle ownership of the property away from Margaret, though the court only deigned to give her half, after which Margaret subsequently purchased the widow's portion.

On August 8th, 1984, Margaret had made a date with a new suitor named Jim Rollins; the pair was going to the opera. But when he arrived to pick her up at about six o'clock that evening, he became alarmed when there was no answer to his knocks, and suspicious that the home was completely dark. The back door was unlocked, so he let himself in.

Peering into Margaret's bedroom, Jim saw what at first appeared to be his date, tucked into her bed asleep. As he drew closer, however, he noticed bruising around her neck, and realized that she wasn't breathing. Recalling with horror that Seana was probably in the house as well, Jim rushed to her room and found the same gruesome scene: the nine-year-old had been strangled and tucked into her bed by an unknown killer. The child had also been savagely raped.

When police arrived, they were met with a disheartening lack of evidence. Though both Margaret and Seana had been strangled with a rope, the murder weapon was nowhere to be found. Further, there was no sign of forced entry, and few significant fingerprints obtained from the home. A few footprints from a brand of sneakers called Dunlop Volleys were recovered, but the shoes were a popular style, and were little help in narrowing down a suspect.

Investigators canvassed the neighborhood for more clues. One neighbor claimed they had heard a strange noise like a muffled scream at around eleven p.m. on August 7th, and further stated that their dog had started barking at around the same time. Other neighbors had witnessed a red utility vehicle, possibly a Ford, parked near the Tapp home that night, though this vehicle was never able to be traced.

Because Margaret was known to date many men, some of whom were married, there was no shortage of suspects, including current or former lovers, her ex-husband, the wives of her suitors, or even men she had rejected at some point in the past. A significant person of interest in this latter category was Margaret's driving instructor, who according to witnesses was obsessed with Margaret but had his advances spurned. Notably, he told police that he had never been in the Tapp home, though his fingerprints were among those recovered from the scene.

Authorities also investigated a teenage neighbor who had done some yard work for Margaret Tapp, but had a reputation around town as a sexually aggressive troublemaker. They also looked into the possibility that the widow of the doctor who had purchased Margaret's home may have perpetrated the crime, though the sexual assault of the nine-year-old Seana cast strong doubt upon this scenario.

DNA had been collected from Seana's body at the time of the murders, and in 2008 it appeared that detectives had cracked the case: the profile seemed to match a Queensland man by the name of Russell John Gesah. But only two weeks after the announcement had been made, authorities were forced to walk back the accusation, as it came to light that the DNA from the case had been contaminated; a second test failed to corroborate the match. Gesah later sued, and Victoria police were obliged to review over six-thousand other cases in Victoria whose outcomes may have been compromised by similar errors. In 2009, another man named Farah Jama was freed after it was determined that the evidence in his rape trial had also been tainted.

The Tapp double murder was reopened in 2015, and two years later, a reward of one-million Australian dollars was offered for any information leading to the conviction of the killer.

****

The blighted area of the Lone Star State known as the Texas Killing Fields would, in September of 1984, consume yet another young victim in the form of sixteen-year-old Laura Miller. On the 10th, she was talking to her boyfriend on the phone—incidentally the same convenience store pay phone in League City that Heide Villareal-Fye had used shortly before disappearing back in October of 1983.

Laura would vanish shortly afterward, and the whereabouts of her remains would not be revealed until more than a year later.

****

Less than a week after Laura Miller disappeared in Texas, a young woman in Arkansas would turn up dead in the second of a possible series of slayings thought to have begun in February of 1983 with the discovery of Wetzel County Jane Doe.

Lisa Nichols was twenty-eight years old, originally from West Virginia but distant from her family. She had apparently been traveling around the United States for a time, and had recently been staying with an unnamed couple in Florida.

On September 16th, 1984, however, her traveling days were found to have come to an end; her body was discovered along Interstate 40 in West Memphis, Arkansas. She had been strangled, and was found clad only in a sweater, though it did not appear as though she had been sexually assaulted. Authorities assumed that she had been hitchhiking and had perhaps been murdered by a truck driver.

Because she had strawberry-blonde hair and had been murdered along a truck route, investigators would later link her death to the earlier Jane Doe slain in 1983, and posit that a serial killer who targeted red-haired women was beginning a killing spree in the American Bible Belt.

****

Miles to the north, in Canada, a little girl would go missing in the middle of a normal afternoon, only to turn up dead just before the year was out.

It was October 3rd, 1984, and nine-year-old Christine Jessop hopped off the school bus at around three-thirty p.m. Neither her parents nor her brother Kenney was home; her father was still at work, and her mother had taken Kenney to the dentist. They expected to be home at four, and Christine's mother had told the girl to wait in the house for them to get back.

Christine, though, apparently had other plans. She and her friend Leslie Chipman had agreed to meet up at nearby Queensville Park with their dolls at four, and before setting out, Christine picked up her family's mail, left it on the kitchen table along with her school book bag, then walked to a convenience store on the corner to buy some gum. She was seen there between three-forty-five and three-fifty p.m. by both the proprietor of the store, and by a customer named Robert Atkinson, who told police she had been in the shop holding her recorder.

Leslie went to the park as planned, but Christine never showed up to meet her. Concerned, Leslie went back home and phoned the Jessop house at around ten minutes past four, but got no answer. She called again at four-twenty, and this time Christine's brother Kenney answered, having just arrived home from the dentist. But Christine wasn't there.

Family and friends fanned out across the neighborhood, but found no sign of her, at which point they reported her disappearance to police. The authorities likewise had no luck in locating the child, though after questioning residents of the area, they thought they might have a suspect in the abduction: a twenty-three-year-old neighbor named Guy Paul Morin.

According to witnesses, Morin was a strange, reclusive young man who kept bees and played in a band. Though he had a girlfriend and a steady job, neighbors thought it odd that he never went to pubs, as most other young men his age did, and detectives' alarm bells were set off by his stoic behavior under interrogation. Further, a police dog tasked with searching Morin's car apparently indicated to handlers that Christine had been in the vehicle.

Though questioning of Morin continued, the case stagnated for the following three months, until a grim find forced the proceedings from a missing persons to a homicide investigation.

****

Across the Atlantic Ocean in the rural backwaters of France, another small child would be murdered, and would kick off an almost unbelievable saga of family jealousy, suicide, and murderous revenge that would come to be known as the Pétit Grégory Affair.

Four-year-old Grégory Villemin lived with his parents, Christine and Jean-Marie, in the small, working-class village of Lepanges, which also housed numerous members of their extended family. While the town was generally fairly poor, Jean-Marie had done a bit better for himself, rising to the rank of supervisor at a local car parts factory, a promotion that apparently stirred up a furious envy in one or more residents of the village. Jean-Marie Villemin, throughout the summer and autumn of 1984, had started receiving anonymous phone calls and letters, threatening vengeance for some unspecified slight. These missives had clearly come from someone close to the family, as they contained accurate details of their lives and relationships, as well as charming sentiments such as, "I hate you so much, the day you die I will spit on your grave."

On the afternoon of October 16th, the letter-writer evidently decided to make good on all of his prior threats. Little Grégory was playing in the front yard of the family's chateau at around five p.m., with his mother watching over him through the front window of the house. She looked away for only a few moments, and when she looked back, the child was gone.

Thirty minutes later, Grégory's uncle Michel received one of the threatening phone calls. The voice on the other end of the line said, "I have taken the boy of the boss. I have thrown him into the Vologne."

Sure enough, when police searched the river later that evening, they discovered the drowned body of the four-year-old, his ankles and wrists bound with rope, his wool hat pulled down over his face. On the day after Grégory's remains were found, another anonymous letter arrived in the Villemin's post box, reading, "I hope you die of grief, boss. Your money will not bring your son back. This is my revenge."

Shortly after the boy was murdered, authorities honed in on a suspect: Jean-Marie's cousin Bernard Laroche. Handwriting analysis suggested that he could have penned the letters, and his niece Muriel informed police that she had witnessed him taking little Grégory to the Vologne in his car.

It seemed an open and shut case, but only days later, Muriel recanted her statement, and the handwriting evidence was deemed inconclusive. Bernard Laroche was released.

Then, in a shocking twist, further handwriting analysis appeared to implicate none other than Christine Villemin, Grégory's twenty-four-year-old mother, in the murder of her own child. And as if this wasn't incredible enough, while she was undergoing an investigation, her husband Jean-Marie shot and killed Bernard Laroche with a hunting rifle, a crime for which he would ultimately serve five years in prison.

Christine, six months pregnant at the time, was indicted in the murder of her son, and endured a roasting by the media, who proclaimed her a "witch." Despite the scorn heaped upon her by the public and an intense probe into her involvement, however, she was ultimately cleared of all charges, as there was no compelling evidence linking her to the slaying.

The case was reopened in 2000, at which point DNA samples were taken from the stamps on the anonymous letters. The results of the tests, though, were inconclusive, as were further DNA tests carried out in 2008 and 2010 on Grégory's clothing and the rope that had been used to bind him.

But in 2017, there was something of a break in the investigation. Based on new evidence that had come to light, three suspects were hauled into custody: Jean-Marie's uncle Marcel Jacob; Jacob's wife Jacqueline; and Jean-Marie's half-sister Ginette Villemin. Jean-Marie's parents were also detained and questioned, but ultimately released. Authorities believe that Marcel, Jacqueline, and Ginette had perhaps conspired with Bernard Laroche to engineer a campaign of terror against Jean-Marie Villemin because they were jealous of his wealth relative to theirs. As of this writing, however, they are still uncertain who actually carried out the murder of little Grégory.

And in a tragic coda to the entire sad incident, shortly following the 2017 reopening of the case, a man named Jean-Michel Lambert, who had served as the magistrate when the case was first being investigated in 1984, committed suicide by putting a plastic bag over his head. A note he left claimed that he could no longer handle the stress that had resulted from the case being reopened.

The Pétit Grégory Affair was a nationwide obsession in France, and remains so to this day, with more than a dozen books and thousands of articles written about the crime.

****

Elsewhere in Europe, before the end of October, a supposed murder would occur whose bizarre and eerie details ensured the case's enduring legacy in the annals of conspiracy theory and paranormal books and websites, even though there have also been rumors that the crime itself is nothing but an elaborate Internet hoax.

The story goes that Günther Stoll, a former food engineer from Anzhausen, Germany, had been having some problems since he'd lost his job. He had been complaining to his wife about an ominous "them," people he said were threatening to hurt or kill him for some unspecified reason. His wife, apparently, had chalked the whole thing up to paranoia, at least until the evening of October 25th.

On that night, at around eleven p.m., Günther suddenly leaped out of his chair and announced, "Now I've got it!" He then proceeded to write a series of letters on a piece of paper that spelled out "YOG'TZE" (or perhaps "YO6'TZE"), before almost instantly scratching out what he wrote.

Günther left the house a short time later, and drove to a nearby pub. He sat on a stool and ordered a beer, but reportedly before he even took a sip, he fell off the stool and bashed his face on the floor, an injury that rendered him unconscious for a brief time.

After he awoke, he left the bar and got back into his VW Golf. He was next seen two hours later in the town of Haigerseelbach, where he had spent his childhood. At one a.m., he allegedly turned up on the doorstep of a woman he had known many years before. She would not open the door to him, but told him to go to his parents' house, after which Günther apparently told her that something horrible was going to happen that night.

Another two hours passed. Then, at around three in the morning, a pair of truck drivers independently spotted a wrecked Volkswagen Golf in a ditch off the side of the Autobahn. One of the truckers ran to the nearest emergency phone, while the other approached the car to see if he could help.

Günther Stoll was still alive, but clearly injured, and most bizarrely, he was completely naked. He told the Good Samaritan that there had been four other men in the car with him, but that they were not his friends, though he would not specify who they were. When authorities arrived, Günther was placed in an ambulance, but died on the way to the hospital.

In an even stranger development, it was later determined that Günther had not been wounded in the car accident, but instead had been run over by a different vehicle while naked, and then placed back in his own car.

The truck drivers who had been the first on the scene told police that they had seen a man in a bright white jacket near the car, but that he had vanished shortly before they approached. One of the truckers also claimed to have seen a man hitchhiking on a nearby off-ramp. Neither of these mysterious men was ever identified.

The meaning of the YOG'TZE clue has also stumped investigators for decades, and it is still unknown if the note had anything to do with Günther's death. Some have speculated that the letters could have been a license plate number, a call sign for a Romanian radio station, a formula for a food additive, or any number of other hypotheses, including the suggestion that the message should actually be read upside down. Everything from industrial espionage to the Dutch drug trade has been bandied about as possible motives for Günther's murder, though it has also been proposed that perhaps the man suffered from a psychotic break, took off his own clothes, and wandered onto the Autobahn where he was hit by a car. The driver of the vehicle who struck him may then have placed Günther back in his own car and taken off to keep from getting into trouble.

Then again, some have discounted the veracity of the entire case, as the only source of it seems to be a report from a popular German crime show that aired in the spring of 1985.

****

Only weeks before Christmas, a young schoolgirl would be waylaid on the way home from a holiday party in England, and her murder would remain unsolved over three decades later.

Fourteen-year-old Lisa Hession had been attending a small celebration with friends, as well as her sixteen-year-old boyfriend Craig Newell, in the town of Leigh in

Greater Manchester on the evening of December 8th. As she had promised her mother she would be home before eleven, she left the party at around half-past ten after kissing Craig goodbye at the front gate. She then began the short walk home, but she never made it there.

When eleven o'clock came and went with no sign of her daughter, Lisa's mother Christine phoned the police, then set out on her own to look for the child. But not long after that, Christine received a phone call that no mother ever wants to receive: authorities summoned her to Leigh Infirmary in order to identify a body.

Lisa Hession had been punched in the face, brutally raped, and strangled with her own t-shirt. Her violated remains had been found in an alley only a few hundred yards from her home.

Several other women had been assaulted in the same area of town over the previous four months, and another victim was attacked five months later. None of these women was killed, and all described a dark-haired, "baby-faced" individual between eighteen and twenty years old with a local accent. One man was arrested a short time after Lisa's murder, but was later released on bail. He died in 2005, but investigators have confirmed that he remains a person of interest.

The case was reopened in 2011, with police offering a reward of fifty-thousand pounds and attempting to obtain DNA swabs from all males in the towns of Leigh and nearby Wigan. So far, there have been no matches, and the investigation is ongoing.

****

On the last day of 1984, the decomposed body of nine-year-old Christine Jessop, last seen at a convenience store near her home in Queensville, Ontario, Canada, was found in a wooded area approximately thirty miles from her last known location. She had been raped and stabbed multiple times. Semen was recovered from the child's underwear, but as DNA testing was still very much in its infancy in 1984, police could do nothing but store the evidence and hope that better technology would soon be able to confirm the identity of the killer.

In the meantime, though, investigators were fairly convinced that Guy Paul Morin was the most likely suspect, despite him having a solid alibi for the time of the homicide, and they arrested him a few months after Christine's remains were recovered. At his trial, a forensic technician claimed that red fibers found in Morin's car had come from Christine's sweater; further circumstantial evidence was given by two inmates at the jail where Morin had been held, who told the assembled jurors that Morin had confessed the murder to them.

Morin was actually acquitted at the first trial, the judge citing lack of compelling evidence, but the Crown appealed the verdict, and Morin stood trial again in 1992, at which point he was convicted of second-degree murder and sentenced to life in prison.

That wasn't the end of the story, however. Three years later, a DNA test was performed on the pair of Christine's underwear that had been recovered from the scene, and the profile of the killer did not match Guy Paul Morin. He was released after spending approximately eighteen months in Kingston Penitentiary, and eventually won more than a million-dollar settlement from the government of Ontario for his wrongful conviction.

But if Guy Paul Morin did not kill Christine Jessop, then who did? Other suspects have been notably difficult to come by, though in 2018 a private investigator named Jay Nicoll told the press that he was looking into a man called Richard Stanley James, who was arrested less than a month after Christine's disappearance for abducting a six-year-old girl named Lynn Ferguson from the parking lot of a convenience store. The little girl was ultimately not harmed, as James's truck broke down and he let his victim go, but it seems significant that James appeared to be driving toward the town of Sonya, not far from where Christine's body would ultimately turn up. Lynn Ferguson also told police that the kidnapper had lured her into his vehicle by telling her he had lost his puppy and would give her two dollars to help him look for it.

The case remains open, though no new leads have emerged as of this writing.

1985

> The Redhead Murders

> Doña Ana County Jane Doe

> Parker County John Doe

On the very first day of 1985, it seemed that the probable serial killer stalking red-haired women in the American Bible Belt had struck for a third time. In this case, a bound and decomposed body was discovered down an embankment off the side of Interstate 75 near the town of Jellico, Tennessee. Like Wetzel County Jane Doe and Lisa Nichols before her, this victim was a redhead, and had been strangled or asphyxiated, though not sexually assaulted.

Additional details about the young woman included the fact that she was somewhere between seventeen and thirty years old, stood between five-foot-one and five-foot-four, weighed around one-hundred-ten pounds, had green eyes and freckles, and wore jeans, a tan shirt, and a tan pull-over-style sweater. Further, she had a partial upper denture replacing two of her front teeth. She was found to be approximately eleven weeks pregnant at the time of her death, which was estimated to have occurred seventy-two hours prior to her remains being recovered on the side of the highway.

For many years, this woman—like many of the victims in the Redhead Murders series—remained unidentified, but in 2018, police finally matched her fingerprints to a set of prints already on file. The unknown victim was twenty-one-year-old Tina Farmer, who had been reported missing from her Indiana home by her parents in late November of 1984. The last known sighting of Tina had been in Indianapolis, when it was believed that she had been spotted in the company of a truck driver heading for Kentucky. This detail strengthened detectives' later suspicions that the serial killer thought to be responsible for the slayings was a trucker, perhaps based around the Knoxville or Nashville areas of Tennessee.

Tina Farmer would be far from the last victim of this elusive killer, and more would turn up as 1985 wore on.

****

On March 10th, 1985, another young woman would be found dead on a roadside, this time in the American Southwest. Unlike Tina Farmer, however, she remains unidentified as of 2019.

A group of three rabbit hunters out patrolling an area off County Road E73 about twenty miles from Hatch, New Mexico stumbled upon the partial skeletal remains of a human being, scattered beneath a layer of thin black plastic in a shallow grave. Though much of the body was never recovered, pathologists were able to determine that the victim was a slim white female between the ages of sixteen and nineteen, with blonde to light brown hair. She was clad in pink underwear, a pink bra from which the underwire had become detached, and a white, Wilson brand sweatshirt with three-quarter-length sleeves. Two of her fingernails were also painted pink.

Notable features included a nose that had been broken at some point in the past but had subsequently healed; and an unusual "wasting" of the second and third lumbar of the spine, an anomaly not commonly seen in teenagers. Because of her designer clothing and expensive dental work, it was almost certain that she was not a transient, and had been well cared for by her family. Authorities surmised that the girl had been murdered approximately three to six months before her remains were unearthed, though specific cause of death is not known.

Dubbed Doña Ana County Jane Doe or Upham Girl, the victim remains unidentified. A composite sketch of her was produced in 2011, but as of this writing, there have been no new leads.

****

Less than a month later, back in Tennessee, another possible victim of the Redhead Murders would come to light. This woman, whose skeletal remains were found on the side of Interstate 24 in Pleasant View, Tennessee on March 31st, and who would become known as Cheatham County Jane Doe, was white, likely between thirty-one and forty years old, and about five-foot-one. Cause of death was undetermined, but thought to have occurred sometime between November of 1984 and January of 1985.

On the following day, April 1st, yet another young woman was found and believed to be related to the same series. Her remains turned up inside an abandoned refrigerator that had been tossed on the side of Route 25 near the town of Gray, Kentucky. The front of the appliance bore a grim hallmark in the form of a sticker reading "Super Woman."

This particular victim, unidentified for decades, was thought to be between twenty-four and thirty-five years old, with long red hair and light brown eyes. She was small, no taller than four-foot-eleven, and sported a scar on her abdomen consistent with a prior C-section.

The girl was found naked save for two pairs of socks and a gold necklace with two pendants, one of an eagle and one of a heart. A pair of boots was also found nearby and believed to have belonged to her. She was thought to have been murdered only a few days before her body was found in the refrigerator.

This victim was known only as Kentucky Jane Doe or The Redhead in the Refrigerator until October of 2018, when DNA evidence finally identified her as twenty-nine-year-old Espy Regina Black-Pilgrim, originally from Spindale, North Carolina. Witnesses later came forward and claimed that they had seen a young woman matching her description at a truck stop in Corbin, Kentucky on March 31st, 1985, and that she had been attempting to hitch a ride back to her home state.

Then, on April 3rd, 1985, there was a sixth discovery: a partial skeleton was found near a strip mine, only four miles from Jellico, Tennessee, where the body of Tina Farmer had been discovered on the first of January. This victim was thought to be much younger than the other casualties of the alleged Bible Belt Strangler, perhaps between nine and fifteen years old, and believed to have been murdered between one and four years prior to her body being found, though cause of death is unverified.

A few articles of clothing, a pair of size five boots, and a necklace and bracelet fashioned from plastic buttons were also recovered from the dump site, though it is uncertain whether these items belonged to the victim.

Though the remains were too decomposed to determine hair or eye color, this victim—known as Campbell County Jane Doe—is usually linked to the other Redhead Murders due to the specific location and circumstances of her death. Facial reconstruction images have been produced, and a later isotopic analysis suggested that the girl likely hailed from either Florida or central Texas, though it appeared that she had recently moved to another area of the country, perhaps the Midwest, the Southwest, or the Pacific Coast.

Eleven days later, a woman thought to be the last known victim of the Bible Belt Strangler was found dead, also in Tennessee, but this time in Greeneville, approximately one-hundred-twenty-five miles away from the sites where Tina Farmer and Campbell County Jane Doe had been dumped. This victim stood around five-foot-five, weighed approximately one-hundred-thirty-five pounds, and was likely between fourteen and twenty years old. She had light brown hair with auburn highlights, and pink-painted fingernails.

Unlike most of the other suspected victims of the Redhead Murders, this young woman had not been strangled or asphyxiated, but had died as a result of blunt force trauma to the head. She also had a single stab wound that may have contributed to her death, which was estimated to have taken place three to six weeks before she was discovered.

In late 2018, the young woman was identified through DNA comparison as seventeen-year-old Elizabeth Lamotte, who was originally from New Hampshire and had gone missing from a group home in Manchester in early April of 1984.

The FBI became involved in this particular string of murders in mid-1985, but it is still not known whether all of these homicides were committed by the same perpetrator.

Complicating the issue further is yet another Tennessee murder, that of the red-haired Nancy Lynn Blankenship, who disappeared in December of 1983 when she was twenty years old and had just discovered she was pregnant. Her strangled body was recovered from the Tennessee River in 1994, but strangely, a post-mortem determined that her remains had only been in the water for five years at most, even though she had been missing for more than a decade. While authorities speculated that her husband may have killed her, it is possible that she might have been yet another statistic in the Redhead Murders series.

Though there are many similarities in these cases, there are also enough differences that it is still just plausible that the crimes are unrelated. That said, there have been some promising persons of interest investigated for the Bible Belt Strangler murders. One of these suspects, a truck driver from Cleveland, Tennessee named Jerry Leon Johns, came to the attention of police when he was arrested for attempting to strangle a red-haired woman named Linda Schacke in Knoxville in March of 1985.

According to the victim, Johns came into the club where she worked and flirted with her, after which she accompanied him back to his hotel after her shift was over. Shortly thereafter, though, Linda stated that the man pulled a gun on her and claimed he was an undercover narcotics officer. He then abducted her, tried to strangle her with a piece of her own t-shirt, and left her for dead in a storm drain.

Johns was questioned regarding twenty unsolved murders across several states, but he denied being the Bible Belt Strangler, though he did manifest a keen interest in serial killers and their psychology, according to investigating officers. He was still in custody when Espy Black-Pilgrim was murdered, however, making it unlikely that he was responsible for the entire series of crimes. He was jailed in 1987 for the kidnapping and attempted murder of Linda Schacke, and eventually died behind bars.

In an eerily similar circumstance, another Tennessee trucker named Thomas Lee Elkins was arrested in 1986 after allegedly kidnapping and raping a red-haired twenty-year-old that he had abducted in either Indiana or Illinois.

She was able to escape his clutches and reported him to authorities. He was also interrogated in the Redhead Murders case, but was ultimately cleared of suspicion.

In 2018, a sociology class at Elizabethton High School in east Tennessee, at the behest of their teacher Alex Campbell, spent an entire semester compiling a profile of the perpetrator of the Redhead Murders; it was this class, in fact, that re-dubbed the killer The Bible Belt Strangler. Their analysis, which was submitted to FBI profilers and believed to be a fairly accurate picture of the probable assailant, hypothesized that the killer was a white male born between 1936 and 1962, of above-average height and weight, who worked as a long-haul commercial truck driver and was likely based out of Knoxville, Tennessee, as that was the geographic center of the dump sites of all the related victims. Further, his trucking route would be concentrated largely along the Interstate 40 corridor and its offshoot highways.

In addition, the class speculated that this serial killer was most likely "mission-oriented" rather than driven by a sexual motive, as none of the victims were thought to have been sexually assaulted or tortured, and there did not appear to be an "overkill" component to their deaths. Mission-oriented killers are those who murder as a means to an end, as a way of essentially punishing people they see as morally or religiously transgressive or somehow a blight on society. Lastly, the profile theorizes that the Bible Belt Strangler is probably of above-average intelligence, may have come from an unstable home, and is likely married or in a long-term relationship.

The FBI investigation into the murders remains open.

****

Later that autumn, an unidentified teenage boy would be found on a ranch in Texas, and sadly, very little about him is known to this day.

It was October 27th, 1985, and a father and son walking across a piece of land off State Highway 51 just south of Springtown, Texas spotted a smattering of human bones in the dirt. Forensic examination determined that the partial skeleton belonged to a white male between the ages of fourteen and twenty-one years old, of indeterminate height and weight, with a pale complexion, short brown hair, and brown or hazel eyes.

The victim was clad in Guess jeans with leather trim on the pocket, a gray shirt with tan corduroy trim, a dark gray jacket, and a white fleece jacket over that. The only other belongings found with the remains was a coin bearing a 1984 date, indicating that the boy had likely been murdered sometime in that year, or in early 1985, though specific cause of death is unclear.

There has been some speculation that this victim—known as Parker County John Doe—may be fourteen-year-old Christopher James Harvey, who was abducted from his home in Colorado in July of 1984, but as of this writing, he remains officially unidentified.

1986

> The Texas Killing Fields

> Pauline Martz

> Willem Klein

> Linda Cook

In 1986, there was a brief callback to the murder of four-teen-year-old Dana Bradley, who had vanished after leaving a friend's house in St. Johns, Newfoundland in December of 1981 and had been found dead four days later.

A man named David Somerton from the town of Mount Pearl confessed to police that he had killed the teenager after picking her up hitchhiking. Authorities looked into his involvement and charged him with the murder, but then Somerton recanted his statement, claiming that it had been coerced. As no other solid evidence of his guilt could be found, he was eventually cleared of suspicion in the slaying, though he did subsequently spend two years in jail on a charge of public mischief stemming from the false confession.

Another possible suspect in the homicide, a convicted pedophile named Tom Carey, came to light in 2014 after a neighbor claimed to have recovered memories of not only being molested by Carey as a child, but also of seeing Carey killing Dana Bradley and stuffing her into the trunk of his car. Investigators looked into these accusations, but failed to substantiate them, and in 2016, DNA confirmed that Carey was not responsible for the crime.

The investigation is ongoing.

****

Back in Texas, February 3rd would reveal the whereabouts of sixteen-year-old Laura Miller, who had disappeared from a League City convenience store after using the pay phone to call her boyfriend in September of 1984. It turned out that not only had Laura last been seen alive at the exact same place as previous Texas Killing Fields victim Heide Villareal-Fye, but her body was found only sixty feet away from where Heide's had been discovered in April of 1984.

And in a macabre illustration of the accuracy of the Texas Killing Fields moniker, yet a third body was found at the site at the same time as Laura's: an unidentified young woman who had been shot in the head approximately seven weeks before, and left leaning against a tree trunk only one-hundred-fifty feet from the location where Heide's body had lain.

In later years, Laura Miller's father Tim founded Texas Equusearch, an organization dedicated to investigating missing persons cases. Tim Miller, as well as several other law enforcement officers and FBI agents, suspected that they knew who killed Laura Miller, Heide Villareal-Fye, and the Jane Doe found alongside them: a man named Robert Abel, who in the 1960s was one of the NASA engineers working on the Apollo moon mission.

Abel had moved to League City in 1983, and had purchased a thousand acres alongside Calder Road, adjacent to where the bodies of the three young women (as well as a fourth victim, found in 1991 and dubbed Janet Doe) had been dumped. He ran a recreation center on the property, with western-themed events and children's pony rides.

When police approached Abel to inspect the pasture next to his land, they were taken aback at how helpful Abel seemed, offering them his horses and backhoe to aid in the search, and asking them endless questions. As the inquiry went on, investigators also fielded statements from two of the man's ex-wives, who claimed that Abel had an explosive temper and often beat his animals.

Police obtained a search warrant to scour Abel's property, but found nothing, at which point Tim Miller decided to take matters into his own hands. He staked out Abel's house, searched his property without permission, and even allegedly pulled a gun on him at one stage, attempting to force a confession out of him. Despite these tactics, Abel did not confess, and no evidence of wrongdoing was ever uncovered in his home or on his land.

Robert Abel eventually filed a restraining order against Miller, but the damage was done; Abel's reputation was ruined, and his business went under. Tim Miller later came to terms with the fact that Abel was likely not guilty, and the two men reconciled, but in 2005, Robert Abel died by deliberately driving his car in front of a train.

After Robert Abel's death, Miller and the FBI began to reexamine evidence surrounding another suspect, who they had ironically passed over in order to focus more fully on Abel. This individual was a man by the name of Clyde Hedrick, who had once lived on the same street as the Miller family, and supposedly knew Laura quite well.

In July of 1984, Hedrick had been seen at a bar with a woman named Ellen Beason, who later turned up missing. When Hedrick was questioned, he told police that Ellen had accidentally drowned that night while they were swimming, and he had panicked and hidden her body.

Investigators did indeed find the remains of Ellen Beason, right where Hedrick said they would be, but since the coroner could not confirm her cause of death as a homicide, Hedrick was only charged with abusing a corpse, a charge for which he spent a year in jail.

But in 1993, a forensic anthropologist took another look at Ellen Beason's skull, and determined that she had probably been murdered by blunt force trauma to the head. This cause of death was corroborated at a 2012 autopsy, and Clyde Hedrick was taken into custody.

During his incarceration, three of his fellow inmates told the prosecutor's office that Hedrick had confessed to beating Ellen Beason to death with a table leg, and then having sex with her dead body. They further claimed that Hedrick had boasted about raping and murdering Laura Miller and Heide Villareal-Fye.

The evidence in the case was ultimately not compelling enough to prove that Hedrick had killed Ellen deliberately, though he was sentenced to twenty years for involuntary manslaughter. From his prison cell, he has repeatedly denied murdering anyone, and has stated that Tim Miller engineered the charges against him.

The case, like so many within the Texas Killing Fields purview, remains open and unsolved.

****

In spring of 1986, the ghastly murder of an elderly widow would lead to the shocking conviction of an innocent man, a breakdown of the justice system that would take nearly a decade to be corrected.

Seventy-nine-year-old Pauline Martz lived alone in the small town of Aurora, Missouri. On April 13th, firefighters were called to her home to extinguish a blaze, and they discovered the dead body of the woman inside. But they very quickly determined that the fire had been no accident: Pauline had been bound and gagged, beaten, possibly sexually assaulted, and then left to the ravages of the flames. Her cause of death was carbon monoxide poisoning.

The murder stunned the entire community, but more unbelievable events were yet to come. A few days after the crime, police picked up a twenty-year-old, mentally challenged man named Johnny Lee Wilson, who had been a friend of Pauline's. According to investigators, a witness named Gary Wall had stated that Johnny had confessed the deed to him. After interrogating Johnny for approximately four hours, officers claimed that the suspect gave in and confessed that he was guilty. A search of the home Johnny shared with his mother turned up further incriminating evidence, such as clothing and jewelry that had supposedly been stolen from Pauline's residence, and a mostly empty can of gasoline.

Few people in town seemed to believe that the gentle Johnny could have possibly killed anyone, and what's more, there were perfectly mundane explanations for the women's clothing and jewelry found in the Wilson home, which belonged to Johnny's mother and grandmother, respectively. Johnny's mother even told police that Johnny had been with her at the grocery store when the fire that killed Pauline Martz was set. In addition, Gary Wall, the witness who had allegedly heard Johnny confess to the murder, walked back his statement as well, claiming that the police had forced him to say it. All evidence of the boy's innocence, however, was ruthlessly set aside.

Johnny, who had an approximate IQ of seventy-six, was initially deemed not mentally fit to stand trial by two psychiatrists, but a third, court-appointed psychiatrist contradicted their findings, and it was his testimony that was heeded. Before the ensuing trial, Johnny Lee Wilson recanted his confession, telling his attorneys that the police had coached him into it by threatening him and asking leading questions, and telling him that he would be allowed to go home if he just said what they wanted him to say. In spite of this, his attorneys still advised him to plead guilty, which he did, reluctantly, and clearly not really understanding the gravity of the situation. He was sentenced to life in prison.

Years later, a man named Chris Brownfield, who was serving time in a Kansas penitentiary for beating, robbing, and killing an elderly woman—a crime which occurred only an hour away from and sixteen days after the murder of Pauline Martz—confessed to police that he and an accomplice had indeed been responsible for Pauline's death, and that Johnny Lee Wilson was completely innocent. Authorities dismissed Brownfield's statement as not credible, however, even though he told them details about the crime—such as the fact that he had left a stun gun behind at the scene—that had not been released to the public.

Brownfield's confession, though, spurred Johnny Wilson to file a motion for a trial by jury in 1989. This motion was denied in 1991, as the judge ruled that Johnny had understood the charges against him and had plead guilty on the basis of that understanding.

In 1995, however, after a year-long investigation headed by governor of Missouri Mel Carnahan, Johnny Lee Wilson was granted a pardon and released. Tapes of the police interrogation that surfaced later on revealed that the examining officers had indeed used intimidation and profoundly leading questions to coerce the mentally-challenged Johnny into confessing to a crime he did not commit.

Though at this stage, it seems most likely that Chris Brownfield and his unknown accomplice were guilty of the murder of Pauline Martz, neither has been charged in the homicide, and the case is officially unresolved.

****

Back amid the Texas Killing Fields, another young woman would go missing and be presumed dead, though in her case, her probable assailants were eventually brought to justice.

Nineteen-year-old Shelley Sikes left her waitressing job at Gaido's seafood restaurant in Texas City on the evening of May 24th, 1986. The following day, her blood-spattered Ford Pinto was discovered stuck in the mud off an I-45 access road near Dickinson, but Shelley herself was nowhere to be found.

Though the whereabouts of her remains are still unknown, two men confessed in 1987 to running Shelley's car off the road before abducting and killing her: Gerald Zwarst and John Robert King. Zwarst drew police a map to where they had buried her body, but authorities were unable to locate it, thus the suspects could only be charged with aggravated kidnapping rather than murder.

King died in prison in 2015. Zwarst remains in custody, and though he applied for parole in 2007, 2012 and again in 2017, he was denied all three times, and is still incarcerated in Huntsville, Texas. It is not known whether either man is responsible for any of the other Texas Killing Fields homicides.

****

Later on, in the summer of 1986, a remarkable Dutch man would mysteriously turn up murdered in his own apartment, in a crime that has sadly been all but forgotten.

Willem "Wim" Klein was born in Amsterdam in 1912, and his physician father initially attempted to push him into the same line of work. Willem did obtain a bachelor's degree in medicine and took the first part of his doctoral exams, but eventually abandoned that career path in order to pursue his true calling: mathematics.

Willem Klein was, in fact, known as a human calculator; in other words, an individual who could do unbelievable mathematical computations in his head within seconds. This talent, incidentally, was shared by his older brother Leo, who died in a Nazi concentration camp in around 1942, after which Willem was forced to go into hiding to escape the same fate.

Willem lived a rather itinerant life after the war ended, performing for circuses around Europe under the stage name Pascal, but in 1952, he was recruited by the Mathematical Center in Amsterdam. Computers were still in their infancy at the time, and often, their powers of calculation were no match for people like Willem Klein, whose amazing feats would later be immortalized in *The Guinness Book of World Records*.

Willem would eventually go on to work at the world-famous CERN, assisting the physicists there with his lightning-fast mathematical processing, but as computers became better and faster, he found himself relegated more to entertainer status, performing for visitors that came through the facility. It should be noted, however, that CERN does recognize Willem Klein as their first "computer."

Dispirited, Willem retired from CERN in 1976 and went back to doing his calculations on the circus stage, this time under the pseudonym Willy Wortel. He drew massive crowds in Europe, Japan, and the United States throughout the 1970s, and despite his alcoholism, kept up a rather rigorous schedule and never seemed to have problems with his mental mathematics at all.

But then, on August 1st, 1986, Willem's housekeeper entered his home on the Brouwersgracht in Amsterdam, and found the seventy-three-year-old genius dead. He had been stabbed multiple times, and it appeared as though his residence had been ransacked, suggesting that the crime had perhaps been a robbery gone wrong.

Though a young man of Willem's acquaintance was arrested for the murder shortly afterward, no evidence could be found linking the suspect to the homicide, and he was summarily released. The brutal death of CERN's first human computer has since faded into relative obscurity, and it appears that no progress whatsoever has been made on the case for more than three decades.

****

Before the year of 1986 was out, a vicious rape and murder in England would eventually lead to a wrongful conviction that took sixteen long years to overturn.

Twenty-four-year-old barmaid Linda Cook lived in the seaside town of Portsmouth with her boyfriend and her boyfriend's mother. At around eleven-thirty p.m. on the night of December 8th, 1986, Linda walked to a friend's house on Sultan Road, a little more than a mile away from her own home on Victoria Road North. She spent less than an hour at her friend's place before heading back, but at some point on her journey home, she was savagely attacked by an unknown assailant.

On the morning of December 9th, the nude body of Linda Cook was discovered on an area of waste ground known as Merry Row. She had been raped and strangled, and as if that wasn't horrifying enough, her killer had also stomped her with his foot so hard that her larynx was crushed, her jaw and backbone were broken, and an imprint of his sneaker was left on her stomach.

The attack on Linda Cook was only the latest in a series of rapes that had been taking place around Portsmouth and had been attributed to an individual dubbed the Beast of Buckland. Police were under enormous pressure to solve the case, and days after Linda's murder, they were pretty sure they had got their man: eighteen-year-old Able Seaman Michael Shirley.

It so happened that on the night that Linda Cook was slain, Michael Shirley had been on shore leave, and was out and about trying to pick up girls at a nearby nightclub called Joanna's. At the bar, he met a girl who told him her name was Sue, though in reality she was called Deena Fogg. She agreed to share a taxi with him, and Michael likely thought he had his night sorted out. But Deena apparently changed her mind at some stage during the cab ride; she told Michael that she needed to be dropped off at her tower block so she could pick up her child, after which she would return to the cab. He agreed, but after Deena got out of the car, she gave Michael the slip and simply went home.

Michael Shirley waited in the taxi for her for about fifteen minutes, then got out of the vehicle and wandered the streets looking for her for a brief time before finally giving up and heading back to his ship, where he was recorded as returning at one-forty-five a.m.

Two days after this incident, Michael ran into Deena again, and apparently, the two of them spoke about how close they had been to the site of Linda Cook's murder. Deena reportedly thought Michael's discussion of the homicide seemed suspicious, and later reported him to police, who hypothesized that Michael had perhaps been sexually frustrated after being ditched by Deena and had then gone on to attack Linda Cook. He was arrested for the crime in early 1987.

Key to the authorities' case against Michael Shirley was the fact that he owned a pair of sneakers of a similar size and bearing the same tread pattern as the shoe that had made the impression on Linda's abdomen. He also had the same blood type as the attacker, which was O positive, and had several minor scratches on his face, arms, and hands. Further, police believed that there was an ample window of thirty minutes between the time when Deena

Fogg claimed she had last seen Michael and when he had arrived back on his ship, during which he could have perpetrated the attack on Linda.

Michael Shirley was convicted of rape and murder in early 1988, and sentenced to life in prison. But even from the beginning, there were those who believed the young seaman was innocent. Indeed, Michael himself campaigned mightily on his own behalf, staging hunger strikes and protests in order to attract attention to his cause.

As supporters looked further into the case, in fact, numerous discrepancies came to light. The thirty-minute time frame in which Michael was thought to have committed the crime, for example, was shown not to exist; Deena Fogg actually misremembered the time that the taxi had picked her and Michael up, placing it half an hour earlier than it actually was.

In addition, the scratches found on Michael's person were essentially a red herring, as Linda's long fingernails showed no signs that she had scratched her attacker at all. And the fact that Michael's blood type matched that of Linda's killer was similarly meaningless, as O positive blood was found in nearly a quarter of British men.

Even the shoe tread, one of the most compelling pieces of evidence presented at the trial, was on second glance not nearly as damning as it seemed, as approximately nine-thousand pairs of the exact same shoes had been sold in the United Kingdom in 1986 alone. Police did recover Michael Shirley's pair from his parents' house, but found no trace of blood or other tissue on them.

At last, in 2002, new DNA tests were performed on pieces of Linda's clothing, and semen that had been recovered at the scene, and these tests eliminated Michael Shirley as the killer of Linda Cook. He was released from prison in 2003, at the age of thirty-four.

Authorities subsequently reopened the homicide investigation and made new appeals to the public to solve the crime once and for all. They made no progress, however, and in later years, retired Norfolk police constable Chris Clark began looking into the case with a view to writing a book. He has stated that he believes Linda Cook's killer is serial rapist and murderer Paul Barry Taylor, who in 2012 was convicted of the 1979 slaying of twenty-two-year-old Sally Ann McGrath, as well as three other rapes and an attempted rape.

Clark points out that wherever Taylor moved to around the country, a spate of sexual assaults would occur there in short order. In fact, Taylor had arrived in the town of Fareham in 1985, which was only six miles away from Portsmouth. Furthermore, a witness claimed to have seen a man resembling Taylor running in front of his car near Merry Row on the night that Linda Cook was killed.

Clark has requested that the police compare the DNA from the crime scene to Taylor's profile, but so far his appeals have gone unanswered. Paul Barry Taylor remains in prison as of this writing.

1987

> Peggy Hettrick

> Daniel Morgan

> Analia Zavodny

> Helen Fleet

> Tracey Hobson

> Simon Dale

> Aiken County Jane Doe

> The Dardeen Family

A little over a month into the new year, a woman would get locked out of her apartment in Fort Collins, Colorado, go bar-hopping, then turn up dead in a field.

It was around nine p.m. on the evening of Tuesday, February 10th, 1987 when thirty-seven-year-old Peggy Hettrick left her job at a clothing store called the Fashion Bar at the Foothills Mall and began walking back to her nearby apartment. Her regular roommate, Barb Kohler, was out of town, but another woman named Sharon Deconick had been staying with her temporarily.

Unfortunately, Sharon had started drinking fairly early, and had passed out inside Peggy's apartment, leaving the door locked. Peggy didn't have her keys, and banged on the door to try and get Sharon to wake up and let her in, but all her efforts were in vain. Annoyed, she walked to the Laughing Dog Saloon nearby, where she had a drink and complained to anyone who would listen about being locked out of her own house. Throughout her stay at the Laughing Dog, both she and the bartender phoned her apartment numerous times, but there was never any answer. At last, Peggy gave up and went to another nearby bar, the Prime Minister, where she repeated the same routine for the next fifteen minutes before setting out into the night.

It was about ten o'clock at this point, and it is believed that Peggy next walked to the home of her ex-boyfriend, Matt Zoellner. He wasn't in, but witnesses later reported seeing Peggy standing around in the parking lot smoking, as though waiting for someone. She also reportedly wrote a note to Matt, telling him that she had been locked out of her apartment and that he shouldn't get angry if she showed back up at his place later that evening.

At around midnight, Peggy was finally able to get back into her place, where she proceeded to change her clothes and then head back out to the Prime Minister, where she arrived at approximately twelve-thirty. Shortly after walking in, she ran into Matt Zoellner, who was there meeting another woman named Dawn for a date. Apparently all three of them had a friendly discussion for a time, and Matt subsequently offered to give Peggy a ride home. According to Matt and Dawn, she initially agreed, but then later left the bar between one and one-thirty a.m. on her own. She was never seen alive again.

At around seven o'clock on the following morning, a man bicycling to work noticed what appeared to be a mannequin in a field, then realized it was a human body when he saw a trail of blood that led to a large red pool on the curb. Police arrived on the scene in short order.

Peggy Hettrick had been murdered by a single stab wound in her upper back that had penetrated and collapsed her left lung. In addition, she had also been gruesomely mutilated; one of her nipples had been removed, perhaps with a scalpel, and she had been subjected to a surgical-level female circumcision as well as a partial vulvectomy, suggesting a killer with some degree of medical training or expertise in butchery. The coroner theorized that the sexual mutilations and the fatal stab wound had been inflicted with two separate implements.

Robbery was clearly not a motive, not only because of the precisely sexual nature of the injuries, but also due to the fact that Peggy's jewelry was untouched and her purse still contained a checkbook and a few dollars in cash. It was also hypothesized that her killer had stabbed her at the curb, then dragged her body by one arm to the spot where it was eventually found. Several sets of footprints facing the curb were discovered near the body, indicating that the killer had been walking backwards as he dragged his victim. These prints were found to have been left by a pair of Thom McCan casual dress shoes.

Another shoe print that would turn out to have massive significance in the case, though unfortunately for all the wrong reasons, was that of a sneaker, left in the dirt facing the body. This sneaker print was found to belong to a fifteen-year-old boy named Tim Masters, who lived in a trailer just across from the field, and had actually been the first to see Peggy Hettrick's body on his way to the school bus stop on the morning of February 11th, though he had not reported it to police. This detail would immediately rocket Tim to the top of the suspect list, even though he claimed that he had not reported the murder because he had initially believed that it was not a real corpse, but that someone was playing a prank.

Authorities probed deeply into the teenager's private life, uncovering a few troubling items during a search of his bedroom. The boy was fond of knives, it seemed, and also enjoyed doing drawings that depicted scenes of bloody violence. Further searches of the Masters home, however, turned up no significant physical evidence, such as blood or fibers, and Tim was not arrested at the time, though police kept him very much on their radar.

In the meantime, a couple of other persons of interest were being investigated. These included a mysterious man named Derrick or Derek, who Peggy had reportedly met at the Laughing Dog Saloon and dated briefly before telling him to get lost. According to friends, Peggy had repeatedly told this man she didn't want to see him anymore, but that he kept calling her and showing up at her apartment. This individual was described as being in his mid-twenties, standing around five-foot-eleven with slightly long hair that was a light, reddish-brown. Despite a canvass of area bars, however, this person was never identified.

Peggy's ex-boyfriend Matt Zoellner was also briefly considered a suspect, and indeed, a later DNA test on Peggy's clothing did find traces of Matt's DNA on her underwear and some items in her purse. However, the pair had been dating off and on for several years, and it is certainly possible that remnants of Matt's DNA would have remained on Peggy's clothing, especially since they were still seeing each other at regular intervals at the time that Peggy was murdered. In addition, Matt was with his date until around three-thirty a.m. on February 11th, and it was estimated that Peggy was most likely killed not long after she was last seen leaving the Prime Minister at approximately one-fifteen. Matt Zoellner was eventually cleared of suspicion.

But a decade after the murder, in 1992, police reverted back to their initial suspect, neighbor Tim Masters, who was now twenty-five years old and serving in the US Navy. Tim had consistently denied having anything to do with the slaying, and there was essentially no physical evidence at all tying him to the crime. There was no blood or hair found in his home or on his person; his fingerprints were not among those recovered from the scene; and he did not own a pair of Thom McCan shoes like those left near the body by the purported killer.

However, Tim had allegedly told a high school friend about the sexual mutilations of Peggy's body, which were not thought to have been released to the public. Investigators questioned Tim about this suspicious detail, but Tim told them that he knew specifics about the crime because he had been a member of the Explorer Scouts in 1987 and had helped police search the scene at the time. His story was later verified, but it seemed that the authorities were bound and determined to pin the murder of Peggy Hettrick on him one way or another.

A forensic psychologist named Dr. J. Reid Maloy was assigned to the case, and even though he lived in California and never met Tim Masters in person, he nonetheless concluded that Tim must be the killer, simply based on the drawings the fifteen-year-old Tim had done at the time of the homicide. Outrageously, based largely on these drawings, Tim Masters was convicted of first-degree murder in 1999 and sentenced to life in prison.

Tim filed several appeals over the years, but none were successful until 2008, when he was finally released, though he was not officially exonerated until 2011.

The gross miscarriage of justice involving Tim Masters aside, there were later two other far more compelling suspects in the murder of Peggy Hettrick. The first of these was an eye surgeon by the name of Dr. Richard Hammond, who in 1995 was arrested for secretly taking photographs of the genitalia of female family members via hidden cameras in the bathroom of his home. Not only did Dr. Hammond live within sight of the field where Peggy's body was dumped, but he did not show up for his scheduled surgeries on the morning following her murder. Additionally, he committed suicide a few days after he was arrested, by injecting cyanide into his thigh. He left behind a cryptic note that read, in part, "My death should satisfy the media's thirst for blood."

An even more intriguing possibility is that Peggy Hettrick may have been an early victim of serial killer Scott Kimball. In 2003 and 2004, Kimball murdered his uncle and three women, crimes for which he is now serving a seventy-year-sentence. But significantly, it is also thought that Kimball may have killed a woman named Catrina Powell in October of 2004. Though unlike Peggy Hettrick, Catrina Powell was beaten and strangled rather than stabbed, she was subjected to very similar post-mortem mutilations to her breasts and genitals, just as Peggy was.

Though Kimball lived in Montana in 1987 and was arrested there three days after Peggy's murder for knocking over mail boxes, he was known to be in Fort Collins, Colorado later in 1987; in fact, he received a ticket there on August 8th for causing a disturbance at a bowling alley and amusement venue called Whirlyball that was located only about a half-mile from the spot where Peggy Hettrick was murdered. Though it is unclear if Kimball was in Colorado at the time Peggy was slain, he has stated that he committed more murders than he is credited with, and other aspects of his psychological profile seem to jibe with the mutilations seen on Peggy's body.

The homicide is still one of Colorado's best-known cold cases, and remains open as of this writing.

****

Early spring of 1987 would feature the heinous slaughter of a private investigator in England, a crime that still resonates throughout the United Kingdom due to its purported association with blatant police and media corruption.

Thirty-seven-year-old Daniel Morgan, originally born in Singapore to Welsh parents, moved to London with his wife sometime in the late 1970s. Though he had initially studied at an agricultural college with a view to going into farming, in the end, his penchant for investigation and his excellent memory eventually led him to open his own private detective firm, called Southern Investigations, in Thornton Heath, London in 1983.

Daniel's partner at the agency was another investigator by the name of Jonathan Rees. On the evening of March 10th, 1987, the two men were talking and having a drink at the Golden Lion pub in Syndenham. According to Rees, he exited the pub at quarter to nine, and left Daniel Morgan sitting at a table writing notes on a piece of paper.

Later that night, people leaving the Golden Lion witnessed the aftermath of a grisly attack: the body of Daniel Morgan lay next to his car in the pub's parking lot. The victim had been savagely smashed in the head several times with an axe; the weapon remained at the scene, still embedded in Daniel's face. The handle of the implement, chillingly, had been wrapped in adhesive bandages, as though the killer had wanted to make sure of having a reliably firm grip as he swung the axe at his intended target.

Though Daniel's Rolex watch was discovered to be missing, robbery was almost immediately ruled out as a motive, for about one-thousand pounds in cash was still in the pocket of the victim's jacket, and his credit cards remained in his wallet. Interestingly, though, a pocket of Daniel's pants had been torn away, leading some investigators to suspect that something besides money had been stolen, perhaps the notes that Jonathan Rees had claimed Daniel was writing.

From the beginning of the inquiry, though, it definitely appeared as though something was amiss. Jonathan Rees, being Daniel's business partner as well as the last person to have seen Daniel alive, was an obvious suspect in his brutal murder, and was duly taken to the nearby Catford police station by Detective Sergeant Sid Fillery. But Fillery, as it happened, was close friends with Rees; in fact, both men had been drinking together at the Golden Lion pub on the night prior to Daniel Morgan's murder, and Fillery, who had been working secretly for Southern Investigations for a time, eventually became Rees's partner at the agency after retiring from the Metropolitan Police on medical grounds.

Not only that, but Daniel's brother Alastair later alleged that when he arrived at the Golden Lion on the morning following the homicide, the area had not been secured or cordoned off. Further, it did not appear that officers at the Catford police station made any attempt to seize the vehicle or clothing of supposed suspect Jonathan Rees in order to obtain forensic evidence.

It began to appear as though Daniel had been murdered for knowing too much, and indeed, there was much speculation going around that he had been looking into police involvement in drug trafficking, robbery, and other crimes when he was killed. A few weeks after his death, six men were taken into custody for the alleged murder conspiracy, including Jonathan Rees, Sid Fillery, Rees's brothers-in-law Glen and Garry Vian, and two Metropolitan Police officers.

According to Kevin Lennon, the bookkeeper at Southern Investigations, Jonathan Rees had stated that he wanted to oust Daniel Morgan from the business, and that he was reportedly first talking with police officers in order to have Daniel framed and arrested for drinking and driving. This plot apparently didn't work out, though, at which point Rees then supposedly began asking about having his partner murdered. Both Rees and Fillery denied any involvement in the slaying of Daniel Morgan, and though Rees and others would eventually be charged, there was insufficient evidence to secure an indictment against anyone.

Over the ensuing years, several more inquiries into the case would be performed that would expose some unbelievably shady dealings between the police and the tabloid media. It eventually came to light, for example, that not only had Jonathan Rees conspired to plant cocaine on a woman involved in a nasty custody battle—a crime for which he served a seven-year prison sentence for perverting the course of justice—but that he had been drawing a salary of approximately one-hundred-fifty-thousand pounds per year from the *News of the World* tabloid for supplying the editor with scandalous information about politicians, royals, and celebrities obtained from his numerous police connections and criminal informants; much of this information, naturally, had been acquired using illegal means.

After another investigation into the murder collapsed in 2011, an independent inquiry was opened in 2013 by then Home Secretary Theresa May. In 2014, Rees and two other suspects sued the Metropolitan Police for four-million pounds, claiming that the continued pursuit of them as conspirators in the murder was essentially harassment. At this hearing, however, officers claimed that they had sufficient reason to believe that Rees had conspired with Sid Fillery to hire Glen and Garry Vian to kill Daniel Morgan to keep him from speaking out about the police corruption he had uncovered. Another man, James Cook, was also named by Metropolitan Police officers as the purported getaway driver.

This lawsuit was settled in 2017, with Sid Fillery receiving twenty-five-thousand pounds in damages, but Rees, Cook, and the Vian brothers receiving nothing. They filed an appeal in 2018, but there has been no further news on the outcome since that time.

The murder of Daniel Morgan remains officially unsolved, though his brother Alastair has been continuing to press for further probes into the homicide case and the alleged police corruption that engendered it.

****

On the morning of March 13th, 1987, in a suburb of Cleveland, Ohio called Bedford, a twenty-four-year-old mother of two was found viciously stabbed to death inside her own apartment. Analia Zavodny was the night manager of the Alamo Apartments on Broadway Avenue.

Three years after she was slain, her boyfriend was put on trial for her murder, but was acquitted shortly thereafter. The case was reopened in 2015 after new evidence surfaced, and police have hinted that they know who the killer is and that he still resides in the Cleveland area, though as of this writing, no arrests have been made. An investigator on the case sent a cryptic message to the murderer via the press, which read in part, "Analia exposed you for the failure that you are. The final nails are being driven in your coffin. Given what I know, I would not go to the store and buy green bananas."

A reward of ten-thousand dollars is still on offer for information leading to the conviction of the killer.

****

A little more than two weeks later, back in England, an older woman out walking her dogs in the woods would be found violently battered to death in a crime that still haunts the nation more than thirty years on.

It was about quarter to eleven on the morning of Saturday, March 28th, 1987. Sixty-six-year-old Helen Fleet had bundled her two dogs, Bilbow and Cindy, into her blue Datsun and was driving out to Worlebury Woods near her home in Weston-super-Mare to take her beloved pets for a walk. She was last seen parking the vehicle at the side of the road at ten-fifty a.m. and setting out into the trees.

Two hours later, another dog walker named Sylvia Lewis came across Helen Fleet lying across the path, not moving. Sylvia, who knew Helen quite well, hurried to a nearby house and called police, but by the time they arrived, it was too late; Helen Fleet was dead.

It appeared that the victim had been beaten, strangled, and stabbed to death. She had been neither robbed nor sexually assaulted, giving authorities little clue as to what the motive for this random, broad-daylight attack could have been.

Several witnesses claimed to have seen a young man running down a few nearby streets on the morning of the murder, and that he looked to be carrying a helmet or a hard hat. Other witnesses stated they had seen two different teenagers—both clad in ski jackets—fleeing through the woods at around eleven-thirty that morning. A composite sketch of the first of these individuals was produced, but led to no significant suspects.

Years later, however, another witness came forward and asserted that Helen Fleet had been talking to a young man in the woods on the day of her death, and that she appeared to know him well. The witness further stated that the teenager had been playing with Helen's dogs. The description of this person of interest very strongly resembled the description of one of the teenagers seen running through the woods by separate witnesses.

The case remains open, with detectives operating under the assumption that Helen Fleet may have known her killer, and that he was a local boy who was familiar with the area and had some unknown grudge against the victim.

However, another possibility being considered is that the murder was the first committed by an as-yet unidentified serial killer. Two later murders—those of fourteen-year-old Kate Bushell in 1997 and forty-one-year-old Lyn Bryant in 1998, both of which will be discussed later on in this book—have been tentatively linked to the killing of Helen Fleet, as the modus operandi was similar enough to warrant further investigation.

****

Back in California late that summer, a young woman would be found dead on the side of a highway and remain unidentified until early 2019, when she finally had her name restored.

It was August 30th, 1987, and a hiker came across the nude and mostly skeletal remains of a woman, lying fifty feet off the side of Santa Ana Canyon Road near the 91 Freeway in Anaheim. It was not immediately clear how she had been killed, though later examination would determine that she had been stabbed in the chest. Time of death was estimated to have been approximately two months prior to the discovery of her body.

No clothing or identification was found alongside the remains; in fact, the only clues as to the victim's identity were a length of cord, a red handkerchief, and a few locks of light brown hair. The woman was thought to be between fifteen and nineteen years old, with a slender build, and standing somewhere between five-foot-one and five-foot-four. She also had six missing teeth, and a chip in one of her remaining front teeth. It further appeared as though her killer had removed her hands.

Police scoured missing persons reports, but came up with no promising matches, and for many years, the victim was known only as Anaheim Jane Doe. Authorities periodically attempted to run her DNA and dental records through the system, but had no luck until late 2018, when, working alongside the non-profit DNA Doe Project, they had a breakthrough: Jane Doe's DNA was found to be a close match to an individual who had submitted their profile to the genealogy website GedMatch. Incidentally, this was the same manner in which notorious Golden State Killer Joseph DeAngelo was finally identified.

It turned out that the stabbing victim was twenty-year-old Tracey Hobson, who had gone missing from her Anaheim home in June of 1987 and had been murdered shortly afterward. Though her family was relieved to be able to lay their daughter to rest at last, her killer remains unknown.

****

As autumn of 1987 descended, a strange and grimly classic English murder mystery would begin to unfold in a crumbling old manor house in rural Shropshire.

Simon Dale had spent much of his career as an architect, mainly focused on restoring country mansions that had fallen into ruin. Back in 1957, when he was thirty-eight years old, he had married the twenty-three-year-old Susan Wilberforce, a haughty society woman who was descended from famed Victorian politician and philanthropist William Wilberforce, best known for his efforts to abolish slavery in Britain in the eighteenth century.

Two years following the wedding, Simon and Susan bought a dilapidated, fifty-room Queen Anne mansion called Heath House, and set about restoring it. The property had been mostly paid for with Susan's family inheritance. For a short time, everything seemed idyllic, and the couple ended up having five children as they lived in and worked on the beautiful old property.

But soon enough, cracks began to appear in the relationship, and Simon and Susan took to living at opposite ends of the enormous home for a while before finally filing for divorce in 1972. By this time, the family's finances were looking fairly dire, as Simon had been losing his eyesight, making it difficult for him to find architectural work; and Susan either could not or would not work at all. It was agreed that Heath House would be sold and the proceeds divided equally, but for more than fifteen years, the unstable housing market insured that there were no interested buyers in the lovely but somewhat remote mansion.

There was also the trifling little detail that Simon Dale seemed to have absolutely no intention of moving out of the house. As he had gotten older, he had developed an all-consuming interest in Arthurian legends, and was unshakably convinced that the grounds around Heath House contained the fabled Holy Grail. He had even written several scholarly papers arguing for his hypothesis, but archaeologists refused to take him seriously, and none of his work was ever published.

By 1987, Simon had become somewhat reclusive, living in two rooms of the mansion while the rest was allowed to slowly deteriorate. His ex-wife Susan had remarried in 1984, to Russian émigré Baron Michael Victor Jossif de Stempel; the pair had divorced in 1985, but Susan retained the title of Baroness. She and two of her and Simon's grown children—Marcus and Sophia—had been occasionally staying in a guest cottage on the property of Heath House, trying to keep the mansion from completely falling into decay; Susan was still hoping to get her fair share of the house or its sale price one day, after all.

However, at some point over the second weekend in September, someone entered Heath House while Simon Dale was in the kitchen cooking and beat the eccentric sixty-eight-year-old man to death with what was thought to be a crowbar. His body was discovered by his assistant, Giselle Wall, on the afternoon of Sunday, September 13th.

Almost immediately, authorities set their sights on Susan, now known as Baroness Susan de Stempel. After all, she had been staying on the property, and she admitted to having broken into Heath House on a few prior occasions in order to retrieve furniture that she felt still belonged to her. Not only that, but she told police that she had been using a crowbar on some of the outside renovation work that she and her children had been undergoing. There had also allegedly been some arguments between the former spouses about Simon's reluctance to leave the home and pay Susan her half of its assessed value. Susan also later claimed that Simon had been abusive to her and the children.

Susan, Marcus, and Sophia were all arrested in the murder, but the grown children were cleared shortly afterward. Though investigators took Susan's crowbar and fireplace poker into evidence, there was no trace of blood on them, and there was likewise no other forensic evidence tying her to the murder. During the entire ordeal, she remained completely calm and aloof, even addressing police officers, lawyers, and judges with a snooty contempt. After only four hours of deliberation at her trial, the jury found her not guilty of the murder of her former husband.

The Baroness didn't get off entirely scot-free, however, although her prison term was mostly unrelated to the murder charge. It so happened that during a series of financial investigations undertaken by police as the trial was going on, it came to light that Susan's wealthy aunt, Lady Margaret Illingworth, was missing a substantial chunk of her considerable fortune. The elderly widow had suffered from dementia, and in 1984 had gone to live with Susan and the Baron at their home in Docklow. During this period, Lady Margaret's valuable paintings and large collection of gold bars disappeared, and shortly after that, many of her antiques were sold at auction. Authorities determined that Susan, Marcus, Sophia, and possibly Baron de Stempel had conspired to forge Lady Margaret's signature on various documents, allowing them to cash out her shares and have money disbursed to them from her accounts. They also apparently forged a new will that left all of Lady Margaret's remaining assets to Susan. In sum, the fraud is thought to have netted the Baroness close to a million pounds.

At the trial in 1990, Susan pled guilty to defrauding her aunt, though Marcus and Sophia insisted they were innocent, on the grounds that they had been unwittingly used by their mother. Despite this, all four defendants were found guilty; Susan received seven years, the Baron four, but Marcus and Sophia were given much lighter sentences, eighteen months and thirty months, respectively.

The murder of Simon Dale, then, remains officially unsolved. Interestingly, Heath House had been the site of another appalling murder back in 1968: Dr. Alan Beach was shot dead in his car in the driveway of the home by a man taking revenge on the physician for not diagnosing his wife's cancer early enough for her to be saved.

As of 2019, Heath House has been beautifully restored, and many of the cottages on the property have been rented out to tenants.

****

On November 16th of 1987, a pair of hunters patrolling an area near Shaw Creek in Eureka, South Carolina stumbled upon a disturbing scene, one that in hindsight may have been the first inkling of a possible serial killer prowling through the forest.

The dead woman had clearly been there for some time, probably between one and five years; there was little left of her but a skeleton, and tree roots had grown through some of her finger bones. She was discovered lying face down, perhaps even posed, in a very shallow grave with no clothing or belongings of any kind. The only item found alongside the body, in fact, was the brass casing from a shotgun shell.

The victim, eventually dubbed Aiken County Jane Doe, was an African-American woman between the ages of seventeen and thirty, standing about five-foot-nine and weighing around one-hundred-fifty-five pounds. She had several teeth missing, and a very prominent overbite. Other identifying features included a healed injury to her right knee, and a healed broken nose. Because the hyoid bone was also found to be missing, authorities speculated that she had perhaps been strangled. Later analysis of the victim's hair tested positive for cocaine.

The woman has so far never been identified, and her killer is likewise a mystery, though as the years went on, other dead women would turn up in the same area, leading some researchers to believe that a serial murderer is responsible for the slaying of Aiken County Jane Doe and more victims that will be discussed later on in this narrative.

****

Two days after the unidentified woman's remains were discovered in South Carolina, the horrific slaughter of an entire family in their own home would shock the Midwestern United States and send a ripple of fear through the residents of the tiny village of Ina, Illinois.

Keith and Elaine Dardeen had bought a mobile home in Ina in 1986, so Keith could be closer to his job as treatment plant operator at the Rend Lake Water Conservancy District facility there. Elaine worked at an office supply store in town. The couple had a two-year-old son named Peter, and in November of 1987, Elaine was pregnant with their second child, a girl who they planned to name Casey.

Ironically, considering what the ghastly fate of the family would be, the Dardeens had recently decided to put their trailer up for sale and move away. The area around where they lived had seen an alarming increase in violent crime over the past two years, with more than two-dozen murders taking place in Jefferson County alone. Keith thought it would be best to move his family somewhere much safer. Unfortunately, he would never get the chance.

On Wednesday, November 18th, 1987, Keith Dardeen didn't show up for work, and his supervisor became concerned; Keith was a conscientious employee, and never would have missed a shift without calling in. The supervisor phoned Keith's parents, but neither of them had seen their son. They called the police and agreed to meet officers at the Dardeens' trailer with their spare copy of the key.

Inside one bedroom of the mobile home, investigators found an absolute bloodbath. Thirty-year-old Elaine and two-year-old Peter were both tucked into bed, their heads obliterated by what was presumed to be Peter's baseball bat. Even more appallingly, it appeared that the killer or killers had beaten Elaine so ferociously that she had gone into labor; the baby girl she had delivered had also been brutally beaten to death and placed in the bed next to her mother and brother.

At first, the whereabouts of twenty-nine-year-old Keith Dardeen and his 1981 red Plymouth were unknown, and detectives initially surmised that he had murdered his family and gone on the run. This hypothesis was only sustained for one more day, as on November 19th, Keith's body was recovered by hunters in a field a short distance from the trailer. He had been shot three times and had his penis cut off. Subsequently, Keith's blood-spattered vehicle was found parked at the Benton police station, eleven miles away from the scene of the crime.

Because of the unbelievable savagery of the quadruple homicide, rumors began to spread that a Satanic cult might be responsible, though police were quick to try to dispel these theories. It seemed that they didn't have many other leads to pursue, however; the Dardeens had been a quiet, well-liked family seemingly untainted by scandal of any sort, and there was no obvious motive for their deaths, particularly in such a beastly fashion. The presence of cash and valuables in the house belied the notion of a robbery, and Elaine had not been sexually assaulted. Further, there was no sign of forced entry. In fact, the only vaguely sketchy evidence discovered in the trailer was a tiny quantity of marijuana, which investigators believed might have been left by the murderer.

The case very quickly began to stagnate, and though Keith's mother Joeann worked tirelessly to keep the homicide in the media, new avenues of inquiry were frustratingly scarce. For a time in the late 1990s, authorities were focused on train-hopping serial killer Ángel Maturino Reséndiz, who turned himself in to Texas police in 1999 and was known to kill people by beating them to death. He was ultimately unable to be linked to the Dardeen slayings, however.

One more promising candidate appeared on investigators' radar a little later that year. In December of 1999, serial killer Tommy Lynn Sells was arrested in Del Rio, Texas after murdering one girl and wounding another by slashing their throats. Sells was eventually convicted and received the death penalty for the Del Rio murder as well as an earlier one in San Antonio, and after he was imprisoned, he began confessing to many other crimes he had allegedly committed as he rode freight trains around the country.

One of the murder cases he admitted responsibility for was the slaughter of the Dardeens, but there were a few glaring problems with his confession. Though he did seem to know a few details about the multiple murder, he changed his story several times and misidentified some aspects of the crime scenes. For example, he first told police that he had met Keith Dardeen at a pool hall or a truck stop, was later invited over to the trailer for dinner, and became enraged when Keith supposedly sexually propositioned him, and/or offered a threesome with Elaine.

In another version of the story, Sells claimed that he had not previously known the Dardeen family at all, but had hopped off a freight train near their trailer and had seen their "For Sale" sign, at which point he had gone to the door and told Keith that he wanted to purchase their house. In this iteration, he gave no compelling reason why he had decided to murder the family, and he also claimed that he had raped Elaine, which the coroner's report suggested was not the case.

He also gave an incorrect answer when asked which seat of Keith's car the victim had been sitting in when he was shot, and he initially misidentified the position in which Elaine's body had been found. Further, friends and family of the Dardeens claimed it was highly unlikely that Keith would have willingly let a stranger inside the trailer for any reason, especially in light of all the previous homicides in the area that had left the family wary and paranoid.

While Tommy Lynn Sells remains the prime suspect, authorities are leaning toward the idea that he was simply confessing to the murders in order to forestall his death sentence. If that was the plan, it ultimately failed; Sells was executed in Texas in 2014, and if he did massacre the Dardeens in Ina, Illinois, he took the knowledge with him to his grave.

1988

> Dade County John Doe

> Jenkins County Jane Doe

> Amar Singh Chamkila
  & Amarjot Kaur

> Debbie Linsley

> Inga Maria Hauser

> Marie Wilks

> Sally McNelly & Shane Stewart

> Julie Ward

> Seymour & Arlene Tankleff

> Jaclyn Dowaliby

> Julie Doe

> The Texas Killing Fields

> Venus Xtravaganza

Less than a week into the new year, the body of a young man would be discovered in a Florida hotel room, and his identity remains an enigma to this day.

It was January 5th, 1988, and a maid entering a room at a Miami hotel was shocked to find the remains of what appeared to be a teenage boy. The victim was white, between the ages of ten and twenty-one years old, stood around five-foot-six and weighed approximately one-hundred-fifty pounds. He had light brown hair that was fairly short in the front and somewhat longer in the back, and his eyes are variously listed as brown or gray.

He was clad in jeans, high-top sneakers, and a white t-shirt with a flag decal on the front. Women's clothing was also discovered in the hotel room, though it was unclear who it belonged to.

The victim—dubbed Dade County John Doe—had been spotted around the hotel by other guests and employees, and from these witnesses, police were able to determine that the boy had told people his name was Robert or Bobby Copeland, that he was a foster child from New York, and that he was part of a group of youngsters selling magazine subscriptions in the area. Though the name and back-story he gave was looked into by investigators, none of the details could be verified.

While John Doe's cause of death is listed as a homicide, details about exactly how he died have not been released to the public. Additionally, the boy had several healed scars on his wrists, forearms, and his right thigh, perhaps indicating prior abuse or possibly self-harm, though these specificities have likewise been of no help in identifying the victim. Both he and his killer are still unknown.

****

More than a month later and miles to the north, yet another unidentified victim would turn up, this time a young woman, shockingly found discarded like garbage.

On Valentine's Day of 1988, authorities were summoned to a dumpster located near the intersection of Kaiser Road and Old Perkins Road in Millen, Georgia. Three people had noticed a foul stench coming from inside the dumpster, and when police investigated, they soon found the source of the odor: inside was a large, nylon duffel bag, and inside the bag was the nude body of a woman wrapped in a sheet of plastic and secured with duct tape.

The victim was an Asian or half-Asian female between the ages of sixteen and twenty-five years old, standing approximately five-foot-five and weighing around one-hundred-forty pounds. She had long, dark brown hair and slightly crooked, though otherwise healthy, teeth. She had also had a molar removed not long before her death.

Christened Jenkins County Jane Doe, the young woman was thought to have been deposited in the dumpster four to seven days prior to her being found, and the state of decomposition of the body meant that neither her eye color nor a definite cause of death could be established, though it was believed she had been asphyxiated, perhaps by being smothered with a pillow.

Several other items assumed to belong to the victim were found alongside the remains, including a towel with a butterfly design, a maroon bedspread with a floral print, and a pale green pillow with a similar floral motif, which was thought to be part of the same bedding set. Authorities surmised that these items had come from the victim's bedroom.

A rape kit was carried out, but produced negative results, though investigators have stated that they cannot rule out the possibility that other forms of more unusual sexual assault were perpetrated on the victim.

Just as in the aforementioned Miami case, Jenkins County Jane Doe remains unidentified, and her case is still open.

****

Early that March, across the globe in northern India, a very different sort of crime would occur, one that took place in broad daylight on a crowded street and claimed the lives of four people, including one of the most famous singer-songwriters to ever emerge from Punjab.

It was around two p.m. on the afternoon of March 8th, 1988, and Amar Singh Chamkila, his wife and singing partner Amarjot Kaur, and their entourage arrived by van for a performance in the village of Mehsampur in Jalandhar. Amar, who had been born Dhanni Ram and had originally wanted to become an electrician before going into music, had a meteoric rise to fame in the early 1980s, writing and singing dozens of songs and duets; touring Dubai, Bahrain, Canada, and the United States; releasing several best-selling folk albums; performing up to three live shows a day at times; and having his music appear in several Punjabi films.

Though much of the popular music of the region during this period was still based around traditional themes, Amar broke the mold and sang about more down-to-earth topics, delving into the problems of drug abuse and alcoholism, extra-marital affairs, and the sometimes toxic masculinity of Punjabi culture. His lyrics were considered rather bawdy and full of double entendres, which more conservative interests did not approve of in the slightest. The youth at the time ate it up, though, easily relating to Amar's soulful voice and heartfelt lyrical examination of day-to-day life; the singer is still widely known, in fact, as "The Elvis of Punjab."

His popularity, though, clearly had its downside, and indeed might have been one of the factors that ultimately put a target on his back. The early 1980s were a time of great strife in the Punjabi region, with the Khalistan movement of Sikh separatists agitating for their demands and sometimes perpetrating assassinations and terrorist-style attacks; honor killings and murders undertaken by police officers were also fairly commonplace. Amar Singh Chamkila had received regular death threats throughout his career, mostly down to the so-called objectionable nature of his lyrical content, as well as his far-reaching fame.

On March 8th, it seemed that whatever powers were conspiring against Amar finally had their revenge. As he, his wife, and his band members exited their van in Mehsampur in front of the venue where they were set to perform, a gang of youths on motorcycles sped by and began firing at them with AK-47s. Twenty-six-year-old Amar was struck in the chest and died at the scene, as did his wife and duet partner Amarjot, another musician in Amar's band, Harjit Singh Gill, and one other member of the couple's entourage. According to survivors of the massacre, several fans who had been waiting to enter the venue for the show attempted to chase down the killers on foot, but were unsuccessful.

Over the years, the appalling quadruple homicide has been the subject of much debate, and several conspiracy theories have emerged as to who could have perpetrated the slaughter. Some have proposed that Amarjot's family was responsible, and that their motivation stemmed from their shame that Amarjot had married someone of a lower caste. Others have speculated that either Khalistani militants or Punjabi police engineered the assassination, as they harshly disapproved of the subject matter of Amar's songs. Yet a third hypothesis holds that rival musicians or disgruntled music promoters might have had it in for Amar due to jealousy or professional rivalry, and may have taken extreme measures to address their grievances. Despite all the conjecture, however, the case remains cold.

A strange mockumentary about the murders, directed by Kabir Singh Chowdhry and called *Mehsampur*, was released in 2018, winning the Grand Jury Prize for Best Film at the Mumbai Film Festival.

****

A little more than two weeks later, back in England, there would be yet another brazenly public attack in the middle of the afternoon, this time against a young woman on a crowded London train.

Twenty-six-year-old Debbie Linsley was originally from Bromley, southeast London, though she had since moved to Edinburgh, Scotland to work as a hotel manager at a Sheraton there. In late March, though, Debbie had taken three days off work to attend a hotel management course in London, and while there, she was spending some time with her family back in Bromley. Her brother Gordon was getting married in a couple of weeks, and Debbie was getting fitted for a bridesmaid's dress and participating in some of the other wedding preparations.

On Wednesday, March 28th, Debbie decided to take a train to Victoria station in order to see about another potential hotel job on Baker Street in London. She made a sandwich to take along on the half-hour journey, and Gordon dropped her off at the Petts Wood station near his work at approximately two p.m. Debbie purchased a ticket and a pack of cigarettes less than five minutes later, then boarded the train when it arrived on the platform at two-eighteen.

Significantly, she sat in a so-called closed carriage, which only had doors on either side allowing access to the platform, but did not allow passage between carriages. Though these types of train cars were on their way out in the late 1980s and were sometimes colloquially referred to as "death traps" because passengers could not move to other carriages while the train was in motion, it is believed that Debbie selected this particular car because it was one of the few on the train that allowed smoking.

Though Debbie was a rather attractive young woman and was clad in a striking blue outfit topped with a black leather jacket on this particular day, there are no witness accounts of her movements after she boarded the train. From a later reconstruction of events, it is known that Debbie smoked at least one cigarette and ate part of her sandwich while she was seated in the car, but it is unclear when her murderer entered the carriage with her.

When the train arrived at Victoria at two-fifty p.m., a porter by the name of Ron Lacey was checking the carriages for lost luggage when he was confronted with the shocking sight of Debbie Linsley lying dead in a massive pool of blood. She had been savagely stabbed nearly a dozen times in the face, neck, chest and abdomen; at least one of these wounds had penetrated her heart.

Unbelievably, the seventy other people on the train had not seen or heard anything suspicious, save for a young French au pair named Helene Jousseline, who had been seated in the next carriage over from Debbie's, and had heard screaming right after the train had departed from the Brixton station. Though the witness was apparently alarmed and considered pulling the communication cord to summon help, in the end she stated that she had been too frozen with fear and shock to do anything.

She did go on to say, however, that when she got off the train at Victoria, she spotted a muscular white man—aged around forty, with red hair and a mustache, and wearing gray pants and a light-colored jacket—getting out of the carriage where the screaming had emitted from. Helene allegedly followed this man, but lost sight of him in the teeming crowds.

After the details of the crime went public, other witnesses came forward and claimed to have seen persons of interest on the day of the slaying. One of these was a five-foot-five-inch white man in his late twenties with long-ash-blond hair and sporting a cut on his left cheek, who was seen on the concourse at Victoria approximately ten minutes after the fatal train had pulled into the platform. It's possible this same individual was seen by another witness a few minutes later in the men's bathroom, cleaning the wound. This could be a critical detail, as police were later able to establish that Debbie's killer had been injured in the struggle with his victim, as his blood was also recovered from the train car. However, authorities were quick to add the caveat that on the day of Debbie's murder, there had been a soccer (football) match between England and Holland at Wembley Stadium, that had engendered a few punch-ups, and it's plausible that the wounded man seen at the station had simply been involved in a sports-related scuffle.

More intriguingly, there had reportedly been a man seen changing carriages, possibly into the car Debbie was seated in, at Penge East station, two stops after Debbie had boarded. This individual was a scruffy-looking white male about thirty years old with dirty blond hair and a stocky build, who was clad in a pale brown jacket.

Yet another suspicious man was allegedly seen at Orpington station, the originating station of the route and one stop before Petts Wood, where Debbie had got on the train. This individual, a description of which was not forthcoming, was said to have been leering at women who boarded the trains.

Though the murder weapon was never recovered, it was believed to be a good quality kitchen knife, measuring between five and seven inches long. The fact that the attacker was apparently carrying this knife with him suggested that he had planned to commit a murder, although it seems unlikely that he had targeted Debbie Linsley specifically, as she no longer lived in the area and did not regularly take this particular train. Detectives have theorized that the crime was perhaps a random sex attack, that turned into a murder after Debbie viciously fought back against her assailant.

The killer's blood, obtained at the scene, was used to construct a complete DNA profile in 2002, but unfortunately, it matches no offender currently in the UK's database. Given the ferocity of the slaying, police are confident that the murder of Debbie Linsley was not this perpetrator's first homicide, but they have been hamstrung by the lack of further leads. The investigation was again reopened in 2013, with a large reward on offer for information leading to the conviction of the killer.

****

Elsewhere in the UK, a woman on a backpacking trip would disappear off a ferry and later be found murdered in a remote forest in Northern Ireland.

Eighteen-year-old Inga Maria Hauser was originally from Munich, Germany, a free-spirited, artistic young woman with a passion for travel. Toward the end of March 1988, her family had dropped her off at the train station, and she had journeyed through Holland before taking a ferry to Harwich, England and then on to London. She had been calling her parents daily and sending postcards along the way to keep them apprised of her movements, but she had no scheduled itinerary at all, enjoying the luxury of being able to wake up every day and go wherever she pleased.

By the time April 6th had rolled around, she was in Scotland, having made her way north from Glasgow to Inverness, and then back down south to Ayr and then Stranraer, where she boarded a ferry bound for Larne, in Northern Ireland. Two later witnesses would remember seeing her aboard the boat, a pretty girl carrying a green backpack that had a pair of white running shoes hanging from it by the laces. It was the last time anyone would see her alive.

Two weeks later, on April 20th, a farmer discovered her beaten body lying face down in an isolated part of Ballypatrick Forest in County Antrim. She had been sexually assaulted and had died of a broken neck.

Authorities assumed that Inga's ultimate destination on this leg of her trip was Belfast, which was approximately fifty-five miles in the opposite direction to the spot where her remains had been dumped. This suggested that whoever had killed her had likely either persuaded or forced her into a vehicle, perhaps on the ferry, and then drove her to this remote location, where she was subsequently murdered.

According to Inga's family, the girl was very worldly and would definitely not have gotten into a car with a man she didn't know, especially considering that she was traveling through a country she had never set foot in before; this tended to support the idea that another passenger or passengers on the ferry with her had strong-armed her into their car and abducted her.

The area where Inga was ultimately found, moreover, was far-flung enough that the assailant must have been very familiar with the lay of the land, and considering the rough terrain, probably drove there in a jeep or a van.

Northern Ireland in 1988 was still in the thick of The Troubles; in fact, that year was one of the most violent of the entire conflict. For this reason, the investigation into Inga's murder was stymied by stretched-thin resources and overworked police officers. That said, some sources reveal that the IRA had looked into the matter themselves shortly after it occurred, and were planning to share the information they had garnered with the Royal Ulster Constabulary, but later decided against it.

The case was reopened in 2018, on the thirtieth anniversary of the murder, and a few new leads did emerge. In May of that year, in fact, two men were arrested in conjunction with the homicide, though after questioning, one of them was released on bond pending further investigation. Authorities had been able to extract a DNA profile of one of the killers, but as of this writing, they have been unable to match it with any known offender in the nationwide database. No updates have been forthcoming since that time.

****

Later on that summer, yet another UK murder would traumatize the nation and ultimately lead to a wrongful conviction.

It was Saturday, June 18th, 1988, and twenty-two-year-old Marie Wilks, seven months pregnant with her second child, had been spending the day in the village of Symonds Yat with her husband Adrian, who was there on a training exercise for the Territorial Army. She was also accompanied by her eleven-year-old sister Georgina, and her and Adrian's thirteen-month-old son Mark.

At approximately seven p.m., Marie bid her husband goodbye and got in her Morris Marina with the two children for the drive back to Worcester. She actually hadn't planned on taking the motorway home—she had only received her driver's license two months previously, and wasn't a very confident driver at this stage—but somewhere along the back roads she became lost, and ultimately had to merge onto the M50.

But as luck would have it, her vehicle broke down shortly afterward. There was an emergency phone box only about seven-hundred yards from where the car gave out, so she left the kids in the car and walked over to it to phone for help. The police operator lodged her call at seven-thirty-seven p.m.

At Marie's request, the dispatcher attempted to call Marie's father Terry so he could come pick her up, but neither of Marie's parents was home. The operator came back on the line to inform Marie of this, but Marie was no longer there; despite repeated summons, all the operator could hear on the phone was the roar of passing traffic.

Twelve minutes after Marie's initial phone call, an officer in a squad car driving past saw the eleven-year-old Georgina walking down the shoulder of the road, carrying baby Mark in her arms. More police descended on the scene after a radio bulletin was issued, but Marie Wilks had seemingly vanished into thin air. Ominously, the receiver of the emergency phone was still hanging at the end of its cord.

A widespread search involving helicopters and tracking dogs was undertaken, but for several hours, nothing at all was found. Shortly after sunrise on Sunday, detectives discovered traces of blood around the phone box, but there was still no sign of Marie.

Then, at six p.m. on the evening of Monday, June 20th, the body of Marie Wilks was found in a patch of thick undergrowth down an embankment, three miles along the motorway from where her vehicle had broken down. She had been severely beaten and kicked around the head and face, her jaw had been broken, and she had been stabbed in the throat, a wound that punctured her carotid artery.

A few days after Marie's remains were recovered, a witness told police that they had seen a silver Renault pulled over on the side of the road near where Marie's car had been on the night she was abducted. They also claimed to have seen a white male walking near the scene of the crime that same evening, and described this individual as being in his twenties, with thin features, a prominent chin, a sharp nose, and spiky blond hair with orange highlights. The witness further stated that the man was dressed for a night out in a blue and white striped dress shirt and dark-colored pants.

Police produced a composite sketch of the suspect, and on the following day, they picked up a thirty-two-year-old Welsh man named Eddie Browning after receiving a tip from an informant.

Authorities found it very suspicious that Browning not only owned a silver Renault and had a history of violence, but had also had an argument with his own pregnant wife on the evening that Marie Wilks was murdered. Further, Browning admitted that he had been driving from his home in Cwmparc, Wales north to Scotland, which detectives speculated could have put him on the same stretch of motorway as Marie Wilks at around the same time as her disappearance.

Eddie Browning actually insisted that he had not taken the M50 to Scotland that night, but had instead taken the M4 to the Severn Bridge, then got on the M5. But his past record of violent behavior and his close resemblance to the composite sketch was enough to secure a conviction, and Browning was eventually handed a life sentence for murder, despite there being no physical evidence tying him to the crime.

However, his conviction was later overturned after it came to light that police had withheld evidence that an off-duty officer, under hypnosis, had actually described the silver Renault he had spotted at the scene as having chrome bumpers and the license plate number C856 HFK. Eddie Browning's Renault, though the same color and style, actually had plastic bumpers and bore the tag number C754 VAD. Browning was released in 1994 and was subsequently awarded a settlement of approximately six-hundred-thousand pounds. He died in 2018, at the age of sixty-three.

After Browning walked free, the case proceeded to go cold. Some researchers have speculated that Marie Wilks might have fallen victim to notorious serial killer couple Fred and Rosemary West, who were familiar with the area where the murder occurred and were not apprehended until 1994. However, detectives on the case are skeptical of this scenario, and while periodic updates on the investigation are still performed at regular intervals, the random slaying of the pregnant woman on the side of the motorway remains unsolved.

****

On Independence Day, back in the United States, a pair of teenagers rekindling their romance would disappear from a Texas lake shore and be found dead four months later.

Eighteen-year-old Sally McNelly and sixteen-year-old Shane Stewart had met in high school and had been dating off and on for a year; they had, in fact, just moved in together in January of 1988, though they had moved out of their apartment in May and spent some time out of town separately before returning to their hometown of San Angelo, Texas that summer. On July 4th, the couple planned to drive Shane's copper-colored 1980 Camaro out to Lake Nasworthy in San Angelo to watch the fireworks.

According to some sources, the teenagers had previously been involved with a questionable circle of friends who were into drugs, sex parties, the occult, and perhaps more serious criminal activities. A few months before their Independence Day excursion, Shane and Sally had reportedly turned in a gun to police that they claimed had been used by a member of the cult to murder someone.

Though authorities were able to determine that the firearm was indeed stolen, they were never able to link it with a specific crime like that Shane and Sally had described. But the deputy who took their statement recalled that the teenagers had seemed nervous, and had told him that the people they hung out with were dangerous and might hurt them.

Likewise, a friend of Sally's named Helen Williams later asserted that two weeks before Independence Day, Sally had expressed fear that someone was trying to kill her.

On the 4th of July, both Shane and Sally were seen at Lake Nasworthy at approximately nine p.m., watching the fireworks display. Less than three hours later, a fisherman named Randall Littlefield spotted Shane and Sally sitting in the Camaro at O.C. Fisher Lake, six miles away from their original destination. Randall told authorities that the couple appeared to be arguing or talking animatedly about not wanting to be "with them people no more," but the conversation was not unusual enough for him to attach any significance to it.

This sighting was the last time that the couple was seen alive. Shane's vehicle was found abandoned on the following day, the keys left on the dashboard and fast food wrappers littering the interior. The whereabouts of Sally McNelly and Shane Stewart would remain unknown until November of 1988.

****

As autumn approached, a young English woman with a passion for photography and adventure would be brutally cut down while on an African safari.

Twenty-eight-year-old Julie Ward worked for a publishing company in Suffolk, England, but had always dreamed of trekking across the Serengeti and capturing the majesty of nature with her camera. In February of 1988, she had finally taken the plunge, securing an extended leave of absence from her job and booking a seven-month trip to Kenya.

She had spent most of her holiday in the capital of Nairobi, but at the start of September, she decided to journey to the Maasai Mara game reserve in order to photograph the annual Great Wildebeest Migration, a breathtaking natural spectacle which saw thousands of zebras, gazelles, and wildebeest making their way across Tanzania. She set out on September 5th, accompanied by her Australian friend, Dr. Glen Burns.

Not long afterward, though, the pair's jeep broke down and the trip had to be postponed somewhat. Glen went back to Nairobi, but Julie stayed at the Mara Serena Safari Lodge overnight while the vehicle was undergoing repairs. The next day, she picked up the jeep, drove to the nearby Sand River Camp where she and Glen had been staying, and picked up their things.

After that, Julie Ward disappeared, and her gruesome fate would not be revealed until a week later.

****

On the following day, back in the United States, there would be a brutal double murder in New York that would result in a controversial familial conviction and later acquittal.

Seymour and Arlene Tankleff lived in the well-heeled village of Belle Terre, on the North Shore of Long Island. Seymour was an insurance broker, and he and his wife often hobnobbed with the other wealthy and influential residents of the area. In fact, on the night of September 6th, 1988, the Tankleffs were hosting their weekly poker night, known as the After Dinner Club, attended by the mayor of Belle Terre, Vincent Bove, as well as many other prominent citizens.

One of the people at the game that night was a businessman by the name of Jerry Steuerman, also known as the Bagel King of Long Island, as he owned about a dozen bagel shops in the vicinity. He and Seymour had been friends and business partners, but apparently, relations between them had cooled somewhat after Jerry had taken out a half-million-dollar loan from Seymour and had yet to pay it back. According to other attendees of the poker game, the two men were civil to each other that evening, but it was clear that their partnership had taken a drastic hit.

Jerry was apparently the last person to leave the Tankleff home that night, at around three a.m. He later told police that nothing had been amiss when he had bid the couple goodbye.

However, just three hours later, on the morning of Wednesday, September 7th, both Seymour and Arlene Tankleff were found stabbed and bludgeoned to death in their Belle Terre home.

From the beginning of the investigation, police seemed less interested in looking into possible motives having to do with Seymour's business interests, and instead focused their attention on the Tankleff's seventeen-year-old son Martin. Under questioning, the teenager apparently gave a confession to authorities on the same day that his parents' bodies were found, though he recanted this statement almost immediately, claiming that police officers had coerced it out of him.

Regardless, investigators pursued Martin, alleging that he had killed his parents in a fit of rage after an argument. Also contributing to the likelihood of his guilt, police felt, was the three-million-dollar inheritance that Martin stood to gain in the event of their deaths.

Despite a lack of physical evidence, Martin Tankleff was eventually charged and convicted of second-degree murder in the double homicide, and would go on to spend seventeen years in prison before finally being exonerated in 2008 after the emergence of new witness testimony that seemed to suggest that someone else was likely responsible for the crime.

This someone, not surprisingly, was Seymour Tankleff's erstwhile business partner Jerry Steuerman. Not only had

Steuerman admitted to being the last person to see the Tankleffs alive, but he was demonstrably in debt to Seymour for a substantial amount of money that Seymour had demanded immediate repayment of. In addition, Arlene Tankleff had reportedly told friends that she was afraid of Steuerman, and that Steuerman had threatened to cut her husband's throat.

This seemed damning enough, but there was also the fact that Steuerman had fled to California shortly after the murders under an assumed name, withdrawing fifteen-thousand dollars from his account and leaving instructions with his estate executor to fake his death and tell his family how to collect his life insurance.

When Steuerman was later tracked down—ironically, in order to testify at Martin Tankleff's murder trial—he claimed that he had only changed his identity because he had derailed his life so much through gambling debts that he had wanted to make a fresh start.

Though Steuerman has never been charged with the murder of Seymour and Arlene Tankleff, many researchers still consider him the prime suspect, speculating that either he killed the couple himself, or hired a pair of hit men to carry out the deed after he left the poker game that night. In the years since the crime, Steuerman has done quite well for himself, opening up a successful chain of bagel shops and living in Florida with his second wife.

Martin Tankleff also believes that Steuerman was responsible for the murder of his parents. He later became a lawyer, and in 2018 was awarded a ten-million-dollar settlement for his wrongful conviction and imprisonment.

The slaying of Seymour and Arlene Tankleff is still officially unresolved.

****

Two days after the Tankleff double homicide, in the Midwestern United States, a little girl would vanish in the middle of the night from her own bedroom, and her own parents would later be suspected in her murder.

Seven-year-old Jaclyn Dowaliby lived in Midlothian, Illinois with her family. She had gone to bed as usual at around ten p.m. on the evening of September 9th, 1988, but on the following morning, the child's stepfather David awoke early and noticed with some alarm that the front door of the house was standing slightly ajar. He initially thought that perhaps his mother had gone out and accidentally left the door open, and so didn't think any more about it.

A few hours later, however, when Jaclyn's mother Cynthia went into her daughter's room to wake up the little girl, she found that the child was not in her bed. But since it was Saturday, Cynthia figured that maybe Jaclyn had also risen early and gone outside to play with her friends. A brief search of the neighborhood, though, turned up no sign of her, and when Cynthia realized that the comforter was missing off the child's bed, and also that a window in the basement had been broken—possibly by an intruder—she and David called the police and reported Jaclyn missing.

She would not be found until four days later.

****

By the 13th of September, back in Kenya, Julie Ward's father John had joined the search party that had formed to find his missing daughter. Horrifically, it was John Ward himself who would actually stumble upon what was left of the vibrant young woman.

Situated near a large tree on the Maasai Mara game reserve was a charred human leg and a jawbone, as well as a few other burned human body parts. Following the recovery of Julie's body, Kenyan authorities attempted to classify the death as a tragic accident, claiming that Julie had perhaps been struck by lightning and partially eaten by a lion (not necessarily in that order), but after a British pathologist was brought in to examine the remains, it was concluded that Julie had actually been cut apart with a machete and then set on fire with gasoline.

Though the case for homicide was fairly airtight, the government of Kenya was still reluctant to concede, trying to essentially sweep the murder under the rug by arguing that Julie had actually committed suicide. A large portion of their reticence could be attributed to public relations; they didn't want to publicize anything that would negatively impact their enormous tourism industry.

Julie's father, however, wasn't going to let the matter rest, and he spent a great deal of his own money traveling back and forth to Kenya and petitioning politicians in the United Kingdom, as well as Scotland Yard, to keep the investigation alive.

Eventually, two Maasai Mara park rangers were arrested and charged with the murder, but both were acquitted at trial. Later on, even the head warden of the game reserve, Simon Makallah, was arrested and placed on trial, but was likewise found not guilty.

In 2004, a female witness came forward and claimed that three men on the reserve had gang-raped and murdered Julie Ward, burying most of her body at an undisclosed location before leaving the rest of the remains where they were found beneath the tree, in order to throw off authorities as to where the killing had actually taken place.

The case stagnated there until 2018, when it turned up in the media again, with John Ward pressing the police to obtain a DNA sample from an unidentified suspect. Since that time, there have been no new developments.

****

The next day, back in Illinois, the body of seven-year-old Jaclyn Dowaliby was discovered in a field in Blue Island, six miles away from her home. She was still clad in her nightgown, and had a length of rope around her neck. The missing comforter from her bed was also found with the remains. An autopsy was unable to determine when the child had been killed.

From the beginning, authorities had their suspicions that Jaclyn's parents might be involved in the death of their daughter. There were some ambiguous clues, such as the fact that the basement window might have been broken from the inside to make it look as though an intruder had entered through it. There were also allegedly hairs belonging to Jaclyn in the trunk of the Dowalibys' car, and blood stains on one of the child's pillowcases. In addition, Jaclyn's four-year-old brother David Jr. claimed that their parents had spanked Jaclyn a lot; he was also reported to have been playing with the very same rope that was later found around the throat of his dead sister.

Jaclyn's parents were ultimately arrested and placed on trial for the murder of their daughter. Besides all the aforementioned evidence, there was also some eyewitness testimony presented on the stand, namely that David Dowaliby had been seen sitting in his car near the site where Jaclyn's body had been dumped. Two witnesses also claimed to have seen Cynthia's vehicle at the same location, but these sightings were later shown to be erroneous, and indeed, even the sighting of David's car could not be confirmed, as the time and the distance from which the witness claimed to have seen him would have made it impossible for him to identify David undeniably.

It was also determined that, contrary to initial suspicions, the basement window had actually been broken from the outside. Further, the hair and blood evidence presented were found to be inconclusive. The case against Cynthia Dowaliby was subsequently dismissed, but David's trial continued, and in 1990, he was found guilty of murdering his daughter and given a sentence of forty-five years. His conviction, however, was overturned on appeal in October of 1991.

Though some investigators still suspect that the Dowalibys were behind the death of their daughter, two other individuals are still considered persons of interest. One of these was another family member: Jaclyn's uncle, Timothy Guess. Guess suffered from schizophrenia, and came under suspicion because his alibi for the night of Jaclyn's disappearance was believed to be false. He also seemed to know a few details about the Dowaliby home, even though he claimed he had never been there. Guess was never arrested for the child's murder, however, and he died in 2002.

Another possible suspect was a known sex offender by the name of Perry Hernandez, who turned up on the police's radar a year after Jaclyn's murder when he perpetrated a nearly identical crime in September of 1989: abducting a little girl from her home in Blue Island. This second child survived, but the modus operandi was too similar to ignore.

The slaying of Jaclyn Dowaliby remains a heartbreaking cold case.

****

Before the month of September was out, another murder victim would turn up, this time in central Florida, though a tragic series of forensic errors would ensure that the woman's identity remained unknown for decades.

It was the morning of Sunday, September 25th, 1988, and a man was driving along Highway 474 in Lake County east of Orlando, searching for a perfect cypress tree to cut down and make furniture out of. Spotting a promising specimen, the man pulled over, but then began to notice a terrible smell wafting out of the woods.

After police arrived on the scene, they discovered the partially skeletonized remains of a woman lying face up in the long weeds. She was clad in an acid-washed denim skirt and a blue-green tank top, and her pantyhose had been rolled down to her knees, suggesting that she had possibly been sexually assaulted.

Though a cause of death could not be conclusively determined, the case was investigated as a homicide, as it appeared that someone had dragged her to the spot where her body was found. Initial post-mortem examinations concluded that the victim was white, between twenty-two and thirty-five years old, standing around five-foot-ten and weighing approximately one-hundred-seventy pounds. The coroner also surmised that the woman had given birth to at least one child.

Dubbed Julie Doe, the victim also had a few other unique characteristics. Her naturally brown hair had been bleached blonde, for example, and she had had a nose job and breast implants that had been put in prior to 1984. She also had several previously healed fractures, including one to her cheekbone, one to her nose, and another to one of her ribs.

Public appeals over the ensuing years failed to identify either the victim or her possible killer, and the case subsequently went fallow. But in 2015, Julie Doe's DNA was reexamined as part of a push to solve cold cases in Lake County, and it was then that investigators got something of a surprise: Julie Doe was a transgender woman who had undergone gender reassignment surgery.

It turned out that the pits on the pelvis that the initial autopsy demonstrated were evidence of childbirth were not as clear-cut an indication as had once been believed. Further testing also established that Julie Doe had probably been undergoing hormonal treatment for several years prior to her death.

Because gender reassignment surgery was much more unusual in the early 1980s, it is almost certain that Julie received it in either Miami, New York City, New Orleans, Atlanta, or Los Angeles. Isotope testing suggested that the victim hailed from south Florida, indicating that perhaps her surgeries had taken place in Miami, though other possibilities are being explored.

Authorities are hopeful that this new information will eventually lead to Julie Doe having her true name restored and her killer being brought to justice.

****

Miles to the west, in Texas, the notorious Killing Fields would devour another young woman, though in this case her body has never been found.

Twenty-two-year-old Suzanne Rene Richerson worked as a night clerk at the Casa Del Mar Condominiums in Galveston. When her shift ended at six a.m., she left the premises, and was never seen again. The only trace of her that remained was a single shoe in the parking lot. It was October 7th, 1988.

****

More than a month later, also in Texas, there would be some resolution in the disappearance of Sally McNelly and Shane Stewart, who had vanished after watching the fireworks at Lake Nasworthy on Independence Day.

On November 11th, 1988, the skeletal remains of Sally McNelly were found near the Twin Buttes Reservoir, about four miles from where the couple had last been seen. Three days later, Shane's body was also found in the same area.

It appeared that both victims had been murdered by shotgun blasts to the head.

Though the cult angle has been a focus of the investigation from the start, the case got a massive break in 2017, when a forty-seven-year-old man named John Gilbreath was pulled over in San Angelo on suspicion of marijuana possession. His girlfriend informed police that Gilbreath was a dealer, at which point authorities filed for a search warrant and conducted an inspection of his property. In the course of their search, they turned up blood, a lock of hair, and a fingernail that possibly could be linked to the McNelly-Stewart homicide. Also present in Gilbreath's home was a notebook allegedly containing the teenagers' names, and three audio tapes which bore the initials SS.

Gilbreath remains a person of interest in the double murder, though it is unclear whether he had been acquainted with the victims in 1988 and had been a part of the purported cult, that they believed was out for revenge against them. The case is ongoing.

****

As the holiday season of 1988 approached, a transgender performer would be savagely murdered in a New York City hotel room in a crime that would be immortalized in an iconic 1990 documentary.

Born Thomas Pellagatti in New Jersey, Venus Xtravaganza moved out of her conservative family home in the early 1980s and made her way to New York City, where she became involved with the burgeoning ballrooms of the underground LBGTQ community. Like many other gay and transgender teenagers at the time, Venus found a new family in the ballrooms, specifically at the House of Xtravaganza, an influential hub of dance, visual arts, and flourishing creativity that would put on lavish events featuring competitions in modeling, dance, costume design, and drag.

By 1988, Venus had become a fixture as a drag performer and had won several competitions in Harlem. She was saving up for gender reassignment surgery, and had also been extensively interviewed for Jennie Livingston's documentary *Paris Is Burning*, which would go on to become something of a cultural milestone.

But it all came crashing down on Christmas Day, when the body of Venus Xtravaganza was found stuffed beneath a bed in a room at the Duchess Hotel. She had been strangled to death approximately four days prior to being discovered.

Venus had made no secret of being involved in sex work, and it is generally believed that she was murdered by a client; indeed, transgender women were (and are) disproportionately likely to be victims of violence and murder. And Venus herself, in one of her filmed interviews, relates an experience whereby she narrowly escaped a john who became enraged after he discovered she was transgender.

The case has never come close to being solved, though Venus's legacy lives on, and the House of Xtravaganza remains a significant force in the LGBTQ community of New York City and beyond.

1989

> Jessie Earl

> The Highway of Tears

> Darleen Messer

> Amy Mihaljevic

In the spring of 1989, a body would be discovered in England that would bring a nine-year search for a missing woman to a heartbreaking close.

It was March on Beachy Head, East Sussex, and a local man was in the area flying a kite with his daughter and enjoying the sunshine. At some stage, the kite blew off into a thicket of brambles, and the man went to retrieve it. While attempting to free the kite from the tangled bushes, he spotted a smattering of human bones in the underbrush.

Upon examining the skull, the remains were soon identified through dental records as belonging to twenty-two-year-old Jessie Earl, who had vanished from her Eastbourne bedsit back in May of 1980 after making plans to visit her parents in London for the weekend. The only other piece of evidence recovered from the site was a knotted brown bra, which a post-mortem suggested might have been used to bind the young woman's wrists, perhaps even to tie her to the tree near where her body was found. It was almost certain that she had died at that same spot, perhaps by strangulation.

Despite the suspicious circumstances surrounding Jessie's death, however, the coroner officially left the verdict open as to whether the victim had been murdered. Jessie Earl's parents campaigned for years to get the case recognized as a homicide, and were finally successful when the case was reopened in 2000.

It would be 2007, though, before a possible suspect in the crime emerged. This was infamous Scottish serial killer Peter Tobin, who was convicted in that year of raping and murdering a twenty-three-year-old Polish woman by the name of Angelika Kluk, and was subsequently found to have killed at least two more victims: eighteen-year-old Dinah McNichol, and fifteen-year-old Vicky Hamilton. Tobin's modus operandi—targeting petite women at random and using articles of their own clothing to restrain and kill them—was compellingly similar to the details of Jessie's death.

Police launched Operation Anagram in 2007 in order to try to link Tobin with other unsolved homicides in the area, and though they investigated him in connection with the Jessie Earl murder, no solid evidence of his involvement could be unearthed. As of this writing, there are no other known suspects, and the murder of Jessie Earl is still unresolved.

****

Later on that summer, the Highway of Tears in British Columbia would live up to its name once again. Its first casualties of 1989, in fact, would be an entire family of four.

It was early August of 1989, and the Jack family—twenty-six-year-old Ronald, his twenty-six-year-old wife Doreen, and the couple's two children, nine-year-old Russell and four-year-old Ryan—were at their home on Strathcona Road in Prince George. On the evening of the 1st, Ronald was spotted in the First Litre Pub not far from the Jack home, and it was later determined that an unidentified man there had offered Ronald work, a ten-to-fourteen-day stint at a logging camp near Cluculz Lake. The pay was good, the man said, and there would also be work there for Doreen and a day care on site for the children. Ronald, who had been looking for employment for some time, was excited about the prospect, and shortly after one-thirty a.m. on the morning of August 2nd, phoned his mother and told her about the job. It was the last time anyone would hear from the family.

After the Jacks disappeared, witnesses who had been in the pub came forward and described the man who had ostensibly offered Ronald the logging gig. This individual was a tall white male in his late thirties with a hefty build, reddish-brown hair, and a mustache and short beard. He had been wearing a red, checkered shirt, jeans, a blue nylon jacket, and work boots with leather fringe.

The vanishing of the Jacks is usually linked to the other Highway of Tears murders by virtue of the location of the disappearance as well as the fact that the victims were of aboriginal descent. The only possible clue as to their whereabouts came in 2002, when investigators fielded an anonymous phone call from a man claiming that the family was buried "at the south end of Gordie's ranch."

Though this call was traced to a home in Stoney Creek, no solid evidence could be found linking the residents to the Jacks' disappearance. The location of the purported bodies was also thoroughly searched, but nothing of note was discovered. No sign of any member of the family has ever turned up.

Less than a month later, however, another victim of the Highway of Tears would go missing, though in her case her remains would be found fairly quickly.

Twenty-four-year-old Alberta Gail Williams had been living with her sister in Vancouver, but both young women were spending the summer working in northern British Columbia. Abigail was last seen on August 25th, 1989, and her fate would be unknown until late September.

****

Miles to the south in Florida, a woman would disappear from her workplace and turn up dead two days later, the possible victim of a serial offender responsible for several abductions and murders in the area.

Thirty-six-year-old Darleen Messer was a clerk at the Suwannee Swifty convenience store in Lake City, and at some point on the night of September 18th, 1989, she was kidnapped from the store amid signs of a struggle and evidence of a robbery.

On September 20th, her body was discovered face down in the water beneath Swift Creek Bridge. She had been bludgeoned to death, though notably, one newspaper reported the cause of death as a single gunshot to the back of the head.

The murder of Darleen Messer is suspected to be linked with a few other cases of workplace abductions that took place in the same area of Florida in 1989 and 1990. On August 6th of 1989, in fact, a twenty-nine-year-old pregnant convenience store clerk named Donna Callahan had likewise been abducted from her store in Gulf Breeze, though in this case, the perpetrators were eventually captured: William Alex Wells and his half-brother, suspected serial killer Mark Riebe, were arrested years after the crime and led police to Donna's remains. Both men received life sentences, though their possible involvement in the murder of Darleen Messer is unclear.

And only a day after Darleen was taken, another woman would fall victim to the same type of crime. Fifty-year-old Eileen Mangold was the manager of a gas station in Riverview, Florida who was abducted during a robbery on the evening of September 19th. Her body was found only hours later; she had been raped and bludgeoned to death. A man named Franklin Alfred Smith was arrested and tried for the murder in 1999; he was a career criminal who lived near the store from which Eileen was abducted, and his fingerprints were discovered on Eileen's car. Smith was ultimately acquitted of the murder, but investigators still consider him the prime suspect.

It is not certain whether any of these other crimes were related to the murder of Darleen Messer. Her death has also been linked to yet another similar case, that of the disappearance of Deborah Poe, which would take place shortly afterward, in early 1990.

****

Back in British Columbia, the body of Alberta Gail Williams, missing since August 25th, was found on the 25th of September near the Tyee Overpass, approximately twenty-three miles east of Prince Rupert. She had been raped and strangled.

And on October 1st, another young woman would vanish along the Highway of Tears: this time it was eighteen-year-old Cicilia Anne Nikal, who had also been living in Vancouver but was reportedly last seen near Highway 16 in Smithers, British Columbia. Cicilia has never been found.

****

Only a few days before Halloween, a mysterious phone call would arrive at the home of the Mihaljevic family in Bay Village, Ohio, just outside of Cleveland. Ten-year-old Amy Mihaljevic answered the phone, and presumably knew the man at the other end of the line. This unidentified individual told Amy to meet him at the Bay Ridge Shopping Center later that afternoon, as he wanted her to help him pick out a gift for her mother to celebrate her recent promotion at *Trading Times* magazine. Amy agreed, and set out to keep the appointment.

Later witnesses would report that Amy was spotted on the afternoon of October 27th, talking calmly to a man in front of a barbershop at Bay Village Square. Two friends of Amy's from school also claimed they had seen Amy walking with a man, and that nothing at all appeared amiss.

But something was, in fact, dreadfully amiss. Only moments after her friends saw her walking alongside this mystery man, Amy completely disappeared, and despite a massive search, FBI involvement, and a detailed composite sketch of her companion, Amy's whereabouts would be unknown for more than three months.

****

The year would be only weeks from ending when the Highway of Tears claimed yet another victim, though in this particular case, her killer was eventually caught and convicted.

Eighteen-year-old Marnie Blanchard was last spotted at the Rock Pit Cabaret in Prince George at approximately two a.m. on the morning of November 22nd, 1989. Witnesses later confirmed that Marnie had gotten into a gray Toyota pickup truck with a white canopy, driven by a man with long, black hair. The vehicle pulled out of the bar's parking lot and headed west, and Marnie would subsequently never be seen alive again.

On December 11th, a pair of cross-country skiers stumbled across Marnie's remains west of Foothills Boulevard. Only months later, serial killer Brian Peter Arp was arrested for her murder, and though he was initially released due to lack of evidence, improved DNA technology later assured that he was convicted of killing Marnie Blanchard, as well as another woman named Theresa Umphrey, in 1993.

1990

> Eileen Jones

> Deborah Poe

> The Highway of Tears

> Amy Mihaljevic

> Susan Poupart

> Leonard Gomm

> Joseph Doucé

> Penny Doe

> Ann Heron

> Hillsborough Jane Doe

> William Arnold Newton

Not long after the dawn of the new decade, an elderly woman looking forward to a sunny Florida retirement would instead turn up murdered in her own home.

Sixty-seven-year-old Eileen Jones had only moved to Gainesville, in north Florida, in 1989. She had always been something of a loner, and had never married; she lived with her two cats in a mobile home off Archer Road, and largely kept to herself, though she had several friends in the neighborhood.

On the morning of Saturday, January 13th, 1990, these friends noticed that the door to her trailer was standing wide open, and they thought they had better go investigate. Now that they thought about it, in fact, none of them had seen Eileen around for a couple of days.

As soon as the neighbors peered inside, they understood why: Eileen was lying face down on the floor of her bedroom, and she wasn't moving.

When police arrived, they found that the victim had been strangled and possibly sexually assaulted. There were signs of a struggle in the home, and the sheets were missing from Eileen's bed.

Authorities honed in on a person of interest rather quickly. This suspect has not been named, but he was known to have committed sexual battery on another older woman in Lantana, Florida, and shortly after moving to Gainesville, was arrested again for sexual battery, this time on an elderly woman who lived in the Wind Meadows mobile home park, the same park that Eileen lived in.

While investigators were certain that this was their man, they did not have the technology to prove it definitively in 1990, and the individual in question has since passed away, leaving the murder of Eileen Jones officially unresolved.

****

In early February of 1990, elsewhere in central Florida, there would be another young woman who was likely abducted from the store where she was working, much like in the earlier case of Darleen Messer from September of 1989. In this particular instance, however, the victim's remains were never found, and it is still uncertain whether the disappearance is related to the other convenience store clerk murders occurring throughout central Florida at the time.

Twenty-six-year-old Deborah Poe had just moved to the Orlando area from her native Virginia less than a year before, and shared an apartment with a friend by the name of Lori Tillman. During the day, Deborah worked as a retail sales associate for the *Orlando Sentinel*, and by night she worked the graveyard shift at the Circle K store at Hall Road and Aloma Avenue. Her family had tried to discourage her from keeping such late hours at the convenience store, citing the dangers she could face, and the little time she had for sleep, but Deborah was working hard to save money; she was planning on buying a house in nearby Volusia County, and she wanted some seed money set aside to get her catering business off the ground.

On the evening of February 3rd, 1990, Deborah arrived at the store for her usual shift at a little before eleven p.m. Her boyfriend, Scott Iaggi, also worked at the Circle K; his shift ended as Deborah's began. He had also warned Deborah about working alone at the store, particularly because of the regular creeps and weirdos that would often harass her; for a time, in fact, he had actually worked the same shift as she did, to keep an eye on her. Eventually she told him that she didn't need his protection, however, and he switched to an earlier shift. He was still in the habit of dropping by every few hours to check on her, though.

Shortly after Deborah started work, another friend of hers dropped by to chat about some house plans. And two hours later, Scott drove by the store and saw Deborah inside, standing behind the counter. Another friend passed the Circle K at about three a.m., and also saw Deborah working as usual.

But a brief time after this sighting, something mysterious and tragic must have occurred. According to a woman who entered the store between three-fifteen and three-thirty a.m. to buy some cigarettes, there wasn't a young woman working behind the counter at the time she came in. Instead, there was a tall, thin young man with dark hair, dark eyes, and a black Megadeth t-shirt standing behind the counter. The woman asked him for cigarettes, and the young man rang up her purchase, although the witness later told police that the man had seemed uncertain about the location of the cigarettes she wanted. He didn't seem to have any problems using the cash register, however, so the woman simply assumed that he was a new clerk, and didn't think much more about it.

At four in the morning, yet another customer walked into the store, and found no one at all, either working or shopping. The cash register was locked and untouched, a Circle K employee smock was neatly folded behind the counter, and a bottle of chocolate milk and a partially drunk cup of coffee was still sitting on top of a small pile of house plans. But Deborah Poe, as well as the enigmatic "Megadeth Man," had completely vanished.

When authorities arrived, they found that Deborah's new red Toyota was still parked out back, and contained Deborah's purse, keys, and paycheck in the back seat. Tracking dogs were brought to the site to try to determine where Deborah might have gone, and the dogs indicated that she had probably either walked willingly or been taken through a gap in the wooden fence behind the store that led to the parking lot of an adjacent apartment complex then called The Shoals. After that, though, the dogs lost the trail, suggesting that Deborah had perhaps been herded into a vehicle and driven away.

The mystifying disappearance was never solved, and the identity of the young man reportedly working the counter in Deborah's absence was never established. Some reports at the time claimed that there had also been a black van in the parking lot with a Megadeth mural painted on the side, but this has never been substantiated, and seems somewhat unlikely, as such a vehicle would have made it much easier for law enforcement to locate the phantom clerk.

Though police were seeking the man as a suspect in the initial stages of the investigation, they later stated that they believed the man might have only been a witness, and not the actual kidnapper. They further implied that he may have been a boyfriend of another Circle K employee who had perhaps filled in on his girlfriend's shift from time to time and thus would have known his way around a convenience store cash register.

In August of 1990, a set of skeletal remains was discovered only two miles from the store from which Deborah disappeared, but it was later found that the body was not hers.

In spring of 2002, authorities announced that they had a suspect in the case, and undertook a massive search of a plot of ground behind the Chapel Hill Baptist Church, only about three-and-a-half miles from the Circle K. Despite their efforts, however, Deborah's remains eluded them once again, and she has still not been found.

Interestingly, detectives noted at the time that their suspect lived near the church whose grounds they had searched. One individual who lived across the street from the church at the time was Deborah's boyfriend, Scott Iaggi, though as of this writing, he has never been charged, and it is not known whether he was involved with her disappearance.

****

The day after Deborah Poe went missing in Florida, a sinister house fire would occur in British Columbia, Canada and claim four lives. The case is generally regarded as falling under the Highway of Tears umbrella, though the modus operandi is obviously drastically different.

Very early on the morning of February 5th, 1990, firefighters responded to a blaze at the Brooks Bank Building in Prince Rupert. Upon extinguishing the flames, they discovered four dead bodies among the ruins: forty-five-year-old Helga Rochon, her twenty-six-year-old daughter Sherri, nineteen-year-old daughter Pauline, and seven-month-old granddaughter Kimberly Dumais. Helga had lived in a third-floor apartment in the building, and her daughters and baby granddaughter had been enjoying an overnight visit.

The fire was later determined by investigators to be arson, and many years after the incident, the remainder of the Rochon family received an anonymous letter taking credit for the quadruple homicide, though no reason for the attack was given. Significantly, the building had also been deliberately set on fire a few months previously, back in October of 1989, leading detectives to theorize that one or more of the women who died in the fire had been a specific target of the arsonist.

The case was renewed in 2009, but as of this writing, there have been no further developments.

****

Only days later, back in Ohio on February 8th, the body of ten-year-old Amy Mihaljevic was found by a jogger, lying face down in a field in Ruggles Township, not far off County Road 1181. Amy had disappeared in late October of 1989, following a phone call from an unknown man who urged her to meet him at the Bay Square Shopping Center near her home in suburban Cleveland.

Amy had been sexually assaulted and stabbed multiple times, and her killer appeared to have taken several items of clothing and jewelry from her body, including her boots and earrings, perhaps as souvenirs. It was also announced that tan-colored fibers from the interior of a General Motors vehicle manufactured between 1976 and 1978 were discovered on the girl's remains.

Despite numerous leads and witness statements describing the man who had been seen with Amy before she disappeared, the investigation essentially spun its wheels until 2006, when law enforcement officers divulged that several other girls had claimed to have received similar phone calls as that preceding Amy's kidnapping. Authorities speculated that the killer may have gotten the girls' names and phone numbers from the visitor's book at the Lake Erie Nature and Science Center, as all the targeted individuals had visited there shortly before Amy went missing.

Ten years later, in 2016, police officers held a press conference to inform the public that an olive green curtain that appeared to have been made out of a bedspread was likely linked to the case, and may have been used to wrap Amy's body before it was dumped. The curtain held traces of dog hair that was similar to the hair from Amy's dog.

And in 2019, there was a further lead in the form of three hairs recovered from the victim's clothing that contained a partial DNA profile. Investigators hope that the DNA evidence can be used to rule out suspects in the murder of Amy Mihaljevic. The case remains open.

****

As the spring of 1990 began heading into summer, a Native American woman in the Midwestern United States would leave a party with two men and disappear shortly thereafter, only to turn up dead in late autumn of the same year.

Twenty-nine-year-old mother of two Susan "Suzy" Poupart had been spending the evening of Saturday, May 19th out on the town, and as the night wore on, she was seen by several witnesses at an after-hours party on the Makwa Trail that ran through the Ojibwe Indian Reservation in Lac Du Flambeau, Wisconsin.

At approximately four a.m. on the morning of May 20th, other partygoers reported that Susan either got into or was forced into a vehicle in front of the building; the two men who got into the car with her were identified as Joe Cobb and Robert Elm, who had also been attending the party. After the car drove away, Susan was never seen alive again, and it would in fact be Thanksgiving Day before her sad fate would be revealed.

****

A little less than a month later, in the United Kingdom, the random murder of an elderly taxi driver would frustrate authorities' efforts to track down either suspect or motive.

Leonard Gomm, a seventy-five-year-old husband, and a father of three grown daughters, had lived in the Oxford area for most of his life, and after retiring from the Cowley motor works some time before, had begun driving a taxi to earn some extra money and get him out of the house. By all accounts, it was a job he very much enjoyed.

At approximately six-thirty-five on the morning of Wednesday, June 13th, 1990, Leonard radioed to his employer, ABC Taxis, that he was picking up a fare near Gloucester Green in the Oxford city center. The passenger had requested to be taken to Bicester.

More than four hours later, a truck driver named David Crisp was traveling down Hampton Gay Lane near Bletchingdon when he noticed the taxi pulled over on the side of the road, and the body of Leonard Gomm lying only five yards away from the vehicle. The victim had been stabbed once through the heart.

Though police initially suspected a robbery had gone drastically awry, they very quickly realized that this was likely not the case. Leonard still had cash in his wallet, and the cash box in the taxi was untouched. There also appeared to be no signs of a struggle.

It seemed obvious that the fare Leonard had picked up that morning was the most promising person of interest, but authorities could never trace him. They were also seeking a hitchhiker who had allegedly been picked up by a motorist on the same morning as the murder, only eight miles away from the crime scene. This individual also reportedly had injuries on his face that suggested he had been in a fight. Though the motorist recalled that the hitchhiker had been heading for Glasgow and that he had dropped the man off in Banbury, he was likewise never able to be tracked down.

It remains possible that Leonard Gomm was targeted by someone he knew, though it is just as possible that the attack was completely random. Many oddities about the case stood out, such as the fact that nothing whatsoever was stolen from the taxi; that Leonard had been stabbed outside of the vehicle, as though the killer had lured him out in some fashion; that the location where the body was found was a less direct and much more rural itinerary to travel from Oxford to Bicester, suggesting that the assailant had requested a more secluded route; and that the killer must have either wandered off on foot after the murder, had another car stowed nearby, or arranged for someone to pick him up.

The case went cold only months after it occurred, but was reopened in 2010 on the twentieth anniversary. At that time, investigators announced that they had obtained DNA evidence sufficient to rule suspects out, but are still asking for the public's help in bringing the murderer of Leonard Gomm to justice.

****

On the same day as taxi driver Leonard Gomm was murdered, another young woman would vanish along British Columbia's infamous Highway of Tears.

Fifteen-year-old Delphine Nikal phoned her uncle at about ten p.m. on the night of June 13th, 1990 and told him that she was making her way from Smithers back to her home in Telkwa. She was last seen hitchhiking along Highway 16, and thereafter disappeared. Her body has never been found.

Delphine Nikal, incidentally, was the cousin of fifteen-year-old Cicilia Anne Nikal, who disappeared back in October of 1989, either from the area around Highway 16, or perhaps from Vancouver. Sadly, there would be one more member of the Nikal family who would also fall victim to the seeming curse surrounding the Highway of Tears: one Roberta Nikal, another of Delphine's cousins who was found murdered a few years after Delphine's disappearance.

****

Later that summer, in France, a gay pastor would be spirited away by supposed police officers and later be found dead, possibly the victim of a nefarious conspiracy.

Joseph Doucé had been born to a Catholic family in Belgium, but in later years converted to the Baptist faith, studied to become a pastor, and eventually settled in Paris. He was also interested in psychology, particularly sexual psychology, and in 1976 founded an organization known as the Centre du Christ Libérateur, or CCL. Its stated goal was to provide a support network for sexual minorities, helping them obtain various social services. He also performed blessing ceremonies for both gay and straight couples, published several books on topics of sexual diversity, helped to pass laws prohibiting discrimination against transgender individuals, and was instrumental in educating people about the then fairly new AIDS epidemic.

Though he was a controversial figure for many reasons—not least of which was the fact that he wrote about and held support meetings for pedophiles—his work was undoubtedly a crucial component in the acceptance of those in society with differing sexual identities.

By the late 1980s, Joseph and his partner Guy Bondar had opened a bookstore in Paris called Autres Cultures (Different Cultures), which sold rare volumes on various sexual topics. The shop had been the target of vandalism on more than one occasion, including rocks thrown through the windows, but on the evening of July 19th, 1990, something much more ominous seemed to be afoot.

Two men in plain clothes knocked on the door of the bookshop, flashed badges, and told Joseph that they were police officers, and that he would need to accompany them to the station for questioning. Joseph, likely wary but trusting enough, went with them. He was never seen alive again.

****

Three days after Joseph Doucé disappeared in France, two boys out looking for berries in a remote area of Pennsylvania would come across a grisly find.

It was July 22nd, 1990, and the teenagers were exploring an area of Monroe Township, about three miles south of Interstate 80. They had just passed under a small railroad trestle when they noticed what they initially thought was a dead deer, lying in a shallow stream. But as they grew closer, they realized the body was actually that of a young woman, face down in the mud.

The victim was white and thought to be between fifteen and twenty-two years old, but possibly as old as forty. She was about five feet tall, weighed between one-hundred-five and one-hundred-twenty pounds, and had long, dark brown hair. She also had near-perfect teeth, though she still had baby teeth behind her adult ones that hadn't fallen out. She also had one tooth that was chipped, and one that was rotated nearly one-hundred-eighty degrees.

It was believed she had been murdered between one to two months prior to being found, and the cause of death was blunt force trauma to the right side of the head. She had also suffered a broken leg.

She was clad in a black, button-down shirt, a vest with a floral pattern, and Gitano brand jeans, though she had no bra, shoes, socks, or jewelry. Because she was found with one penny in each of her two jeans pockets, she was eventually christened Penny Doe. It was never established whether the pennies had been placed in her pockets deliberately by her killer as some sort of message, or whether the coins had perhaps just been left there after he had rifled through her pockets for valuables.

Authorities were doubtful that the woman was local to the area, but they were convinced that the assailant almost certainly was, due to the isolated location where the victim was found, which would indicate a killer with an intimate knowledge of the terrain. Then again, since the remains were discovered close to a railroad trestle, there was still a slim possibility that the perpetrator had reached the location by train.

Because there had been an outdoor music festival held fifteen miles away from the dump site over the previous Memorial Day weekend—which would have jibed well with the time Penny Doe was thought to have died—there has been speculation that the victim traveled to the area to attend the concert and met with her killer there, though this scenario is simply conjecture at this point.

In the summer of 2002, twelve years after the body was found, police received an anonymous letter referring to the Penny Doe case. Though law enforcement encouraged the letter writer to contact them again with more details, this never came to pass. But interestingly, the letter arrived at police headquarters right around the same time that authorities had reopened the case of missing person Barbara Miller, a thirty-year-old woman who had vanished after attending a wedding in Mifflinburg, Pennsylvania back in late June of 1989. It has been hypothesized that Barbara Miller was murdered for being a drug informant, and though her body has yet to be found, some investigators believe that Penny Doe may be Barbara Miller. As of 2018, results of DNA tests are still pending, and Penny Doe's identity remains unknown.

****

August 3rd, 1990 was a Friday, and just as he usually did, Peter Heron headed out for his job at GE Stiller Transport, a haulage firm in the town of Darlington in northeast England. His wife, forty-four-year-old Ann Heron, was off work that day, and had been running some errands that morning, though she had arrived back at the house by the time Peter came home for lunch at one p.m.

After her husband went back to work at two that afternoon, Ann decided to do some sunbathing on the lawn of the couple's luxurious home, known as Aeolian House. She stretched out on her lounge chair, her cigarettes and a drink by her side, a book about ghosts in her hand. Her beloved collie sat contentedly in the grass next to her. At approximately three p.m., a friend of Ann's who was riding past the house on the second level of a double-decker bus spotted the bikini-clad woman enjoying the sunshine in her garden.

About an hour and fifteen minutes later, another friend saw Ann driving her car in front of Aeolian House, and preparing to turn into the driveway. Two other people were in the car with her, but the friend didn't recognize them; one of them was a man in the passenger seat, who had his hands on the dashboard, while the other was in the back seat. Ann didn't appear distressed, and waved to her friend as he passed by in his own car. The friend flashed his headlights at her in response.

At five o'clock p.m., witnesses reported seeing a jogger pass by the house, but in light of later events, this wasn't the most sinister sighting. Other witnesses told police that they had seen a tanned, dark-haired man in his early thirties speeding out of the driveway of Aeolian House in a blue Ford Sierra.

When Peter Heron arrived home from work at six p.m., he found the front door open, the dog outside, and Ann's lounge chair abandoned on the front lawn. Her cigarettes and a half-empty glass were next to the chair, while her book and a pair of her shoes were lying under a tree several yards away.

When Peter went inside the house, he was confronted with the shocking scene of his wife lying dead in a widening pool of blood on the living room floor. Her throat had been slit from ear to ear, possibly with a razor or a Stanley knife. She was still wearing her bikini top, though the bottoms had been removed. Despite this, there was no indication that Ann had been raped. Further, there were absolutely no signs of a struggle or of forced entry, and nothing whatsoever had been stolen from the home, leaving investigators baffled as to what the motive for the crime had been.

Authorities attempted to locate the individuals seen by witnesses at around five p.m., the time Ann was thought to have been killed. The jogger, the man in the blue Sierra, and the two people allegedly seen with Ann in her own vehicle were sought, but none came forward, and to this day are all unidentified.

From the very beginning of the inquiry, Peter Heron was a person of interest in the murder of his wife, a common enough situation in spousal murder cases. He had a fairly solid alibi for the time of her death—several witnesses placed him at a work meeting in the village of Cleveland Bridge until four-thirty, at which point he had driven back to his own office, and then began driving home at a little past five o'clock.

However, police officers uncovered the fact that Peter had been having an affair with a much younger woman who worked as a barmaid at his golf club. Indeed, Peter had taken an unusual route home on the day of his wife's death, and it later came to light that he had stopped by to visit his mistress along the way. The affair, detectives felt, might have been enough incentive for Peter to have paid someone to get rid of his wife. Conversely, it is also possible that Peter's mistress may have contracted a hit on her romantic rival so that she could have Peter all to herself.

On the other hand, some researchers speculated that perhaps Ann was also having an affair and had been slain by her lover, though no evidence exists to substantiate this, and friends and family deny the possibility. While it is true that both Peter and Ann had cheated on their respective first spouses with each other before ultimately marrying, there is no more compelling reason to believe that Ann was two-timing her current husband.

A few more bizarre details about the homicide would emerge in ensuing years. In late 1992 or early 1993, for example, a woman known only as Sylvia came forward and informed police that a man had come into the card shop in Newton Aycliffe where she worked and bragged about murdering Ann Heron. Sylvia asserted that this individual looked very much like the person described as leaving the scene of the crime in the blue Ford Sierra, and further stated that the man had told her that he would never be punished for the crime because he was moving to Australia.

And in 1994, an anonymous letter arrived at police headquarters as well as at the offices of the *Northern Echo*; it read, "Hello editor, it's me. Ann Heron's killer." The writer of this missive has never been traced.

But in 2005, there was a massive twist in the case when Peter Heron, then seventy years old, was arrested and charged with the murder of his wife. Apparently the only solid evidence presented at his subsequent arraignment was the fact that his DNA was found on Ann's body, and that his bloody fingerprints had been discovered on the receiver of the home's telephone.

However, it seemed clear that Peter's DNA on Ann's body would not be unusual, given that they were married, and Peter explained the fingerprint evidence by admitting that he had touched Ann to ascertain whether or not she was alive, thus getting her blood on his hands before picking up the phone to call the police. The charges against Peter were dropped in early 2006, due to lack of evidence, though some researchers still consider him a person of interest. His children are adamant, however, that their father is innocent, and it is certainly feasible that Ann might have simply been the unlucky victim of a completely random attack.

The strange case, sometimes known as the Beauty in the Bikini Murder, is Durham County's only unsolved homicide.

****

In early fall, in the southeastern United States, an inmate work crew picking up garbage alongside Interstate 40 in Hillsborough, North Carolina discovered the decomposed body of a young woman down an embankment just off the highway. It was September 19th, 1990.

The victim, eventually dubbed Hillsborough Jane Doe or "Hope," was white, aged between fourteen and twenty-five, standing around five-foot-four and weighing approximately one-hundred-eight pounds. She had light brown or strawberry blonde hair that was frosted with blonde highlights, and was cut in a layered style that fell to her shoulders. She had three fillings in her teeth, and a three-inch appendectomy scar on her abdomen.

When found, Jane Doe was clad in a bright pink sweatshirt with three cartoon rabbits—two of them on bicycles and one on a unicycle—printed on the front. She also wore a white bra and clean white ankle socks, though her shoes were missing, indicating that perhaps her killer had taken them as a souvenir. Her jewelry included a handmade yellow metal ring on her left ring finger, and a similar bracelet made of thin, twisted metal on her left wrist.

After an autopsy, it was determined that Jane Doe had been murdered by strangulation, probably between four to six days prior to her remains being recovered.

Once the homicide was made public, a few witnesses came forward and stated that they had seen a girl matching the victim's description walking near a Ramada Inn on Interstate 85, and that she may have been a hitchhiker. Another witness thought they had seen her at a truck stop in Alamance County.

There are few leads in the case of Hillsborough County Jane Doe. Authorities have theorized that she may have been a victim of a taxi driver who was arrested in Guilford County not long after the murder; this individual was a suspect in several other similar homicides in the area, but he committed suicide before he could be further investigated.

As of this writing, nearly fifty missing persons have been ruled out as the Hillsborough Jane Doe, but the case is still cold, and the victim has yet to have her identity restored.

****

On October 24th, 1990, back in France, the decomposed body of forty-five-year-old Joseph Doucé—who had vanished from his bookshop after leaving with two purported police officers—was discovered in a remote area in the forest of Fountainebleau, southwest of Paris. Though his remains were far too degraded to determine cause of death, there was speculation that he had been strangled.

Over the years, the most persistent theory concerning the death of Joseph Doucé was that he was targeted by the Rensignements Generaux, or RG, the branch of the French police that dealt with political matters. The RG at the time was rumored to be irredeemably corrupt, and there have since been whispers that they had been keeping Joseph Doucé's bookstore under surveillance and had been tapping his phone. One of the inspectors who was allegedly keeping tabs on Joseph Doucé, Jean-Marc Dufourg, was reportedly later fired from his position and subsequently convicted of falsifying documents and misusing a firearm.

In fact, in the wake of Joseph Doucé's murder and the suspicions surrounding the RG, the French interior minister later disbanded the branch, but probes into the organization did little to solve the shocking slaying of Joseph Doucé, and the crime remains unresolved to this day.

****

A few days before Halloween of 1990, there would be a horrific murder of a handsome gay man in the streets of Tinseltown, a crime that is sadly all but forgotten today.

William Arnold Newton was originally from Wisconsin, but eventually ended up in Los Angeles in 1985 after wandering around the country for a time. He wanted to be an artist and write poetry, but took a job at a gay bathhouse to make ends meet. It was there that he made the acquaintance of David Rey, an adult film producer who would later become his boyfriend and business partner.

William began starring in adult films under the stage names Billy London and Billy Porter, and even produced some of his own films, using the pseudonym Bill E. London. As producer, he racked up six film credits, and seven as an actor; his last film was 1990's *The Grip of Passion*.

On October 28th, a homeless man digging through a dumpster in an alley off Santa Monica Boulevard came across the severed head and feet of porn star Billy London. The remainder of his body was never found, and neither motive nor suspect in the gruesome crime has ever been established.

The case was reopened in 2015, but so far, there have been no new developments.

****

Back in the Midwestern United States, six months had passed since twenty-nine-year-old Susan Poupart had gotten into a car with two men after a party and later turned up missing. On November 22nd, 1990, which happened to be Thanksgiving Day, two hunters walking through the Chequamegon-Nicolet National Forest in northern Wisconsin noticed something strange hidden underneath a log. This discovery proved to be a woman's purse, a jacket, and a tribal ID bearing the name of Susan Poupart. When the jacket was pulled out of the hole, the hunters spotted a human jawbone underneath it. A wider search revealed more skeletal fragments in the area, though some of Susan's remains were never recovered, presumably because the bones had been scattered by animals.

Because duct tape and scraps of plastic were also found at the site, investigators assumed that Susan's body had been wrapped and stashed beneath the log by her killer or killers. The coroner also stated that she had likely been sexually assaulted.

Joe Cobb and Robert Elm, the two men allegedly seen putting Susan into a car after a party back in May, had testified that they had not kidnapped her, but had instead been giving her a ride home. They both claimed to have dropped her off in front of Lac Du Flambeau Elementary School. Cobb and Elm were never charged, as there was not enough evidence to tie the men to Susan's disappearance and subsequent murder.

Another local individual, Fritz Schuman, was questioned extensively after an inmate at the Vilas County Jail told authorities that Schuman had admitted to him that he and two other men had taken Susan out into the woods to rape her and beat her to death. But just as in the case of Robert Elm and Joe Cobb, there was insufficient evidence to actually charge Schuman with any wrongdoing, and he has steadfastly refused to answer any and all questions about the slaying.

Law enforcement officers are hoping that DNA evidence might help them to crack the case, but obtaining DNA has been particularly difficult in Susan Poupart's murder, and what little has been recovered has not been much help. A billboard displaying Susan's picture and a plea for help in the case has greeted drivers on Route 47 in Lac Du Flambeau for years, and a twenty-thousand-dollar reward for information is still on offer in the unsolved crime.

1991

> Valentine Doe

> Jackie Council

> The Frog Boys

> Rachael Johnson

> Karmein Chan

> Penny Bell

> Lynne Trenholm

> Sandy Drummond

> Los Angeles County Jane Doe

> The Bolney Torso

> The Austin Yogurt Shop Murders

> Katrien de Cuyper

> Joe Cole

On the day after Valentine's Day of 1991, a group of windsurfers was enjoying a camping trip at the Bahia Honda State Recreation area on West Summerland Key in South Florida. The location where they had set up camp was a thickly wooded copse not far off the beach and quite close to the Bahia Honda Channel Bridge, an area known locally as "the horseshoe."

As they headed down toward the shore on that particular winter day, they spotted something strange in the underbrush, and sadly, this turned out to be the nude, dead body of a young woman.

The victim, later christened Florida Jane Doe or Valentine Doe, was likely white, estimated to be between sixteen and twenty-five years old, standing approximately five-foot-four to five-foot seven, and weighing around one-hundred-forty pounds. She had straight, dark brown hair that was cut to collar-length, and eyes that were light brown or green. She also wore a silver Timex watch, had her ears pierced four times in each ear, and wore silver ball and imitation pearl earrings.

Distinguishing marks included a small, crude tattoo of a cross with sun-rays emitting from it, etched into the girl's left hand, between her thumb and forefinger; and another, larger tattoo on her upper left arm, of a heart with the word "love" inside. Both tattoos were amateur-quality and had been done in blue ink.

When police officers arrived at the scene, they noted drag marks in the dirt and droplets of blood near the body. Following the trail, they discovered Valentine Doe's scattered clothing, articles of which included a reddish-pink-and-dark-blue-striped cardigan sweater, a pair of knee-length denim shorts, a bikini top, and a pair of black, ankle-high moccasins with red stitching, turquoise bead-work, and leather fringe on the back seams.

After an autopsy was performed, it was determined that the victim had been raped and badly beaten, then strangled to death with her own bikini top, probably only the day before her body was discovered. Additionally, she was thought to have suffered from both anemia, and painful cysts on her ovaries and fallopian tubes; and she had perhaps been pregnant at some stage, judging by stretch marks on her abdomen. Her teeth were in excellent shape, save for one filling, though it appeared that she had had two top teeth extracted when she was around ten years old.

After news of the murder went public, several witnesses came forward and asserted that they had seen Valentine Doe at various points along US 1 on February 14th; the last sighting was thought to have been at around six-thirty p.m., approximately eighteen miles away from the site where her body was eventually found. It was believed that she had been hitchhiking north, and that she was not native to the area, as her lack of tan lines and her atypical clothing—particularly the sweater and moccasins—did not suggest someone who lived in South Florida.

Witnesses also reported having seen an older-model white pickup truck with a camper shell in the area in the days prior to the murder, and this vehicle was believed to contain two white males, though neither has been identified.

No progress has been made on the case since shortly after its occurrence, and the identity of Valentine Doe and her killer are still a mystery.

****

On the morning of March 22nd, 1991, a crew of loggers cutting down pine trees near Highway 191 south of Eureka, South Carolina happened upon a set of skeletal remains not far from the banks of Shaw Creek, the very same location where the body of the unidentified Aiken County Jane Doe had been discovered back in November of 1987.

Like that former victim, this one also appeared to be an African-American woman in her mid-to-late twenties who had been dead for several years and had been dumped at the site with no clothing or belongings, and no other clues as to her identity or that of her killer. Cause of death was likewise unable to be determined.

For several years, the body of this particular victim was unidentified, but in 1997, a pathologist concluded that the remains most likely belonged to thirty-year-old Jacquelyn "Jackie" Council, who had vanished on November 10th, 1986 after dropping her five-year-old off at school. In 1999, DNA evidence confirmed the identification.

In the years following the finding of Jackie Council's and Aiken County Jane Doe's bodies, at least one more victim would be discovered in the same area of South Carolina, in 1993, and one other nearby case, that of Risteen Durden in 1992, may also be tangentially related. These three—or possibly four—women might very well have been casualties of an as-yet-unknown serial killer, one that Micheal Whelen of the *Unresolved* podcast has dubbed the Shaw Creek Killer.

The other two related homicides, and suspects in the slayings, will be discussed later on in this narrative.

****

Four days later, on the opposite side of the globe, five schoolboys would set out to enjoy the outdoors on a day off from school, and would later vanish into thin air.

It was Tuesday, March 26th, 1991 in Daegu, South Korea, and due to local elections, schools and many workplaces were closed for the day. Six young boys, who were all students at Seongseo Elementary School—nine-year-old Kim Jong-sik, ten-year-old Park Chan-in, ten-year-old Kim Tae-ryong, eleven-year-old Kim Yeong-gyu, twelve-year-old Jo Ho-yeon, and thirteen-year-old U Cheol-won—decided to take a hike out to nearby Mount Waryong to look for salamander eggs.

At the last minute, Kim Tae-ryong was called back home by his mother to finish his breakfast, so he told his friends he would catch up with them later. The remaining five boys went on their way, carrying walking sticks and tin cans to hold any eggs they might find. They were never seen alive again.

When evening began to fall and the boys had not returned home, their worried parents began scouring the area for them, but could discover no sign. Police officers were called in, and authorities soon marshaled a massive search for the missing children, utilizing thousands of officers, volunteers, and tracking dogs. But still, no trace of the boys could be found.

Months went by, and though there were hundreds of false leads and reported sightings of the children—who would come to be known as the "Frog Boys," as it was later mistakenly believed that they had gone out hunting for frogs rather than salamander eggs—no progress at all was made on the shocking case. One man even phoned the police anonymously and said that he had kidnapped the boys and was starving them until he was paid a ransom, but this confession was found to be fraudulent.

The disappearance of the Frog Boys became a national sensation throughout South Korea, with the children's photographs appearing on posters, milk cartons, the sides of buses, and even candy wrappers. Several of the boys' parents quit their jobs in order to search for the boys full time. But despite everyone's best efforts, the location of the missing children remained unknown.

Then, in late September of 2002—more than a decade after the disappearance—two men out searching for acorns on Mount Waryong came across some children's clothing and shoes lying in the leaves on the mountainside. After a more thorough search of the site by police investigators, the bodies of all five boys were unearthed from a shallow grave, only a little more than a mile away from their homes.

Because the bodies had been discovered entwined together, authorities initially speculated that the children had simply become lost and had died of hypothermia after attempting to huddle together for warmth. However, the boys' parents were immediately suspicious of this scenario, as the area where the bodies were found was not only close to their homes, but also close to another village that all the boys were very familiar with, the lights of which would have been perfectly visible from the mountainside.

When a more thorough examination of the remains was undertaken, the parents were vindicated: three of the boys' skulls showed signs of blunt force trauma, though the implement used to administer the blows is still unknown, but was perhaps a work tool such as a screwdriver. Most sources also report that one of the skulls contained what appeared to be two bullet holes, probably from shotgun shells, and two of the skulls also had traces of blood on them. In addition, the boys' clothing was tied in knots, leading some to suggest that the children had been bound together before being murdered.

One of the stranger aspects of the discovery of the bodies was the fact that the area of Mount Waryong where the skeletons were eventually found had been searched more than five-hundred times in the ten years since the Frog Boys vanished. It seemed bizarre that the remains had not been revealed much earlier, leaving open the possibility that the killer had perhaps moved the bodies from their initial location. Forensic examination of mold found inside the skulls, however, seemed to suggest that the remains had been there the entire time.

After the bodies of the Frog Boys were found, numerous theories began to swirl about what had become of them on that sunlit mountain excursion in 1991. One of these theories held that a man at the shooting range nearby had accidentally shot one or more of the boys, then killed the others to avoid having to fess up to the crime. Although the shooting range had been closed on the day the children disappeared because of the election day holiday, it was hypothesized that perhaps someone had been using the site illegally. The shooting range had been closed permanently in 1994.

Another supposition was that the children had been murdered by a group of lepers who believed the common superstition that the livers of children could cure their disease. And yet another rumor held that perhaps one of the boys' fathers had killed his own son, and also murdered the other boys to keep from drawing attention to himself. This particular hypothesis, put forward by a criminal psychologist, was investigated, but found to have little merit, as there was no evidence to suggest that any of the children's parents were involved in the deaths.

In South Korea, the statute of limitations on murder is fifteen years, and so the case of the Frog Boys was closed in 2006 with no resolution. However, in 2015, this particular statute was waived, meaning that investigation of the slayings may still go forward, though as of this writing, there have been no further developments.

Two films about the crime have been made, one of which—titled *Come Back, Frog Boys*—was released only a year after they disappeared. The other was simply called *Children* and came out in 2011. There was also a novel published in 2005 titled *The Boys Never Went to the Mountain*, which is a fictionalized retelling of the famous case.

****

One day before the end of March, back in the Midwestern United States, a woman would be savagely murdered after leaving a nightclub, and her killer may possibly be responsible for as many as seven other similar crimes.

Twenty-four-year-old Rachael Johnson lived in Tallmadge, Ohio with her three-year-old daughter Katelin. On the evening of Friday, March 29th, 1991, Rachael had hired a babysitter and went out on the town with her best friend. The two women were seen leaving the El Cid bar at about two-thirty a.m. on the morning of Saturday, March 30th.

On their way back home, the friend's car got a flat tire, and she pulled the vehicle off the road into the parking lot of a Dairy Mart at the intersection of Dan Street and Glenwood Avenue. A faded gray car was seen to follow them into the lot.

The friend apparently decided that she would be able to get home on the flat tire, but Rachael decided to walk the rest of the short way back to her own residence, as she didn't like the burning rubber smell that was permeating the inside of the vehicle. Rachael's friend drove off into the night, while Rachael herself was either lured or forced into the mysterious gray car that had driven into the lot behind them.

The next morning, the burned body of Rachael Johnson was discovered lying in the middle of Weller Avenue. She had been beaten, raped, stabbed ten times in the chest, and then set on fire while still alive.

The only solid suspect in the case was a then-twenty-one-year-old man by the name of Daniel E. Wilson. He was arrested and charged with aggravated murder in May of 1991, following the killing of twenty-four-year-old Carol Lutz, who was left for dead in the trunk of her car, which was subsequently set on fire.

Though Wilson's DNA was compared to DNA found at the Rachael Johnson crime scene, the results were inconclusive, and though Wilson did admit to murdering Carol Lutz, he denied involvement in any other killings.

Significantly, though, police have looked into the possibility that whoever killed Rachael Johnson—whether Daniel Wilson or some other suspect—may have perpetrated many other comparable crimes spanning a fairly large geographical area. For example, two other Ohio women—thirty-two-year-old Elaine Graham of Hambden Township and thirty-seven-year-old Jean Eddy of Lakewood—were murdered and found in the trunks of their burning cars, in November and December of 1990, respectively.

Further, a twenty-one-year-old woman named Lynda Shaw was beaten, stabbed, and burned to death in London, Ontario, Canada in April of the same year. And earlier still, four other victims—twenty-two-year-old Catherine Corkery, twenty-nine-year-old Brenda Bloom, twenty-year-old Rafaella Bryant, and one unidentified woman—were murdered in very similar ways in Pennsylvania, Maryland, Virginia, and California between the years of 1984 and 1989.

The investigation into the brutal slaying of Rachael Johnson was reopened in 2013, and authorities hope that DNA evidence in the case may help them to finally bring the killer to justice.

****

As the spring of 1991 continued, a chilling abduction in Australia would lead to a renewed push to locate the as-yet-unidentified serial rapist and possible murderer known only as Mr. Cruel.

It was the evening of April 13th, and thirteen-year-old Karmein Chan was at her home in the affluent Victorian suburb of Templestowe, babysitting her two younger sisters—nine-year-old Karly and seven-year-old Karen—while their parents worked at the Chinese restaurant they owned, only a ten-minute drive away.

The girls had been watching a documentary about Marilyn Monroe in Karmein's bedroom, and at around nine p.m., they decided it was time for a little snack. But as they walked down the hall toward the kitchen, they were confronted with the terrifying sight of a man whose face was covered with a black ski mask and who was brandishing a gun and a large hunting knife.

He grabbed the girls by the hair, and forced Karly and Karen into a nearby cupboard, sealing them in by shoving a heavy bed against the doors. According to the girls, the man had said, "I won't hurt you." After a time, the girls were able to free themselves from their prison, but by the time they escaped, both the intruder and their older sister Karmein had disappeared.

When authorities arrived, they discovered that the perpetrator had spray-painted the words "payback," "Asian drug deal," and "more to come" on the side of the Chan family's Toyota Camry, which was parked in the driveway. Police dogs deployed at the scene were only able to track Karmein's movements to a vacant lot about three-hundred-twenty-five yards from the house before the trail went cold.

From the very beginning of the investigation, police were operating under the assumption that Karmein Chan had likely been abducted by the assailant nicknamed Mr. Cruel. This unknown individual had been responsible for at least three other similar crimes, and had been under investigation by a task force known as Operation Challenge. In August of 1987, for example, he had forced his way into a house in Lower Plenty, tied up the parents and a young boy, cut the phone lines, and raped an eleven-year-old girl.

Then, two days after Christmas of 1988, the same attacker broke into a family home in Ringwood, bound and gagged the parents, and abducted ten-year-old Sharon Wills. The girl was raped multiple times, and released alive eighteen hours later; she was found behind Bayswater High School, clad in garbage bags.

And in early July of 1990, the man the media had dubbed Mr. Cruel apparently struck again, kidnapping thirteen-year-old Nicola Lynas from her home in Canterbury, repeatedly sexually assaulting her, then releasing her fifty hours later.

In an intriguing coincidence, police had actually been scaling back Operation Challenge in the days prior to Karmein Chan's disappearance, leading some to posit that the kidnapper may have had some inside knowledge about police matters. There were also speculations that Mr. Cruel may have had some involvement with the educational system, as all of the attacks had taken place during school holidays.

Following the abduction of Karmein Chan, detectives reinvigorated Operation Challenge, renaming it Spectrum Taskforce and placing particular emphasis on locating Karmein. They also offered a one-hundred-thousand-dollar reward for any information in the case.

In spite of all their efforts, though, it would be almost a year before the tragic fate of Karmein Chan would be revealed.

****

The first week of June of 1991 would see the appalling slaughter of a successful businesswoman in broad daylight in a parking lot in England.

Ruth Penelope Bell, better known to family and friends as Penny, was a forty-three-year-old woman who ran a thriving employment agency called Coverstaff Limited, which placed candidates in catering positions. Her husband Alistair was an estate agent, and the couple lived in an elegant detached home near Denham in Buckinghamshire with two children: eleven-year-old Matthew (from Penny's previous marriage), and nine-year-old Lauren.

On the morning of Thursday, June 6th, the family was getting ready for the workday, as they normally did. The household had been in a bit of disarray since the previous November, as the Bells had hired builders to renovate portions of the home, but by this point they seemed to have gotten used to the disruptions. On this particular day, workers were continuing construction in the kitchen, which was undergoing a significant expansion.

Alistair left for work at approximately eight-thirty a.m., and though his wife usually waved goodbye to him from the kitchen window as he drove off, on that day she failed to do so. Alistair didn't think a great deal about it, as perhaps the kitchen renovations were preoccupying her. In addition, he noticed that she had seemed a little more stressed out than usual the past couple of days, though again, nothing that struck him as overly alarming.

A little more than an hour later, at around nine-forty a.m., Penny told the builders that she was heading out for an appointment; she was late, she said, and had to meet the client in ten minutes. The workers, at least one of whom was also a close family friend, later reported that nothing at all seemed to be amiss; Penny was acting completely normally. She took her handbag and some wallpaper samples and climbed into her powder blue Jaguar to drive to her scheduled meeting.

At around ten o'clock, several witnesses later reported seeing Penny's car driving very slowly down Greenford Road in west London, and observed that the hazard lights were on. In light of subsequent events, the location of the vehicle was noted as unusual, as Penny's office was in the opposite direction of where she was seen to be driving.

A half-hour after that, another witness who later came

forward stated that he saw Penny's Jaguar pulling into the parking lot of the Gurnell Leisure Centre. There was a man in the passenger seat of the vehicle, the witness said, and this man and Penny appeared to be struggling. The witness even claimed that Penny had mouthed the words, "Help me," out the window at him, but that he had not heeded her pleas at the time. The witness also hadn't got a very good look at the man in the Jaguar's passenger seat, saying only that he looked to be in his forties, with dark hair and possibly a beard, clad in a dark-colored blazer and wearing a bracelet on his right wrist.

Two women walking through the parking lot to go swimming at the leisure centre at around eleven a.m. noticed Penny slumped over the steering wheel of her car, but initially thought she was only sleeping. However, when they exited the building at a little past noon, they saw that Penny hadn't moved, and also spotted some blood spatter inside the vehicle. They phoned the police at approximately twelve-fifteen p.m.

Authorities arrived to a scene of almost unimaginable brutality. Penny Bell had been stabbed upwards of fifty times in the chest and arms by a knife with a three- to four-inch blade. From the position of the wounds, it appeared that the killer had begun stabbing her from the passenger seat, then had exited the vehicle, walked around it, and continued stabbing her from the driver's side, either through the window or after opening the driver's side door.

Penny's handbag was discovered inside the vehicle untouched, indicating that robbery had probably not been the primary motive. The wallpaper samples that Penny had taken with her were spread out in the car, as though she had been showing them to someone. Penny had not been sexually assaulted, though the frenzied nature of the attack did seem to indicate a personal vendetta of some kind.

From the very beginning of the investigation, police were baffled by the bizarre details surrounding the crime. One of the most puzzling was how the murderer—who would have been covered in blood—had managed to get out of the parking lot without being seen by anyone. The spot where the Jaguar was parked faced a high hedge that concealed it from view from the front side, but the lot was nearly full, and people had been coming and going all morning. Though the Jaguar's back window was small enough to have partially masked the slaying as it was happening, and though the car was largely soundproof, which would have muffled any screams, it still seemed very odd that no one had seen or heard anything unusual. This has led some researchers to surmise that the killer may have already had a getaway car parked at the site, and left the scene in that, rather than fleeing on foot.

And as the inquiry continued, more and weirder aspects of the case began to come to light. For instance, it was discovered that three days prior to the murder of Penny Bell, she had withdrawn the sum of eight-thousand-five-hundred pounds from the joint bank account she shared with her husband. Apparently she had not told Alistair about the withdrawal or made a note of it anywhere, which was unprecedented for her, though a few of the builders who had been working in the Bell home told police that Penny had the cash in an envelope which she took with her to her purported appointment on the morning she was killed. The cash has never been recovered.

The appointment was yet another bone of contention, as Penny hadn't made mention of it in her diary, which she was usually meticulous about doing. Alistair later suggested that perhaps the meeting had been set up by a last-minute phone call, but workers in the home claimed they had not heard any phone call on the morning of June 6th.

Alistair Bell was initially scrutinized as a person of interest, especially since he inherited the bulk of his wife's estate after her death, and also received a substantial payout on her life insurance policy. Alistair had a solid alibi for the morning of the murder, and seemingly had no motive to kill his wife, as the marriage appeared to be stable. However, when police discovered that prior to marrying Penny in 1981, Alistair had been in an eleven-year relationship with a man, they redoubled their investigative efforts, suspecting that perhaps Alistair's former lover had been responsible for the slaying, either of his own accord or at Alistair's behest.

It seems, though, that some amount of homophobia may have played a part in this particular avenue of questioning, as according to everyone who knew the Bells, Alistair had never made a secret of his bisexuality, and in fact, his former boyfriend had attended his and Penny's wedding. Both Alistair and his ex-partner were eventually cleared.

The following year, though, a strange twist in the case would occur. A family friend of the Bells named John Richmond approached a tabloid newspaper and told them that he knew who had killed Penny, and would reveal this information for the sum of eighty-thousand pounds. He alleged that Penny's murder had been a contract hit; he and Penny had been having an affair, he claimed, and had met on the morning that Penny was murdered. He further stated that Penny had asked him to recommend a hit man, which he apparently did. He said that he had not killed Penny, but knew who had.

Police did arrest John Richmond, and his fingerprints were found in Penny's Jaguar, but as he and Penny were friends, this particular clue was not all that significant, and many of his other claims could not be corroborated. While his involvement in some capacity has not been ruled out, investigators seem to think it highly unlikely that he and Penny were seeing each other, and equally implausible that he knew who killed her.

The mystery surrounding Penny Bell's death endures, and while the possibility remains that she was the victim of a random attack, perhaps perpetrated by killer Robert Napper, also believed to be responsible for the similar stabbing murders of between three and six other victims, the Bell family as well as investigators are leaning toward the theory that she was killed by someone she knew. The case remains one of the UK's most infamous unsolved murders.

****

Only three days later, in another part of England, yet another woman would be viciously stabbed to death in the course of their workday.

Twenty-nine-year-old Lynne Trenholm lived in the town of Failsworth, in Greater Manchester. Though she had always told her family that she worked as a receptionist, she was actually a sex worker, using the pseudonyms Blondie and Marilyn, and plying her trade out of a brothel-slash-massage-parlor known as Pinky's, in Boughton.

On the morning of Sunday, June 9th, 1991, the body of Lynne Trenholm was discovered in an upstairs room at her place of employment. She had been savagely stabbed to death.

The only clue found at the scene was a single, bloody fingerprint. This print is periodically run through the nationwide database, but so far has produced no matches. Police have also interviewed several hundred men who were known to frequent Pinky's, but no suspects at all have been forthcoming, and the case has not been reexamined since 2013.

****

Elsewhere in the British Isles, the month of June would feature yet a third mysterious murder, this time of an unassuming Scottish man.

Thirty-three-year-old Sandy Drummond lived in a cottage in the village of Boarhills, near Fife, Scotland, with his brother James. Sandy had worked as a laborer at the nearby Guardbridge Paper Mill for the past seven years, but in late June, he abruptly quit his job, and also withdrew a large sum of money from his bank account for unknown reasons.

Only days later, on the evening of June 24th, 1991, Sandy was found dead on a farm track near his home. Though at first authorities believed he may have died of natural causes, later examination demonstrated that he had been strangled, perhaps by someone performing a jiu jitsu move on him.

After Sandy's death, police found most of the money he had withdrawn inside his home, and also fielded tips from people who had seen an orange Morris Marina parked outside of the cottage on several occasions. Some sources further reported that Sandy had been spotted in the hours prior to his death running from his house to a field opposite, and that he was carrying a blue sports bag, which has never been found.

Investigators also attempted to locate a man who had boarded a bus near Falside Farm at around two-thirty p.m. on the afternoon of Sandy's murder; this individual was said to be carrying a handkerchief that appeared to have blood on it, though as of this writing, this man has never been identified.

Sandy's brother James suspects that Sandy may have been being blackmailed, but admits he has no idea why, or what possible motive anyone could have had for killing him.

****

Back in the United States that fall, a young woman would be found dead in a California park and remain unidentified to this day.

At around six-thirty a.m. on the morning of September 11th, 1991, passersby strolling through Green Meadows Park in Los Angeles stumbled across the dead body of a young white or Hispanic woman.

The victim—eventually dubbed Los Angeles County Jane Doe—was between fifteen and twenty years old, stood approximately five-foot-two, and weighed around one-hundred-seventy pounds. She had long, dark, wavy hair that was layered in the front, brown eyes, and telltale marks and tan lines on her face that suggested she wore glasses or sunglasses with some regularity. She was fully dressed when found, clad in a blue striped t-shirt, denim shorts, black socks, and black hiking boots with white laces.

In addition, she had several distinguishing scars, including one on her right clavicle, one on her right knee, and one on the calf of her left leg. Her teeth showed signs of an infection in her upper right lateral incisor; this infection likely would have caused the girl significant discomfort in life.

Though Jane Doe's cause of death was not released to the public, she was believed to have been murdered four to six hours prior to her body being found in the park. As of this writing, neither victim nor killer has been identified.

****

As autumn of 1991 wore on, a grisly mystery would begin to unfold in the English county of Sussex with the discovery of a still-unidentified murder victim.

On October 11th, a sixty-two-year-old man by the name of Colin Oliver was walking from Cuckfield back to his home in Burgess Hill, via Broxmead Lane in the village of Bolney, in Sussex. As he wandered a little way off the road to urinate, he was horrified to discover part of a human body rolled up in a scrap of bloody carpet.

The victim was found to have been beheaded, and his

hands had also been removed, either with an axe or with bolt cutters. Neither the head nor the hands have ever been found, and police speculated that the killer had removed the body parts in order to complicate identification.

The dead man—who would eventually be christened the Bolney Torso—was believed to be between thirty-five and forty-five years old, but most likely in his late thirties. He was white, stood about five-foot-seven with a strong upper body but a protruding belly, and had a somewhat Scandinavian appearance. He also had a mole that was vaguely star-shaped on his right thigh.

Investigators were making no progress on identifying the victim, but before the year was out, they did get an intriguing lead on a suspect.

It so happened that a real estate agent who had been in charge of a property on Copyhold Lane—about a mile and a half from where the Bolney Torso was found—became suspicious when the tenants who had been renting the house suddenly abandoned it on October 9th. The tenants had been a German man named Gunter Josef Knieper and his girlfriend, Kornelia Maria Teusel. The pair had rented the house in September of 1991, paying six months' rent in advance; a sum of about ten-thousand pounds.

During the inquiry into these individuals, police discovered that Knieper had been using an alias—Dr. Matthias Herrman—and additionally was wanted for questioning in connection with a series of fraud charges in Ireland and Germany.

Not only that, but when investigators searched the rental house in Sussex, they found an issue of *Penthouse* magazine that had an article about dismembering bodies in it, and the pages containing the article had various numbers written on them.

Knieper, as well as three other German nationals thought to be involved in the prior fraud allegations, were eventually arrested, though all denied having anything to do with the murder of the Bolney victim. Aside from the magazine, no other physical evidence tying Knieper to the crime has ever been discovered, and he has never been charged in the case.

In 1995, an anonymous person left flowers and a note on the grave of the Bolney Torso victim. The note read, "For the unknown male, Peter and team, remember our loss." This clue has never been unraveled.

In 2009, there was a small breakthrough in the case when DNA analysis of the remains suggested that the victim was originally from southern Germany, but had likely spent the last year of his life in the United Kingdom, or living somewhere along the French-German border. Detectives were also later able to establish that the victim had likely been dressed after he was already dead, and that the clothing he was found in did not belong to him.

The case seems to have hit a wall as of 2011, and no further developments have been announced.

****

Many crimes over the years have been described as a "loss of innocence" of one particular city or town, and in the case of Austin, Texas, this crime is inarguably the horrific quadruple murder that took place on the night of December 6th, 1991.

Seventeen-year-old girls Eliza Thomas and Jennifer Harbison worked at the I Can't Believe It's Yogurt store, located in the Hillside strip mall on West Anderson Lane. On December 6th, they were working the closing shift; Eliza's parents had both dropped by the shop to check on their daughter at separate times between nine-thirty and ten p.m.

At some point before the store closed, Jennifer's fifteen-year-old sister Sarah, and Sarah's thirteen-year-old friend Amy Ayers, came to the shop as well. They had been hanging out at the Northcross Mall down the street all evening; all four girls were planning a sleep-over at the Harbison home, and Sarah and Amy were going to help close the store and then get a ride with the older girls. The shop was closed at its regular time of eleven p.m., with the cash register being rung out with a "no sale" tag at three minutes past the hour.

About forty-five minutes later, a police officer cruising by the strip mall noticed that the yogurt shop was ablaze, and contacted the fire department, who arrived six minutes after the call. When firefighters forced their way into the store, they discovered the stacked and burned bodies of four teenage girls. All were nude, and had been bound and gagged with pieces of their own clothing.

As the investigation commenced, authorities began trying to piece together what had happened, though because the scene had first been processed as a fire and not as a homicide, much crucial evidence was lost or contaminated. It appeared that at least two assailants had either entered the store after closing, or had been in the store previously and had forced the girls into the stockroom at gunpoint. Though robbery was initially thought to be the motive, a bank bag full of money was found beneath the front counter. Sources differ, however, on how much cash was taken from the premises, with some claiming only fourteen dollars was stolen from the register, and some stating it was five-hundred-forty dollars.

After the four victims were autopsied, it was discovered that at least two of them—Amy and Jennifer—had been raped. All had been shot in the head with either a .22 or .380 caliber semi-automatic pistol; Amy had been shot twice, perhaps because she had struggled. After the girls were dead, the killers had partially stacked their bodies and then started a fire in the corner nearest the victims, though it is unclear if any accelerant, such as lighter fluid, was used.

The crime understandably shocked the city of Austin, and police were immediately placed under enormous pressure to solve the case as quickly as possible. Amid a flood of useless tips and bizarre false confessions, investigators did get a few promising leads in the days following the murders.

The first of these came from a man named Dearl Croft, a former police officer who had been eating yogurt in the shop a few hours before the girls were killed. He said that he had noticed a somewhat suspicious individual wearing a large green jacket, similar to Army fatigues, walking toward the rear of the shop. Croft said he asked Eliza Thomas where the young man was going, and Eliza answered that he was going to use the restroom. Croft further said that the man in the green jacket had emerged from the bathroom and sat at a booth with another young man wearing a black jacket. The witness described the first man as being about five-foot-six with dirty blond hair, while the second man was of a larger build. Both men, Croft said, appeared to be in their late twenties or early thirties, and were definitely still in the shop as of ten-forty-seven p.m.

While neither of these two men was identified, police did link a suspect to the murders fairly swiftly: this was sixteen-year-old Maurice Pierce, who had been picked up carrying a .22 caliber pistol at the Northcross Mall, the same mall where Sarah and Amy had been hanging out prior to their deaths.

When questioned about the yogurt shop murders, Pierce claimed that he personally didn't know anything about the crime, but that his fifteen-year-old friend Forrest Welborn had borrowed the gun and perpetrated the slaughter.

Pierce also implicated two other friends, seventeen-year-olds Michael Scott and Robert Springsteen; the four teenagers had stolen a Nissan Pathfinder from a car lot on the night the girls were killed and driven it to San Antonio.

Though ballistics on the .22 found in Pierce's possession did not appear to match the firearm used in the killings, police eventually corralled all four young men into custody and began grilling them about the quadruple homicide. It should be noted from the outset that a large portion of the interrogation was handled by officer Hector Polanco, who would later be temporarily suspended from the force after it came to light that he had coerced confessions in a 1988 rape and murder case, though he was later reinstated.

After several hours of questioning, all four suspects in the Austin yogurt shop murders confessed to their part in the crime, though even from the beginning, it appeared that their accounts of the homicides were somewhat contradictory, with details being fed to them by police after they failed to correctly "guess" the right answers. Even after the confessions, though, Maurice Pierce and Forrest Welborn were never prosecuted, as a grand jury felt that there was insufficient evidence to try them. The cases against Michael Scott and Robert Springsteen, however, proceeded; Springsteen was convicted in 2001 and given a death sentence, while Scott was convicted in 2002 and received life in prison.

In 2006, Springsteen's conviction was overturned on the basis of an unfair trial, and in 2008, attorneys for Scott and Springsteen petitioned to get more stringent DNA testing performed on their clients for a comparison to DNA recovered from the scene. The DNA profile of the unknown man (or men) that had been obtained from the yogurt shop victims did not match the DNA of any of the four initial suspects. Both Scott and Springsteen were released in 2009.

A year later, Maurice Pierce, whose firearm possession had first led authorities to questioning the four suspects, was pulled over in a routine traffic stop in Austin. Pierce took off running, was tackled by police officer Frank Wilson, and ended up stabbing Wilson during the ensuing struggle. Wilson subsequently shot Pierce dead. Frank Wilson recovered from his injuries.

While some researchers remain convinced that Pierce, Welborn, Scott, and Springsteen were indeed the perpetrators of the gruesome slayings, others maintain that the most likely suspects were the two mysterious individuals seen in the yogurt shop by Dearl Croft. To this day, neither of these men has been identified.

For a time, investigators speculated that Jennifer, Eliza, Sarah, and Amy had been murdered by serial killer Kenneth McDuff, also known as the Broomstick Murderer, who had been convicted in 1966 of three homicides, but was paroled in 1989 and suspected of committing many more crimes after his release. Though he initially confessed to the yogurt shop murders, he later recanted, saying that if he really had done it he would have been proud of it. McDuff was executed by lethal injection in 1998 after being convicted of a separate murder.

The heartbreaking case of the Austin yogurt shop murders is still open, and remains a source of lingering trauma in the city.

****

Less than two weeks after four teenage girls were slain in Texas, a teenager in Belgium would vanish and not be discovered for six long months.

It was the evening of Tuesday, December 17th, 1991, and fifteen-year-old Katrien de Cuyper had been visiting her boyfriend in Antwerp. She was planning to take the bus home, as she usually did, but it was pouring down rain that night, and Katrien didn't want her boyfriend to have to go out in the weather just to walk her to the nearby bus stop. She told him she'd be just fine alone.

She phoned her parents at about nine-thirty p.m. and told them that she was catching the next bus, but for whatever reason, she missed it. At around ten-forty-five, the proprietor of a bar called Café Les Routiers stated that Katrien had come in out of the rain and asked to use the pay phone. He gave his assent, and she called someone and spoke to them briefly, though it is unknown who she phoned. After she hung up, she left the establishment, and disappeared into the night.

It would be the following summer before any trace of her was found.

****

Two days later, back in the United States, a prominent member of California's punk rock community would be gunned down on the street in front of his home.

Thirty-year-old Joe Cole was the son of well-known actor Dennis Cole, and was making quite a name for himself in his own right. An actor and writer, Joe also worked as a roadie for Black Flag, the Rollins Band, and Hole, and shared a house in Venice Beach with Black Flag / Rollins Band front man Henry Rollins.

In the early morning hours of December 19th, 1991, Joe and Henry had been attending a Hole concert at the Whisky A Go Go, and after the show was over, stopped by an all-night grocery store on their walk back home.

But no sooner had they arrived in front of their house than they were set upon by two armed individuals, who ordered them onto their knees and demanded money, further telling them to keep quiet or they would be shot.

Once Joe and Henry were on the ground, the assailants

went through their pockets, and expressed their displeasure that the two men had less than fifty dollars between them. They told Henry to go into the house and get more money, but as Henry approached the front door, the attackers shot Joe in the face at point blank range. They also shot at Henry's back as he fled into the house, but missed, and thereafter ran off on foot as Henry escaped out the back door of the house.

Henry quickly phoned the police, but by the time officers arrived, Joe was already dead. The suspects were described as two African-American males in their late twenties or early thirties, one of whom was about five-foot-eleven, weighed approximately one-hundred-sixty-five pounds, had a trimmed beard and mustache, and wore a baseball cap.

In the years since the senseless crime, Henry Rollins has written and spoken of the death of his friend many times, and published a book of Joe Cole's writings, called *Planet Joe*, in 1997. Joe Cole's murder has also been the inspiration for two Sonic Youth songs, "100%" and "JC," and footage and interviews with Venice Beach residents that Joe filmed before his death was later compiled into a documentary titled *Raves - God's Movie, Volume 1*.

1992

> Bitter Creek Betty

> Risteen Durden

> Karmein Chan

> Sheridan County Jane Doe

> Katrien de Cuyper

> Nikki Allan

> The Alcàsser Girls

> Natalie Pearman

> Johanna Young

On the afternoon of March 1st, 1992, a truck driver named Barbara Leverton, who had pulled over to the side of Interstate 80 in Sweetwater, Wyoming to change out her fuel tanks, beheld the appalling sight of a naked, frozen corpse lying face down at the bottom of a slope off the roadside, near an area known as Bitter Creek.

The victim—who would eventually be nicknamed Rose Doe or Bitter Creek Betty—was believed to be white or Hispanic, between twenty-four and thirty-two years of age, standing about five-foot-eight and weighing approximately one-hundred-twenty-five pounds. She had dark brown hair, brown eyes, and a tattoo of a rose on her right breast. Other distinguishing marks included a scar from a former Caesarean section, and a scar on the calf of her left leg. She wore a gold necklace, and a gold ring on her left ring finger. In addition, a pair of pink underwear and a pair of sweat pants were recovered near the body and presumed to belong to the victim.

A post-mortem examination revealed that Bitter Creek Betty had endured unimaginable suffering before her death. She had been raped and sodomized, severely beaten about the face, and partially strangled, before finally being dispatched by being stabbed through the nostril with an ice pick or similar implement. The coroner determined that the victim had been dead for anywhere from a few weeks to five months, and that her body had likely been dumped from a moving vehicle.

During the course of the ensuing investigation, it was discovered that the victim had obtained her tattoo at a shop in Tucson, Arizona. The artist who inked the tattoo remembered the girl had been wearing a brown dress with yellow flowers on it when she came in the shop, and also that she had told him she had been hitchhiking from place to place.

All that is known about the killer of Bitter Creek Betty is that he had type O blood, and was probably responsible for yet another murder in Wyoming, which would take place shortly afterward, in mid-April.

****

Meanwhile, weeks after the discovery of Bitter Creek Betty, another dead woman would be found in South Carolina, who may or may not be related to the elusive Shaw Creek Killer, two victims of which have already been discussed.

Sometime in March, a set of skeletal remains was discovered in Aiken County, just off Uncle Duck Road. Though the site where the bones turned up lay about fifteen miles from Shaw Creek—where Aiken County Jane Doe and

Jackie Council had been found in 1987 and 1991 respectively—there were too many other similarities to ignore.

Like the previous two victims, this was an African-American woman in her late twenties, whose body was found nude and with no personal belongings, situated near a body of water.

Authorities would eventually identify this latest victim as twenty-nine-year-old Risteen Durden, who had vanished from her home in Avera, Georgia back in March of 1989 and had been reported missing by her family. Dental records would later confirm her identity.

Though Risteen is generally not officially linked to the Shaw Creek murders, due to the location of her remains, it seems plausible that she may have been killed by the same shadowy assailant responsible for the previous crimes. Another body would come to light the following year, bringing the serial killer's possible tally to four.

****

Days later, on the opposite side of the globe, there would be some measure of tragic closure in the disappearance of thirteen-year-old Karmein Chan, who had been abducted from her home in Templestowe, Victoria, Australia in April of 1991.

On April 9th, 1992, a man out walking a dog near Edgars Creek in Thomastown noticed what appeared to be a human skull poking out of a landfill. Police combed the area, but were only able to recover the skull, a few vertebrae, and a jawbone. These limited remains, however, would be sufficient to prove that the final resting place of Karmein Chan had been found at last. The girl had died from three gunshot wounds to the back of the head.

Authorities were still convinced that the man known as Mr. Cruel was responsible for killing Karmein Chan, and after her body was discovered, the Spectrum Taskforce kicked into high gear to try and apprehend him. All they knew was that the suspect wore a black ski mask with white stitching around the eyes and mouth, that he lived in a house near an airport, and that it was likely he had videotaped his kidnapping victims in order to make his own child pornography.

But despite countless man-hours and millions of dollars spent, police grew no closer to identifying Mr. Cruel, and the case slowly began to stagnate. In recent years, theories have begun to circulate that Joseph James DeAngelo, allegedly the Golden State Killer who raped and murdered numerous victims in California between the years of 1974 and 1986, may have moved to Australia for a time after his last known American crime and subsequently perpetrated the Mr. Cruel attacks. The modus operandi of the two killers, it must be said, is startlingly similar: both offenders broke into family homes wearing ski masks and armed with a knife and gun; both tied up their victims using complicated knots; both were allegedly heard to speak to imaginary people; and both sometimes stopped in the midst of their assaults in order to eat a meal in their victims' homes.

Though the FBI are still keeping open the possibility that the Golden State Killer and Mr. Cruel are the same man, it seems that police in Victoria have dismissed the supposition. The identity of Mr. Cruel, then, is still unknown, and it is not even clear whether it was indeed Mr. Cruel who shot and killed little Karmein Chan.

****

Back in Wyoming, another young woman would turn up dead on the side of a road, her death bearing chilling similarities to the case of Bitter Creek Betty from the beginning of March.

On April 13th, 1992, a decomposed body was recovered from a ditch parallel to Interstate 90, only five miles from the border between Wyoming and Montana. The victim—still unidentified and referred to as Sheridan County Jane Doe—was white, between sixteen and twenty-one years old, standing about five-foot-five and weighing one-hundred-ten pounds. She had shoulder-length brown hair that was bleached by the sun, and was clad in a blue and white checkered midriff shirt, jeans, and a white plastic belt with a silver buckle. No shoes or socks were found.

It appeared that the victim had been killed by blunt force trauma to the head and face, though it is not known whether she was sexually assaulted. Authorities determined she had been murdered elsewhere, likely about two months before, and then dumped from a vehicle into the ditch where she was later discovered.

Later DNA tests would show that her killer and that of Bitter Creek Betty were the same man, but this individual has so far not been identified, and the case remains open.

****

Two months later, in Belgium, June 19th would reveal the grim fate of fifteen-year-old Katrien de Cuyper, who had vanished after making a phone call from a bar called the Café Les Routiers.

A construction worker digging near the port of Antwerp unearthed the decomposed remains of the missing girl, who had been strangled and buried at the site, though it could never be established with any certainty whether she had been sexually assaulted. Some sources assert that the body had been soaked in hydrochloric acid in order to hasten decomposition.

Less than a month after Katrien's body was found, a magazine called *Blik* received a bizarre anonymous letter concerning the case. The writer, a man describing himself as a light-haired young man between the ages of eighteen and twenty-five who lived in the local area, claimed to have been soliciting prostitutes on the night Katrien disappeared. He further wrote that he had seen Katrien walking down the street and had picked her up and given her a ride, dropping her off near an unnamed highway, though he stated that she hadn't wanted to go home. Katrien's parents also received a copy of this strange missive, and the writer apparently wasn't finished yet, either.

The second letter was more lurid than the first, and accused Katrien's parents of neglecting and abusing the girl, allowing her to run around alone at night with no supervision. The writer said that on the night Katrien disappeared, she had actually called her father from the bar, but her father had allegedly told her that he wasn't going to come pick her up and that she should handle her own business. Though the letter writer insisted that he had not killed Katrien, he went on to say that she was a beautiful girl and that he regularly visited her grave.

Obviously, police were fervently seeking the man who wrote these letters, as he seemed a prime suspect in the homicide, but he was not identified until 2006, and before that occurred, there was an even more shocking development in the case.

In 1997, a woman named Regina Louf also wrote a letter to authorities, taking responsibility for murdering Katrien de Cuyper. She maintained that she had been kidnapped and held prisoner by an international pedophile ring comprised of high-ranking members of Belgian society and other powerful individuals, who met in an unspecified castle in Antwerp to abuse and kill children, as well as produce child pornography and snuff films.

Regina went on to say that many children were abducted by this organization, and that some of them, like her, were groomed to torture and murder other victims. She alleged that she had been forced to kill Katrien during an orgy at the castle.

While investigators were skeptical of the claims put forth in Regina's letter, and indeed later dismissed them as unfounded, there was some other circumstantial evidence to suggest that there might have been some measure of truth to her assertions. Firstly, a man named Marc Dutroux, who was convicted in 2004 of multiple abduction, rape, murder, and child pornography charges that took place between 1986 and 1996, was widely believed to be involved with a far-reaching pedophile network much like the one described by Regina Louf.

Secondly, the early days of January 1994 would see two young siblings—eleven-year-old Kim Heyrman and her eight-year-old brother Ken—abducted from the streets of Antwerp. Kim would subsequently turn up raped and murdered, while Ken's remains have never been found. Some researchers surmise that this particular crime could have been linked to the murder of Katrien de Cuyper. The case will be discussed in more detail later on in this book.

Thirdly, some sources suggest that the bar where Katrien de Cuyper was last seen, the Café Les Routiers, was an intensely sketchy place that housed an illicit photography studio—said to be used for child porn—on its upper floor. On a related note, a known German porn producer named Gerry Ulrich was, in 1998, shot and killed in Italy by a Belgian man named Robert van der Plancken, who claimed that he had been sexually abused as a child by Ulrich and an organized cabal of pedophiles. When Ulrich's property was searched, there was a pornographic photo among his belongings that bore a passing resemblance to Katrien de Cuyper, though experts have stated that the child in the picture is a few years younger than Katrien, and may in fact be a boy.

Despite widespread rumors that the murder of Katrien de Cuyper might be related to an underground pedophile ring, though, a chance occurrence in 2006 would focus detectives' attention back on the writer of the weird letters that had appeared in July of 1992, only a month after Katrien's body was discovered.

In August of 2006, police arrested a thirty-five-year-old man known as Karl V.R. on an unrelated stalking charge, and upon searching his home, found a large stash of child pornography, as well as several news clippings about the murder of Katrien de Cuyper, and copies of the anonymous letters. A later DNA comparison demonstrated that Karl V.R. had licked the stamp on one of the letters sent to police headquarters and to the de Cuyper family.

The suspect denied everything at first, but eventually confessed to writing the letters. He insisted, however, that he had not killed Katrien, and in fact had never even laid eyes on her. He told authorities that at the time the letters were written, he was going through a rough time in his life and had simply made the whole story up. Significantly, it is also believed that Karl's brother Kurt may have written a bogus suicide letter in an attempt to cover up the fact that he had murdered his ex-girlfriend's new partner in 2002. The ruse didn't work; Kurt V.R. was subsequently convicted of the murder.

Conversely, Karl V.R. was never charged with killing Katrien de Cuyper, as the odd letters he'd written were the only evidence linking him to the crime. He did, however, serve six months in prison in 2007 for possession of child pornography.

Whether Katrien de Cuyper was the victim of a coordinated association of pedophiles, a disturbed older man who chose her on a whim, or some other random killer is still not known. The case retains an air of conspiratorial mystery in Belgium right up until the present day.

****

Later on that autumn, elsewhere in Europe, a little girl would vanish during a brief walk home and be found brutally butchered the following morning.

Seven-year-old Nikki Allan lived in the Wear Garths block of flats in Sunderland, northeast England, with her mother Sharon and her three sisters. On the evening of October 7th, 1992, the whole family was visiting Sharon's parents, who occupied a residence in the same complex, only a short distance away from the Allan home.

At some time between eight-thirty and ten p.m., little Nikki decided she would like to go back to their own apartment. Though her mother Sharon normally wouldn't allow the girl to walk there alone, the homes were so close together and the surrounding community so tight-knit that Sharon thought it would be all right just this once. She let Nikki set out for the one-hundred-fifty-yard trek to the family's flat, and said she'd only be a few minutes behind.

True to her word, Sharon and the other three girls followed Nikki out the door only about ten minutes later. But by the time they arrived back at their home, Nikki had disappeared.

Police were called immediately, and neighbors fanned out in all directions, searching for the missing seven-year-old. The hunt continued all through the night and into the following day, when a chilling clue alerted searchers to Nikki's location.

A party that included Nikki's aunt noticed that a pair of child's shoes had been placed neatly outside of the abandoned Quayside Exchange building, a derelict structure only about three-hundred yards from the block of flats where the Allans lived. When investigators entered the building, they found the body of Nikki

Allan lying in a puddle of blood. She had been bashed in the head with a brick and stabbed thirty-seven times in the chest and abdomen.

Shortly after the appalling crime occurred, police seemed to have found their man: twenty-four-year-old George Heron, who had just moved to the Wear Garths flats a few months before and was staying with his sister. Numerous pieces of circumstantial evidence appeared to highlight his guilt: a knife found in his home was the same type as that used to kill Nikki Allan; blood spatter was discovered on his shoes; and more than one witness claimed they had seen George Heron in the nearby Boar's Head pub on the night of the murder buying a bag of cheese and onion crisps, which were Nikki's favorite snack.

In addition, George's sister told authorities that when George had come home from the pub that night, he had gone straight up to the bathroom and had been in there washing for half an hour, which was unusual behavior for him. And some locals even alleged that George had been seen hanging around the Quayside Exchange building on more than one occasion prior to Nikki's slaying.

George Heron was duly arrested and questioned, and though at first he said he had not gone to the Boar's Head at all that night, and categorically denied having anything to do with Nikki Allan's murder, after three days of intense interrogation, he finally buckled and confessed that he had killed the child.

His trial took place in Leeds, as it was believed that he would not receive a fair hearing in Sunderland. The judge immediately ruled that several of the police interview tapes—including the one containing Heron's confession—were inadmissible, as Heron had not had a solicitor present at the questioning; the judge further opined that the police had used "oppressive tactics" and misrepresented the evidence they had in order to secure the confession from the suspect.

Moreover, there were some contradictory witness statements, and even people who claimed they had seen the killer on the night of the crime had given wildly differing descriptions of the man they saw, and most importantly had failed to pick Heron out of a lineup. Another witness later came forward and said that they had seen a man covered in blood in the neighborhood on the night of October 7th; this man also did not resemble Heron.

George Heron was eventually acquitted of the murder, much to the dismay of the Allan family and the community at large. Heron was later given a new identity and moved to a different location, due to the rancor that still festered in Sunderland. Nikki's mother Sharon brought a civil lawsuit against him in 1994, which Heron did not show up to contest. Sharon was awarded seven-thousand pounds, but never received the money.

The tragic case then went dormant until 2014, when serial killer Steven Grieveson was arrested and questioned in connection with the murder. Though Grieveson—also known as the Sunderland Strangler—had been in the area at the time of Nikki's death, he was thought to exclusively target young boys, and strangled them to death rather than stabbing them, though one of his known victims had been battered in the head in a similar fashion to Nikki Allan. Police ultimately dismissed his involvement, however.

In 2017, authorities announced that they had uncovered new male DNA relating to the case, and urged anyone involved in the investigation to come forward and have their own DNA tested in order to rule them out as suspects. And a year later, in April of 2018, police raided a house in Teesside and arrested an unnamed individual who they believed may have been linked to the case. As of this writing, however, there have been no further updates, and the murder of seven-year-old Nikki Allan is still an active inquiry.

****

Back on the continent, this time in small-town Spain, three girls would go missing on their way to a party, in a case that would draw worldwide attention, and would also just recently inspire a true crime series on Netflix titled *The Alcàsser Murders*.

It was the afternoon of Friday, November 13th, 1992, and three friends—sixteen-year-old Antonia Gomez Rodriguez, better known as Toni; fifteen-year-old María Deseada Hernández Folch, better known as Desirée; and fifteen-year-old Miriam Garcia Iborra—met up at the home of a fourth friend, a girl named Esther Diez, in the town of Alcàsser, in Valencia.

Toni, Desirée, and Miriam were planning to attend a fund-raising party that night at a club called Coolor, which was located in the next town over, Picassent. Esther had come down with the flu the day before, and so opted to stay home; incidentally, Miriam's father Fernando was also suffering from the same malady, which meant that he could not give the three girls a ride to the party as he had planned to. Undaunted, the girls decided to hitchhike, which they had done countless times before.

According to Esther, they left her home at around eight o'clock p.m. Approximately fifteen minutes later, they were spotted by an acquaintance of theirs, Francisco Hervas, who was driving by with his girlfriend Maria Garcia. The pair offered to give the three girls a lift part of the way, as Francisco was heading to an auto repair shop to get a fuel tank leak looked at. According to him, he dropped the girls off a few blocks away from the Coolor nightclub, and this sequence of events was corroborated by another witness who saw them a little further down the street several minutes later.

Toni, Desirée, and Miriam never arrived at the club. The only other sighting of them came from an elderly woman by the name of Maria Soria, who later told authorities that she had seen the girls walk by her house in Picassent and then witnessed them getting into a white sedan, possibly an Opel Corsa, which contained three or four men.

The three girls vanished at some point thereafter, and would not be found until early into the following year.

****

Back in England, and more specifically in the sleepy town of Norwich, a teenaged sex worker was allegedly seen getting into a car on Rouen Road at approximately one-fifteen a.m. on the morning of November 20th, 1992. A little more than two hours later, she would be dead.

A truck driver passing through the area at ten minutes before four a.m. spotted the remains, which were soon found to belong to sixteen-year-old Natalie Pearman. She had engaged in sexual activity shortly before her death, though it is unknown if it was consensual. She had then been asphyxiated.

Police conducted over four-thousand interviews and obtained DNA samples from hundreds of potential suspects, but as of this writing, Natalie's murderer has not been apprehended. Links to serial killers Peter Tobin and Steve Wright have also been investigated, but have not produced significant leads so far. The case is still open.

****

A month later, elsewhere in Norfolk, another teenage girl would leave home days before Christmas and later be found dead, with little clue what had happened to her.

It was about seven-thirty p.m. on the frigid, foggy evening of December 23rd, 1992, and fourteen-year-old Johanna Young set out from her home in Watton, presumably to visit her boyfriend, Ryan Firman. She was spotted near a chip shop in the city center by a handful of witnesses over the ensuing hour, but by eight-thirty, she had seemingly vanished into the night.

When the girl hadn't come home by the following morning to go on her paper route, her parents summoned the police, and a massive search commenced. Despite their efforts, no trace of the girl was discovered until the day after Christmas, when a dog walker saw a pair of girls' black sneakers in a hedge on Griston Road. A wider exploration of the surrounding area soon turned up Johanna's remains, lying face down in a pool of shallow, icy water at the bottom of a clay pit. She was naked from the waist down, and her body was covered in scratches. An autopsy demonstrated that she had died from drowning after having her skull fractured, an injury that had rendered her unconscious. Despite the disarray of her clothing, however, it did not appear that she had been raped.

Investigators first questioned Johanna's boyfriend, Ryan Firman, though they soon discovered that he and Johanna had broken up only a few days before, and that it was likely not his house to which Johanna had been heading on the night she died, even though the area where her body was found was quite near to Ryan's home. But there was no physical evidence linking him with the crime, and numerous witnesses placed him at a pub playing snooker on the night of December 23rd, so he was promptly released.

On December 31st, the *Eastern Daily Press* newspaper received an eerie postcard that seemed to make cryptic reference to the murder, reading, "Griston Rd. Watton 23/12" and featuring two crude stick figures labeled "Youth" and "girl," as well as a sketch of a motorcycle. This lead was pursued, but generated little progress.

For a time, police were looking into an unnamed older teenager, who other area kids reported sold them weed, had a violent temper, and had a crush on Johanna. This suspect allegedly left his job abruptly a few days after Christmas, and coworkers told investigators that he had scratches on his face the last time they saw him. It was also later discovered that he had repainted his car only a few days after the murder. The boy was arrested and questioned, but refused to cooperate. Prosecutors eventually concluded that there was insufficient evidence to charge him, and he was released.

The most recent developments in the case occurred in 2014, when two men from the Watton area—one in his thirties and one in his forties—were taken into custody. It is not clear whether one of these men was the same individual questioned at the time of the murder, when he would have been seventeen years old.

There has been no movement on the investigation in the past five years, though police are still hopeful that the killer will soon be brought to justice.

1993

> Aiken County Jane Doe #2

> The Alcàsser Girls

> Doris Shelley

> The Highway of Tears

> Colin Ridgway

> Rainbow Falls Doe

> Brett Cantor

> Holly Piirainen

> Karen Hales

> Gary Flanagan

On the morning of January 25th, 1993, another set of skeletal remains would turn up around the area of Shaw Creek in South Carolina, the same location which had earlier seen the discovery of two very similar bodies: that of Jackie Council, who had disappeared in 1986 and was found dead in 1991; and Aiken County Jane Doe, found dead in 1987 and still unidentified. This third, likely related, murder victim was later dubbed Aiken County Jane Doe Two.

Just as in the previous cases, this Jane Doe was an African-American woman who was left nude near the banks of Shaw Creek, with no items at the site that would help to confirm her identity. According to forensic examination, her death had occurred at some time between 1990 and 1992.

The victim was thought to be between twenty-five and thirty-two years old, standing around five-foot-four to five-foot-seven, with a slim to medium build. Her hair and eye color were unable to be determined, due to the extent of the decomposition.

Cause of death appeared to be a stab wound in the back of the neck, and the remains had also been burned, though whether the killer had attempted to burn the body or there had simply been a brush fire in the area that had singed the bones at some point was not clear.

Thus far, the main person of interest in the interconnected Shaw Creek cases seems to be serial killer Henry Louis Wallace, also known as the "Taco Bell Strangler," who admitted to murdering ten women in Charlotte, North Carolina in the 1990s. Though he claimed to have killed one woman in South Carolina, at this stage it does not appear that he has confessed to any of the Shaw Creek killings, and he has not been charged with any of them. As of this writing, he is on death row at Central Prison in Raleigh, North Carolina.

Other serial killers whose names have been mentioned in relation to the Shaw Creek crimes include Joseph Patrick Washington of Augusta, Georgia, who in 1995 received multiple life sentences for several rapes, kidnappings, and murders perpetrated between 1991 and 1993. Washington died in prison in 1999, reportedly from complications stemming from AIDS.

John Wayne Boyer, also from Augusta and better known as the "Long Haul Territory Killer," has also been considered, though his victim profile does not closely resemble that seen in the Shaw Creek cases. Boyer was imprisoned in 2007 for killing a woman named Scarlett Wood, but police soon discovered that the trucker was likely responsible for many more murders, including those of Michelle Haggadone in 2000 and Jennifer Smith in 2005.

The deaths of the three women near Shaw Creek, as well as the death of Risteen Durden, are all unresolved.

****

Two days after the discovery of Aiken County Jane Doe Two, the bodies of three young women missing since November of 1992 would turn up in rural Spain.

On January 27th, two beekeepers were checking out their hives in a remote, hilly area known as La Romana when one of them spotted something shiny glinting at him from a ditch. Upon closer examination, this object was found to be a watch, which was worn on the skeletal wrist of a corpse.

When authorities arrived and surveyed the site, they discovered the stacked and decomposed remains of the three girls—sixteen-year-old Toni Rodriguez, fifteen-year-old Desirée Folch, and fifteen-year-old Miriam Iborra—who had vanished two-and-a-half months before while hitchhiking to a party at the Coolor nightclub in Picassent. Their bodies lay roughly a half-hour drive away from where the three girls had last been seen.

It appeared that the victims had undergone unimaginable torture and various indignities both before and after their deaths. The girls' wrists were all bound together with rope, two of the victims had been beheaded, and one had her hands removed. Later evidence would suggest that all had been raped, sodomized, and beaten severely, and Desirée had her right nipple amputated, perhaps with a pair of pliers. In addition, it looked as though Miriam had had a sharp object inserted into her vagina, though it was not clear if this happened pre- or post-mortem.

Among the objects recovered from around the crime scene were a single nine-millimeter shell casing, a man's glove, and a Social Security outpatient pamphlet bearing the name Enrique Anglés.

Though Spanish police would later be raked over the coals by the press and the public for their seemingly lackadaisical approach to collecting forensic evidence—failing to photograph items found at the scene, for example, and sealing some pieces of damp evidence into plastic bags for hours, leading to mold growing on them—they had enough presence of mind to realize that the name of Enrique Anglés immediately rang a bell. For though Enrique didn't have much of a rap sheet, his brother Antonio most certainly did.

Antonio Anglés, in fact, had a long and storied criminal career, beginning with relatively minor charges related to receiving stolen property and drug trafficking, and eventually escalating to armed robbery. But in 1991, he had kidnapped a woman named Nuria Pera, who had stolen heroin from him, and chained her to a post in the back room of his family home, where he beat her savagely.

A handful of Antonio's friends and family members were charged with aiding and abetting Antonio in this crime, though in the end, only Antonio was convicted, and sentenced to six years. Only one year later, however, he was released on a furlough and simply never returned to prison. Significantly, at least in the eyes of the authorities, he was still running around loose when Toni, Desirée, and Miriam were abducted in Picassent.

Police descended on the Anglés home, ultimately arresting Antonio's brothers Enrique, Mauricio, and Ricardo, along with his sister Kelly and her boyfriend. Also taken into custody was a friend of the family named Miguel Ricart, who investigators focused their attention on almost immediately, as he owned a white Opel Corsa similar to the vehicle that a witness had seen the three Alcàsser girls getting into prior to their disappearance. Miguel had also been charged in the earlier kidnapping case involving Antonio and victim Nuria Pera, though he was subsequently cleared.

Under questioning, Miguel Ricart at first denied knowing anything about the murders or the current whereabouts of Antonio Anglés, and claimed that he himself had been in prison on the night that the Alcàsser girls were taken. When police attempted to corroborate this story, they found that they could not; Miguel had indeed been in jail throughout most of December of 1992 on a charge of car theft, but prison officials couldn't find a record that he was incarcerated on the night of November 13th. Miguel was thereafter officially charged as an accomplice in the triple homicide.

Approximately twenty-four hours after his arrest, Miguel began to open up about what had allegedly happened to the three girls from Alcàsser. He initially claimed that he and Antonio had picked up the girls at a gas station near the Coolor nightclub, and that the three girls had come along with them willingly on the drive out to La Romana. He stated that he had consensual sex with Desirée once they arrived at their destination, and that Antonio went off to have sex with Toni and Miriam.

Miguel then said that he had heard three gunshots from a distance, implying that Antonio had killed Toni and Miriam out of his view. This is where his confession got confusing, however, because he didn't say who had killed Desirée, or if she had been murdered at the same location as the other two victims. He simply asserted that he and Antonio had then dug a pit into which they deposited the bodies of the three girls.

But hours later, after a second autopsy was performed on the bodies that revealed the extent of the appalling violence that had been visited upon the young women, Miguel changed his story somewhat, maintaining that actually, he and Antonio had lured the three girls into their vehicle under false pretenses, after which Antonio had pistol-whipped them into silence when they started to scream. He further said that the two men had then driven out to an abandoned house near the remote area of La Romana, where they had raped and tortured the three girls before forcing them to walk to a pit they had dug. According to this account, Miguel and Antonio had then shot the girls and hastily buried the bodies in the pit, after wrapping them in a greenish-brown rug.

Whichever of these accounts was true—if indeed either one of them was—Miguel would later recant his entire testimony, claiming that his confession had been coerced. To many outside observers who have looked into the case, in fact, it appears that Miguel would change his story whenever a new autopsy was performed or a new piece of evidence in the case would turn up; for example, in a later iteration of his account, he stated that even though he had been present at La Romana, he had nothing to do with raping or killing the girls, an act which he claimed had been entirely perpetrated by Antonio, his brother Mauricio, and a third teenager known only as El Nano. Miguel had not mentioned these latter two individuals in any previous statement. This constant evolution of Miguel's narrative has led some to speculate that he was being railroaded by the police.

Miguel Ricart would stand trial for the crimes in 1997. Before the trial began, though, Fernando Garcia, the father of victim Miriam Garcia Iborra, requested that the proceedings be delayed, as he did not think the police had been diligent in their investigation and were guilty of ignoring or manufacturing evidence. Garcia further believed that there was insufficient cause to try Miguel; while he was not certain if Miguel or Antonio were guilty, he surmised that there might have been more people involved, and that the scope of the investigation should perhaps be widened.

There were some later developments in the case that seemed to bolster his assertions; witnesses came forward and stated that they had seen Miguel at a restaurant in another town on the night the Alcàsser girls were abducted, for instance, and DNA analysis on several pubic hairs found at the scene did not match the profiles of Miguel Ricart, Antonio Anglés, or any of the other named suspects.

Despite this, Miguel Ricart would ultimately be sentenced to one-hundred-seventy years in prison for his part in the murders of the Alcàsser girls. He was released in 2013, after a new European Union ruling that deemed sentences over thirty years to be cruel and unusual punishment. Since his release, he has gone off the grid, but insisted upon his innocence in the crimes before doing so.

Authorities would continue to search for the elusive Antonio Anglés, who was spotted numerous times in the ensuing years, and whose whereabouts are still unknown. He remains on Interpol's list of most wanted fugitives. One of the most persistent rumors concerning Antonio Anglés is that he leaped to his death from a ship crossing into Dublin, though this tale has never been substantiated.

In the time since the murders, numerous theories about what really happened to the Alcàsser girls have been splashed all over the media. Some believe that several prominent individuals, such as politicians and wealthy businessmen, were complicit in the killings, and that Miguel Ricart was simply used as a scapegoat. Conspiracy theories of this type were only strengthened by the Spanish government's refusal to test further DNA evidence discovered on the rug used to wrap the bodies, and their banning of a book co-authored by Fernando Garcia and criminologist Juan Ignacio Blanco in which the writers named specific individuals who they believed knew what really happened. There has also been ongoing strife between the parents of all the victims, some of whom still allege that Miguel Ricart was nothing but a patsy, and others who simply want to be left alone to put the entire tragedy behind them.

Though with the conviction of Miguel Ricart, the murders are officially considered solved, so much controversy exists concerning the case that it is likely the truth may never come out. The labyrinthine details of the investigation and its profound impact on the nation of Spain were the subject of a Netflix miniseries in 2019, titled *The Alcàsser Murders*.

****

Back in England that February, an elderly woman who had been the victim of a previous attack would succumb to a second one that eventually led to her death.

On the early afternoon of February 11th, 1993, a neighbor entered the bungalow of eighty-two-year-old Doris Shelley in Martlesham, Suffolk. Ever since Doris had been beaten and robbed of all her life savings in a home invasion back in June of 1991—the amount stolen in excess of twelve-thousand pounds—she had been a terrified recluse, and her neighbors would generally go out of their way to pop in on her regularly and see if she was doing all right.

But on this particular day, Doris Shelley was not all right. The neighbor found her cowering in a corner of the kitchen, blood pouring down from her head. The elderly widow was taken to the hospital, but died from her injuries eleven days later. Forensic examination determined that the victim had been beaten and kicked multiple times before having her skull fractured by some unknown blunt instrument.

The investigation into the savage and random murder ended up going nowhere, the only possible clue to the assailant a mysterious red Ford Sierra that witnesses had seen in the driveway of Doris's home on the day of the attack.

For a time, authorities believed that the killing of Doris Shelley might have been carried out by the same offender who perpetrated at least one violent robbery in September of 1992, in which a female postal carrier was hit over the head and robbed, but later forensic evidence seemed to discount this notion.

The inquiry was given a renewed push in 2018, on the twenty-fifth anniversary of Doris's death, but so far, no new leads have been forthcoming.

****

On Valentine's Day of 1993, across the Atlantic in British Columbia, Canada, the Highway of Tears would serve up yet another victim, though in her case, the killer would eventually be caught.

Thirty-nine-year-old Theresa Umphrey was last spotted in front of a convenience store in Prince George on the morning of February 14th; witnesses reported that she appeared intoxicated. Two unnamed men would later inform police that they had attempted to give the woman a ride, but that when they asked her where they should drop her off, she couldn't remember her home address. They claimed they subsequently drove her back to the same convenience store and left her there.

Only hours later, her nude and frozen body was discovered about thirty miles away from where she was last seen. A post-mortem determined that she had been killed by manual strangulation, followed by ligature strangulation, perhaps by a shoelace.

Later in 1993, serial killer Brian Peter Arp was arrested and charged with the murder of Theresa Umphrey, as well as that of Marnie Blanchard, who was killed in November of 1989 and whose case was discussed earlier.

The Highway of Tears would subsequently go quiet, but not for long, as another young woman would meet her end there in the summer of 1994.

****

As the spring of 1993 came into full blossom, a distinguished athlete would be gunned down in his own home in Texas.

Fifty-six-year-old Colin Ridgway had been born in Melbourne, Australia, where he began his sports career playing Australian-rules football and representing his country as a high jumper in the 1956 Olympics.

In 1965, he was recruited by the American football team the Dallas Cowboys, and played one season as a punter, making him the first Australian to play for the NFL. After retiring from football, he moved to University Park, Texas with his wife Joan and opened up a string of successful travel agencies.

On the evening of May 13th, 1993, Colin and Joan had been out for a late dinner. They had driven to the restaurant in separate cars; Joan reportedly arrived home first, and went out on the back patio to water some flowers.

When her husband Colin arrived home a short time later, he opened the front door and was immediately shot eight times at close range. He died at the scene, and neither Joan nor any of the neighbors claimed to have seen or heard anything suspicious; in fact, Joan initially reported to 911 dispatchers that she thought Colin had collapsed from a heart attack or a stroke.

From the outset, police did not believe Joan's account of what had happened, and began looking into the possibility that she had hired a hit man to kill Colin Ridgway. Said hit man was thought to be an individual by the name of Kenneth Bicking III.

Fueling detectives' suspicions in this regard was the fact that Bicking was a known associate of Joan's, had deposited five-thousand dollars into his personal checking account four days after the murder, and had bought a boat and made a down payment on a house over the subsequent few months. In addition, Bicking was known to have been in the area on the night of the murder, and was ratted out by his own wife, who told police that he had confessed the killing to her. Further, Bicking's father and Joan Ridgway held a joint bank account that contained a sum of about one-hundred-thousand dollars. From these intriguing tendrils, investigators surmised that Joan and Kenneth Bicking Jr. had hired Kenneth Bicking III to carry out the deed.

Joan vigorously denied the accusations, and subsequently passed a polygraph test. It was her opinion that her husband had gotten mixed up in drug trafficking, and that it was this involvement that had led to his death. The district attorney ultimately declined to press charges against Joan due to lack of evidence, and she was later released.

But Bicking did not get off the hook so easily. He was arrested for the murder of Colin Ridgway in 1996, but after his wife's testimony was deemed inadmissible, the charges against him were dropped. He thereafter moved to Florida, where he was arrested numerous times over the following years, usually for robberies. One of his accomplices in a 1994 burglary, William Wells III, would later be convicted of murdering five people, and Bicking himself is also suspected of perpetrating the 1983 murder of drug kingpin Eugene Hicks in south Florida.

It would later come to light through DNA comparison that Bicking had perpetrated a violent, home invasion-style rape in April of 1992. He was eventually convicted of this crime in 2014, and while police were hoping to link him definitively with the slaying of Colin Ridgway through further DNA testing, the comparison of his profile with that of a hair found at Colin's home did not produce a match. The case is therefore unresolved.

****

In early summer of 1993, a young woman would be found dead at a Colorado campsite, and her identity remains a mystery.

It was June 15th, and a hiker walking through the Rainbow Falls Campground in the Pike San Isabel National Forest near Castle Rock, Colorado, spotted the partially clad body of a young woman dumped in the underbrush.

The victim, later christened Rainbow Falls Doe, was a white female between the ages of thirteen and twenty-five years old with light brown hair that had possibly been dyed blonde. She was about five-foot-seven, with a stocky build, large breasts and wide hips. Other distinguishing features included near-perfect teeth, fingernails that had been cut or bitten very short, and a horizontal scar on her abdomen from a former splenectomy.

When found, Rainbow Falls Doe was clad in a black, short-sleeved Harley-Davidson shirt and several pieces of jewelry, including a gold pinkie ring, a gold necklace with a long black crystal pendant, and another necklace with a pendant depicting a pair of wizard's hands holding a brown tiger's eye.

The victim had been murdered by blunt force trauma to the head, probably two to three days prior to her remains being discovered. It was believed she had been killed elsewhere and then dumped at the unmarked campsite. It did not appear as though she was sexually assaulted, and there was no trace of drugs found in her system.

Because of the Harley-Davidson shirt, authorities tried to connect her with a nearby convention of the Vietnam Vets Motorcycle Club that had been going on over the weekend of June 12th and 13th at the Horse Creek Campground, not far from the dump site. This association was never able to be made, however. Witness statements seemed to imply that the victim had told people she was from Louisiana, but later isotopic analysis suggested she was probably from Alaska or Canada. Authorities suspect she might have been a runaway.

Though her remains were exhumed in 2012 to extract DNA, neither her identity nor that of her murderer have yet been uncovered.

****

Six weeks later, many miles to the west in Los Angeles, a well-known club promoter and record executive would be found brutally butchered in his apartment, in a crime that some have sought to link with one of the most high profile murders in American history.

Twenty-five-year-old Brett Cantor was originally from New York, but moved with his family to Los Angeles, California when he was only four years old. Brett's father Paul was an agent for the prestigious William Morris Agency, and later managed several musical performers, including Dionne Warwick.

Brett was well on his way to following in his father's footsteps. He first worked as an A&R executive for Chrysalis Music Group, famously signing Jane's Addiction and helping Rage Against the Machine obtain their first record contract. Both bands would go on to become massive stars of the alternative rock scene of the 1990s.

Brett then went into business for himself, organizing successful raves around Los Angeles under the auspices of his own company, Underground Entertainment. Subsequently, he purchased a ten-percent share in the wildly successful Dragonfly nightclub on Santa Monica Boulevard, which was mainly owned by Steve Edelson. Shortly afterward, Brett began dating actress Rose McGowan, who he met at Dragonfly in the spring of 1993.

Life appeared to be on an upward trajectory for Brett Cantor, but then came the early morning of July 30th. Brett was spotted leaving another nightspot, Club 434, in the small hours of that morning, but it was the last time he was seen alive.

Later on in the day, the body of Brett Cantor was discovered lying just inside the front door of his home in West Hollywood, which was only a short distance from Dragonfly. He had been stabbed nearly two dozen times in the upper body, and his throat had been slashed so deeply that he was nearly decapitated. Though some sources include the grisly detail that he was also given a Colombian necktie, the official report does not contain a description of this specific wound, and it's possible this was a later exaggeration.

The inquiry into the murder of Brett Cantor stalled almost before it began, though its notoriety would be given an enormous boost a year later, when Nicole Brown Simpson and Ron Goldman were found slain outside of Nicole's Brentwood home. When ex-football star O.J. Simpson was later put on trial for the infamous double homicide, his defense team began searching for similar cases in the area that could plausibly be argued might be the work of the same killer. One of these cases was the murder of Brett Cantor.

There were, it must be said, a few tenuous links between the murder of Brett Cantor and those of Brown and Goldman. All three victims had been stabbed multiple times in the upper body. The knife used in all three killings was said to possess a long, thin blade. And Ron Goldman's throat had been slit in a comparable fashion to Brett Cantor's.

There were some other connections as well. Ron Goldman had briefly worked part-time as a waiter at Dragonfly, and Nicole Brown Simpson sometimes went there to dance. Though there was no evidence that either one of them was acquainted with Brett Cantor, the link seemed worth exploring.

In the end, though, O.J. Simpson's defense team never brought Brett Cantor's murder up at the trial, and of course it didn't end up mattering, as Simpson was acquitted in October of 1995.

Conspiracy theories about the alleged association between the murders of Brett Cantor, Nicole Brown, and Ron Goldman persist, and were given renewed life in September of 1995, when waiter Michael Nigg was shot and killed during an apparent robbery in Hollywood. Nigg had worked at another restaurant, Mezzaluna, and was friends with Ron Goldman, who also worked there before his death. Some researchers have speculated that the victims of all four homicides were involved in drug trafficking, though there is no compelling evidence to support this hypothesis.

For their part, the Cantor family has gone on record as stating that they do not believe Brett's murder was connected to the slayings of Nicole Brown and Ronald Goldman. But apart from the dubious claims circulating around the Internet, it seems that authorities in Los Angeles are no closer to solving the homicide than they were in 1993.

****

In early August, a little girl visiting her grandmother in Massachusetts would vanish off a neighborhood street, only to turn up dead more than two months later.

Ten-year-old Holly Piirainen lived with her family in Grafton, Massachusetts, but on August 5th, she, her father, and her two younger brothers were staying at their grandmother's summer cottage in Sturbridge. On this particular day, a Thursday, Holly and her five-year-old brother Zachary had walked to a neighbor's house at a little before noon to see some new puppies.

A short time later, though, Zachary returned to the cottage without his older sister. Holly's father sent eight-year-old Andrew to the neighbor's place to fetch her, but ominously, the only sign of Holly that Andrew saw was one of her red sneakers, lying forlornly in the road.

A massive search of the area was undertaken immediately, but despite the quick response by police and the hundreds of volunteers who aided in the quest to find the child, weeks and then months passed with no trace of Holly.

Then, on October 23rd, 1993, hunters in the thick woods near Brimfield, Massachusetts—about five miles away from where Holly had last been seen—stumbled across her skeletal remains. Cause of death was uncertain, but presumably homicide.

Over the ensuing years, as the case began to grow cold, at least three persons of interest were named in the abduction and murder of Holly Piirainen. One of these was serial killer Lewis L. Lent, Jr., thought to have murdered between two and eight victims between 1983 and 1994, all of whom were children and teenagers. Lent was convicted of numerous counts of kidnapping, rape, and murder in Massachusetts in 1995, and in New York in 1997.

Another suspect interrogated in the slaying was Randy Stanger, who would be arrested in 2009 for the murder of his girlfriend and would subsequently be questioned in regards to the June 2000 abduction and murder of sixteen-year-old Molly Bish of Warren, Massachusetts. Molly Bish had been the same age as Holly Piirainen in 1993, and eerily, had even sent Holly's parents a sympathetic letter shortly after the child's disappearance, in which she had written, "I am very sorry. I wish I could make it up to you. Holly is a very pretty girl. She is almost as tall as me. I hope they found her."

Randy Stanger was never charged with either the murder of Holly Piirainen or that of Molly Bish, though he was convicted in Florida of the murder of his girlfriend.

In 2012, the Holly Piirainen case made news once again when authorities announced that they had some unspecified forensic evidence linking a man named David Pouliot to the site where her body had been dumped. Pouliot, a carpenter and avid outdoorsman who often hunted and fished in the woods near Brimfield, had died in 2003 and could not be questioned in the murder. Police have stressed that David Pouliot is not necessarily a suspect, and have not formally named him as such.

The kidnapping and murder of the ten-year-old remains an open investigation.

****

In late November of 1993, there would be another shocking and horrific crime in Suffolk, southeast England, only seven miles from the site of the brutal murder of Doris Shelley back in February.

It was the snowy afternoon of Sunday, November 21st, and twenty-one-year-old Karen Hales was at the home she shared on Lavenham Road in Ipswich with her fiancé Peter Ruffles and the pair's eighteen-month-old daughter Emily.

At a little before four o'clock, it was already starting to get dark, and Peter left for work. Karen was a little jumpy about being alone, as she thought she had seen someone turning the knob of the front door the previous evening, but she likely thought little about it as she settled in for the night with her child.

Slightly less than an hour later, at around four-forty p.m., Karen's parents Graham and Geraldine dropped by the Lavenham Road house for a visit, and were initially unsettled at finding the front door unlocked. They entered the home, and immediately smelled smoke.

Upon entering the kitchen, they discovered a large blaze, with their daughter Karen lying motionless in the middle of it. Baby Emily, sitting goggle-eyed on the kitchen floor, was unharmed, so the Hales scooped the infant up and quickly phoned police and firefighters.

When authorities arrived, they determined that Karen had actually been stabbed multiple times by an unknown assailant, who had then attempted to set her body on fire. Two Laser 7 brand kitchen knives were missing from the home, and these were presumed to be the murder weapons, though neither was ever recovered. Karen's purse had also vanished, and was never found.

Though there was a fairly heavy snowfall on the ground outside the home, there were no footprints leading away from the back of the house, and as there was also no sign of forced entry, police assumed that Karen was possibly acquainted with her killer and had let him in willingly. Alternately, he may have been posing as an authority figure and gained entry that way.

There were very few clues in the seemingly random attack. One witness claimed to have seen a man clad in a blue parka with a fur-lined hood, lurking in an alleyway between Lavenham Road and London Road at around the same time as the murder, but this man was never traced. In early 1994, two separate men—one in his twenties and one a thirty-year-old—were arrested and questioned, but released shortly afterward.

A later composite sketch of the man in the alley was produced, and a reward of fifty-thousand pounds was offered for information. In 1997, criminal profilers released a psychological description of the possible assailant, stating that he was likely in his late twenties to early thirties, lived or worked in Ipswich, was perhaps an acquaintance of Karen's, such as a coworker, and had a volatile temper triggered by relatively minor stresses.

In late 2018, authorities made a renewed appeal in the murder, and told the press they were encouraged by some new leads that had emerged in the wake of their announcement. But as of this writing, the case remains unsolved.

****

Shortly before the end of the year, a man would be found dead in a wooded area in central Florida, though very little is known about him or his probable killer.

Gary Flanagan was from Nashville, Tennessee, but arrived on a flight to Gainesville, Florida on December 22nd. He may have been coming to visit his brother for the holidays, but this is not known with any certainty.

A week later, on December 29th, his body was discovered in the woods near State Road 24 and Northeast 69th Avenue. Cause of death was unknown, but it was presumed that he had been murdered. 2018 marked the twenty-fifth anniversary of his slaying, and the case is still open and unresolved.

1994

- Kim & Ken Heyrman
- Kori Lamaster
- Inokashira Park Dismemberment Incident
- The Highway of Tears
- The Bain Family Murders
- Kathryn Menendez & Sarah Rae Boehm
- Lindsay Rimer
- Rikki Neave
- Michael Meenaghan
- Tracey Mertens

Less than a week into the new year, there would be an eerie disappearance of two children from the chilly streets of Antwerp, Belgium, a crime that might have possible links to the case of Katrien de Cuyper, who was abducted from the same area in December of 1991 and found murdered more than six months later.

It was a little past six p.m. on the evening of Tuesday, January 4th, 1994. Eleven-year-old Kim Heyrman and her eight-year-old brother Ken left their Antwerp home and went to visit their friends David and Natacha Musik. David was not at home, though, having earlier traveled to the nearby town of Merksem to play football. Kim and Ken boarded a tram to the football pitch so they could watch the game; numerous witnesses saw the siblings on the tram and confirmed that they had gotten off at Schijnpoort. After they disembarked, the children's whereabouts were unclear.

Over the following few days, there were some reported sightings of Kim and Ken; one person claimed to have seen them in a movie theater on Wednesday, January 5th; another witness asserted that the siblings had been in a café on Thursday, January 6th; and still another individual purportedly saw them on a bus bound for Putte on Friday, January 7th. None of these sightings could be confirmed, and indeed, in light of later events, it would seem that the witness accounts might have been erroneous.

Hundreds of volunteers in Antwerp fanned out all over the city looking for the missing children, but for more than a month, they would have no luck.

****

More than three weeks after the Heyrman children vanished off the streets of Antwerp, two students in California would stumble upon a gruesome find on a sunny afternoon.

It was January 29th, 1994, and two young women— Monika Maeir and Lauri Duncan—were hiking through Pogonip Park in Santa Cruz, California, looking for wild mushrooms in the woods. What they found instead was the partially buried and decomposed remains of an unknown teenage girl.

The victim was white, with short brown hair, pink nail polish, and a tiny tattoo of a heart etched between her left thumb and index finger. She had been bludgeoned to death, apparently with a metal pipe, and her skull was almost completely crushed, making facial reconstruction extremely difficult.

For many years, the girl's identity remained a mystery; she seemed to match no missing persons on file, and no one came forward to claim her, so she eventually came to be known as Pogonip Jane. A later isotopic analysis of the girl's hair seemed to indicate that she had traveled between Santa Barbara and Santa Cruz shortly before her death.

In 2013, interest in the case was reinvigorated after the lead investigator on the murder, Officer Loran "Butch" Baker, was tragically gunned down along with his partner, Detective Elizabeth Butler, when they attempted to apprehend a suspect in an unrelated sexual assault. Other officers on the force remembered how the Pogonip Jane case had haunted Baker, and renewed their efforts to solve the crime in honor of their fallen comrade.

Through DNA profiling, the victim was finally identified as seventeen-year-old Kori Lamaster, who had run away from her home in Pacifica, California in late December of 1993. Though many sources state that her parents had not filed a missing persons report on Kori until 2007, the website maintained by the family states that Kori had run away from home several times after starting high school, and that missing persons reports had been filed after each of these incidents. At the time of her murder, they seemed unaware that there was not a current report on file, and therefore did not think to file a new one until many years later.

Once Kori's remains were definitively identified and laid to rest, investigators began trying to discover who might have killed the troubled seventeen-year-old. Their most promising lead concerned a father and son, Wayne and Greg White, who witnesses claim had been seen with Kori before she disappeared. Greg White has since passed away. Wayne White was known to have been living in east Tennessee as of 2015, though some sources assert that he has also died. No other suspects have been publicly named.

****

Back in Belgium, February 11th saw the discovery of the body of eleven-year-old Kim Heyrman, who had vanished along with her younger brother Ken after getting off a tram in Schijnpoort. The little girl had been raped and viciously stabbed numerous times in the neck, chest, and abdomen. A mariner found her floating in the Asiadok at the port of Antwerp, her bra ripped off, her underwear around her ankles. No sign of her eight-year-old brother Ken was apparent.

As Kim was found clad in the same clothes she had been wearing on the day she went missing, it was presumed that the subsequent sightings of her that had taken place on the days following her disappearance had been cases of mistaken identity. Significantly, Kim's remains were recovered only a little more than one-hundred yards from where the body of fifteen-year-old Katrien de Cuyper had been found back in June of 1992.

Despite a massive search in the years since the incident, Ken Heyrman has never been found. He was presumed murdered alongside his sister, and he was declared dead in 2004. Ominously, two weeks after Kim's body was fished out of the water, someone dumped Ken's jacket in the same area, and several weeks after that, this same mysterious individual also pushed Ken's football gloves through the mail slot at the Heyrman family home. Though it seems obvious that this person was likely the killer, and that he was possibly taunting law enforcement and the family of the murdered children, no hint of his identity has ever been established.

However, Belgian police did have one fairly solid suspect: Manuel Heyrman, who was Ken's biological father and Kim's adopted father. Manuel had divorced the children's mother Tinny Mast several years before, and had an extremely weak alibi for the time of the siblings' disappearance. In addition, he also sent a letter to investigating authorities, claiming that the children had been murdered and then thrown into the Albert Canal, a location not far from the actual spot where Kim's body would later turn up. In addition, Manuel Heyrman attempted suicide only four days prior to his adopted daughter's body being recovered. Though Manuel was extensively questioned, it seemed there was not enough physical evidence to tie him directly to the crime, particularly since Kim's remains had been too decomposed to obtain a semen sample from her murderer.

Another person of interest was Belgian serial killer Ronald Janssen, who was convicted in 2011 of three murders: that of eighteen-year-old Annick Van Uytsel in April of 2007, and the double murder of eighteen-year-old Shana Appeltans and her twenty-two-year-old boyfriend Kevin Paulus in early January of 2010. Janssen also admitted to committing at least five other rapes, though authorities speculate he may have perpetrated four times that many between the years of 2001 and 2010.

Ronald Janssen is currently serving a life sentence at a prison in Limbourg, Belgium. He has not admitted to the slayings of Kim and Ken Heyrman, and their murders remain an open investigation.

****

Thousands of miles to the east and much later on in the spring of 1994, an almost unimaginable crime would be uncovered in a picturesque park in Japan.

It was the morning of April 23rd, and a cleaning woman at Inokashira Park in Tokyo was emptying out the garbage cans when she came across a plastic bag that smelled particularly foul. At first believing it contained rotten fish, she opened the bag to take a peek inside, but was instead horrified to behold what was clearly a human ankle.

When authorities arrived at the scene and catalogued the contents of the bag, they discovered a total of twenty-four pieces of a human body, including a shoulder, two feet, two hands, and several other fragments sliced neatly into eight-inch chunks, all of which had been drained of blood and thoroughly washed. No head, torso, or genitalia were ever found.

Days later, the victim of this appalling murder was identified as thirty-five-year-old architect Seiichi Kawamura, who lived not far from the park. He had last been seen leaving a nearby karaoke bar alone at around eleven p.m. on the night of April 21st. His family had reported him missing on the morning of the 22nd when he had failed to come home after his night out.

An autopsy determined that Seiichi's body had likely been cut apart with an electric saw and possibly a knife like those commonly used by fishermen. It was also suspected that his killer or killers had begun cutting him up while he was still alive. No trace of drugs or alcohol was found in his system, and because of the state of the remains, an exact cause of death could not be determined.

After the grisly crime went public, a handful of witnesses reported seeing a man who resembled Seiichi going into the park, and then later seeing two suspicious men carrying a bag around the park at roughly four a.m. Another witness also claimed they heard what sounded like a car hitting something near the park on the night Seiichi was murdered, leading some to speculate that perhaps Seiichi had been struck by a vehicle, after which the driver had cut up the body to hide the crime. The lack of blood found at the scene and the intricacy of the post-mortem mutilations, however, seem to rule out this possibility.

Other theories have it that perhaps the architect had been targeted by the Yakuza for some reason, or had fallen afoul of an organ-dealing gang. There have also been rumors that he had been involved with some bizarre religious cult and was ritualistically murdered by them when he attempted to leave the sect.

The horrific crime, known as the Inokashira Park Dismemberment Incident, remains a baffling unsolved homicide in Japan, and it seems no progress at all has been made on the case since it occurred a quarter-century ago.

****

On the first day of June 1994, back in British Columbia, Canada along the Highway of Tears, sixteen-year-old Ramona Wilson was hitchhiking from her home in Smithers to the town of Hazelton, a journey of a little less than forty miles. She had been planning to visit friends and go out to a dance. But Ramona never arrived at her friends' place, and her remains would not turn up until nearly a year later.

****

A few weeks after Ramona's disappearance, on the other side of the globe in New Zealand, an entire family would be gunned down in one of the most divisive crimes the country had ever seen.

It was the early morning of Monday, June 20th, 1994. Twenty-two-year-old David Bain, a student at Otago University in Dunedin who had been studying classical music and singing, set out on his part-time paper route, ostensibly leaving the rest of his family sleeping at home.

According to his later account, David arrived back at the Every Street residence at around six-forty-five a.m. and entered the house quietly, without turning on any lights. He went into a downstairs bathroom to wash the newspaper ink off his hands, and while down there, he also put a load of clothes into the washing machine, including an olive green sweater whose significance would be hotly debated at the later murder trial.

Once the laundry was going, David went to his room and there noticed a few bullets and the trigger lock from his .22 caliber rifle lying on the floor. He wasn't initially alarmed at seeing this, but after turning on the lights in the house and making his way upstairs, he soon discovered that his entire family had been brutally massacred.

Fifty-year-old Margaret Bain, David's mother, was sitting upright in her bed. She had been shot in the face. David's sisters, nineteen-year-old Arawa and eighteen-year-old Laniet, had both been shot in their beds, presumably while they slept. His fourteen-year-old brother Stephen was dead in his room; he appeared to have been the only victim who had put up a fight against the killer, for he had been partially strangled before being shot, and fibers were found beneath his fingernails. Lastly, David's fifty-eight-year-old father Robin was prone on the floor of the lounge, the rifle lying beside him, blood and brain matter spattered all about.

Eerily, someone had typed a message on the computer in the lounge where Robin's body was found. It read, "Sorry, you are the only one who deserves to stay." A shocked David Bain phoned police at nine minutes past seven a.m., telling authorities, "They're all dead."

During the initial stages of the investigation, it was suspected that Robin Bain had actually killed the family and then turned the gun on himself after David had left on his paper route that day. The family dynamic of the Bains, it should be noted, was somewhat bizarre. They were stringently religious, and also appeared to have hoarding tendencies. Robin and Margaret were essentially estranged; Robin, in fact, lived at the school he taught at during the week, and when he was home on the weekends, he slept in a filthy trailer in the backyard.

Even more to the point, daughter Laniet, who lived elsewhere and reportedly worked as a prostitute, told at least four separate people that Robin had been molesting her for years, and indeed, she had supposedly come home on that particular weekend for the specific purpose of telling the family what had been going on.

However, only a few days after the multiple murder, son David Bain was arrested and charged with the crime. Authorities believed that he had a motive for killing his family: namely, the substantial sum of money they had set aside in order to build a new house to replace the derelict one they were living in, a sum that would now go directly to David.

The police put forth a scenario whereby David had shot his mother and siblings before going out on his paper route, then after he returned, had waited in the house for his father Robin to come in from the trailer for his daily prayers and had then shot him as well. Afterwards, he purportedly typed the cryptic message on the computer to make the whole scene look like a murder-suicide.

Investigators further pointed out that the rifle used to perpetrate the slayings unquestionably belonged to David, though the ammunition and the key to the trigger lock were apparently kept in David's room, and Robin also had easy access to them; in fact, some later evidence suggested that Robin had used David's rifle before.

Another point of contention was the green sweater that David had thrown into the washing machine before allegedly finding the bodies of his family. Fibers from this sweater were found beneath the fingernails of fourteen-year-old Stephen Bain, all but confirming the fact that Stephen had struggled with the attacker. The sweater actually belonged to Robin, and when David was asked to try it on at the ensuing trial, it appeared too small for him, though the prosecution argued that David had put on weight during his stint in jail.

Also at issue was an unaccounted-for twenty-five minutes between the time David arrived back at his family home and the time he phoned the police for help. On the stand, David simply explained that he was in shock upon finding the bodies of his parents and siblings, and spent some time going from room to room to check if any of them were still alive. This would also account for the fact, said the defense, that there were smears of blood from several of his family members on the back lower hem of David's t-shirt and the crotch of his black shorts.

A few other confusing clues muddied the waters of the investigation. For instance, the left lens off a pair of glasses ostensibly worn by David were found in Stephen's room, and the prosecution maintained that the lens had popped out during the death struggle between Stephen and David. The glasses actually belonged to David's mother Margaret, but David had been wearing them off and on; the frame and right lens were discovered in his bedroom. However, other sources assert that the lens was found beneath an ice skate and covered with dust, suggesting it had been lost a significant amount of time before the murders.

A pair of white gloves that supposedly belonged to David was likewise found in Stephen's room, with the fourteen-year-old's blood smeared on them. It is unknown whether David or Robin was wearing the gloves; the only fingerprints found on the rifle were Stephen's, as he had obviously grabbed the barrel of the firearm during the struggle.

On the other hand, some evidence that seemed to point more in the direction of Robin Bain's guilt was considered inadmissible and not presented at the trial, including the supposition that Robin had been molesting his daughter and that she had been planning to confront the family about it. Also not mentioned was the fact that Robin had been suffering from a profound depression, had been neglecting his personal hygiene, had been recently reprimanded at work for striking a student, and had published some strange and violent stories in the school newspaper, one of which involved a character who murdered his entire family.

Ultimately, David Bain was found guilty of the five murders and sentenced to life in prison in 1995. However, former rugby player and businessman Joe Karam believed that David was innocent, and took it upon himself to get the case retried. In 2009, he was successful, and this time around, David was found not guilty, and released after serving thirteen years in prison. He later attempted to get compensation from the New Zealand government for wrongful imprisonment, but was instead given a one-time ex-gratia payment of nine-hundred-twenty-five-thousand New Zealand dollars and told to drop the whole thing.

The Bain family murders remain a controversial topic in New Zealand, and opinion seems neatly divided between those who believe David killed his family and those who believe Robin committed the crime before turning the rifle on himself. Undoubtedly, both men had motive, means, and opportunity, but the evidence seems ambiguous on either score. David Bain later changed his name, married a schoolteacher, had a son and moved to Australia with his new family, but doubts about his guilt still remain, and the case has been a source of fascination for more than twenty years, spawning several books, podcasts, and a stage play produced in 2010.

****

Back in British Columbia, another teenage girl would vanish along the Highway of Tears. This time the victim was fifteen-year-old sometime prostitute Roxanne Thiara, who disappeared over a long weekend in July after walking off with a client in Prince George. Her remains were found later on that summer, on August 17th, along Highway 16 less than four miles from Burns Lake. A friend of hers, another fifteen-year-old named Alishia "Leah" Germaine, would subsequently be murdered not far away, in December of the same year.

****

That summer and autumn, in a wooded park in Ohio, two teenage girls would be found dead more than three months apart, but only eight-hundred yards from one another. To this day, it is unclear whether their murders were related, and both cases have tragically gone cold.

Fourteen-year-old Sarah Rae Boehm lived with her family in Beaver County, Pennsylvania. By all accounts, she was a bright, conscientious student, a cheerleader and active in her school band. Her family was apparently unaware of any particular troubles she was going through.

At around ten p.m. on the night of July 14th, 1994, Sarah told her mother she was going to a friend's house, and she set out on foot. When the following day dawned and Sarah had not returned, her parents discovered that their daughter had actually never arrived at her friend's house, and what's more, the friend had not even been expecting her, suggesting that Sarah might have lied about her destination. The Boehm family reported Sarah missing on July 15th.

A few days after her disappearance, the girl's uncle told authorities that he had found a note hidden beneath a pillow in the teenager's bedroom. This bizarre letter, written in several different colors of ink, seemed to imply that Sarah felt as though she was a burden on her family and believed they would be better off if she ran away. She also claimed that she had been seeing a much older man who, while abusive, supposedly gave her the love she felt she was lacking and had promised to take care of her. Because of this strange note, investigators assumed that Sarah was a runaway, and therefore did not feel the need to enter her details into the database of missing and endangered children.

A little more than a month later, seventeen-year-old Kathryn Menendez disappeared from her home in Portage County, Ohio. According to her mother, Kathryn had also been planning to visit friends on the evening of August 20th, but had never arrived at her destination and had never come home. Although Kathryn had run away from home before, her parents believed that this time was different, and reported their daughter missing on August 21st.

Days after that, on the 25th, the nude body of Kathryn Menendez was discovered on a track off Fewtown Road that led to an oil well. She had been stabbed, strangled and bludgeoned, though authorities never reported if she had been raped. Witnesses reported seeing her in Alliance, Ohio a day or two prior to her body being found, and it was assumed that she had been killed there and then dumped at this particular spot, near Berlin Reservoir in a state park in Portage County.

Kathryn's mother believed that her daughter was murdered by someone who knew her, perhaps a scorned suitor with a violent temper. Police did investigate this angle, but came up with few solid leads. And later that fall, they would be confronted with another crime that led them to suspect that a serial killer might be at work in the area.

On November 4th, 1994, the remains of a fourteen-year-old girl turned up near the Berlin Reservoir, only about half a mile from where Kathryn's body had been found. Though this victim would be identified as Sarah Boehm in 2003, for many years, investigative miscommunications and other errors ensured that the Boehm family had no idea where their daughter was. Since Sarah had never been entered into the missing children database, and because the body was found a two-hour drive away from the Boehm household, a match was not made until nearly a decade after the girl vanished, and in the interim, the family made numerous reports to police that they had seen Sarah alive at various places before anyone realized that she was the unidentified body lying in cold storage in Ohio.

In an unsettling twist to the case, Sarah's father would later be investigated for allegedly confessing to inappropriate behavior with a thirteen-year-old girl. The FBI was brought in on the Sarah Boehm case, as it constituted kidnapping over a state line, and they began to suspect that the mysterious letter found in the girl's bedroom might have been planted. The letter contained not only Sarah's father's fingerprints, but also a lipstick print belonging to the father's girlfriend.

Although it would seem that the proximity of the two bodies suggests the work of a single killer, there were some differences between the cases as well. For instance, Sarah was found clothed, while Kathryn was found nude; her clothing has never been recovered. In addition, the somewhat odd behavior of some of the Boehm family members has led some to believe that one or more of them might have been involved in the girl's death.

In a sinister harbinger of the case, it came to light that in late 1993, Sarah claimed to have been accosted by a man in a Rochester Borough alley who attempted to abduct her before she fought him off. This incident was reported to police at the time, but authorities believed the girl might have made the story up and didn't investigate any further.

The cases are still being investigated as connected crimes, in spite of all the complicating factors.

****

A few days after Sarah Boehm's body was discovered in Ohio, a young girl would disappear after visiting a shop in West Yorkshire, England.

Thirteen-year-old Lindsay Rimer lived with her parents and three siblings in a house on Cambridge Street in the market town of Hebden Bridge. She had been there on the night of Monday, November 7th, 1994, but at about ten p.m., she decided to walk to a nearby supermarket to buy a package of cereal.

On her way to the store, she dropped into the local pub, the Trades Club, where her mother was having a drink with a friend, to say hello. Lindsay's mother asked the girl to stay and have a soda, but Lindsay declined, and headed back out into the street.

At ten-twenty-two p.m., Lindsay appeared on the CCTV footage at the Spar Supermarket as she paid for her corn-flakes at the front counter. After that, she mysteriously disappeared into the night. Though authorities initially believed she had been having problems at home and had simply run away, her family denied this assertion, and feared the child had been abducted.

Lindsay's whereabouts would not be established until five months later.

****

Elsewhere in England later that month, the heartbreaking murder of a schoolboy would bring to light an appalling litany of abuse and possible occult ties on a downtrodden council estate in Peterborough.

Rikki Neave was six years old, and already hardened beyond his tender age. His mother Ruth, who had been the victim of abuse and neglect herself as a child and whose own parents had died in a bizarre suicide pact, was tragically repeating the cycle. She was a known amphetamine addict, and no stranger to Peterborough social services. She had admittedly physically abused Rikki as well as her other two children; the list of atrocities she had committed against her defenseless six-year-old makes for sickening reading. She routinely kicked and punched him, burned him with matches, dangled him off bridges by his feet, locked him out of the house barefoot in freezing weather, squirted dish soap into his mouth to punish him for swearing, scrawled the word "idiot" on his forehead with a felt-tip pen, and sometimes sent him out at night alone to pick up her drugs. The ever-changing roster of boyfriends cycling through the house was also an issue, and the man she was married to in 1994, whose name was Dean, actively hated little Rikki and made no secret of this fact.

On the morning of Thursday, November 28th, Rikki Neave left his home at Redmile Walk, Welland, at about nine a.m., ostensibly to go to school. But the child was often truant, and it didn't appear that he was planning on attending school on this particular day, as none of his teachers reported seeing him. No one is quite sure what he was doing all day, though a few of the neighborhood kids claimed they had seen him wandering around the estate with some of his friends as late as seven p.m.

Rikki's mother Ruth, despite her habitual neglect, apparently became concerned when the child hadn't come home by tea time, and reported him missing to police at six p.m.

A search was undertaken, but Rikki Neave was not found until about noon on the following day. His nude body was discovered spread-eagled in a wooded area off Eye Road, only about five-hundred yards from his house. He had not been sexually assaulted, but he had been strangled to death. His clothing—including gray pants, a white shirt, black shoes, a blue coat, and possibly his red school sweater—were later found in a nearby garbage can.

From very early on in the inquiry, authorities suspected that Ruth Neave had killed her six-year-old son. Her abuse of him was well known, after all, and according to several witnesses, she had repeatedly stated that she wanted to kill him. Further, she had told numerous people that she was an "occult high priestess," a claim that resonated with a public still somewhat in the grips of the so-called Satanic Panic; the way Rikki's body was found spread out suggested to some a pentagram or other ritualistic aspect to the crime.

Police also found her behavior strange after her son was found, and noted that she had declined to participate in the search for him. And they took particular interest in Ruth's fascination with true crime and her tendency to write stories about gruesome murders.

Ruth Neave was arrested and stood trial for the murder of her son in 1996. On the stand, she openly admitted her interest in the occult, her previous abuse of Rikki and her other two children, and her devastating drug habit, but asserted that she had not killed the boy. She believed that he had been murdered by a group of older children in the neighborhood, and that police were using her as an easy scapegoat.

This contention wasn't entirely unfounded, it must be said; only the year before, in Merseyside, England, two ten-year-old boys had abducted two-year-old Jamie Bulger from a mall, tortured and murdered him, then placed his body on train tracks to be sliced in half. And many in the United Kingdom still remembered the chilling case of Mary Bell, the ten-year-old girl who strangled two toddlers in Newcastle upon Tyne back in 1968. Some have speculated that the murder of Rikki Neave, in fact, might have been a sort of copycat crime, perpetrated by other children living in the rather squalid, negligent atmosphere of the council estate.

Though Ruth's testimony at the murder trial horrified the jury, they were ultimately not convinced that she had killed Rikki. She was acquitted of the murder, but was sentenced to seven years in prison on charges of abuse and neglect.

After Ruth's release, she campaigned for authorities to reopen the investigation, which they did in June of 2015. In April of 2016, a thirty-six-year-old man named James Watson was arrested in connection with the case; tellingly, he had been fourteen years old when Rikki Neave was murdered, suggesting that police were now pursuing the angle of a child killer. Watson fled to Portugal while out on bail, but was re-arrested and brought back to England for further questioning.

However, in June of 2018, authorities concluded that there was insufficient evidence to prosecute James Watson for the crime, and released him. Since that time, there have been no new announcements in the case.

****

On December 9th, not far from the Highway of Tears in British Columbia, the body of fifteen-year-old Alishia "Leah" Germaine was discovered behind Haldi Road Elementary School in Prince George. She had been stabbed to death. She was the third Highway of Tears victim of 1994, and the second whose remains were found. The haunted highway would claim many more souls as the nineties wore on.

****

Back in England, the seemingly motiveless shooting of a handsome young scientist would baffle even the sharpest of detectives.

Thirty-three-year-old Dr. Michael Meenaghan, nick-named Spike by his friends, was originally from Glasgow, but had been living in Oxford for quite some time. He was, in fact, a lecturer and research scientist at the Sir William Dunn School of Pathology at Oxford University; molecular biology was his area of expertise.

At about four-thirty p.m. on the afternoon of Saturday, December 10th, 1994, Michael was making a pot of tea in the kitchen of his pleasant home on the Blackbird Leys estate when an unknown assailant approached the house and shot him through the window with a shotgun.

Michael managed to call emergency services, but could not get any words out; police dispatchers heard only strangled breathing. When officers arrived at the house, they stormed inside, only to find the scientist dead on the kitchen floor, his chest nothing but a massive bloody wound.

The details in the shocking slaying were frustratingly obtuse. Though neighbors told investigators that Michael had seemed a little nervous lately, keeping his doors locked and his curtains closed at all hours, and changing his phone number to unlisted, none of his friends or co-workers reported any unusual behavior at all, claiming that he had seemed just as friendly and normal as always.

A probe of the scientist's private life likewise yielded no clues at all as to who might have wanted him dead. Michael had become estranged from his first wife and son some time before, and had dated several women in the years since, but there was nothing particularly strange about that, and none of his former girlfriends reported anything amiss. In fact, police informed the press that Michael Meenaghan's private life had been essentially "exemplary," as far as they could determine.

The possibility arose that he may have been murdered because of something to do with his work, but police quickly dismissed the idea, as Michael's area of study was not controversial in the least and was funded by modest research grants. Rumors that Dr. Meenaghan was involved in studying DNA techniques used to catch criminals were erroneous.

There has also been speculation that Michael's murder was a case of mistaken identity carried out by a hit man targeting another individual. Given the lack of motive and Michael's unimpeachable background, this would seem a likely scenario, though authorities have not been able to discover if this was indeed the case, and if so, who may have been the intended mark.

A new appeal to solve the crime was made in 2014, and a large reward was offered, but so far, no new leads have been reported.

****

Weeks later, also in the UK, there would be yet another murder of someone who apparently feared for their life beforehand; but this time, it was a young woman who would be killed in an unbelievably grim fashion.

Thirty-one-year-old cafeteria worker Tracey Mertens had been in an on-again, off-again relationship with her boyfriend Joey Kavanaugh since both were teenagers. They had two children together, Daniel and Kelly, but Joey, it seemed, was not the most responsible father; he was an admitted drug addict, and often borrowed money from some unsavory characters in order to feed his habit.

In 1992, Tracey and Joey had moved from Rochdale to Birmingham, but things had gotten rather strained after that point. In the summer of 1994, Tracey returned to Rochdale with her children and spent some time staying with her sister Sharon. She told Sharon and their mother Barbara that she had left Joey, and that she didn't want him to find her. According to her family, Tracey acted strange and fearful that summer, taping up the windows and sealing the mailbox shut.

A few weeks later, though, Tracey decided to get back together with Joey, and went back to Birmingham to be with him. In November, the couple moved back to Rochdale, perhaps to be closer to Tracey's family.

A few days before Christmas, on December 22nd, Tracey drove back to Birmingham to pick up a few things, including a child benefits book, from her and Joey's former home. Upon arriving in Birmingham, she first spent the night at the home of Joey's sister, then went to the old house on Cattells Grove the following morning.

She arrived at a little before noon on December 23rd, and had only been in the home for about ten minutes when there was a loud knock on the door. When Tracey answered it, she was confronted with two overweight black men in their early thirties, clad in leather jackets and brown leather caps. They immediately demanded, "Where's Joey?"

The men then snatched the terrified Tracey, blindfolded her, and hustled her into a car parked along the street. The vehicle was described as a bright yellow, Mark II Ford Escort with a stuffed animal stuck to the back window.

Tracey's whereabouts were unaccounted for over the next several hours, but at around four-ten p.m., a woman walking near a church in Eaton, Cheshire—about sixty miles away from where Tracey had been kidnapped— heard someone screaming and rushed to help.

Tracey Mertens had been doused with gasoline and set alight on the front steps of Christ Church.

Though she was burned over ninety percent of her body, Tracey lived long enough to give police a description of her attackers, who she said spoke English with a Birmingham accent, but also spoke in a "foreign language" she couldn't identify. Investigators suspected that the language was a patois spoken by Jamaican immigrants.

Twelve hours after being taken to the hospital, Tracey died from her injuries. It was Christmas Eve. Although detectives interrogated her boyfriend Joey Kavanaugh, surmising that his drug debts were the most likely cause of the vicious attack against Tracey, Joey denied knowing who had killed her, though he admitted owing money to several different individuals. As the investigation progressed, it was also discovered that there had been a break-in at Tracey and Joey's former home only a few weeks before her slaying, and that someone had written the word "death" on a window with white paint.

A short time later, a Birmingham man was arrested on charges of conspiracy to commit murder, but was subsequently released due to lack of evidence. The homicide investigation was reopened in 2009, and authorities are still convinced that Joey's illegal activities contributed to the brutal murder of his girlfriend. Though a thirty-thousand-pound reward is still on offer, the case remains unresolved.

1995

> Melanie Carpenter

> Deanna Cremin

> The Highway of Tears

> Lindsay Rimer

> Michael Nigg

> Randi Stacey Boothe-Wilson

> Barbara Barnes

T he besieged province of British Columbia, Canada would once again make headlines in early 1995, though this time around the crime had nothing to do with the notorious Highway of Tears.

Twenty-three-year-old Melanie Carpenter lived in her native Vancouver with her boyfriend, and managed a tanning salon called Island Tan in the suburb of Surrey. On the afternoon of January 6th, in fact, she was working at the salon alone, and had received several phone calls, purportedly from a man representing a Japanese investment firm that was interested in purchasing a franchise. The man asked Melanie if she could close the store for an hour between one and two p.m. so the potential investors could come in and have a look around.

It is unclear whether Melanie believed this story, but what is known without a doubt is that sometime before two p.m., she was abducted from the salon. A little while later, two truck drivers reported seeing her in a red Hyundai Excel driven by a man; the car was spotted in the area of Hope, British Columbia.

Later on that same day, the man and the red car were captured on camera as the individual in question withdrew three-hundred dollars from Melanie's account using her bank card. Melanie Carpenter was nowhere to be seen. The following day, the same man was spotted accosting two teenage girls in a doughnut shop in Lethbridge, Alberta.

The man on the security camera was no stranger to police; he was thirty-seven-year-old Fernand Auger, who was originally from Ontario and had been working as a waiter in a Greek restaurant in Calgary until shortly before Melanie's abduction.

Even more to the point, Auger had recently served sixteen months of a two-year prison sentence for armed robbery; he had been released from jail in Bowden, Alberta in August of 1994, and told friends that he was going to be moving soon, though he didn't specify where. The conviction hadn't been his first; he had also served time back in 1985 for sexual assault against a fourteen-year-old prostitute.

Investigators were certain they had their culprit, but only nine days after Melanie's kidnapping, on January 15th, a real estate agent showing a vacant property in High River, Alberta discovered the dead, frozen body of Fernand Auger in the garage of the empty house. He had committed suicide by inhaling carbon monoxide fumes from the tailpipe of his rented Hyundai Excel.

A search of the vehicle turned up a few blonde hairs believed to belong to Melanie Carpenter, but her whereabouts were still unknown. All that would change on Thursday, January 26th.

Two men—Art Tooke and Steve Emery—were out looking for old fishing nets in Fraser Canyon near Hope, British Columbia when they spotted a rope hanging down from the steep riverbank. Upon moving closer, the men realized that there was something covered in a white blanket lying in a rock cleft near the water, and this turned out to be the body of Melanie Carpenter. She was found fully clothed, with her hands tied behind her back. She had been stabbed to death, though it was unclear if she had been sexually assaulted.

Though authorities were convinced that Fernand Auger had murdered Melanie Carpenter, his suicide meant that he could never be tried for the crime. No motive for the homicide was ever established, and the case is regarded as unsolved.

****

Seventeen-year-old Deanna Cremin lived with her parents and five siblings in Somerville, Massachusetts; she was a petite, attractive girl who volunteered for a local cable access station, worked part-time at the Star Market, and planned to go into teaching or social work after her graduation.

On the evening of Wednesday, March 29th, 1995, Deanna had walked to the home of her boyfriend Tommy LeBlanc, as she normally did on weeknights. She had a ten o'clock curfew, but on this particular night, Deanna phoned her mother and told her that she and Tommy were watching a program on television, and said she might be a little late. Her mother assented, and then fell asleep on the sofa.

Two hours later, at around midnight, Deanna's mother awoke and realized that her daughter had not come home. She attempted to contact her pager, but got no reply, and when she called Tommy, he claimed that he had walked Deanna halfway home and then returned to his own house. This struck Deanna's mother as strange, since Tommy was usually in the habit of walking Deanna all the way home, then calling to check on her when he arrived back at his own residence.

At around eight a.m. on the following morning, two school girls who Deanna had previously baby-sat for were taking a shortcut behind a senior housing complex on Jaques Street when they discovered the nearly-nude body of Deanna Cremin, lying only a block from her own home. She had been raped and strangled.

The investigation immediately focused on three promising suspects. The first of these was Tommy LeBlanc, who alleged that he had parted from Deanna halfway to her house, a site only about four-hundred yards from the spot where her body would ultimately be found. LeBlanc was said to be uncooperative under questioning, never showed his face at any of the subsequent memorials for Deanna, and even had a restraining order placed against him by his own mother only a few months after the slaying; LeBlanc's mother asserted that he had become bad-tempered and experienced wild mood swings since the murder occurred.

Though Deanna's family remains convinced that Tommy was the killer, there were two other prospects being looked into. One of these was an unnamed older man, a local firefighter more than twice Deanna's age who was said to be obsessed with her.

The other was a man who had been spotted lurking around the area where Deanna's body had been found in the very early morning hours of March 30th. Though this man has likewise never been named, authorities confirm that he was later imprisoned for a separate crime at the Massachusetts Correctional Institution at Cedar Junction.

The Cremin family maintains a billboard offering a twenty-thousand-dollar reward for information, and though new evidence supposedly came to light in 2005, no arrests have yet been made.

****

Back in British Columbia, a dreadful double murder took place that is often tied in with the Highway of Tears crimes, though the modus operandi was drastically different, and the killer almost certainly known.

On April 5th, 1995, the strangled bodies of twenty-five-year-old Sheila Faye Kinequon and her three-year-old daughter Christine were found in their apartment in Prince George.

On the same day, the remains of twenty-six-year-old John Joseph Seymour were discovered in a dirt lot beneath the Alex Fraser Bridge in Delta. Seymour had been the estranged common-law husband of Sheila Kinequon, and it was presumed that he had killed his wife and daughter and then committed suicide by throwing himself the fifty feet off the bridge.

Also that April, in a case more in line with the other Highway of Tears homicides, the remains of Ramona Wilson turned up near the Smithers Airport north of Yellich Road. She had disappeared while hitchhiking to Hazelton, British Columbia on June 1st of 1994.

Discovered neatly arranged in a pile near her body were three nylon ties, a small length of rope, and a pink water pistol with a handle shaped like brass knuckles. Her killer has never been found.

****

Across the Atlantic, April of 1995 would bring a grim end to the search for thirteen-year-old Lindsay Rimer, last spotted on a security camera purchasing cornflakes from a supermarket on November 7th, 1994 near her home in Hebden Bridge, West Yorkshire, England.

On April 12th, two workers dredged the remains of the teenage girl from Rochdale Canal. Her body had been weighed down with a concrete block, and was discovered about a mile upstream from where Lindsay had last been seen alive. Though it did not appear that she had been sexually assaulted, she had been strangled to death.

Authorities looked into possible links with several local killers and rapists, including John Oswin, who was convicted of two rapes in 1998; and John Taylor, convicted in 2002 of the murder of Leanne Tiernan in Leeds. Unfortunately, none of these avenues of inquiry panned out.

In April of 2016, investigators announced that they had successfully extracted a DNA profile of the probable murderer, and approximately seven months later, arrested an unnamed, sixty-three-year-old man in connection with the slaying. He was later bonded out, and his current status is unknown. A second suspect, a sixty-eight-year-old Bradford man, was arrested in April of 2017. The investigation is still ongoing.

****

Back in California, another crime would occur that some have attempted to link with the extremely high-profile murders of Ronald Goldman and Nicole Brown Simpson, not to mention the mysterious 1993 slaying of record promoter Brett Cantor, discussed earlier in this book.

Twenty-six-year-old Michael Nigg was originally from Colorado, but had moved to Los Angeles after graduating from college to try to make it as an actor or model. He had obtained a few low-key acting gigs, such as a recurring role on the mostly-forgotten syndicated television program *Liars*, but he mostly supported himself by waiting tables, just as many aspiring actors in the City of Angels do.

In fact, Michael had worked as a waiter at Mezzaluna Trattoria, where Ronald Goldman also worked for a time, and the two were said to be friends. Michael had quit his job there a month before Ronald Goldman was murdered, and went to work at another restaurant called Sanctuary, in Hollywood.

On the evening of September 8th, 1995, Michael Nigg and his girlfriend Julie Long were planning on going out to dinner. Michael stopped at an ATM in Hollywood to withdraw some cash; Julie waited for him in the car.

As Michael walked away from the bank, he was set upon by two men who waved guns in his face and demanded money. However, Michael did not even have enough time to hand over the cash, for one of the men shot him in the head, and then both assailants jumped into a waiting car driven by a third man. The supposed robbers had not stolen any money, and Julie Long was unharmed.

Though the crime initially appeared to be nothing more than a botched robbery, Michael Nigg's tenuous links with Ronald Goldman and the Mezzaluna restaurant gave some later researchers pause. Theories began to swirl that Mezzaluna was the center for a drug trafficking empire run by Mafia-affiliated cocaine dealer Joey Ippolito, and that several waiters there were part of the operation. In this scenario, it was hypothesized that Ron Goldman, Nicole Brown Simpson, Brett Cantor, and possibly Michael Nigg were involved in setting up a rival narcotics network, and were essentially assassinated. Evidence for this particular series of events is scant, however, and relies mostly on nebulous relationships and the fact that Michael Nigg was not robbed in spite of the fact that his attackers had specifically demanded money.

Three suspects were later arrested for the murder, but summarily released due to lack of evidence. The case has seen no further progress since that time.

****

October of 1995 would see another young woman vanish along the Highway of Tears; this time it was nineteen-year-old Lana Derrick, last seen in Thornhill at a gas station. A later witness claimed that she had gotten into a vehicle with two unidentified men, but this has not been substantiated. Lana Derrick has never been found.

****

About a month before the year was out, a woman's body would be discovered in North Carolina; her identity would not be established until early 2019, and the circumstances surrounding her death still remain a puzzling mystery.

It was December 6th, 1995, and the skeletal remains were discovered in a field in Jacksonville, North Carolina. At the time the body was found, authorities believed that the decedent was a Caucasian woman between the ages of twenty-five and forty years old, who stood between five-foot-five and five-foot-eight. She was believed to have reddish hair, and had a great deal of expensive dental work. She was clad in a yellow shirt with shoulder pads, an additional red shirt, also with shoulder pads, black jeans, and one white Nike sneaker. In addition, she wore an eighteen-karat gold necklace, several gold bracelets, and a black watch. Gold hoop earrings were found nearby, as were two New York Transit Authority tokens and a set of two hotel keys on a ring with a burned tag attached.

Though cause of death was unable to be determined, the positioning of the body suggested homicide. According to the coroner, the woman had likely died about two years previously.

For more than two decades, the victim, dubbed Jacksonville Jane Doe, remained unidentified, but in February of 2019, a DNA comparison uncovered the fact that the victim was actually thirty-three-year-old Randi Stacey Boothe-

Wilson, primarily known as Stacey, an African-American woman from Greenburgh, New York.

Stacey was a former Marine who had left the service in August of 1994. She had been married to another Marine, Earle Wilson, until their divorce shortly after her discharge. The couple had three children, Earl III, Elliot, and Leslye. Stacey had been living in New York with her daughter and two sons, and working as a security guard at a museum in Manhattan.

In late October of 1994, though, Stacey told her children that she was going to visit her sister in Queens, but she never arrived there. Her vehicle was later found abandoned. Even weirder, her estranged husband found letters, supposedly written by Stacey, in which she claimed that she was leaving her children. Earle also told police that Stacey had sent him her debit and credit cards in the mail before she vanished. She was reported missing shortly afterward.

Since the victim's identity was proven, detectives have been stumped as to how Stacey Boothe-Wilson ended up dead nearly six-hundred miles away from home, and whether she had either voluntarily abandoned her old life and perhaps committed suicide, or was alternately abducted and murdered by someone who staged the entire scenario.

The most compelling lead thus far concerns a connection between Stacey's death and the crimes committed by another former Marine, possible serial killer Matthew Lorne Alder. Alder was convicted in 1995 of raping and murdering nineteen-year-old Lisa Gipson, who he had picked up from a nightclub and later burned alive. Alder was also charged with the 1993 murder of nineteen-year-old Wanda Musk in Genesee Township, and is further suspected in the 1992 slaying of twenty-five-year-old Camille Marie Whalen.

The inquiry is still active.

****

On the following day, a little girl in Ohio would vanish while walking to school. She would not be found until two months into the following year.

Thirteen-year-old Barbara Barnes was a quiet, conscientious child who volunteered at the Salvation Army and was a favorite of her teachers at Harding Middle School, where she was an eighth-grader.

Apparently, Barbara had become a much more circumspect child since her father had been murdered in 1989. She rarely spoke about the crime, and kept to herself in general, not sharing a great deal about her life with her classmates.

On the morning of December 7th, Barbara was walking to school, as she did every morning, along with several other children who only lived blocks away from the school building. Apparently, the girl was abducted at some point before she reached the school, though no one seemed to realize she had disappeared until about three o'clock that afternoon, when she failed to return home. Her mother had not received the several phone calls from the school administration informing her that Barbara had not shown up for classes.

It would be late February before her fate was discovered.

1996

In the first two weeks of 1996, a little girl would be snatched by a stranger in broad daylight, and although she would later be found murdered, her abduction led to some of the most sweeping changes in how law enforcement interfaced with the public concerning kidnapped and endangered children.

It was January 13th in Arlington, Texas. Nine-year-old Amber Hagerman and her five-year-old brother Ricky were spending some time at their grandparents' house on a Sunday afternoon when they decided to take a bike ride around the neighborhood. They set out at about three p.m., heading for the parking lot of an abandoned Winn-Dixie grocery store, where some local kids had set up a wooden bike ramp.

Amber and Ricky did a few jumps on their bikes, and then Ricky decided he was ready to head back home. Amber wanted to stay a little longer, so she told him to go ahead home without her. Their grandparents' house was only a couple of blocks away.

Minutes after Ricky left the parking lot, Jim Kevil, a seventy-eight-year-old retiree who lived nearby, saw Amber riding her bike up and down in the parking lot while he was working in his backyard. Then, quite suddenly, he saw a dark blue or black American-made pickup truck pull up alongside the child. The man in the truck jumped out, pulled Amber off her bike, and stuffed her into the cab of the vehicle before peeling out. Amber screamed briefly and kicked at her attacker, but she was no match for him.

Jim Kevil immediately phoned the police, describing the truck as well as the kidnapper, who he said was a white or Hispanic male between the ages of twenty-five and forty, with a medium build and standing less than six feet tall.

Authorities arrived on the scene immediately, even before Amber's grandparents were aware that she had been taken. When her grandfather Jimmie Whitson got to the parking lot, having become worried when Ricky had come home without his sister, he was met with swarms of police cars and officers. A search fanned out from there.

It turned out that no one other than Jim Kevil had seen the girl being abducted, or at least were not willing to come forward and claim they had. There was a busy laundromat in the same parking lot as the former grocery store, but many of the customers were suspected to be in the United States illegally, and were perhaps reluctant to come forward and expose themselves to law enforcement. One witness did say they had seen a dark-colored pickup parked in front of the laundromat that afternoon, but other than this one nebulous lead, investigators were left with nothing at all to go on.

Amber's distraught parents, Donna and Richard, took to the media to beg the kidnapper to return their little girl unharmed, but all of their pleas seemingly fell on deaf ears. And sadly, four days after she went missing, Amber Hagerman would be found dead.

On January 17th, a man out walking his dog near the Forest Hill apartment complex, less than five miles away from the parking lot from which Amber was abducted, saw the child's body lying in a creek bed. She was nude except for one sock, and her throat had been slashed.

After an autopsy was performed, the coroner determined that Amber had been held for two days prior to her murder. She had been sexually assaulted multiple times while in captivity. But because her remains were found in a creek, any further potential evidence had been washed away by the water.

Though police investigated thousands of leads and attempted to track down the man in the dark pickup truck who had taken the girl, no suspect was ever identified, and the case is still unsolved, more than twenty years later.

One positive development did emerge from the horrific crime shortly afterward, however. Only a few days following the funeral of Amber Hagerman, a woman named Diana Simone, who was a mother herself but did not know the Hagerman family personally, called a radio station in Dallas and asked them why the public was immediately alerted when dangerous weather was approaching, but not when a child was abducted. She pointed out that had locals in the surrounding area been informed of Amber's kidnapping and told the type of vehicle and perpetrator to look for, then perhaps someone could have intervened before Amber was killed.

The idea quickly spread through the Dallas-Fort Worth area, and eventually went national, then international; at this writing, more than twenty countries besides the United States also utilize this child abduction alert system, called the AMBER Alert in Amber Hagerman's honor. The system sends immediate notifications to the cell phones of all individuals in the area of the kidnapping, along with a description of the child, the vehicle, and the perpetrator, if known. The same alert is also posted on electronic billboards on all nearby highways. To date, the AMBER Alert system is estimated to have recovered nearly nine-hundred abducted or endangered children.

****

Elsewhere in the Lone Star State, two teenage girls would fall prey to one or more of the human predators stalking the Texas Killing Fields.

It was February 1st, 1996, and fourteen-year-old Lynette Bibbs was attending an event at a teen club in Houston with her fifteen-year-old friend, Tamara Fisher. The pair was reportedly seen in the company of a twenty-two-year-old man who was thought to be a friend of theirs; this man told police that he had been with the girls at the club, and then had dropped them off at a motel on Old Spanish Trail.

Two days later, on February 3rd, the bodies of both girls where found lying on the side of a dirt road in Cleveland, Texas. Both had been shot, though police suspected that there were two assailants, one of whom shot Lynette, and the other who shot Tamara.

It was the first Texas Killing Fields-adjacent crime in a long while, the last one being the disappearance of Suzanne Rene Richerson back in October of 1988. There would be a handful of others before the 1990s ended.

****

Later on that winter, back in Steubenville, Ohio, police were still investigating the troubling disappearance of thirteen-year-old Barbara Barnes, who had gone missing on her way to school back in early December of 1995.

But on February 22nd, a surveyor working in an area near the Pittsburgh International Airport found the partially frozen remains of the murdered teenager in a dry creek bed. She had been raped and strangled.

Initially, suspicion fell on the child's uncle, Louis Boyce, incidentally also a person of interest in the 1989 shooting death of Barbara's father. The child's body was found near Boyce's property, and he allegedly failed a polygraph test when questioned about the homicide. However, no physical evidence could be found that linked him to either crime, and he was never charged.

Authorities generally believed that Barbara had been killed by someone local to the area, and perhaps someone responsible for other, similar murders. At least one researcher has attempted to make the case that Barbara Barnes might have been slain by the same assailant who kidnapped and murdered ten-year-old Amy Mihaljevic in 1989. This individual was speculated to be an Akron man by the name of Robert Anthony Buell, who murdered twelve-year-old Tina Harmon in 1981, eleven-year-old Krista Harrison in 1982, and ten-year-old Debora Kaye Smith in 1983.

Buell was executed in Lucasville, Ohio in September of 2002. It is unknown whether he was involved in the death of Barbara Barnes.

****

Later that autumn, back in Texas, the decomposed remains of a young woman would be found in the underbrush. It would take two years to identify her, and once that occurred, her sad life up until the time of her murder would be tragically revealed.

On October 8th, 1996, a farmer in Decatur, Texas stumbled upon the nude body in a pile of dead branches. It appeared the girl had been raped and strangled, though cause of death was not entirely clear, due to the state of decay. The victim bore no particular distinguishing marks, and would eventually come to be dubbed Brush Girl. Authorities at first believed that she was between twenty and forty years old, of a small build, and with hair that was bleached blonde.

However, in 1998, a facial reconstruction and a comparison of dental records confirmed the identity of the victim as fourteen-year-old April Dawn Lacy, who had been reported missing by her mother only five days before she was found dead.

April had never really had a chance in life. Born in Oklahoma City in 1982, her parents were both drug addicts and lived an itinerant existence in cheap motel after cheap motel, shoplifting and scrounging through garbage cans to find items to sell for a few dollars. April's mother Jacqueline allegedly worked as a prostitute, and may have pimped out April as well, though Jacqueline denied this strenuously. The Lacys also had a younger child, a boy, who had earlier been removed from their care by the Department of Human Services.

On October 3rd, Jacqueline told police, she and April had had an argument, supposedly about the marital problems that Jacqueline was having with her husband Dale. April had run away before, she said, and threatened to again on this particular day. Jacqueline claimed that she left the motel room where the pair of them had been staying, and when she returned, April was gone. She had not been alarmed at first, she asserted, because April had not taken her purse with her, but after a few hours, Jacqueline purportedly became concerned and phoned police to report her daughter missing. Dale Lacy also reported April missing, in January of 1997; at this point, April's body had already been found, but she was still unidentified.

Once investigators surmised that Brush Girl was actually April Lacy, they attempted to inform Jacqueline and Dale of this fact, but the couple refused to believe it, not only because they deemed the dental and facial reconstruction comparisons insufficient, but also because initially, authorities thought the victim was much older than fourteen.

There was also the seemingly inconsistent fact that April's body was found dramatically decomposed only five days after her mother claimed to have last seen her. Though the Lacys used this as another argument as to why they needed more proof that the body actually belonged to their missing daughter, detectives looking into the case hypothesized that perhaps April had been dead far longer than five days, and that her parents might have known more about her death than they were letting on, or at least had not reported her missing until long after she had vanished.

A DNA test was eventually performed on the girl's remains, which definitively confirmed that Brush Girl was April Lacy. It is uncertain whether Jacqueline or Dale Lacy knew anything about their daughter's disappearance or murder. Authorities have also pursued a few other leads, including the possibility that April might have been slain by a serial killer. Some speculation has her death linked to the Redhead Murders, though this series is thought to have ended in 1992 at the latest.

The grim saga of April's life and death is still a mystery.

****

On the day after Christmas of 1996, a crime occurred that would go on to become one of the most iconic and hotly-debated child murders in the history of American crime, a baffling case of a six-year-old beauty queen, her affluent parents, a bizarre ransom note, and a less-than-ideal police investigation.

JonBenét Ramsey had been born in Atlanta, Georgia in 1990, but only a year later, moved with her parents John and Patsy and her older brother Burke to a wealthy suburb in Boulder, Colorado. John Ramsey was the CEO of a computer systems company called Access Graphics, a firm that would later be purchased by Lockheed Martin. Ramsey was a multi-millionaire, and the family lived accordingly.

Patsy Ramsey, formerly Miss West Virginia of 1977, enjoyed traveling around the country with JonBenét and entering her in numerous pageants, many of which she won. By the time she was six years old, JonBenét had several pageant titles to her name, including Little Miss Colorado, America's Royale Miss, Colorado All-Star Kids Cover Girl, and National Tiny Miss Beauty.

Early on the morning of December 26th, 1996, Patsy Ramsey awoke to prepare for a trip the family would be taking later that day, but she noticed that JonBenét was not in her bed. She didn't become particularly alarmed until she found a strange, two-and-a-half-page ransom letter lying on the staircase in the kitchen. It was addressed to "Mr. Ramsey," and read:

"Listen carefully! We are a group of individuals that represent a small foreign faction. We respect your bussiness [sic] but not the country that it serves. At this time we have your daughter in our posession [sic]. She is safe and unharmed and if you want her to see 1997, you must follow our instructions to the letter.

"You will withdraw $118,000.00 from your account. $100,000 will be in $100 bills and the remaining $18,000 in $20 bills. Make sure that you bring an adequate size attaché to the bank. When you get home you will put the money in a brown paper bag. I will call you between 8 and 10 am tomorrow to instruct you on delivery. The delivery will be exhausting so I advise you to be rested. If we monitor you getting the money early, we might call you early to arrange an earlier delivery of the money and hence a [sic] earlier pick-up of your daughter.

"Any deviation of my instructions will result in the immediate execution of your daughter. You will also be denied her remains for proper burial. The two gentlemen watching over your daughter do not particularly like you so I advise you not to provoke them. Speaking to anyone about your situation, such as Police, F.B.I., etc., will result in your daughter being beheaded. If we catch you talking to a stray dog, she dies. If you alert bank authorities, she dies. If the money is in any way marked or tampered with, she dies. You will be scanned for electronic devices and if any are found, she dies. You can try to deceive us but be warned that we are familiar with law enforcement countermeasures and tactics. You stand a 99% chance of killing your daughter if you try to out smart [sic] us. Follow our instructions and you stand a 100% chance of getting her back. You and your family are under constant scrutiny as well as the authorities. Don't try to grow a brain John. You are not the only fat cat around so don't think that killing will be difficult. Don't underestimate us John. Use that good southern common sense of yours. It is up to you now John!

Victory!

S.B.T.C."

Despite the warnings in the ransom letter, Patsy phoned police at a little before six a.m., telling them her daughter had been abducted. She also phoned family members and friends, ostensibly for support and to get them to come help in the search. Police arrived only three minutes after the initial 911 call.

Because the case was first perceived as a kidnapping, officers did not take particular care to search the entire house or secure the area as a crime scene, though JonBenét's bedroom was cordoned off, as it was assumed that this was where the child had been taken from. However, numerous individuals—including police officers, FBI agents, relatives, victim advocates, and the family's minister—were essentially allowed to mill around the house looking for clues and trying to help in the investigation, thereby contaminating any physical evidence that might have been present. Most notably, authorities did not immediately search the basement.

As the morning wore on, John Ramsey began making arrangements to pay the ransom, although the phone call promised by the writer of the letter never materialized. At around one p.m. on December 26th, at something of a loss as to what else to do, the police advised John and a friend of the family to search the house again and see if they could see anything out of the ordinary that might suggest what had happened to little JonBenét. It was at this point that John Ramsey, opening a latched door to an unsearched basement room, discovered the body of his six-year-old daughter.

JonBenét was found partially covered with a white blanket, with a piece of duct tape over her mouth. Her wrists had been bound with nylon cord, and a length of this same cord, along with a segment of a broken paintbrush handle, and been used to make a crude garrote that had been used to strangle the child. Her skull was also fractured, an injury that likely would have eventually killed her even if the strangulation had not been brought into play. Though a later examination found no semen on the remains, it was believed that she had been sexually assaulted in some fashion, as there were signs that her vaginal area had been wiped clean. Some sources also reported wooden splinters from the paintbrush handle were recovered from the girl's vagina.

John Ramsey removed the duct tape and carried the body of his daughter upstairs, again contaminating crucial evidence. In the basement, police officers found a partial boot print and a broken window, suggesting that perhaps an intruder had entered the home and murdered the child. It was also believed that whoever had killed her had likely subdued her with a stun gun prior to committing the crime.

Authorities, though, were not so sure that the Ramseys themselves weren't in some way involved in the death of their daughter. The FBI made particular note of the fact that the ransom letter was very suspicious, as it was unusually long and verbose, had been written at the scene with paper and a pen taken from the Ramsey home, and most significantly, asked for the troublingly specific amount of one-hundred-eighteen-thousand dollars—which just happened to be the exact sum that John Ramsey had just received as a bonus at work.

John, Patsy, and nine-year-old Burke all gave handwriting samples to investigators, as well as blood and hair. Both John and Burke were definitively ruled out of having written the ransom letter, as their handwriting did not match, and though Patsy's handwriting was similar enough that investigators could not rule her out, they were unable to prove she had penned it.

From the very early stages of the investigation, there were two distinct lines of inquiry. The first of these, which seemed to be the primary focus shortly after the crime occurred and for many years afterward, was that the Ramseys themselves had killed their daughter and attempted to stage the crime to look like a kidnapping gone wrong. Those who supported this hypothesis noted the peculiar ransom letter, the perceived lack of cooperation by John and Patsy Ramsey, and other clues found at the scene, including the fact that the broken paintbrush handle used to strangle JonBenét was found to correspond to the bristle end of a paintbrush found among Patsy's art supplies.

Additionally, at autopsy, JonBenét was found to have eaten pineapple shortly before her death. Though neither John nor Patsy could recall feeding pineapple to the child, crime scene photographs demonstrate that there was actually a bowl of pineapple chunks left on the kitchen table with a spoon still in it. The bowl was found to have Burke's fingerprints on it.

Detectives who believed the family was somehow involved speculated that John or Patsy was abusive and had killed their daughter accidentally, after which they staged an intruder murder to cover up the incident. Alternately, they proposed, nine-year-old Burke may have hit his younger sister in the head with something, inadvertently killing her.

In the wake of the tragedy, the media ran with the family involvement angle, playing up the sordid "pageant culture" aspect and implying that even if the family had not killed the girl outright, then their supposed "flaunting" of her on the pageant stage may have placed her in danger by exposing her to pedophiles. The Ramseys were repeatedly raked over the coals, with every nook and cranny of their private lives and parenting skills exposed and picked over. The Ramseys were involved in several libel lawsuits over the years, particularly after Burke became the target of the media's attacks.

But although the family was the main target of the inquiry, authorities did also explore the possibility that JonBenét had been murdered by a random intruder, or by someone known to the family. To this end, they questioned more than fifteen-hundred people as persons of interest in the case, noting in particular that at the time of the murder, nearly forty sex offenders were living within a two-mile radius of the Ramsey home. There had also been a series of approximately one-hundred burglaries in the same area in just the few months before JonBenét was slain.

One of the individuals examined early on by police was a neighbor and family friend named Bill McReynolds, who had played Santa Claus at the Ramseys' holiday party on December 23rd and had a particularly close friendship with JonBenét. Though his name emerged during the initial stages of the investigation, as the Ramseys were attempting to come up with anyone they knew who might have had a motive, however slim, for killing the child, McReynolds was in relatively poor health and would likely not have had the physical strength to have administered the blow to the head that had fractured JonBenét's skull. In addition, he had a large beard, which would undoubtedly have left copious hair evidence at the scene had he been the culprit.

Likewise, the Ramseys' former housekeeper Linda Hoffman-Pugh, as well as her husband, handyman Mervin Pugh, were briefly examined, as it was discovered that Linda had recently asked the Ramseys for a loan and was denied; she could also have known the amount of the holiday bonus that John Ramsey had received, and would have had keys to the house. The Ramseys themselves, though, did not believe that either of the Pughs would have harmed their daughter.

There was also a twenty-six-year-old electrician named Michael Helgoth, who worked in a nearby auto salvage yard and had previously been involved in a property dispute with the Ramseys. Helgoth died, apparently by suicide, on Valentine's Day of 1997. Significantly, a stun gun was found near his body, as was a baseball cap bearing the initials SBTC, the same letters that the ransom letter writer had ended his missive with. Helgoth also owned a pair of boots similar to the ones that made the print in the Ramseys' basement. Some sources also reported that a few dog hairs found at the scene of the murder matched two wolfdog puppies that Helgoth owned.

There has been further speculation that if Helgoth was the killer, he may have had an accomplice named John Steven Gigax, who had been convicted of sexually assaulting a young girl some time before. Receipts and other records, however, seem to demonstrate that Gigax was not in Colorado at the time of the murder, and even Helgoth's involvement has been dismissed by a number of investigators, as many believe the boot print was not an exact match, and that Helgoth likely killed himself because of a recent break-up with a girlfriend, and not because he thought he was going to be arrested for killing JonBenét Ramsey.

A more promising suspect who came to light slightly later on was Gary Oliva, a paranoid schizophrenic who had been living as a transient and collected his mail from a church only a block from the Ramsey home. Oliva was reportedly obsessed with JonBenét, carrying around magazine photos of her in his backpack, as well as a poem to her that he had written. He was also photographed attending a memorial vigil for the child that took place in December of 1997.

What's more, Oliva was a registered sex offender in Oregon, convicted of molesting a little girl. He also stood trial later on for possession of child pornography. Perhaps even more significantly, he carried a stun gun in his backpack, and was suspected of trying to strangle his own mother with a garrote similar to the one used to throttle JonBenét. Further, a friend of Oliva's told police that Oliva had confessed tearfully to him that he had "hurt a little girl."

As of 2019, Oliva remains in a Colorado prison on child pornography charges, and though he supposedly confessed to killing JonBenét in a letter to a longtime friend, police apparently have no record of his confession, though he remains a person of interest.

Though the Boulder District Attorney's office as well as several investigators involved with the case strongly suspected that the murder had been committed by an intruder, a grand jury was convened against John and Patsy Ramsey in September of 1998, prompting some detectives to quit the investigation in protest. In 1999, however, the District Attorney declined to prosecute, claiming that there was insufficient evidence to charge the Ramseys with any wrongdoing. Several other investigators, as well as a federal judge who presided over a later libel case involving the homicide, agreed that the evidence seemed more consistent with an intruder murder rather than one committed by any immediate member of the Ramsey family.

In 2006, an American teacher living in Thailand by the name of John Mark Karr confessed to the crime, claiming he had drugged JonBenét, sexually assaulted her, then killed her accidentally. Karr was taken into custody, but his confession was not consistent with specific details of the crime scene—for example, no drugs were found in JonBenét's system—and a later DNA comparison failed to find a match to his profile. Karr was released.

Also in 2006, Patsy Ramsey, still lingering under a cloud of suspicion, died of cancer at the age of forty-nine.

In 2008, DNA evidence definitively absolved John, Patsy, and Burke Ramsey of the murder of JonBenét. The DNA profile recovered from the child's remains belonged to one (or possibly two) unknown males. A match to this DNA profile has so far not been discovered.

In 2010, the investigation was reopened. Six years after that, Burke Ramsey filed several defamation lawsuits stemming from a CBS documentary that had accused him of killing his younger sister, in spite of his earlier DNA exoneration. The lawsuits were settled in early 2019.

As of this writing, the slaying of JonBenét Ramsey remains one of the most infamous murder cases in the history of American crime, and has been the subject of countless books, documentaries, news articles, and blog posts. Speculation is still rife as to who might have killed the little blonde beauty queen on the day after Christmas of 1996, but it appears that the answer to that question might still be a long way off.

1997

In early February of 1997, a man would be randomly shot on the side of a highway in New York State, and though he was able to describe his killer to police before he died, the case remains unsolved.

It was around six p.m. on the evening of Wednesday, February 5th, and forty-seven-year-old Richard Aderson—a husband and father who worked as the assistant superintendent of the Valley Central School District in Orange County, New York—was driving his 1995 gray Volvo sedan home along Interstate 84.

At some point, he apparently became involved in a minor fender-bender, and both he and the other driver pulled over to the shoulder of the highway about a fifth of a mile from exit twelve in Fishkill. Passing motorists later reported seeing the two men arguing, but evidently none of them saw what happened next.

The man in the other vehicle pulled out a gun and shot Richard Aderson square in the chest, then jumped into his own car and sped off eastbound on Interstate 84. Richard was able to make his way back to his own vehicle and call 911 on his cell phone.

Richard described the man who had shot him as a white male in his late forties to early fifties, standing around six feet tall with a very thin build and a generally slovenly appearance. The man had a receding hairline, a scruffy beard, and wore large, aviator-style eyeglasses. Richard also reported that the man had been driving a green Jeep Cherokee, model year 1995 to 1997, with possibly New Hampshire plates.

Though police arrived at the scene quickly, Richard Aderson succumbed to his injuries before he could be transported to the hospital. A sketch of the perpetrator was immediately produced and released to the public, resulting in thousands of leads, but unfortunately none of them were to pan out. Repeated pleas to the public also yielded no significant information; though several witnesses admitted to seeing the argument between Richard Aderson and his killer, no one would cop to seeing either the original accident or the actual shooting.

In later years, rumors began to swirl that the murderer may have been a corrupt police officer from New Hampshire, but so far these stories have not been substantiated. Law enforcement is still hoping that the case can one day be put to bed at last.

****

Months later, back in Texas, the so-called Killing Fields would swallow up yet another young victim.

On the morning of Thursday, April 3rd, 1997, twelve-year-old Laura Smither told her mother that she was going for a short run along their street in Friendswood, Texas, a suburb of Houston. Laura was an aspiring dancer, had just been accepted to a prestigious ballet school in Houston, and had read that running was a great way to strengthen the leg muscles. She set out before breakfast.

A handful of witnesses spotted her on her jog, but at some point, she completely vanished. Her parents immediately panicked when their daughter did not return home, and reported her disappearance to police.

Her gruesome fate would not be discovered for nearly three weeks.

****

Only hours after Laura Smither disappeared in Texas, a man in Germany would die in what for many years was believed to be a tragic accident.

At around four-thirty a.m. on the morning of April 4th, 1997, police in the area received a report of a serious car crash in the region of Wetterau; evidently, a black BMW had careened off a country road and slammed into a tree. When authorities arrived at the scene, they found a man dead behind the wheel, his injuries seemingly consistent with a one-car wreck.

The man, forty-five-year-old Adem Bozkurt, was originally from Turkey, but had lived in the town of Bad Nauheim, in the western German state of Hesse, for some time. After his death, his remains were shipped back to his hometown of Izmir for burial.

However, in 2014, a witness came forward and claimed that the accident that had killed Adem was no accident at all, but had been staged to appear as such. This individual apparently had enough evidence of this to convince investigators to travel to Turkey and have the victim's remains exhumed, at which point they discovered that Adem had indeed been shot in the neck prior to the crash.

Though police were criticized for not initially recognizing the crime as a murder, officers defended themselves by pointing out that the firearm used in the crime was of a very small caliber, and that the bullet hole was only a millimeter across and hidden beneath the victim's hair. At the time of the crash, they noted, there was absolutely no reason to believe that the driver had not simply died as a result of the impact with the tree.

As the inquiry continued, leads began to surface suggesting that Adem Bozkurt might have been targeted as the result of a business rivalry, and in 2016, the homes of three suspects were searched in conjunction with the homicide investigation. However, no charges were laid at the time, and the mysterious case remains very much up in the air, though there is currently a reward of ten-thousand Euros on offer for information leading to the conviction of the killer or killers.

****

Later that same month, back in the northeastern United States, a truly bizarre murder mystery would begin to unfold whose every detail seems to suggest ever more improbable scenarios and whose outcome appears just as muddled today as it did when it first occurred.

Fifty-year-old Judy Smith was a successful home-care nurse who lived in a wealthy suburb of Boston with her third husband Jeffrey, a corporate lawyer. Judy had two adult children from a previous marriage, while Jeffrey had an older teenage daughter from his first. Judy and Jeffrey had actually met and started dating ten years prior, when

Judy was hired to care for Jeffrey's father after a cancer-related surgery, and the pair had lived together for three years before finally tying the knot in September of 1996.

On Wednesday, April 9th, the couple travelled to Boston's Logan International Airport for a scheduled flight to Philadelphia. Jeffrey was involved in a three-day pharmaceutical conference there, and as Judy had never been to Philadelphia before, she decided to tag along and do some sightseeing on her own while Jeffrey attended workshops and sat on panels at the conference. They also planned to stop by and visit some friends in New Jersey over the weekend, after the conference had ended.

However, before Judy could board the plane, she discovered that she had forgotten her driver's license, necessitating a ride back home to pick it up. The Smiths agreed that Jeffrey would go on and board the flight alone, as he was expected at a panel at the conference that afternoon, while Judy would take a later flight and meet up with him at the Double Tree hotel in Center City Philadelphia, where they already had reservations.

This seems to have gone as planned; Judy supposedly went home and picked up her identification, then caught a seven-thirty flight to Philadelphia, arriving at the hotel at around ten p.m. She had even brought her husband some flowers, to apologize for the trouble she'd caused.

The following morning, Jeffrey awoke much earlier than his wife and went down to take advantage of the hotel's free breakfast. He returned to the room at around nine a.m., at which point he claimed that his wife was in the shower. He told her that the breakfast was very good and that she should go down and get some, at which point she apparently joked that perhaps she should go downstairs just as she was, naked and wet from the shower.

Jeffrey then left the room and went to attend the conference. Judy had expressed a desire to see some of the sights around the city, in particular the Liberty Bell and Independence Hall. The couple arranged to meet back at the hotel room before six p.m., so they could change and go to the conference cocktail party being held at the Double Tree that evening.

After a full day of activities and sessions, Jeffrey returned to the room at around five-thirty p.m., but found that Judy wasn't there. At first he wasn't unduly alarmed, surmising that she had either been delayed in her sightseeing, or had become confused about their plans and had returned earlier and gone down to the cocktail party ahead of him. So thinking, he changed and headed down to the conference room where the party was being held, but he didn't see her; he asked some of his colleagues, but they hadn't spotted her either.

Jeffrey spent the next forty-five minutes going back and forth from the party to the couple's room, hoping Judy would return, but when she didn't, he began to worry. He went out and summoned a cab, telling the driver to very slowly drive the route that the local tourist bus would have taken, while he peered out the windows, searching for any sign of his wife. He also phoned his stepchildren back in Boston to ask if she had called them, and asked them to check the answering machines at the couple's home on the off chance that she had called there and left a message. All of his efforts were in vain; Judy Smith had disappeared.

Jeffrey then proceeded to the police station at around midnight and attempted to file a missing persons report, but officers apparently informed him that he could not do so until his wife had been gone for twenty-four hours. According to him, the police seemed dismissive of his concerns, implicitly conveying to him their belief that the woman had simply taken off of her own volition. Jeffrey returned to the hotel and spoke to some of his colleagues who were attending the same conference, one of whom was the then-mayor of Philadelphia, and the other of whom was a member of the Pennsylvania House of Representatives. They told Jeffrey they would put in a word with the Philadelphia police, and when Jeffrey returned to the station early the following morning, officers were much more receptive, and allowed him to file the report. Over the ensuing days, detectives also began interviewing witnesses at the hotel and around the area to try to determine the whereabouts of the missing woman.

According to a desk clerk at the Double Tree, Judy had approached him on the late morning of April 10th and asked him where would be the best place to catch the PHLASH bus, which made stops at all the significant tourist sites around the city. This jibed with Judy's reported plans to spend the day sightseeing. A PHLASH driver also claimed he had picked Judy up at the intersection of Front and South Streets early in the afternoon, and further said he had dropped her off near the Double Tree later in the day. Another conference attendee also allegedly spotted her in the hotel lobby, though he admitted he didn't know Judy Smith very well.

Other witnesses also reported seeing Judy going into and coming out of the Philadelphia Greyhound bus terminal, where she may have gone to use the restroom. Her family later speculated that Judy might have been in that area because it was very close to Chinatown, and Judy often sought out Chinese or Thai restaurants when out traveling. Notably, though, no one working in the establishments in Chinatown ever came forward claiming to have seen her that day.

There were a few weirder sightings of her as well, though these may have been cases of mistaken identity. For example, staff members at the Society Hill Hotel claimed that a woman who closely resembled Judy had stayed there from April 13th to the 15th, checking in under the name

H.K. Rich/Collins. Employees remembered this woman specifically because she had been behaving very strangely, reportedly speaking in tongues, masturbating in front of a hotel window, and referring to someone called "the emperor" who was going to wire her money so that she could stay at the hotel longer.

In addition, a handful of individuals reported a similar-looking woman who appeared disoriented, walking around the intersection of Locust and Broad Streets at around three p.m. on the afternoon of April 10th. This same woman was apparently spotted near Penn's Landing on the same day, acting in a bizarre fashion. Further, a homeless man in the vicinity, when shown a photograph of Judy, told police that she had slept on a bench next to him on the night of April 14th.

However, it should be noted that there was a homeless woman, well known in the area, who looked so much like Judy Smith that even her own son had mistaken her for his mother when he spotted her from across the street. This raised the possibility that many of the sightings of Judy on the day of her disappearance, particularly the ones where she was reportedly disoriented, might have actually been sightings of the homeless woman, although the homeless man who asserted that he'd seen her sleeping on the bench was insistent that the woman he saw was not the homeless woman, who he had seen before, but was in fact Judy Smith. If this was the case, the prospect arose that Judy had suffered some type of mental breakdown, a stroke, or perhaps had hit her head and lost her memory.

Over the next few days, there were a handful of other accounts from farther afield. A retail clerk at a Macy's department store in Deptford, New Jersey, for instance, stated that she had seen Judy there shopping for dresses. The clerk maintained that she had spoken to this woman, who had told her she was buying a dress for her daughter and lamenting that her daughter never liked anything that she bought for her. This unknown woman had not appeared distressed, though the clerk further claimed that the woman had attempted to get another younger woman, presumably the daughter, to leave the store with her. While it was possible that Judy could have traveled to Deptford from Philadelphia in a very short time by taking the New Jersey Transit Bus Route 400, there was no way of knowing if this woman was actually Judy Smith or simply a woman who resembled her.

Likewise, a woman who looked like Judy was spotted in Easton, Pennsylvania—more than fifty miles from Philadelphia—shortly after the disappearance, and another witness reported seeing her sitting in front of a grocery store in Philadelphia at around six a.m. a few days after Judy went missing. None of these eyewitness accounts could be corroborated as actually being sightings of Judy Smith.

Jeffrey Smith spent the next several months searching for his wife, hiring three private investigators and printing thousands of flyers, which he faxed to police departments and hospitals all around the country. Despite his efforts, it would be September of 1997 before she was found, and her discovery would only deepen the mystery of what had transpired in Philadelphia on that fateful April afternoon.

****

Back in Texas, on April 20th, the body of twelve-year-old Laura Smither was found by a father and son who were walking past a retention pond in Pasadena. The site lay approximately fourteen miles away from where the victim had last been seen jogging along her own street in her hometown of Friendswood.

Less than a month after Laura's remains were discovered, a nineteen-year-old pregnant woman named Sandra

Sapaugh was kidnapped at knifepoint in Webster, Texas after she discovered that the tires on her car had been slashed. She was thankfully able to escape by throwing herself out of her abductor's truck, and later identified her assailant as thirty-eight-year-old William Reece.

Police suspected that Reece might have also been responsible for the murder of Laura Smither, but had insufficient evidence to charge him with the homicide. He would later be convicted on the kidnapping charge, however, and as the years went on, it came to light that Reece may not only have been the killer of Laura Smither, but also of an Oklahoma City woman, another Texas woman, and an additional Texas Killing Fields victim who would disappear later in 1997.

****

A couple of months later, on June 14th, 1997, a woman named Bilynda Williams was going to a party not far from her home in Newborough, Victoria, Australia. She left her fourteen-month-old son, Jaidyn Leskie, in the care of her casual boyfriend, Greg Domaszewicz, at his residence at around two p.m. Greg was, by most accounts, quite fond of the boy, and had baby-sat him on at least eight prior occasions over the preceding few months.

Although the child had sustained relatively minor injuries, such as bruises and scrapes, while under the care of Greg Domaszewicz before, so much so that Bilynda was becoming wary of leaving her son alone with him, she evidently was not concerned enough on this occasion to find another babysitter. It should be noted also that the boy had sustained injuries while under the care of his mother as well, who actually admitted to kicking him in at least one instance when the boy would not stop fussing.

On June 14th, Bilynda had dressed the child in warm clothes, provided a bag with extra diapers, a bottle, and snacks, and left him with Greg, stating that Greg was to bring the child with him when he came to pick her up later on that evening.

According to Greg, he worked on his car all day until darkness fell, and claimed that Jaidyn had spent the time playing with the dogs in the backyard, and wandering in and out of the house through the open back door. Some later accounts contradicted his story, as some acquaintances asserted they had driven by Greg's home during the afternoon and had not seen his car there.

Greg's neighbor Alan Sparks later alleged that he had seen the child in the yard with a bloody lip. Greg had spoken to Bilynda on the phone and told her that Jaidyn had fallen down, though he apparently did not mention the fact that the child's lip had been bleeding, only that he had cleaned the boy up after his fall. Bilynda had heard Jaidyn's voice in the background during this phone call, which occurred some time around eight p.m.

Some time after this conversation, Bilynda evidently had an argument with her sister Katie. She had been planning to have Greg bring Jaidyn to pick her up and then all of them were going to go to Katie's house, but after the argument, Bilynda tried to phone Greg again to tell him to just bring the toddler straight back to her own house, as she had walked home in the meantime.

However, at this stage, there was no answer to her phone calls at Greg's residence, though she apparently called there between fifteen and twenty times. A neighbor named Mariann McKinnon tried to phone him at around eight p.m. and also got no answer, though she later informed police that Greg had always been somewhat lax about answering his phone. She later told investigators that Greg had called her at around ten p.m., though, and said that Greg asked if she had any extra diapers he could borrow and what size she thought Jaidyn would be. Mariann also claimed to hear Jaidyn laughing in the background during the telephone call.

Bilynda, meanwhile, had reconciled with her sister and ended up at a hotel bar, where she called Greg again after eleven p.m. This time she was able to get hold of him, and asked if Jaidyn was all right. Greg said something to the effect of, "Shit's happened," telling her that Jaidyn had got a minor burn from standing too close to a space heater and that he had taken the child to a local hospital, Moe Casualty, to have ointment applied to the wound. He then told her that the nurses there hadn't treated the injury properly, and that he had been obliged to take the child somewhere else.

Bilynda later stated to police that she had heard the sound of a Nintendo video game in the background of this call, and when she phoned Greg again, reportedly around three a.m. on the morning of June 15th, she thought she heard Jaidyn talking in the background, though she had been refused further drinks at the hotel bar some time earlier and might have been too inebriated to remember.

Shortly after this exchange, Greg decided to go pick up Bilynda from the hotel. According to his own account, he left Jaidyn asleep on the sofa, with the television going and the heater on. He said he had put the dogs outside and locked all the doors, and that no one else was present in the house at the time.

Upon arriving at the hotel, he noted that Bilynda was drunk, and continued to drink from a container of whiskey he had in his car. When she asked where Jaidyn was, Greg told her that he was at Maryvale Hospital, and when she asked to be driven there, Greg refused, telling her she was too drunk.

When Greg and Bilynda pulled up in front of Greg's residence on Narracan Street, Bilynda saw that the front windows were broken, though the front and back doors remained locked. Upon entering the home, Greg apparently began looking through the cabinets, but did not mention Jaidyn's whereabouts, and Bilynda could not find the child anywhere. She asked Greg to call the police, but he wouldn't; he later said that he did not want to tell Bilynda that Jaidyn was missing because he was afraid it would alarm her, though he did tell her that he suspected his ex-girlfriend Yvonne Penfold might have been responsible for the break-in. Bizarrely, there was also a severed pig's head in a flower bed just outside the front lounge window.

Greg drove the drunken Bilynda home, where she fell asleep on the floor in front of the heater. Greg left for a period of about two hours, then returned to her house at approximately five a.m. to inform her that Jaidyn was missing. He told her he was sorry that he had lied about the child being at the hospital, and asked her to come to the police station with him to report the abduction, reiterating that he believed Yvonne Penfold was somehow responsible.

In regards to the strange detail of the break-in and the pig's head at Greg's residence, it seemed that while Greg and Bilynda had been engaging in their strange song and dance about the whereabouts of little Jaidyn Leskie, several other individuals had been on a sinister adventure of their own. Yvonne Penfold, her brother Kenneth, his roommates Dean Ross and Raymond Hopkinson, and another friend, Darrin Wilson, had all been at a party nearby, and had got to talking about Greg's alleged harassment of Yvonne during their recent breakup. At some point, Kenneth Penfold got the idea that they should go to Greg's place to "give him a scare."

The group supposedly drove to the Narracan Drive residence and waited in the bushes across the street until they saw Greg leave, at which point Kenneth and Darrin approached the house, threw rocks through the windows, attempted to throw the pig's head through the window but were unsuccessful, tossed an axe handle into the shrubbery in front of the house, then made their way back to where Yvonne had parked the car to wait for them. The men alleged that they had heard Greg's three dogs barking from the backyard, but had not heard a baby crying, and all denied going into the house and taking the child. Several other witnesses who were passing through the area at the relevant time later told police that they had seen two men running down Narracan Street toward a red car at around the time Kenneth and Darrin had claimed, thus corroborating aspects of their account. None of the neighbors or other witnesses remembered hearing a child crying at the time of the incident.

Investigators quickly performed forensic searches of Greg Domaszewicz's home to try and piece together what had happened to the missing toddler. They found a small particle of skin on the space heater, consistent with the injury Greg claimed the child had sustained earlier that evening. They also discovered several blood spots on the bathroom wall of the home, which later analysis established belonged to Yvonne Penfold. Bloodstained tissues were also found in a plastic bag sitting near a wheeled garbage bin in front of the house. This blood reportedly belonged to Jaidyn.

Authorities also conducted a search of Gregg's vehicle, a green Falcon XC sedan with the plate number IRS 680. During the search, detectives found that the carpet on the floor of the car was wet, and there was a wet jacket found on the floor beneath the back seat. In addition, a wallet, which was soaked through with water, was recovered from underneath the accelerator pedal. Bilynda later explained the water to police by claiming that the window on the front passenger side of Greg's car didn't close all the way, and rain leaked in when the car was left exposed to the elements.

During a search of Bilynda Williams's home, detectives found an overturned garbage bin out front with tire tracks next to it. Inside the house, the mattress and blanket from Jaidyn's cot had been pulled out and were lying next to the cot on the floor, though Bilynda insisted that the cot had looked normal when she left the house to go to the party on the afternoon of June 14th.

Jaidyn Leskie was reported missing at approximately five a.m. on the morning of June 15th, though his body would not be found for several more months, and the resulting murder investigation would be one of the most complex and frustrating in the history of crime in Victoria.

****

Back in the United States, a macabre discovery in New York would serve as a possible early hint of the presence of a serial killer who would go on to terrorize Long Island well into the 2000s and beyond, and as of this writing, has never been caught.

It was June 28th, 1997, and a hiker making his way through a wooded area of Hempstead Lake State Park in Lakeview, New York happened upon a large, green Rubbermaid container lying just west of Lake Drive and north of Peninsula Boulevard. Inside the container was the dismembered torso of a woman, along with a floral pillowcase and a red towel.

Investigators conducted a thorough search of the area in an attempt to locate the rest of the body, but the head, arms, and lower legs of the victim have never been found. Because of a distinctive tattoo the woman sported on her left breast—of a two-inch-wide, heart-shaped peach with a bite taken out of it and two droplets dripping from the middle—police dubbed the unknown victim "Peaches."

The only other distinguishing feature was an abdominal scar, presumably from a Cesarean section. The woman was believed to be African-American or mixed race, and somewhere between sixteen and thirty years old. She was thought to have been murdered no more than three days before her partial remains were found.

After authorities published a photograph of the woman's tattoo in a nationwide tattoo magazine, an artist named Steve Cullen from Connecticut contacted police and said that he remembered giving the tattoo to a young black woman, approximately nineteen years old, who had come into his shop accompanied by her aunt and her cousin. She had reportedly told him that she was from Long Island or the Bronx, but that she was in Connecticut staying with relatives because she was having problems with her boyfriend.

Despite this promising lead, the young woman's identity remained a mystery. Then, in 2011, another set of partial skeletal remains was recovered in Jones Beach State Park, about thirteen-and-a-half miles from where the torso had been dumped. Five years later, these bones were definitively linked to Peaches, as were two gold bracelets found alongside the fragments.

What's more, the remains of a one- to four-year-old child found at around the same time in nearby Gilgo Beach were proven via DNA to be Peaches's child. The site where the toddler's remains were discovered also yielded a gold necklace and gold hoop earrings believed to belong to Peaches.

The discovery of the child's body, in fact, came about following a missing persons investigation launched in May of 2010, when authorities were looking for twenty-four-year-old escort Shannan Gilbert, who vanished after fleeing from a client's home in Oak Beach, New York.

Though the body of Shannan Gilbert was not found until late December of 2011, and her death may have been accidental, the investigation into her disappearance unearthed several more bodies that had been dumped in Oak Beach, Gilgo Beach, and other areas along the South Shore of Long Island. In all, the remains of at least ten victims (including the partial skeleton belonging to Peaches) were recovered, many of whom are still unidentified, and authorities were forced to deal with the fact that they had stumbled upon the previously unrecognized killing grounds of a serial murderer, who has been variously dubbed the Long Island Serial Killer, the Gilgo Beach Killer, or the Craigslist Ripper.

Peaches and her baby are considered victims of this elusive slayer, who is believed responsible for perhaps as many as sixteen murders in the area. As most of this unknown killer's victims were slaughtered in the 2000s, his crimes lie just outside the scope of this book, but the investigation into the case continues.

****

Later that summer, the Texas Killing Fields would again make headlines, though in this case, the victim would not be found for nearly two decades.

Seventeen-year-old Jessica Cain had been hanging out with friends on the evening of Saturday, August 16th, and the group of them apparently ended the night with a meal at the Bennigan's restaurant in Clear Lake, Texas, near the Baybrook Mall. According to her companions, Jessica left the restaurant at about one-thirty a.m. on Sunday, August 17th and got into her father's truck, which she had borrowed for the night. She subsequently disappeared.

After the truck was found abandoned along South Interstate 45 in Tiki Island, with Jessica's purse still inside, a massive search commenced, but for almost twenty years, no sign of Jessica Cain could be found.

Then, on March 18th, 2016, suspected serial killer William Reece, who was serving time on rape and kidnapping charges at Huntsville State Penitentiary in Texas, suddenly informed police that he would lead them to the bodies of two women he had murdered in Houston. Reece had already been the prime suspect in the killing of twelve-year-old Laura Smither, kidnapped from her own street in Friendswood, though there had never been enough evidence to charge him.

With Reece in tow, authorities finally unearthed the body of Jessica Cain in a field on East Orem Road in Houston, not far from Hobby Airport. Reece also led investigators to another of his victims, a twenty-year-old woman named Kelli Cox, who had vanished while using a pay phone at a gas station in Denton, Texas in 1997. And in 2015, DNA evidence confirmed Reece's involvement in yet another slaying, that of eighteen-year-old newlywed Tiffany Johnston, who had gone missing from a car wash in Bethany, Oklahoma in July of 1997.

In September of 2016, a grand jury indicted William Reece on two counts of murder, stemming from the deaths of both Jessica Cain and Laura Smither. A month later, he was transferred to Oklahoma to stand trial for the killing of Tiffany Johnston. Though the trial was initially supposed to begin on October 22nd, 2018, it was postponed until June 17th, 2019. Pending the outcome of the Oklahoma trial, Reece is set to be transferred back to Texas to face justice in the slayings of Jessica Cain, Kelli Cox, and Laura Smither.

There have been no further updates as of this writing.

****

On the afternoon of September 7th, 1997, a father and son who were deer hunting out of season in the Pisgah National Forest near Asheville, North Carolina stumbled across a set of human bones not far from the Stoney Creek picnic area. The body had been buried in a shallow grave, and appeared to have been scattered by animals. Punctures and slashes in the bra, as well as cut marks on the bones, suggested the victim had been stabbed to death.

When the skeleton was examined, it was found to belong to a white woman between forty and fifty-five years old, with extensive dental work and a severely arthritic knee. The coroner estimated that the woman had been dead for perhaps a year, maybe as long as two years.

A North Carolina doctor, who read about the finding of the body in the newspaper, remembered a faxed flyer he had received a few months before, concerning a fifty-year-old Boston woman named Judy Smith, who had gone missing from Philadelphia while on a trip there with her husband. The doctor contacted the authorities, who were soon able to obtain Judy Smith's dental records. It was a match; the dead woman was Judy Smith.

The discovery of the remains opened up a whole host of mystifying questions. How had Judy Smith ended up dead on a somewhat remote hiking trail nearly six-hundred miles from where she had last been seen alive? Stranger still, why was her body found dressed in clothing more appropriate for cold-weather hiking—jeans, long underwear, and hiking boots—rather than the clothing Judy Smith had last been seen in, which had been more appropriate for sightseeing in spring in Philadelphia? And why were there various items found alongside the body—such as a pair of expensive Bollé sunglasses and a blue vinyl backpack containing winter clothing—which appeared new and reportedly did not belong to Judy?

North Carolina police were quickly able to establish a few facts. Firstly, robbery had not been the motive for the slaying; though no wallet or identification was found with the remains, the backpack contained eighty dollars in cash, and a shirt buried nearby contained a further eighty-seven dollars in the front pocket. Judy was also still wearing her wedding ring. Oddly, though, Judy's trademark bright red backpack—which she had been wearing in Philadelphia and always carried when she traveled—was never found.

Secondly, several people in the Asheville area claimed to have seen a woman resembling Judy Smith in April of 1997, and none of them reported that she seemed to be under duress or suffering from any type of mental impairment. A retail clerk at a Christmas store, for example, said the woman had shopped there and had seemed very friendly, saying that she was from Boston, that her husband was a lawyer, and that he was attending a conference in Philadelphia. She also allegedly told the clerk that she had decided to come to Asheville, though she didn't give a specific reason.

The proprietor of an Asheville deli also came forward and said that this same woman had spent thirty dollars there, buying a toy truck and several sandwiches. And a woman who worked at the popular Biltmore Estate tourist attraction informed police that a woman resembling Judy had driven to a nearby campground in a gray sedan and asked if she could park the car there and sleep in it overnight. The vehicle, the witness said, had been full of boxes and bags. After the employee had told the woman that she couldn't sleep in her car there, the woman had driven off. None of the witnesses remembered this woman being accompanied by anyone else, though a few of them did report that she had been wearing the distinctive red backpack.

If the witness sightings were actually of Judy Smith, this would seem to imply that she had traveled to North Carolina on her own for some reason known only to her, without informing her husband, her children, her friends, or her coworkers where she was going. Curiously, Judy had never expressed a desire to visit North Carolina before, at least as far as anyone who knew her could recall, and the only other time she had even been to the state was a few years prior, when she had stayed there for a week while her husband was getting treatment at a weight loss clinic in Raleigh-Durham, about two-hundred-fifty miles away from where her body would eventually turn up.

According to Jeffrey, his wife had taken two-hundred dollars in cash with her on her supposed sightseeing tour of Philadelphia on April 10th, though she had left another five-hundred dollars in cash back at the hotel room. She had a credit card, but apparently it had not been used at any time after her disappearance, whether to rent a car or take a bus or train to North Carolina. She might have had some amount of cash and a credit card that Jeffrey was unaware of, however.

At this stage, police were looking into two distinct lines of inquiry. On the one hand, since most of Judy's movements after arriving in Philadelphia were attested to by her husband Jeffrey, there were some investigators who favored the idea that Judy had never come to Philadelphia at all, but that Jeffrey had either killed his wife prior to leaving for the conference, or hired someone to kill her after he had already left.

Those who supported this theory pointed out that whenever a woman was murdered, there was an eighty-five to ninety percent chance of her having been killed by her spouse, boyfriend, or other male acquaintance. There was also the reported refusal of Jeffrey Smith to take a polygraph test. Though Jeffrey claimed that he would take a test if it was administered by the FBI, apparently this condition was not met, and when he was asked to take one later on, he declined due to his fear that his heart medication would interfere with the results.

Police had also made note of the fact that when they searched the couple's Philadelphia hotel room, there were no female toiletries or cosmetics in the room and no dirty clothes. Judy's luggage was still there with some of her clothing in it, but apparently none of it had been worn. Jeffrey claimed that Judy had simply redressed in the clothes she had traveled in before going on her excursion, and her children informed police that Judy never wore much makeup, and what little she did wear would have been in the red backpack she reportedly took with her.

Working against the hypothesis that Jeffrey was the killer was the fact that he was morbidly obese, and would not have been able to hike the quarter-mile up the steep hiking trail where Judy's body was ultimately found. Not only that, but his movements were accounted for by numerous other colleagues at the conference, as well as hotel employees. Further, Jeffrey spent a great deal of his own money hiring private investigators and printing and faxing flyers for months after his wife's disappearance, and though one of Judy's friends told police that the Smiths' marriage was "tenuous," everyone else familiar with the couple didn't see any problems at all between Judy and Jeffrey that would have suggested he had a motive for killing her.

Lastly, Judy was apparently seen alive by her children on the evening before the couple had left on their trip, and nothing had seemed amiss. Her ticket on the seven-thirty flight to Philadelphia on April 9th had been used, the plane had held the correct number of passengers, and some of the other people on the plane remembered seeing Judy—or someone who closely resembled her—on the later flight; not to mention the desk clerk, the conference attendee, and the PHLASH bus driver in the city who claimed to see Judy on April 10th, going about her business according to her stated plans while in Philadelphia.

Jeffrey Smith died in 2005, and though he was still considered a person of interest in the murder of his wife, he was never charged in any capacity, and while his involvement is certainly possible, it seems somewhat unlikely.

The other line of inquiry pursued by detectives was that Judy was murdered by a stranger, or someone she had made plans to meet up with. Though she could have potentially been abducted from Philadelphia while out sightseeing and subsequently been taken to North Carolina before she was murdered, this seemed implausible in light of the several sightings of her in Asheville, where she appeared to be alone, untroubled, and in her right mind.

This left police with the theory that Judy had gone to North Carolina on her own, perhaps on a whim, where she then came across a stranger who had murdered her. Alternately, she may have pre-planned the whole escapade in order to meet up with someone secretly, who later killed her. It did appear, from the clothing Judy was found wearing, that she had planned the hiking trip; she also had a blanket with her, other articles of warm clothing, and some sources reported that she also had a flashlight and a paperback book. It further did not look as though her body had been dragged to the site where it was found, indicating that she had gone there voluntarily.

For a time, detectives considered the possibility that Judy had run into serial killer Gary Michael Hilton, who in 2007 murdered an elderly couple in Pisgah National Forest in North Carolina, and was later convicted of killing and beheading two other hikers in Florida and Georgia. Though the murder of Judy Smith predated Hilton's other known crimes by a decade, the area and modus operandi was similar enough that his involvement could not be ruled out. Hilton remains on Florida's death row, and has not confessed to killing Judy Smith.

The bizarre homicide case has been featured on the *Unsolved Mysteries* television program, and a reward of seventeen-thousand dollars is still on offer for information leading to a conviction, but as of this writing, police are still spinning their wheels in the investigation, and the questions concerning why Judy Smith suddenly took off for North Carolina and who exactly ended up killing her remain unanswered.

****

In early November of 1997, in a suburb of Victoria, Australia, a woman would be coldly gunned down in her driveway in the middle of the afternoon, in a shocking crime that is now suspected to have been a case of mistaken identity.

It was just after three-thirty p.m. on Thursday, November 6th, when thirty-four-year-old Jane Thurgood-Dove pulled her four-wheel-drive vehicle into the driveway of her home on Muriel Street in the Melbourne suburb of Niddrie. She had just returned from picking up her three children—eleven-year-old Scott, six-year-old Ashley, and four-year-old Holly—from school.

Suddenly, a blue Holden Commodore squealed into the driveway behind her, and a heavyset masked man jumped out. Jane attempted to run from him, but tripped and fell, at which point the assailant shot her several times in the back of the head with a large caliber handgun. The killer then jumped back into the getaway vehicle, driven by a second, slimmer man, and both perpetrators sped away. The horrified children, who had witnessed the entire incident, ran down the street to a local milk bar for help.

Jane Thurgood-Dove was pronounced dead at the scene. Because of the ruthless efficiency of the crime, authorities surmised that it was a professional hit. Initially, they focused on Jane's husband Mark as the mastermind behind his wife's killing, but the couple—who had been high school sweethearts—did not appear to be having any marital difficulties, and there seemed no reason for Mark to want Jane dead. After passing a polygraph test, he was dismissed as a suspect.

The next person of interest to capture investigators' attention was a police officer who was known to be obsessed with Jane, to the point where he had directly asked her to leave her husband for him, and had attempted to buy a burial plot next to hers. He reportedly also had a shrine to her in his home, and had based his cell phone number and his computer passwords around Jane's birth date.

Most intriguingly, the unnamed policeman failed a polygraph test, and in particular seemed very nervous when asked if he was involved in Jane's death. Though he was not believed to have killed the victim himself, he was suspected of hiring the two hit men to gun her down after she had rejected his advances.

Though he remained on the authorities' radar, there was insufficient evidence to charge him with the crime, and he was even allowed to keep his position on the police force after undertaking medical and psychological analyses that suggested he was still fit to serve.

As the years went on with no arrests made, a third possibility for the seemingly random crime began to present itself, and it is this theory that is now most widely presumed to be true. It so happened that there was another blonde woman, named Carmel Kyprianou, who closely resembled Jane and lived on the same street; most significantly, Carmel's husband Peter was involved in some intensely shady business dealings.

According to an anonymous tip, which was later corroborated by other evidence, the two hit men had been hired to kill a blonde woman who lived three houses from the corner of Muriel Street, as retaliation for some criminal deal gone wrong. Peter Kyprianou, in fact, was a known associate of several underworld figures, and had been provably targeted for death before by a man named Philip Peters, also known as Mr. Laundry. Peters served three years for conspiracy to commit murder in that case, but had been released after a plea bargain; in fact, his release from prison had occurred only a few months before the slaying of Jane Thurgood-Dove.

Jane's actual assassins were thought to be bikers from the port city of Geelong who were associates of an amphetamines dealer that Philip Peters had served time with. Apparently, the instructions they had been given for the hit were unclear, and they had mistakenly targeted the woman in the house at the wrong end of the street. Bolstering this speculative series of events was the fact that one of the suspected hit men was beaten to a pulp not long after the crime, suggesting that he had been punished for his mistake.

Sadly, by the time all of this information came out, the man who was believed to have pulled the trigger that day—Steven John Mordy, a member of the Rebels Motorcycle Club—was already dead, having succumbed to a drug overdose in September of 2001. Likewise, the individual thought to have stolen the getaway car, James Ian Reynolds, died in a supposed boating accident in 2004, before police could get to him. A third man, believed to be the getaway driver, is still unidentified, though authorities have offered leniency if he will come forward and confess to his part in the slaying. Philip Peters, hypothesized to be the man pulling the strings, has repeatedly denied any involvement.

The case remains one of Victoria's most frustrating unsolved homicides.

****

At around four-thirty p.m. on the afternoon of Saturday, November 15th, 1997, fourteen-year-old Kate Bushell left her home in the small village of Exwick in Devon, England to take her neighbors' dog—a Jack Russell terrier named

Gemma—for a walk. Her neighbors were away on vacation, and Kate had promised to walk their dog as a favor.

Approximately twenty minutes later, locals spotted Kate and Gemma walking down Exeter Lane, but at some point shortly after that, both the teenager and the dog disappeared.

When Kate had not returned home by six-thirty p.m., her parents Jerry and Suzanne became alarmed and began searching the area for her. Failing to find her, they phoned police at seven o'clock. Only half an hour later, during a search conducted by police officers, family members, and volunteers, Kate's father himself came across the dead body of his daughter, lying in a field not far off Exwick Lane, only a few hundred yards from her family's home. Her throat had been savagely slashed.

The tight-knit community was appalled by the randomness and violence of the slaughter. It didn't appear as though Kate had been raped, though an attempted rape could not be ruled out, as her clothing was reportedly "disordered." The wound to her throat had been administered by a large knife with a six-inch blade, most likely a standard kitchen knife. The murder weapon was never found. The only other significant forensic evidence recovered from Kate's remains was a sizable number of very distinctive orange fibers, thought to have come from some work-related article of clothing, such as an apron, a boiler suit, or perhaps a pair of work gloves.

Gemma the dog was later discovered unharmed, and though the animal was also examined for forensic evidence, none was found that would result in any leads.

After the slaying of Kate Bushell was made public, several witnesses came forward and reported various sightings of two different men at around the time the girl was killed. The first of these individuals was a thirty- to forty-year-old white male, of average height and weight, with dark, collar-length hair, who was standing by a blue car parked in a layby near the walking path where the teenager's body was ultimately found. Another couple who drove through the area only a few minutes later spotted the same car, but noted that they had not seen the man. This individual was sought for questioning, but did not come forward and has never been identified.

Two other witnesses separately reported seeing a man running very quickly from the direction of the field where Kate was found, somewhere between five-ten and five-forty p.m. This individual allegedly looked disheveled and possibly had blood on his clothes; he was last seen entering a nearby housing estate. The identity of this man was likewise never established.

Because the site where Kate's remains lay was a somewhat remote walking path accessed by passing through at least two stiles, authorities surmised that the killer was perhaps someone who lived or worked in the area, as the path was unknown to outsiders, but was commonly used by local dog-walkers. However, despite a massive investigation of the surrounding area, including five-thousand DNA tests, five-thousand interviews, and two-thousand vehicle inquiries, the case remains unresolved. Three suspects were arrested over the course of the early investigation, but all were quickly dismissed.

Though it seems that police are still focusing on suspects who lived or worked in the Exwick area, at least one investigator has put forward the theory that Kate Bushell may have been slain by a serial killer, specifically the same assailant also responsible for the murders of sixty-six-year-old Helen Fleet in March of 1987, and forty-one-year-old Lyn Bryant in October of 1998. Though the victims were all of different ages and lived a significant distance apart—Helen Fleet was killed in Weston-super-Mare, Lyn Bryant in Truro, Cornwall—some have speculated that because the women were all targeted while walking dogs and none of them were robbed or sexually assaulted, there is a possibility that the same attacker murdered all three victims. The latter two cases also reportedly featured sightings of a pale-colored van.

A new push to solve the case was commenced in 2017, on the twentieth anniversary of the schoolgirl's tragic murder, and the investigation is still open.

****

Back in the United States, a formerly troubled young teenager with a bright future ahead of him was gunned down in the streets of New York City.

Ali He'Shun Forney, also known as Luscious, was a transgender youth who was originally from North Carolina, but moved with his mother to Brooklyn, New York when he was still quite young. After being rejected by his family when they found out about his sexuality, Ali went to live in a series of foster homes, but eventually decided that he would rather live on the streets. He began engaging in sex work when he was thirteen years old, and began using drugs soon afterward as a way of dealing with the trauma of the way he made his living.

By the time he was seventeen, though, he seemed to be turning his life around. He got his GED, and also joined the Safe Horizon program, a nonprofit that sought to help victims of abuse and violent crime. Through their auspices, he soon became a peer counselor, teaching street kids about safety and AIDS prevention. He was also quite vocal about advocating for more police investigation into the killings of non-gender-conforming youth on the streets of New York.

But at approximately four a.m. on December 5th, 1997, Ali Forney, then twenty-two-years old, was found dead of a single gunshot wound to the head in front of a housing project on East 131st Street in Harlem. Authorities noted that his was the third murder of a transgender sex worker over the previous year and two months: twenty-one-year-old Dion Webster had been stabbed in the head in East Harlem in November of 1996, while twenty-five-year-old Kevin "Kiki" Freeman was stabbed with a screwdriver in May of 1997, in the same area. None of these murders has been solved.

In 2002, a man named Carl Siciliano, who had been friends with Ali, founded the Ali Forney Center in New York City, in order to provide aid, shelter, food, and social services for homeless LBGTQ youth. The Center now provides help to over one thousand homeless teens in Manhattan and Brooklyn every year.

1998

> Jaidyn Leskie

> Stephanie Crowe

> Alfred Kunz

> Tristan Brübach

> Lois Roberts

> Lyn Bryant

> Christine Mirzayan

> Suzanne Jovin

> Kirsty Bentley

On the first day of 1998, the answer to one mystery concerning the disappearance of Australian toddler Jaidyn Leskie would be discovered, but sadly, many more questions would follow in the wake of the find.

On January 1st, a man named Samuel Payne, who was enjoying a picnic with his family, spotted the partially frozen body of the fourteen-month-old boy floating in the waters beneath Blue Rock Dam, a site approximately nineteen miles from the house on Narracan Street in Moe from which the child had presumably vanished.

Jaidyn was found fully clothed, and there was also a bandage on the boy's arm from the elbow to the wrist; the child's arm had reportedly been broken and sloppily bandaged. A further search of the water around the dam also yielded an adult-size sleeping bag with a long crowbar tied around it with rope, and a plastic bag containing more of Jaidyn's clothing, as well as the bottle and the green apple that his mother had left with him when she had dropped him off with Greg Domaszewicz back in June of 1997. Investigators theorized that both the plastic bag and the body had all been wrapped in the sleeping bag and then weighed down with the crowbar, but that both bag and corpse had popped free of the sleeping bag at around the same time. The coroner established that Jaidyn Leskie had died from a blow to the base of the skull.

Clearly, Greg Domaszewicz was the prime suspect in the murder, and was placed on trial in late 1998. Among the numerous pieces of circumstantial evidence presented on the stand were the facts that the boy had last been seen alive in Greg's care; that Greg had behaved in a bizarre and sketchy manner concerning the child's whereabouts, even lying to his mother Bilynda Williams about where the boy was; and that his movements on the night in question couldn't be established with any certainty.

For example, at approximately three-thirty a.m. on the day of Jaidyn's disappearance, a police officer had stopped Greg as he drove his green Falcon down Lloyd Street, away from Moe. When asked where he had been, he would only say, "Nowhere." The officer claimed that Greg had seemed "cautious," and had not mentioned a missing child at the time.

Further, there was a period of about ninety minutes to two hours between the time the officer saw Greg in his car, and the time when Greg stated that he had returned to Bilynda Williams's house to inform her that her son was missing. When asked to account for the discrepancy, Greg said that he had dropped Bilynda off at home, driven back to his own house for about twenty minutes, then drove to the residence of his ex-girlfriend Yvonne Penfold to stake it out, as he apparently believed she was involved in kidnapping Jaidyn Leskie.

In addition, the crowbar used to weigh down the sleeping bag was thought to have been taken from Greg's backyard; though the implement did not belong to him, a neighbor stated that Greg had borrowed it, as well as a few other tools, some time before the murder.

There was also the matter of the wet jacket and the wet wallet found in Greg's vehicle shortly after the boy's disappearance. Though this would seem to suggest that Greg might have waded into the water beneath the dam in order to dispose of the bundle containing the body, there was a complicating issue, as his wallet was not found to contain any diatoms, which would likely have been present had the wallet been submerged in the waters below the dam where the body was recovered. Moreover, the police officer who had stopped Greg in his vehicle on the night in question had specifically stated that Greg had not appeared wet.

Many years after the murder, a witness who had been fishing on the night of the incident reported to police that he had seen a green Falcon sedan with the partial license plate IRS parked near Blue Rock Dam on the night Jaidyn Leskie vanished. This sighting seemed damning, but when police attempted to replicate the circumstances, they found that they were unable to clearly see the vehicle or its license plate in their headlights under the same atmospheric and light conditions, and they were also forced to take the claim with a grain of salt, as the witness had waited so long to come forward with the information.

After deliberating for about seventy-four hours, the jury at Greg Domaszewicz's murder trial returned with a not guilty verdict. Although jurors had been informed that they could have fallen back on the lesser charge of manslaughter if they believed that Greg had killed the child accidentally, apparently they were still not convinced that Greg had been involved in the death of Jaidyn Leskie, perhaps because they felt that there was more evidence to implicate a member of the so-called "pig's head team," who had demonstrably been at Greg's residence that night with malicious intent and may have taken the boy themselves.

In the face of an outcry from the media as well as Jaidyn's family, another inquest into the child's death was commenced in 2005, at which point the coroner announced that in his opinion, Greg Domaszewicz had been responsible for the boy's death, either accidentally or deliberately, and had also disposed of the child's body at Blue Rock Dam. Due to the double jeopardy laws on the books in Victoria, Australia, however, Greg Domaszewicz cannot be tried for the crime again, though Jaidyn's family members have been attempting to get the law overturned.

For his part, Greg still vehemently denies direct involvement, maintaining that one of the "pig's head team" abducted and killed the toddler. He has told the press that he still feels as though the child's death was his fault, however, because he states that he should never have left the boy in the house alone while he went to pick up Bilynda from the hotel bar.

The case remains one of the most controversial in the history of Victorian crime.

****

Three weeks after Jaidyn Leskie's body was found in Australia, a young girl in California would be brutally butchered in her bed, and for a time, it was believed that a member of her own household was responsible.

At six-thirty a.m. on the morning of January 21st, 1998, an alarm clock went off in the bedroom of twelve-year-old Stephanie Crowe, who lived in Escondido with her family. After several minutes of the clock buzzing loudly throughout the house, the girl's grandmother went to Stephanie's room to see why she wasn't up yet.

Horrifyingly, the bloodied body of the twelve-year-old was lying in the open doorway of her bedroom. It appeared that the girl had been stabbed nine times while she was still in her bed, then had attempted to crawl to her bedroom door for help before she succumbed to blood loss.

Because there was no sign of forced entry into the house, police initially focused their attention on members of the girl's immediate family, and confiscated all of their clothing for testing. Additionally, authorities separated Stephanie's parents from their other children—fourteen-year-old Michael and ten-year-old Shannon—who were taken into protective custody and questioned about the crime without their parents' consent and without an attorney present.

From the beginning, investigators were suspicious of the teenaged Michael, who appeared distant and allegedly unconcerned about his sister's death, reportedly playing a hand-held video game while the rest of his family reacted with anguish to Stephanie's murder. They were also skeptical of Michael's account of his movements that night; he claimed that he had awoken at four-thirty a.m. with a headache, and had gone down the hall to get a painkiller, but had not seen his sister's body at that time. Detectives were doubtful that Michael could have completely missed seeing her, as his bedroom was right across the hall from hers, and she was lying very clearly in the open doorway of her own room.

Michael Crowe was subjected to an intense, several-hour interrogation, in which officers informed him that Stephanie's blood had been found in his room, that a clump of his hair had been found clutched in her hand, and that the computer voice stress analyzer utilized during the questioning demonstrated that he was being deceptive. None of these allegations was true, but California law does allow for interrogating investigators to lie to suspects in order to elicit a confession. After a full day's session, Michael was returned to the Polinsky Children's Center where he and his younger sister were being held; then the following day, he was brought back for further interrogation.

After many more hours, Michael Crowe finally cracked and told police that he must have killed his sister because of all the purported evidence that he had done so, though he told them that he could not remember doing it, and was unable to provide specific details. At the encouragement of law enforcement, Michael wrote an apology letter to his sister, and informed detectives that he had killed her because he was jealous of her for being more popular and better at everything than he was.

It didn't help that Michael was an introverted kid who wore black, liked video games and fantasy literature, and had written a story in which a character named Odinwrath was plotting to kill his sister. Partly due to his demeanor, police seemed adamant that he was the culprit, and apparently went to ridiculous lengths to fit the fourteen-year-old into their narrative of the crime.

The murder weapon was still an issue, however, as it had never been found. As it happened, though, the mother of a fifteen-year-old friend of Michael's named Aaron Houser phoned police about a week after the slaying and claimed that a knife had been stolen from her son's collection. Investigators undertook an all-out hunt for it, finally discovering it hidden under the bed of another one of Michael's friends, fifteen-year-old Joshua Treadway. Joshua admitted that he had always liked the knife and had stolen it last time he was visiting Aaron, and on the strength of this confession, officers arrested Joshua on petty theft charges and then relentlessly grilled him for eleven hours about the murder of Stephanie Crowe.

Joshua initially insisted that he had only stolen the knife, but as the questioning went on—and as officers reportedly denied the teenager sleep and food over yet another marathon session the following day—he eventually buckled, claiming first that Aaron had actually given him the knife to hide because it had been used in the murder, then finally caving in completely and giving police the story they seemed to want: that all three boys had planned and ruthlessly carried out the slaying of Stephanie Crowe. All three boys were subsequently arrested and charged with murder.

Right from the beginning, though, the prosecution's case encountered problems. The judge presiding over the proceedings ruled all of Joshua's confession, save for the last two hours, inadmissible, on the grounds that it had been coerced. Since the final two hours were when the boy had given the detailed plan behind the murder, though, Joshua was set to stand trial first, though his confession could only be used against him and not the other two boys. Michael Crowe's confession was also ruled inadmissible for the same reason; he and Aaron were to be tried together, after Joshua's day in court.

As jury selection began in Joshua's trial, however, there was a momentous break that completely cut the legs out from beneath the authorities' favored scenario.

It turned out that on the same morning that Stephanie's body was discovered, another woman living on the same street had called 911 to report that a man who seemed threatening was following her back to her residence. When police arrived, they found that the man was Richard Tuite, a transient with mental health issues and a criminal record. Tuite was taken back to the station and questioned, and his clothing was also confiscated, but he was eventually released.

However, it turned out that Richard Tuite had provably been in the Crowes' neighborhood on the night of Stephanie's murder, and that morning's 911 call had not been the first one. The night before, as a matter of fact, two other residents of the same street had phoned to report the drifter, who was walking around the neighborhood, behaving erratically, knocking on doors, peering in windows, and asking for a girl named Tracy. Tracy, incidentally, was Tracy Nelson, a former friend of Tuite's when they were both teenagers. Tuite had apparently fallen deeply in love with Tracy, but she had not felt the same way, and he had become so enraged at her gentle refusal of him that she had been obliged to cut off all contact because she had begun to fear him.

One caller to 911 on the night Stephanie was killed even alleged that Tuite was in the middle of the street, shouting to no one that, "I'll kill you, you fucking bitch."

Not only that, but a police officer who had come to investigate the disturbances had actually pulled into the Crowes' driveway at around ten p.m. and had seen the laundry room door to their house closing, but did not find it prudent to investigate. The family had told authorities that they were actually in the habit of leaving the laundry room door unlocked, and suggested that the killer could have entered through this door without having to break in.

Though a cursory examination of Richard Tuite's clothing on the day of his arrest had not yielded anything unusual, a more thorough analysis revealed three drops of Stephanie's blood on Tuite's red sweatshirt, as well as a tiny amount on the white t-shirt he had been wearing underneath it. Tuite was arrested for Stephanie's murder, and a sheepish police department released traumatized teenagers Michael Crowe, Aaron Houser, and Joshua Treadway. Two of the boys' families would eventually sue the police department over the affair, and would be awarded substantial sums in 2011: more than seven million dollars to the Crowes, and four million dollars to the Housers. The Treadway family had abandoned the lawsuit years prior.

Richard Tuite was convicted of voluntary manslaughter in the Stephanie Crowe case in 2004, and was sentenced to thirteen years, though because he had attempted to escape from custody prior to his trial (he was re-apprehended after only a few hours), he was saddled with an additional four years. Had that been the end of the story, the Stephanie Crowe homicide would be considered a solved case, but more twists and turns were yet to come.

In 2011, the manslaughter charge was overturned on appeal, with the judge citing the lack of physical evidence tying Tuite to the crime and several other factors. A retrial was ordered, which commenced in 2013.

At the second trial, the prosecution leaned heavily on the fact that Richard Tuite was demonstrably less than five-hundred yards from the Crowe house on the night of the murder, had been behaving in a frightening and violent manner according to numerous witnesses, and likely could have entered the Crowes' home through an unlocked door. They also pointed out that Stephanie's blood had been found on his clothes, and further that he was found to have an unusual brand of cough drop in his pocket that was of the same brand as the ones that had been sitting on the Crowes' kitchen counter, suggesting that he had indeed been in their home that night.

The defense responded with the fact that none of Tuite's fingerprints or hair had been found in the Crowe home, that he would never have been able to find Stephanie's bedroom in the dark in an unfamiliar house, and that the family's dog had apparently not barked to alert the Crowes to an intruder. They also claimed that the blood evidence could have been later cross-contamination from another piece of evidence being placed in the same locker, as it was allegedly not noticed when Tuite's clothing was first confiscated. Further, they attempted to demonstrate that Stephanie must have been killed by at least two attackers, using the pattern of the stab wounds to posit that at least one person must have been holding the girl down while another person stabbed her.

Whether any of this was true or not, evidently enough reasonable doubt was engendered by the defense's arguments that Tuite was found not guilty at this second trial, and summarily released. The Crowe family was furious, but the jury had spoken. The question remains, then, whether the case is truly unsolved, or whether the killer of Stephanie Crowe simply got away with murder.

****

Early that spring, a priest would be slaughtered in cold blood for reasons which are still unclear, though everything from cult sacrifice to a crime of passion to a vast conspiracy has been put forward in the years since.

Sixty-seven-year-old Father Alfred Kunz was a traditionalist, Roman Catholic priest who served at a church in the small community of Dane, Wisconsin, approximately fifteen miles from the capital city of Madison. Father Kunz co-hosted a local Catholic radio show, was closely associated with well-known exorcist Malachi Martin, and was also involved in attempting to root out both homosexual priests and pedophiles in the diocese of Springfield, Illinois.

On the night of Tuesday, March 3rd, 1998, Father Kunz was going about his normal routine; he had just finished recording an installment of his radio show that would be broadcast the following Sunday, and as usual, his friend and colleague Father Charles Fiore had just dropped him off in front of St. Michael School, where he had an office and living quarters. It was around ten p.m. A little more than twenty minutes later, Father Kunz spoke to another associate on the phone, and at that time, nothing at all seemed amiss. It was the last time anyone would ever talk to the doomed priest.

At seven o'clock on the morning of March 4th, teacher Brian Jackson arrived at St. Michael's and unlocked the door to begin the day. As he entered the school, he was horrified to discover the body of Father Kunz lying face down in a large pool of blood, in a hallway outside his office. The priest's throat had been raggedly slashed on one side, severing his carotid artery.

Because there was no sign of forced entry, investigators believed that the killer was someone known to Father Kunz, or someone who had been able to persuade the priest to allow him inside after hours. Judging by injuries to Father's Kunz's hands, it appeared that the priest, who had been an accomplished boxer in his youth, had fought back savagely against his attacker. When police solicited help from the public in trying to find the killer, they stated that whoever had committed the crime would have been not only covered in blood from his victim's wound, but would also have facial bruising and lacerations consistent with having been in a fight.

Detectives investigated several different lines of inquiry in regards to the motives behind the slaying. Malachi Martin and others were convinced that a group of Luciferians or a Satanic cult was responsible, claiming that Father Kunz had been involved in numerous exorcisms that were kept quiet. He also asserted that Father Kunz had told him that he feared for his life only weeks before he died, and that there were ritualistic wounds on Father Kunz's dead body. Though the first allegation might very well have been true, the second was on shakier ground, as authorities insisted that the only injury to Father Kunz was the slash wound on his throat that had killed him.

There were also rumors that the priest might have been silenced by someone who disliked his vocal opposition to gay relationships between priests, or his role in helping to expose pedophiles and other sexual abusers in the diocese. Though many of Father Kunz's colleagues maintain that his connection to these high-profile investigations contributed to his death, police have found no solid evidence to support this hypothesis.

Likewise, theories about Father Kunz being a "ladies man" who was intimately entangled with one or more parishioners didn't have much of a leg to stand on either; although a handful of women did come forward, claiming to have had relations with Father Kunz, there was seemingly nothing to suggest that these alleged relationships had led to his murder.

Authorities contend that the most likely motive behind the killing of the priest was nothing more than a robbery gone wrong, and further state that the murderer probably did not even enter the church that night with the intention of killing Father Kunz. They point out that the priest's office had been robbed before, four years prior, and also noted that bags of money collected during Sunday services would sometimes remain on the premises for weeks at a time. Further, Father Kunz was well known in the community and kept to a regular schedule, meaning that someone familiar with his routine might have approached him under false pretenses with the goal of robbing him, but panicked when the priest fought back.

Several suspects along this line were examined shortly after the incident. One of these individuals was a man named Jeffrey Maas, who would later be imprisoned on theft charges for stealing various items, such as statues and candles, from churches around Wisconsin.

Another thief by the name of Robert Pulvermacher was arrested not long after Father Kunz's murder, and would later serve time for burglary, though he escaped from prison in late 1998 and subsequently assaulted a police officer. He was eventually caught and sentenced to eleven years. In 2019, though, he was thrust back into the headlines once again when he was charged with first-degree murder in the stabbing death of eighty-eight-year-old Harold Johnson in a casino parking lot in Portage, Wisconsin. That case is still ongoing.

Then there was Joseph Cavanaugh, of La Crosse, Wisconsin. Cavanaugh came to the attention of authorities because he was known to be in the Dane area at the time Father Kunz was slain, and because he had also allegedly told his father that he had "roughed up" the priest after he asked him for money but was refused. He had also reportedly asked his grandfather for money, and had likewise "roughed him up" when his grandfather said no.

Though there was no evidence to arrest Cavanaugh for the murder of Father Kunz, years later, in 2002, Cavanaugh was arrested for sexually assaulting his ex-girlfriend, stealing money from her, and then leading police on a high-speed chase through La Crosse. He never stood trial on any of the charges, however, because he hanged himself in jail before he had his day in court. Though he had remained a person of interest in the Father Kunz homicide case, DNA evidence exonerated him definitively in March of 2019. Incidentally, DNA also eliminated teacher Brian Jackson, the man who had found the priest's body, as a suspect.

As of this writing, the murder of Father Alfred Kunz remains as mysterious as ever.

****

Thursday, March 26th, 1998 was the last day of school before Easter break in Frankfurt, Germany. At a little before eight o'clock that morning, thirteen-year-old Tristan Brübach got up for classes; his father Bernd had left for work nearly four hours before, as usual. Tristan was being raised by his father and grandmother, after enduring the loss of his mother Iris two years prior.

Tristan phoned his father at work that morning and told him that he was having severe back pain, and didn't want to attend school that day. His father, perhaps suspicious of Tristan's excuse, told the boy to go ahead to his classes, and then if he was still in pain later on, he could go to see the doctor then.

Tristan appeared to comply, though on his way to school, he reportedly ran into his friend Boris, and the two boys smoked a couple of cigarettes before finally turning up for their second-period class at around nine a.m. Tristan attended classes as normal until lunchtime, but about fifteen minutes into his first class after lunch, he complained to the teacher that his back was bothering him, and asked to be dismissed. When the teacher asked what had happened, Tristan claimed that he had fallen out of a tree the day before, though later evidence suggested that he had actually hurt his back whilst engaging in a rock fight with another boy; Tristan was allegedly the frequent victim of bullies, though he seemed to prefer to keep this fact to himself as much as possible.

The teacher gave permission, and Tristan left the school grounds alone at around one-thirty p.m., taking a local bus and getting off at the Frankfurt-Höchst train station, where he would apparently spend the last two hours of his life.

At one-forty-six p.m., CCTV footage at the busy train station showed Tristan inside a shop, possibly moving toward a pay phone. There was an unknown adult male near the boy, but the footage was too unclear to determine whether the man was interacting with Tristan, or just happened to be standing there. Tristan would also be spotted twice more at the train station, both times by separate classmates, between two-fifteen and two-forty-five p.m. One of the witnesses said that Tristan might have been waiting for someone, but wasn't entirely sure of that.

It is believed that the last sighting of Tristan alive was at approximately three-twenty p.m. A woman walking her dog through a park near the train station said that Tristan had been sitting on a bench smoking a cigarette and had spoken to her as she passed, asking if he could pet her dog. She said the boy was very friendly and told her that he was quite fond of animals, a personality trait vouched for by essentially everyone else who knew him; he even had a pet rabbit named Hoppelfried back at home. This same woman also claimed that after this encounter, she had looked back and seen Tristan sitting on a bench at the park with two adult males, one sitting on either side of him. The woman stated that the men looked "foreign."

About ninety minutes later, a group of children were passing through Liederbach Tunnel, a dimly lit but often-used shortcut that lay underneath a train overpass and ran parallel to the Liederbach River. What the children found within caused them to flee from the tunnel in terror.

After the children reported their find to their teachers at the day care they had been heading toward, the teachers went into the tunnel themselves to confirm the veracity of the children's story. Seeing the carnage with their own eyes, they phoned the police at eight minutes past five p.m.

Approximately halfway through the tunnel, the body of Tristan Brübach lay, posed as though he was sleeping. A closer examination of the remains, however, revealed the horrific truth: Tristan had been beaten and choked into unconsciousness, dragged into the tunnel, then had his throat slashed from ear to ear, deeply enough that the cut nearly reached his spine. The killer had then bled the boy out into the water flowing alongside the walkway of the tunnel.

As if that wasn't gruesome enough, the murderer had then excised the child's testicles from his scrotum, and sliced substantial chunks of flesh off the boy's thigh and buttocks. As Tristan's backpack was not recovered from the scene, authorities theorized that the killer had used the backpack to carry away the pieces of the boy's body, perhaps to keep as trophies, or to use for cannibalistic purposes.

Eerily, it appeared that one of the boy's shoes had come off during the hypothesized struggle, and after the boy was dead, the assailant had gone to the mouth of the tunnel to fetch the shoe, which he then placed deliberately on the boy's posed body. The only other evidence of the killer's presence was a single bloody fingerprint recovered from near the remains.

Investigators were shaken to the core by the savagery of the crime, which was unprecedented in that region of Germany. Even more shocking was the fact that such a brutal murder had occurred in the middle of a normal afternoon in a well-trafficked area, and that the entire grisly slaughter was believed to have been perpetrated inside of fifteen minutes.

As details of the case began to go public, several individuals came forward with further details about what might have happened on that fateful day. Three children who had been planning on cutting through the Leiderbach Tunnel on their way to a soccer field that afternoon, for example, said that as they approached the tunnel entrance, they had seen a man leaning over an "object" about halfway along the tunnel. Though they couldn't see what the object was, the scene looked so odd that they decided to take the long way around rather than risk walking through the tunnel. Since this sighting occurred at around three-thirty p.m., detectives presumed that these three children, who were about the same age as Tristan, had actually witnessed the murder taking place, but hadn't realized what they were seeing.

All three children described the man they saw as being about five-foot-seven, with a lean build, light-colored eyes, and long blond hair pulled back in a ponytail or braid. They said he was wearing a baseball cap, looked disheveled or dirty, and most notably had either a harelip or a very large scar in the space between his upper lip and the bottom of his nose. Another woman who had been passing through the area described what seemed to be the same man emerging from the tunnel at approximately the same time. Police used these witness statements to produce a detailed composite image of the suspected murderer, and released it to the public with further profile information, such as the fact that he was likely in his mid-twenties to mid-thirties, antisocial with pedophilic tendencies, and may have had prior interactions with Tristan. But despite the purported killer's very distinctive appearance and qualities, no one came forward to identify him.

And the case only got weirder from there. Only a few days after Tristan's funeral, officers at the Frankfurt police station fielded a call from a man who claimed to be Tristan's killer. He said that he wanted to turn himself in for the crime, and asserted that he was calling from a pay phone at the Frankfurt-Höchst train station. He described himself as five-foot-eleven with long black hair, a very different appearance than the man seen by at least four witnesses on the day of Tristan's slaying. The mysterious caller abruptly ended the conversation with, "Arrest me."

Police officers naturally rushed to the train station, but failed to find the caller or any evidence that he had actually been there. To this day it is unknown whether the man who called was actually the murderer or simply someone playing a sick joke. Some amateur sleuths who have listened to the recording of the phone call maintain that the man sounds drunk or otherwise not entirely lucid.

As the investigation progressed, Frankfurt police fingerprinted more than ten-thousand men in the surrounding area, attempting to find a match with the bloody fingerprint recovered from the scene. As of this writing, no match has been found, and DNA evidence has likewise produced no helpful leads.

In March of 1999, detectives found Tristan's backpack in the woods about sixteen miles from Leiderbach Tunnel. Inside the backpack, they discovered a map of Germany that was printed in Czech, a language that Tristan apparently did not know. This led authorities to surmise that the map belonged to the killer, and that perhaps the assailant had indeed been "foreign," just as the woman walking her dog had stated.

The finding of the Czech-language map caused another witness to come forward. This woman claimed that she had been in the woods where the backpack was found on the same day as Tristan was murdered. While there, she reportedly came across a man who was acting belligerently, ranting about trying to find his lost sheep and divulging that he was in the French Foreign Legion. The witness also told police that this man had mentioned being from the Czech Republic.

Authorities investigated this lead, but it turned out that the French Foreign Legion already knew who this man was, and later determined that he could not have been Tristan's killer, as he was recorded as being accounted for by his army unit that day.

The case took a ghoulish turn later in 1999, when Tristan's grandmother, upon visiting the child's grave one day in October, found that someone had attempted to dig up the boy's body. It looked as though an unknown individual had come to the cemetery, laid a tarp down next to the grave, then dug a few feet down into the earth. Although this person had not reached the coffin, he had left the grave open and the tarp alongside, with dirt piled on top of it. This unsettling development was also looked into, but it was never determined whether the killer had come to the grave to "reclaim" the victim, or if some random vandal had simply targeted the grave because of the notoriety of the crime.

Later leads that were explored and abandoned included a tip from an American woman who claimed that her German ex-husband was the murderer; police eventually established that the woman was simply bitter about her ex and was trying to take revenge on him. She was fined for filing a false report.

There was also the glimmer of hope that the murder of Tristan Brübach might be related to two other similar crimes that had taken place in the surrounding area: the disappearance of eleven-year-old Annika Seidel in 1996, and the disappearance and murder of thirteen-year-old Melanie Frank in 1999. Though some aspects of all three crimes were comparable, including the fact that a witness thought they had seen a car with Eastern European license plates at the site of Annika's abduction, police were never able to establish a definitive link.

One of the more promising avenues of inquiry, at least until fairly recently, was that Tristan might have been murdered by suspected German serial killer Manfred Seel, who was actually not revealed to be a murderer until after his death from esophageal cancer in 2014.

Seel had lived what appeared to be a completely normal life, working in a printing company, marrying, and fathering a daughter. Shortly after his death, his daughter was cleaning out his rented storage unit when she discovered human body parts inside a large blue barrel. The remains were found to belong to a prostitute named Simone Diallo, who had disappeared in 2003.

As investigators looked further into Seel's past, they established that he often visited prostitutes, some of whom reported being violently abused by him. He is also suspected of murdering two women he worked with back in 1971, and in general is believed to be responsible for between five and nine murders, mostly of prostitutes and drug addicts, between the years of 1971 and 2004. He has posthumously been nicknamed the Hesse Ripper or Jack the Ripper of Schwalbach.

Authorities sought a connection between Manfred Seel and the murder of Tristan Brübach due to the similar mutilations visited upon Seel's victims and the body of the thirteen-year-old boy. All of the women Seel murdered exhibited evidence of extreme sexual sadism, with their genitals and breasts often maimed or removed altogether.

However, some detectives doubted Seel's involvement in the Tristan Brübach case, as Seel was believed to only target adult women, not pre-adolescent boys. And in 2017, these doubters were apparently vindicated, as it was discovered that Seel's fingerprints did not match the print found near Tristan Brübach's remains.

The Leiderbach Tunnel was gated off in late 1998, and in the years since the murder of Tristan Brübach, numerous theories and urban legends about the slaying have sprung up in Frankfurt. One of the most persistent is that Tristan— an independent thirteen-year-old who lived a somewhat hard life and was used to walking around unsupervised— was perhaps a drug mule or a prostitute, and that one or both of these "professions" contributed to his murder.

Bolstering this dubious hypothesis were the claims of a few other witnesses who reported seeing Tristan talking to various adult men in the days and weeks before his death, and other accounts that reported seeing the blond man with the harelip stalking Tristan or otherwise hanging around the train station appearing to follow other kids. Some amateur sleuths have even taken the detail of Tristan's reported back pain on the day he was murdered as evidence that he was being sexually abused, either at home or by some shadowy cabal of pedophiles on the street. Though these scenarios are of course possible, there is little to no evidence to support them, and many of the rumors that have emerged in the years since the crime are predicated upon exaggerations of Tristan as a neglected "street kid," when family members assert that this was definitely not the case.

The murder is still unsolved, and a large reward is on offer for information leading to the arrest of the killer.

****

Four months later, in Australia, a woman would vanish off a city street and remain undiscovered until well into the following year.

Thirty-eight-year-old Lois Roberts was a vivacious, independent woman, the daughter of a pastor and Aboriginal activist. At the age of twenty-one, Lois had been involved in a devastating car accident that had left her brain-damaged, but with therapy, she had managed to recover enough to resume a relatively normal life, living on her own in Lismore, New South Wales, and eventually giving birth to two children, who were raised by her mother and her twin sister Rhoda.

At around five-thirty p.m. on July 31st, 1998, Lois was seen on the street outside the police station in Nimbin, evidently trying to thumb a lift home to Lismore. Witnesses reported seeing her climbing into a white car, and after that, she mysteriously vanished without a trace.

She would not be found until January of 1999.

****

On the following day, in the United States capitol of Washington DC, a young intern would be brutally attacked on the street, in a crime that was initially linked to two later, and far more famous, cases.

Twenty-nine-year-old Christine Mirzayan was the daughter of Iranian immigrants, a newlywed, a Congressional fellow with the American Association for the Advancement of Science, and a graduate student in biology at Georgetown University. On the evening of August 1st, 1998, in fact, she was walking back to her dormitory building on campus after attending a friend's cookout, when she was set upon by an unknown assailant.

The next day, passersby discovered the young woman's battered body near a wooded pathway. She had been savagely raped, and her skull had been bashed in with a massive rock. Months later, it was discovered that the killer had also taken the victim's purse, placed a brick in it, and thrown it into a canal, perhaps in an effort to make the crime look like a robbery.

Though the investigation stagnated for some time afterward, the slaying was later tenuously connected with the 1999 murder of lawyer and DC intern Joyce Chiang, discussed in the next chapter, and the notorious 2001 killing of Chandra Levy, another intern from the same neighborhood who was believed to have been romantically involved with California congressman Gary Condit.

In 2009, though, the inquiry into Christine Mirzayan's death took a different turn when it was established that DNA evidence recovered from her remains suggested that she had been killed by the so-called Potomac River Rapist, an unapprehended individual believed to have committed at least nine other sexual assaults in the surrounding region between May of 1991 and November of 1997. Christine Mirzayan was the perpetrator's only known murder.

The FBI is still seeking to apprehend the elusive suspect, described as an African-American man in his forties or fifties with a medium build.

****

Later that autumn, back in England, another female victim would be stabbed to death while walking a dog in a country lane, a crime that harkened back to the grisly murder of fourteen-year-old Kate Bushell from November of 1997.

Forty-year-old Lyn Bryant of Truro, Cornwall set out to walk her dog Jay on the early afternoon of Tuesday, October 20th, 1998, but at some point along her journey, she ran across a killer. Only an hour later, at approximately two-thirty p.m., her body was discovered lying in the gateway to a field in the village of Ruan High Lanes. She had been stabbed multiple times in the back, chest, and neck, possibly with a small kitchen knife or penknife, and though she had not been raped, her clothing was in disorder, just as in the prior case of Kate Bushell. Also like the earlier crime, some witnesses reported seeing a pale-colored car or van near the scene of the slaying.

Another witness reported seeing a bearded male in a shabby white van pulled into the same gas station as the one Lyn Bryant was seen at before she went for her walk. According to this witness, the same man had been spotted around the area a few times in the days prior to the murder, and was probably not a local.

Yet another witness reported seeing Lyn speaking to a clean-shaven man in his early thirties outside Ruan High

Lanes Methodist Church between one-forty-five and two p.m. on the day she was killed. A farmer saw what might have been the same man walking through the field near the murder scene at some time between two-forty-five and three p.m.; the farmer noticed this individual because he didn't appear to be dressed for walking, and was not in an area with a foot path. None of these men has been identified.

Investigators speculated that another dog-walker murder—that of fifty-two-year-old Julia Webb of Northwich, who was bludgeoned to death while walking her dog in July of 1998—might possibly be linked, as witnesses also reported seeing a bearded man, this time carrying a cane, in the vicinity of the crime scene.

In an odd twist, investigators found Lyn Bryant's tortoiseshell glasses in the mud near the gate where her body was found, four months after her murder. The glasses had not been noticed at the time, and authorities presumed that the killer had returned to the scene to place them there as a taunting rebuke, or alternately that a random citizen had found the glasses and just left them there so they wouldn't have to become involved in the investigation.

In July of 2000, a forty-six-year-old woman named Carmen Boxwell was walking her dog near Salcombe, Devon, and reported that the killer might have actually followed her for a time, but was evidently frightened away by the growling of her Alsatian, Topsy. Carmen claimed that the man was about forty years old, tanned, and clean-shaven, wearing green corduroy pants and a blue sweatshirt, and carrying a six-inch knife. She further asserted that he had emerged from a blue Volvo, a vehicle similar to that seen by two witnesses parked near the site where Kate Bushell was murdered.

A partial DNA profile of the killer has been extracted, but no match has been determined thus far. Police also recovered some distinctive, bright blue fibers from Lyn's remains, which they believe to have come from the murderer's clothing. These fibers are of a type commonly seen in sweaters and polo-style shirts.

In 2018, there was a renewed push to solve the case on the twentieth anniversary of its occurrence, but despite new leads and a large reward on offer, the stabbing death of Lyn Bryant remains cold and unresolved.

**

As winter of 1998 descended, a brilliant and promising young woman would be viciously slain in the street near the campus of one of the most prestigious universities in the world.

Suzanne Jovin was twenty-one years old, a senior majoring in political science and international studies at Yale University in Connecticut. She had been born in Germany, to American parents who were both well-regarded scientists, and Suzanne had initially been planning to follow in her mother's footsteps, studying cell biology, but after having trouble in some of her initial science classes, decided to switch to politics, with a view to eventually going into diplomatic service.

Suzanne was a popular, hard-working student who spoke four languages, played the cello and the piano, and was active in various sports. Her friends remember her as a fun, compassionate young woman with a beautiful singing voice, strong opinions, and a fervent desire to help others. While at Yale, in fact, she became very active in a volunteer program called Best Buddies, which matched college students with disabled adults, and by her senior year, she was directing the program on her campus.

On the evening of December 4th, 1998, Suzanne had organized a pizza party for Best Buddies at the Trinity Lutheran

Church on Orange Street in New Haven, Connecticut, and after it was over, she stayed until around eight-thirty p.m., cleaning up after the function. She then drove another volunteer home in the Yale-owned vehicle she had borrowed for the occasion, and afterward dropped the car off at the lot on the corner of Howe Street and Edgewood Avenue at around eight-forty-five p.m. Suzanne then walked the two blocks back to her own apartment, which was on the second floor of a building on Park Street whose ground floor housed the Yale police substation.

Only five minutes after she arrived home, some of her friends passed by the building and shouted up to her window to ask her if she wanted to go to the movies with them. Suzanne declined the invitation, telling them she had a lot of work to do. She then sat down at her computer and wrote an email, in German, to a friend of hers, in which she said that she could loan her some books after she retrieved them from "someone" who had borrowed them. Suzanne wrote that she would leave the books in a locker in the lobby of the apartment building, and gave the recipient of the email the access code for the door of the building.

Apparently, Suzanne then realized that she had forgotten to drop off the keys to the vehicle she had borrowed and returned earlier, so she set out on foot a few minutes later to take the keys back to the Yale-owned lot. At around nine-twenty-two p.m., she encountered a friend of hers named Peter Stein, who was out for a walk. They only spoke for a few minutes, but Peter later stated that Suzanne had told him she was exhausted and was looking forward to getting back home and getting some sleep. He said she was carrying some papers in her hand and did not appear to be distressed or nervous in any way.

Another student who was returning from a hockey game also spotted Suzanne about three minutes later, though she was reportedly walking north on College Street, not necessarily the direction she would be traveling if she were going back toward her apartment. Apparently she did return the keys to the borrowed vehicle at some time between nine-twenty-five and nine-thirty.

Less than half an hour later, though, a call came in to 911 dispatchers, reporting that a young woman was lying face down and bleeding at the corner of East Rock and Edgehill Roads, in a wealthy neighborhood less than two miles from the Yale campus. When police arrived, they found Suzanne Jovin with her feet in the road and the upper half of her body lying on the grass. She had been stabbed in the neck and the back of the head seventeen times, and her throat had also been cut. Later examination determined that her killer had stabbed her so savagely that the knife point had broken off in her skull. Though Suzanne was just barely alive when authorities reached her, she was pronounced dead shortly afterward.

The victim was found fully clothed, and had not been raped. There was still money in her pocket, she was still wearing jewelry, and her wallet was later found back at her apartment; this suggested that robbery had not been the motive for the seemingly random attack. Detectives also recovered a Fresca soda bottle from a nearby bush that had both Suzanne's fingerprints and the partial palm print of an unknown individual on its surface. During the post-mortem examination, skin scrapings containing DNA were also obtained from beneath the victim's fingernails.

Several witness accounts of the possible killer were reported in the days following the slaying. A few people reported having seen a tan or brown van parked near the area where Suzanne's body was found. In addition, one woman claimed she saw a blond, athletically-built man in his twenties or thirties with a "chiseled" face, clad in a green jacket and dark pants, running as fast as he could in the opposite direction from the intersection where the remains were discovered. The witness stated that this man had peered quickly into the passenger side window of her car before running off, and that this occurred shortly before ten p.m.

A few locals also reported hearing the sounds of a man and woman arguing in the area and something that sounded like a scream, though it was unknown if this was related to the Suzanne Jovin case. There were also reported sightings of two different men seen walking near Suzanne shortly before she was found stabbed; these included a black or Hispanic man wearing a dark hooded sweatshirt, and a blond-haired white man wearing glasses and "nice" clothes.

Because the site where Suzanne's body was found lay nearly two miles from the spot where she was last seen alive, investigators assumed that she must have gotten into a vehicle, either voluntarily or under threat, and been driven to the place where she was murdered, as there was no way she could have reached the site by walking or running there in such a brief amount of time. If she had gotten into a car willingly, police theorized, then there was a possibility that the killer was someone who knew her.

To that end, investigators initially focused on a popular lecturer at Yale and a man who happened to be Suzanne's senior essay adviser: James Van de Velde, who was then thirty-eight years old. Van de Velde had a Ph.D. in international security studies, had previously done work for the Pentagon and the State Department, and was a member of the US Naval Intelligence Reserves.

Friends and colleagues were shocked that Van de Velde's name had come up as a suspect in such a vicious crime, for the man was the very picture of professionalism and propriety. Though it seemed that investigators were so keen to solve the crime that they were willing to insinuate all kinds of things about the well-liked professor—including the supposition that he had been having an affair with Suzanne Jovin that eventually went sour—there was in reality no reason to believe that Van de Velde had perpetrated the attack. There was not even a whiff of a rumor that Suzanne and Van de Velde were romantically involved, and besides, Suzanne had seemed quite happy with her long-time boyfriend Roman Caudillo, who had been ruled out of the investigation early on because he had demonstrably been in New York City on the night of Suzanne's slaying.

Though Suzanne had reportedly been extremely frustrated with what she perceived as Van de Velde's lack of interest in her senior essay, and had complained to friends and family that he had been putting her off and delaying getting back to her about discussing it, this seemed a very thin motive for murder. Van de Velde was initially very cooperative with police, offering to take a polygraph and a blood test, and giving authorities free license to search his car and apartment. Apparently, nothing untoward was discovered. Despite the flimsy evidence, however, police dogged the professor for probably far longer than they should have, and Yale University was forced to suspend him so that he wouldn't be a distraction in his classes, a move which damaged his reputation and career for quite a long time afterward.

The investigation was thereafter plagued by unexplained secrecy and inaction, and forensic examination on the palm print and the DNA evidence recovered from the scene was not even performed until late 2000. At that time, it was discovered that neither the DNA nor the palm print on the Fresca bottle matched James Van de Velde; indeed, the fingernail scrapings taken from Suzanne Jovin's body actually matched a technician at the crime lab, suggesting that the DNA evidence had been tainted.

James Van de Velde later sued both Yale University and the New Haven Police Department, and ended up with a settlement of approximately two-hundred-thousand dollars, though outrageously, the State's Attorney did not admit publicly that Van de Velde was no longer a suspect in the murder until mid-2013. James Van de Velde was ultimately able to get his career back on track, going on to teach at Johns Hopkins University.

As for other suspects in the murder, there have been very few, though a composite sketch of the square-jawed young blond man seen running away from the scene of the crime has been released to the public. There was also some speculation about a former Yale student known only by the pseudonym "Billy," who committed suicide in 2012 and allegedly told friends that he was afraid he would get arrested for the murder. Billy also spoke German, as Suzanne did, reportedly owned a green jacket like that seen on the man running from the scene, and allegedly had problems with women.

There have also been theories that Suzanne was murdered by a police officer, perhaps one that worked in the station on the ground floor of her apartment building. This hypothesis is admittedly tenuous, with only the baffling mishandling of the case and the detrimental focus on James Van der Velde to support it; proponents argue that the police department was attempting to cover up for one of their own by deliberately sabotaging the investigation.

Another possibility was that Suzanne was murdered by a complete stranger for totally random reasons, or that she was slain by the unknown "someone" who had borrowed her books and who she had mentioned in the email to her friend a short time before she died.

Some investigators have even asserted that Suzanne Jovin's killing might have been motivated by terrorism, as her senior thesis was about Osama bin Laden and Al Qaeda, though the majority of the detectives working the case consider this angle to be farfetched at best.

The case is still open, and a new appeal for information was launched in 2018. So far, there have been no new developments.

****

On the very last day of 1998, on the South Island of New Zealand, yet another young woman would disappear while walking her dog. Her body would not be found until weeks into the new year.

Fifteen-year-old Kirsty Bentley lived in the town of Ashburton with her parents, Jill and Sidney, and her older brother John. She was a creative, fun-loving teenager with a flair for poetry and drama, a girl who, according to her mother, had "only two speeds—top gear and stop."

On December 31st, 1998, Kirsty had been spending the day with a close friend; the two girls had been at the Ashburton library all morning, then proceeded to do some shopping before dropping into a local McDonald's for lunch. Kirsty was excited to celebrate New Year's Eve with her boyfriend Graeme Offord, who was planning to come over to have dinner with her family that evening.

At around two-thirty p.m., Kirsty's friend's sister dropped her off at home, at which point her nineteen-year-old brother John was the only other person in the house. John told Kirsty that Graeme had called while she was out; Kirsty called him back at about two-thirty-eight, but he wasn't home, so she left a message. She then decided to take the family's black Labrador mix, Abby, out for a walk.

John later told police that he had not seen or heard Kirsty leave the house with the dog, but a neighbor did spot the girl walking Abby down the street at about five minutes past three in the afternoon. After that, though, Kirsty Bentley's movements are unknown.

At around four-thirty p.m., back at the Bentley household, Graeme called back, at which point John realized that his sister had not returned. When their mother Jill came home at a quarter past five, both she and John began searching the neighborhood for her, to no avail. As soon as Kirsty's father arrived home at six p.m., and after several more searches had failed to turn up any sign of his vanished daughter, Kirsty was reported to police as a missing person.

Police and volunteers combed the streets all night, but found nothing until ten a.m. on January 1st, 1999. At that point, Abby the dog was found alive, tied to a tree by her leash. The area where the dog was abandoned had been searched the previous night, though Abby had not been there at that time.

Even more hauntingly, in the same location, authorities recovered a pair of underwear and a pair of boxer shorts that belonged to Kirsty; her mother had given Kirsty the items for Christmas, as a matter of fact. Now certain that their worst fears were likely to be realized, the family and investigators continued the hunt, but would not get a definitive answer to the mystery of Kirsty's whereabouts until much later in the month.

1999

- > Lois Roberts
- > Joyce Chiang
- > Kirsty Bentley
- > Jill Dando
- > Ricky McCormick
- > Sampson County Jane Doe
- > Racine County Jane Doe
- > Raonaid Murray
- > Larry Dale Lee
- > The Highway of Tears

Early in 1999, back in New South Wales, Australia, a bushwalker making his way through the Whian Whian State Forest near the village of Dunoon happened upon the remains of thirty-eight-year-old Lois Roberts, last seen hitchhiking in front of a police station in Nimbin in late July of 1998. Her body was bound with electrical cord, and an autopsy suggested that the victim had been held captive, raped, and tortured for a substantial period of time, possibly as long as ten days, before she was killed.

It appears that very little progress has been made into the murder of Lois Roberts in the years since it took place. Authorities seem to have pursued the possibilities that Lois was slain by someone who was obsessed with her twin sister Rhoda Roberts, a well-known television presenter; or that she might have been the victim of an unknown serial killer also believed to be responsible for several other murders in the Northern Rivers area that occurred in around the same time period. Some investigators have even speculated that Lois was threatening to expose a pedophile ring in the region and was silenced to prevent her accusations from coming out.

Whatever the case, the homicide investigation remains open and unresolved. In 2006, a documentary called *A Sister's Love*, directed by Ivan Sen and featuring Rhoda Roberts, was released, and was part of a wider call by the public for Australian law enforcement to take crimes against indigenous people more seriously.

****

Back in Washington DC, another young intern would go missing, in a case that recalled the savage rape and murder of Christine Mirzayan from the previous August.

Twenty-eight-year-old Joyce Chiang was the daughter of Taiwanese immigrants, and worked as a lawyer for what was then called the Immigration and Naturalization Service, or INS. On the evening of January 9th, 1999, Joyce had been out to dinner and a movie with friends, and one of them had offered to give her a ride home back to her apartment in Dupont Circle, which she shared with her brother Roger.

Joyce, though, asked to be dropped off in front of the Starbucks coffee shop four blocks from her building so she could get some tea; the Starbucks was a regular hangout of hers. The friend obliged, and Joyce got out of the car, but disappeared some time before arriving back at her residence.

The next day, a couple walking through Washington DC's Anacostia Park found Joyce's billfold, and a later search of the park by the FBI—who became involved in the case early on because Joyce was a federal employee—also turned up the victim's apartment keys, gloves, video rental card, and grocery store card. In addition, Joyce's green suede jacket was also found, ominously torn up the back.

There would be no other sign of Joyce's fate for three long months.

****

On January 17th, 1999, back in New Zealand, two men out looking for a cannabis patch stumbled across a decomposed body in Rakaia, about twenty-five miles from the town of Ashburton. Dental records identified the remains as belonging to fifteen-year-old Kirsty Bentley, who had vanished while walking her dog on the afternoon of December 31st, 1998.

The body was found fully clothed—save for the underwear and boxer shorts previously recovered—and posed in a fetal position. Cause of death was determined to be blunt force trauma to the right side of the skull.

The case caused a media frenzy in New Zealand, and many leads and suspects were ultimately investigated. Perhaps the most controversial aspect of the case was the naming of Kirsty's father Sid and her brother John as persons of interest in her murder. Authorities were initially suspicious because Sid could not provide a concrete alibi for his whereabouts on the day his daughter disappeared, and seemed reluctant to tell police where he had been and what he was doing. Likewise, John was considered a suspect because he had been the only person home in the time before Kirsty vanished. Both men were interrogated and a thorough search of the family home was undertaken, but no solid evidence was found to link either of them to the crime. Sid Bentley died in 2015, and in 2018, investigators confirmed that neither he nor John were suspects any longer.

Another man named Russell John Tully was also the focus of intense scrutiny. Tully had been convicted of two counts of murder for slaying two employees of the Ashburton Work and Income office in 2014, and further was known to sometimes camp out in the area near where Kirsty Bentley's body was found. However, police later dismissed him as a suspect after his alibi was confirmed.

Investigators also sought the driver of a mysterious blue or blue-green van seen by multiple witnesses both in Ashburton and in the Camp Gully area near where Kirsty's remains were dumped. The vehicle—a very distinctive model believed to be one of only two examples in the whole of New Zealand—was described as a 1961 Commer FC, kitted out as a camper and bearing the license plate number EP9888. It was last registered with the New Zealand Transport Agency in 1995. Despite its unique appearance, however, neither the vehicle nor its driver has ever been located.

The inquiry into the death of Kirsty Bentley remains an open and active investigation.

****

Back in Washington DC in April of 1999, an individual canoeing down the Potomac River spotted a badly decomposed body lying along the riverbank in Fairfax County. Later examination would determine that these were the remains of twenty-eight-year-old Joyce Chiang, who had vanished back in early January only four blocks from her apartment after a night out with friends. The site where the body was found lay about eight miles down-river from where Joyce had last been seen alive.

Because cause of death could not be determined, authorities initially believed that Joyce had either committed suicide or had slipped and accidentally drowned in the river. Her family vehemently disagreed, stressing the unlikelihood of Joyce taking her own life, and citing the torn jacket found in the park only days after her disappearance. In spite of their insistence, Joyce's death was not considered a homicide for many years afterward.

New life was breathed into the investigation following the 2001 slaying of DC intern Chandra Levy, a murder case that captured the national imagination due to the victim's alleged romantic links to California congressman Gary Condit and rumors of a conspiracy surrounding the killing. Investigators pointed out that the murders of Chandra Levy and Joyce Chiang did bear some striking similarities, including the fact that both victims were attractive young interns with dark hair, both lived within a few blocks of each other in Dupont Circle (though Chandra did not move there until after Joyce's death), and both were known to hang out at the same Starbucks, the one where Joyce was last seen alive (though again, Chandra did not live in the area until after Joyce was killed).

In 2011, authorities finally vindicated the Chiang family by stating that Joyce had most likely been the victim of a homicide, and not only that, but asserted that they almost certainly knew who the perpetrators were. One of them, they stated, was a man named Steve Allen, who was already in prison in Maryland for a sexual assault; while the other was Neil Joaquin, who had subsequently moved to Guyana—which has no extradition treaty with the United States—and was therefore out of reach. Investigators put forth the theory that the two men often worked as a team on the streets of DC, targeting women at random for abduction, rape, and robbery. A very similar crime, thought to have been carried out by the same two attackers, occurred only a short time after Joyce went missing.

Though no charges have been filed against the two suspects, authorities seem confident that they are the most likely assailants. Though a link to the murder of Chandra Levy is still possible, most investigators seem to believe that the two crimes are unrelated.

****

In the spring of 1999, in London, England, a crime occurred that took the nation by storm: the seemingly random assassination of a beloved British celebrity in broad daylight. Media coverage of the murder in the weeks and months afterward rivaled the frenzy following the death of Princess Diana in August of 1997.

Thirty-seven-year-old Jill Dando was a familiar face to millions of people in the UK. Born in Weston-super-Mare, she began working as a journalist for her local newspaper before making her way up to the BBC, first as a regional radio news-reader, then onto a national platform as a TV presenter on such programs as *Breakfast Time*, *Breakfast News*, several other daily newscasts, and the travel show *Holiday*. The BBC had even named her their Personality of the Year in 1997. By the time 1999 rolled around, however, she was probably most famous for co-hosting the popular *Crimewatch* series, which she had been presenting with Nick Ross since 1995.

On the morning of Monday, April 26th, 1999, Jill left the home of her fiancé, gynecologist Alan Farthing, in Chiswick. The couple had announced their engagement the previous January, and their wedding was set to take place on September 25th of 1999.

Jill drove back to the house she owned in Fulham, in southwest London. She wasn't really living there anymore; the property had been put up for sale that month, and Jill was in the process of moving out.

At a little past eleven-thirty a.m., Jill approached the front door of her former home, and then, quite suddenly, a man grabbed her from behind, forced her down to the ground, and shot her in the left temple at point blank range before vanishing back into the surrounding landscape. The body of Jill Dando was found by a neighbor fifteen minutes later.

When police arrived on the scene, they found very little physical evidence to identify the killer or the motive for the slaying. Jill Dando had died from a single bullet wound to the head, fired from a 9mm semi-automatic pistol, which had actually been either a modified starter pistol or a decommissioned firearm that someone had restored to usability.

A canvass of the neighborhood produced only one sighting of the assailant, described as a six-foot-tall white man who was about forty years of age. No one had heard a gunshot, though next-door neighbor Richard Hughes— the only person who had caught a glimpse of the killer— said that he had heard Jill exclaim in what sounded like a friendly manner, as though she had been suddenly approached by someone she knew.

Though the area Jill had traveled through that day was awash in CCTV cameras, an examination of the footage seemed to rule out the possibility that the victim had been followed on the day of her death.

The whole of Britain was terribly shaken by the senseless murder of a woman who was so familiar to so many, and Metropolitan Police were under immense pressure to get to the bottom of the case. The investigation into Jill Dando's death was dubbed Operation Oxborough, but despite countless man-hours devoted to chasing down leads, the inquiry went nowhere for nearly a year.

Then, acting on a tip, police began to look into a man named Barry George, who lived only about five-hundred yards from Jill's home in Fulham and had something of a checkered past. George was no stranger to the system; when younger, he had been a student at a boarding school for children with emotional problems, and had previously been arrested for impersonating a police officer, indecent assault, and attempted rape. He had even once been picked up hiding in the bushes in front of Kensington Palace—then the residence of Prince Charles and Princess Diana—dressed in military gear and carrying a knife and a weird poem addressed to Charles. Further, George had been diagnosed with several disorders—including epilepsy, ADHD, Asperger syndrome, and antisocial personality disorder, among others—and had a tested IQ of seventy-five.

After placing Barry George under surveillance for a time, police finally arrested him in May of 2000 and charged him with Jill Dando's murder.

At the ensuing trial, much was made of George's prior convictions and bizarre behavior, and the prosecution also leaned hard on the fact that a search of George's flat had uncovered four copies of the memorial issue of *Ariel* magazine featuring Jill Dando on the cover. A forensic specialist, moreover, testified that there was a single particle which was possibly firearm residue discovered in the pocket of George's overcoat.

In July of 2001, Barry George was found guilty, despite his protestations of innocence, and sentenced to life in prison.

After several appeals, though, he was granted a retrial in 2008, and at this second trial, he was acquitted and released. At issue this second time around was the fact that the supposed firearm residue was too small of a sample to be of any use as evidence, and the further supposition that George was not intelligent or organized enough to carry out what appeared to be a fairly efficient and professional assassination.

After Barry George's exoneration, rumors about who might have really killed Jill Dando reached a fever pitch, with some of the scenarios more plausible than others. One of the most enduring hypotheses maintains that Jill was murdered by a Serb hit man in retaliation for hosting a BBC television appeal for refugees fleeing the Kosovo War and the regime of Slobodan Milosevic. The BBC program, which aired nearly three weeks before Jill Dando was slain, raised about one-million pounds.

Proponents of this theory also point to the fact that only a few days before the murder, American and British warplanes had bombed the Radio Television Serbia building in Belgrade, an action that killed sixteen staff members. Tony Hall, then the head of news at the BBC, also claimed that he received a phone call after Jill's death in which a man with an Eastern European accent told him, "Your prime minister Blair butchered innocent young people. We butcher back."

Though this angle was thoroughly investigated and has subsequently been largely dismissed, there are a handful of detectives who still believe it is worth pursuing.

Other avenues of inquiry examined in regards to assassination included the possibility that Jill was silenced by someone at the BBC who apparently did not want her to reveal information she had about a purported pedophile ring at the organization; or the prospect that she was targeted by someone in organized crime after exposing or facilitating the arrest of a suspect featured on the *Crimewatch* program. A few commentators have even speculated that she might have been murdered by a faction of the IRA.

Authorities have also not ruled out more mundane explanations, such as a case of mistaken identity, a botched robbery, the actions of a stalker or obsessed fan, or murderous jealousy on the part of a professional rival. Police also looked into Jill's private life to determine whether an ex-boyfriend or potential suitor might have killed her, but found no evidence to support this.

No other suspects have come to light in the decade since the release of Barry George, and some investigators have publicly opined in the press that the case may never be solved. Jill Dando's legacy lives on, however; a memorial garden dedicated to her stands in her hometown of Weston-super-Mare, a broadcast journalism scholarship in her name is offered to one student every year at University College Falmouth, and in 2001, the Jill Dando Institute of Crime Science was founded at University College London.

****

In late June of 1999, a death would take place in the American Midwest whose details were not excessively remarked upon at the time, though the announcement of a mysterious and still unbroken code discovered on the victim's person would later launch the case into widespread Internet infamy.

Forty-one-year-old Ricky McCormick had been a rather aimless soul throughout his life. A high school dropout who was barely literate and suffered from chronic lung and heart issues, Ricky had spent most of his adulthood living with relatives and bouncing from low-level job to low-level job, even spending some time in prison for statutory rape at one point. In 1999, he was staying with his elderly mother, and possibly unemployed, though some sources have him working part-time at an Amoco gas station in St. Louis, Missouri.

On June 30th, a woman driving along a road off Route 367 in West Alton spotted a dead body lying in a cornfield and reported it to police. The decomposed remains were found to belong to Ricky McCormick, who was believed to have died three days before, although the state of decomposition suggested that he had been dead much longer. Because the body was so degraded, in fact, authorities were unable to determine cause of death, and initially were reluctant to attribute Ricky's demise to homicide.

A few more strange details about the case surfaced in the days following the discovery. First of all, it was unknown how Ricky had ended up in a field at least fifteen miles away from his last known address; he did not own a car, and no public transportation served the area where his body was found. This bolstered the theory that the victim had been murdered, as it was hypothesized that his assailant might have dumped him there after killing him somewhere else.

Secondly, according to his family—who had never reported him missing—Ricky had been acting a little odd in the days before his death, as though he was afraid someone might be after him. On June 25th, 1999, he had gone to the emergency room at Forest Park Hospital in St. Louis and complained of chest pains and shortness of breath. He spent two days at the hospital under observation, and after his release went to stay with his aunt Gloria. The following day, he went to another emergency room at a different hospital with the same complaint, and though they released him in under an hour, he reportedly hung around the hospital anyway, sleeping overnight in the waiting room. According to Gloria, Ricky was acting as though he was trying to stay somewhere safe.

Upon looking further into Ricky's activities in the days before his death, authorities stumbled upon what might have been a motive for the murder. The gas station where Ricky reportedly worked was owned by a drug dealer named Juma Hamdallah, and it was speculated that Ricky might have been acting as a drug mule for his boss's operation. According to a statement by Ricky's girlfriend Sandra, Ricky often took a Greyhound bus to Orlando, Florida to pick up drugs, and that on the trip he took shortly before his death, he may have made some unforgivable mistake that put a target on his back.

Another drug dealer named Gregory Knox, who lived in the same housing complex as Ricky, was also investigated, and though this angle seemed very promising, in the end there was not enough evidence to charge anyone with the crime.

Had that been all there was to the case, then it's likely the murder of Ricky McCormick would have been sadly forgotten. But then, twelve years after the victim's body was found, the FBI made a public appeal for help. They admitted that they had found two pieces of paper in the pocket of Ricky's pants, and these notes appeared to be written in code. FBI cryptanalysts had been working on cracking the cipher for more than a decade, but had had no success, hence their desperate plea to find a member of the public who might be able to solve the mystery.

The code, if that was what it was, consisted of two pages of what seemed to be paragraphs, with some lines set apart with parentheses, and some sections separated by something like word bubbles. Standard code-breaking techniques yielded nothing close to a solution, and investigators were frustrated by the fact that the question of who killed Ricky McCormick might be encoded right in front of their faces.

Theories about the encrypted notes abound. While some adhere to the theory that Ricky McCormick wrote the code himself—perhaps as instructions pertaining to his last alleged drug pickup—it was widely reported that Ricky was illiterate, and according to some family members, only wrote in scribbles or couldn't write anything other than his own name. However, a few other family members did mention that Ricky was known to write in ciphers ever since he was a child, and the possibility remains that his learning disabilities had encouraged him to develop a kind of shorthand that only he understood. If this is the case, then it's likely the code will never be solved.

On the other hand, some have surmised that the killer wrote the note, either as a coded set of directions, or just as a weird, meaningless clue to throw investigators off his trail. It's also plausible that Ricky was simply carrying the coded message from one criminal to another, and personally had no idea what it might have said. Considering that the best minds in the FBI have been attempting to decipher the code since 1999, however, and since amateur cryptographers around the world have been trying their hand at it since it went public in 2011, it seems unlikely that someone hasn't cracked it by now, if it was indeed a standard type of code.

The FBI established a separate website for those wishing to attempt to decipher Ricky McCormick's notes, and as of this writing, more than seven-thousand people have submitted possible solutions, but the code remains one of the most notorious unbroken ciphers at the FBI's Cryptanalysis and Racketeering Records Unit, alongside the thus-far uncracked codes written by the Zodiac Killer.

****

Nearly a month later, in North Carolina on July 20th, a man riding an all-terrain vehicle in the woods near Dunn came across the decomposed body of a young woman who remains unidentified to this day.

The victim, discovered beneath an old mattress, was believed to be white or Hispanic, between seventeen and twenty-five years old, standing between five-foot-four and five-foot-seven, with a slim build, excellent dental health, and long, curly, auburn-colored hair. A post-mortem established that she had probably died about two months prior to her body being found, most likely from a stab wound in her neck.

The victim, later dubbed Sampson County Jane Doe, was clad in a black or navy blue spaghetti-strap tank top, green Calvin Klein jeans, a lacy and padded navy blue bra, lavender-colored underwear with lace around the edges, and a copper- or gold-colored L'Elle brand watch. Her fingernails were painted with an iridescent, blue-green polish. White sandals were also recovered from near the remains and believed to belong to the victim.

The Inez Labor Camp near where the body was found was known to be an area where sex workers plied their trade, so it has been speculated that the victim might have been working as a prostitute.

The identity of both Sampson County Jane Doe and her killer are still unknown.

****

The very next day, yet another unidentified dead woman would be found, this time in Wisconsin.

On July 21st, 1999, two individuals happened upon the remains in a field not far from the town of Raymond in Racine County. The victim would thus be christened Racine County Jane Doe, or more informally as Crystal Rae.

The victim in this case appeared to have suffered from neglect, malnourishment, and abuse for quite a long time before her death, which was estimated to have occurred only about a day before her body was found. She was a white woman, believed to be between eighteen and thirty-five years old, standing around five-foot-eight and weighing around one-hundred-twenty pounds. She had curly, reddish-brown hair that was collar-length and had blonde highlights throughout.

Her teeth were found to be in poor shape; several of them were decayed, and a few were missing. She also had a cauliflower ear, perhaps indicative of intense physical abuse perpetrated against her while she was alive. Her body was also found to have many old cuts and bruises, as well as a broken nose, strengthening the assertions that she had been regularly beaten and sexually assaulted. There was also some speculation that she might have been mentally disabled.

When found, she was clad in a men's gray button-up shirt with floral embroidery on the front, and a pair of black sweat pants, though no shoes were ever found.

In 2013, the victim's remains were exhumed, and a later isotopic analysis was able to establish that Racine County Jane Doe probably hailed from somewhere in Montana, Alaska, or southern Canada. Though authorities held a press conference and announced that further evidence was found, there has been no more information released to the public about the identity of Crystal Rae or that of her suspected murderer.

****

As summer began fading into autumn, a teenage girl would be attacked and murdered on the street, only yards from her home in Ireland.

Seventeen-year-old Raonaid Murray lived in Glenageary, South Dublin, with her parents and two older siblings. She had done well in school, and was planning to go on to University College Dublin, possibly to become a writer. In the meantime, she was working part-time at a ladies' fashion boutique in the coastal town of Dún Laoghaire.

On Friday, September 3rd, 1999, Raonaid left work at about nine p.m. and walked to Scotts pub across the street to socialize with friends, and perhaps to see her boyfriend, who worked there. She left the pub at a little before eleven-thirty and began walking back toward home, a distance of only about a mile.

Less than a half-hour later, witnesses heard a woman's voice saying, "Leave me alone," "go away," and "fuck off;" the voice seemed to be coming from a back lane near Silchester Road. At approximately twelve-twenty a.m. on the morning of September 3rd, Raonaid's sister, out walking with friends near the family home, spotted Raonaid lying dead in the road, only fifty yards from their front door.

Raonaid Murray had been stabbed more than thirty times in the side, chest, and shoulder with a small kitchen knife. It appeared that she had managed to walk about two-hundred yards from the site of the stabbing before she collapsed and succumbed to blood loss.

The area where Raonaid was murdered was a fairly affluent neighborhood in the region with the lowest homicide rate in Dublin, and residents were horrified by the random brutality of the crime. Over the course of the investigation, the Gardaí interviewed approximately three-thousand persons of interest and made at least twelve arrests, but were never able to come up with enough solid evidence to charge anyone with the slaying. Raonaid's boyfriend was immediately dismissed as a suspect, as CCTV footage clearly showed him working at Scotts pub all that night.

The first significant suspect to draw the attention of authorities was a young man who had reportedly been seen arguing with Raonaid in Glenageary Road Upper shortly before she was killed. This individual was said to be in his mid-twenties, standing about five-foot-seven, with sandy blond hair cut in a shaggy style resembling that of Noel Gallagher of Oasis, and clad in a beige shirt and light-colored combat pants.

Another suspicious young man was allegedly picked up by a taxi driver in the center of Dún Laoghaire in the early hours of Saturday morning. The driver told police that his passenger appeared to have blood spattered on his pants, and asked to be taken to what the driver believed was a fake address. This young man apparently acted very strangely after exiting the cab, lurking around near a bush as though waiting for the driver to leave.

Police later identified this man as a cook who worked in an area restaurant. Though there was not enough evidence to charge him with the murder of Raonaid Murray, he was arrested in 2000 in Wicklow for assaulting another young woman.

Yet another man investigated for the slaying was Kenyan immigrant Farah Swaleh Noor, who would infamously be murdered himself in March of 2005 by so-called "Scissor Sisters" Linda and Charlotte Mulhall, who also dismembered his body. Noor's name came up because he allegedly threatened to kill Linda and Charlotte's mother Kathleen, "just like I did with Raonaid Murray." Noor, it should be noted, was reportedly drunk when he made the statement, and no further evidence was found that pointed toward his guilt.

Investigators could also not rule out the possibility that Raonaid was killed by a woman, as many of the stab wounds were very shallow. One unnamed woman with purported family ties to the IRA and a violent personality was interrogated, but subsequently dismissed. Notably, female DNA was found underneath Raonaid's fingernails, though this DNA did not match the female suspect, and it is not certain whether the DNA even came from the killer, or was simply there due to Raonaid's work at the ladies' boutique.

Several other shady characters around Dún Laoghaire were also questioned, including a few others who made confessions—perhaps false ones—that they had killed Raonaid. And in later years, detectives looked into the hypothesis that Raonaid might have been murdered by Dublin architect Graham Dwyer, who in 2015 would be convicted of murdering thirty-six-year-old child care worker Elaine O'Hara, last seen alive in a public park in Dublin in August of 2012. DNA analysis, however, seemed to rule out Dwyer as a suspect in the slaying of Raonaid Murray.

The murder of the seventeen-year-old is one of the most iconic unsolved crimes in Ireland, and it remains uncertain whether Raonaid was killed by a random stranger or by someone she knew. The investigation is ongoing.

****

A few days after Christmas of 1999, an American journalist would be mysteriously slain in Guatemala, one of thirty-seven journalists murdered that year, though the motives behind his killing are still unclear.

Forty-one-year-old Larry Dale Lee was originally from Rockford, Illinois, but spent most of his formative years in the small town of Doniphan, Missouri. After obtaining his graduate degree in journalism in 1987, he went on to work for numerous different newspapers in Florida, Texas, Arkansas, and Tennessee. In 1998, he took a position for the second-largest financial news agency in the world, Bridge-News, and moved to Guatemala to act as a correspondent.

After a little more than a year on the job, however, Larry was apparently growing tired of reporting on financial matters, and reportedly told friends that he was planning on selling most of his things and moving to Mexico City, with a view to perhaps getting more into social services. He filed his last story for BridgeNews, about the Guatemalan presidential election, at approximately ten-thirty p.m. on December 26th, 1999.

Two days later, a friend dropped by Larry's apartment in Zone 1 of Guatemala City, but received no answer to his knocks. The friend fetched a janitor to unlock the front door, at which point he discovered Larry Dale Lee lying dead on his bed. He was naked, and had been viciously slashed several times across the throat, chest, back, and wrists.

The investigation into the journalist's death apparently left a great deal to be desired, with some sources reporting that police never even bothered to check the apartment for fingerprints and may have contaminated the crime scene. There were also so many varying lines of inquiry in regards to a motive that the case seemed doomed from the start.

Since Larry was a journalist, the possibility had to be considered that he was murdered for something he had written that someone didn't approve of. Though much of his work centered on money matters, he did write about politics and their intersection with other social and financial issues. He had, in fact, recently penned an article about a former Guatemalan leader and allegations of human rights abuses against him.

As the investigation progressed, detectives also discovered that Larry was gay, which gave them another possible angle to pursue. Though Larry had been out to his friends since 1993, his family was not aware of his sexuality. Police speculated that Larry might have been slain by a current or former lover, or perhaps was the target of a hate crime.

Then again, it was also plausible that Larry had not been specifically targeted at all, but was simply the victim of a robbery or a random attack. The fact that his neighborhood was allegedly fairly dangerous and didn't house a lot of foreigners might have made him an appealing mark, as did the fact that he had advertised some of his possessions for sale in preparation for his move to Mexico, which might have attracted the attention of violent thieves.

Sadly, the murder of Larry Dale Lee seems to have been all but forgotten, and the slapdash investigation by Guatemalan authorities makes it unlikely the crime will ever be resolved.

****

Only hours before 1999 came to a close, the Highway of Tears saw fit to devour one more innocent victim.

Eighteen-year-old Monica McKay was hanging out with friends on New Year's Eve in Prince Rupert, British Columbia, Canada, but apparently left them before midnight struck. Two days later, her family reported her missing after she failed to return home.

A little over a week into the year 2000, on January 8th, the girl's dead body was discovered lying next to a dumpster. Detectives are unsure whether Monica's death is linked to the other Highway of Tears murders, but in any event, no suspects have ever been identified, and her slaying remains unsolved, just like all the cases discussed throughout the course of this series.

About the Author

Jenny Ashford is a writer, graphic designer, and podcaster. Her works include three volumes of the true crime collection *The Faceless Villain*; four paranormal nonfiction books: *House of Fire and Whispers: Investigating the Seattle Demon House*, and *The Rochdale Poltergeist* (both with parapsychologist Steve Mera); *The Mammoth Mountain Poltergeist* (with poltergeist focus Tom Ross); and *The Unseen Hand: A New Exploration of Poltergeist Phenomena*. She has also written three horror novels: *Red Menace*, *Bellwether*, and *The Five Poisons*; two short story collections, *Hopeful Monsters* and *The Associated Villainies*; and a graphic novel, *The Tenebrist*.

She co-hosts a podcast with Tom Ross called 13 O'Clock, on which they discuss true crime, paranormal topics, and other unexplained mysteries. Find her online at www.jennyashford.com or at goddessofhellfire.com, and listen to 13 O'Clock on iTunes, Wordpress, and other podcast outlets, or watch the show on YouTube at 13OClockPodcast.

Bibliography

"11th Red-Haired Victim Found in Series of Baffling Homicides." *Daily News*. April 17, 1985.

"20-Year Murder Mystery: Kirsty's Mum Breaks Her Silence." *Woman's Day*. August 10, 2016.

"20 Years Later, Detectives Have Information To Share On Amber Hagerman Case." *21 CBS DFW*. January 11, 2016.

"25 Years Later: Murder of 4 Austin Teens Still Unsolved." *KXAN.com*. December 6, 2016.

"1323UFNY - Unidentified Female." *The Doe Network*. May 17, 2017.

"151UFNY - Unidentified Female." *The Doe Network*. May 17, 2017.

"154UFCO - Unidentified Female." *The Doe Network*. December 12, 2018.

"The 1994 Heinous Murder of Young Mother Tracey Mertens." *True Crime Diva*. February 19, 2018.

"204UFNC - Unidentified Female." *The Doe Network*. October 14, 2017.

"213UFWY - Unidentified Female." *The Doe Network*. February 24, 2019.

"218UMNY - Unidentified Male." *The Doe Network*. December 11, 2018.

"299UMTX - Unidentified Male." *The Doe Network*. May 10, 2018.

"390UFWY - Unidentified Female." *The Doe Network*. February 24, 2019.

"431UFMO - Unidentified Female." *The Doe Network*. May 2, 2018.

"443UFCA - Unidentified Female." *The Doe Network*. August 13, 2018.

"46UFSC - Unidentified Female." *The Doe Network.* November 8, 2018.

"49UFFL - Unidentified Female." *The Doe Network.* January 28, 2018.

"558UFNC - Unidentified Female." *The Doe Network.* January 14, 2019.

"A1 Murder: Police Issue Appeal Over 1983 Killing of Janice Weston." *BBC News.* September 11, 2018.

"A&R Exec Cantor Slain." *Variety.* August 3, 1993.

Abbott, Matt C. "Did Hanged Rapist Kill Wisconsin Priest?" *Renew America.* January 28, 2006.

Abbott, Matt C. "New Information on Father Alfred Kunz Murder." *Church Militant.* October 11, 2018.

"After Discovery of Taegu Remains, Cause of Death Still Uncertain." *Korea Times.* September 28, 2011.

Agrawal, Nina. "20 Years Later, JonBenet Ramsey Murder Remains Unsolved. Why?" *Los Angeles Times.* December 29, 2016.

"Akron Death Linked With Other Killings." *AP News.* November 25, 1991.

Alderson, Andrew. "New Witness: Julie Ward was Gang Raped Then Killed." *The Telegraph.* June 5, 2004.

Aldrich, Marta W. "Officials Puzzle Over String of Redhead Murders." *Associated Press.* April 25, 1985.

Alexander, Phil. "Gov. Hunt OKs Reward for Case." *Asheville Citizen-Times.* July 21, 1999.

Allman, Megan. "Her Body Was Found on the Side of I-40 in Hillsborough in 1990. Do You Know Who She Is?" *WFMY News 2.* July 11, 2018.

Alpert, Lukas I. "FBI Seeks Public's Help to Crack Killer's Cryptic Code in 1999's Unsolved Murder of Ricky McCormick." *New York Daily News.* March 30, 2011.

Altimari, Dave; Owens, David. "Strong Push On To Solve 1998 Slaying Of Yale Student Suzanne Jovin." *Hartford Courant*. September 26, 2017.

Altman, Howard; Lewis, Frank. "City Beat: Found." *Philadelphia City Paper*. October 2–9, 1997.

Anderson, Christopher. "Burke Ramsey Not Suspect in Killing, DA's Office Says." Daily Camera. May 21, 1999.

Anderson, Mike. "Investigators Still Believe Racine County Jane Doe Case Can Be Solved." *WISN*. October 17, 2013.

Andrews, Suzanna. "Murder Most Yale." *Vanity Fair*. August 1999.

Anthony, Shane. "Body Found in Field Puzzles Police." *St. Louis Post Dispatch*. July 2, 1999.

"Anvers: Sur la Piste de Kim et Ken." *Le Soir*. January 17, 1994.

"Appeal on 20th Anniversary of County Durham Woman Death." *BBC News*. August 3, 2010.

"Appeal Planned." *Montreal Gazette*. March 6, 1986.

Armstrong, Jeremy. "Durham Police's Only Unsolved Murder Raises Questions 25 Years On." *Chronicle Live*. August 8, 2015.

Arntfield, Michael. *Murder City: The Untold Story of Canada's Serial Killer Capital, 1959-1984*. FriesenPress, 2015.

"Arrest Made Raises Hope for Unsolved Murder of Holly Piirainen." *Boston 25 News*. September 25, 2017.

Ashby, Cary. "Unsolved Amy Mihaljevic Kidnapping and Murder Case to be Featured on TV." *Norwalk Reflector*. December 7, 2018.

"At a Glance: A 20-Year Timeline of David Bain." *Newshub*. June 18, 2014.

Atsiaya, Peter. "Key Witness to Julie Ward's Murder Dies." *The Standard*. December 24, 2009.

Babay, Emily. "10th Attack From 1990s Linked to Potomac River Rapist." *Washington Examiner*. June 14, 2012.

"Bain Father and Son Were Suspects." *Otago Daily Times*. March 26, 2009.

Baker, Trevor. "Still Rockin' and Rollins." *The Guardian*. February 2, 2008.

Bandler, Jonathan. "Archive: New Focus Put on Case of Stacey Boothe-Wilson, Mother Missing Since '94." *Lohud. com*. February 27, 2019.

Banerjee, Sidharth. "The Elvis of Punjab." *The Times of India*. July 24, 2016.

Barber, Haylee. "The Amber Behind Amber Alert Still Waiting for Justice 20 Years Later." *NBC News*. January 17, 2016.

Barber, Randy. "Detective: Fingerprints Didn't Belong to Masters." *9news.com*. January 21, 2009.

Barcelona, Ainhoa. "Who Killed Jill Dando? Hitman Claims He Knows Who Murdered Her." *Hello!* April 2, 2019.

Barker, Dennis. "Jill Dando: Broadcaster With Feel-Good Factor." *The Guardian*. April 27, 1999.

Barkham, Patrick. "Julie Ward Death Report Was False, Says Pathologist." *The Guardian*. April 27, 2004.

Barkham, Patrick. "MI6 Agent Hid Role in Julie Ward Murder Case." *The Guardian*. April 30, 2004.

Barlass, Tim. "Murdered Penny's Home is Ransacked." *Evening Standard*. February 11, 1992.

Barnes, Mike. "Paul Cantor, Agent, Manager and Record Label Exec, Dies at 86." *The Hollywood Reporter*. January 29, 2014.

"Baroness Cleared of Murder Charge." *The Herald*. August 2, 1989.

Barrett, Hywel. "Hunt for Killer Continues After 30 Years Since Woman Was Found at Side of A1 Near Huntingdon." *The Hunts Post*. February 7, 2013.

Barton, Gina. "4 Suspects in the Cold-Case Murder of Wisconsin Priest Father Alfred Kunz." *Journal Sentinel*. March 6, 2019.

Barton, Gina. "8 Things to Know About Our Investigation Into the 1998 Unsolved Murder of Wisconsin Priest Father Alfred Kunz." *Journal Sentinel*. March 15, 2019.

Baxter, Stephen. "After 20 Years, Santa Cruz Murder Victim 'Pogonip Jane' Identified as Pacifica Teen." *The Mercury News*. December 5, 2013.

Bayer, Kurt; Davison, Isaac. "No Compensation for David Bain; $925,000 Ex Gratia Payment." *The New Zealand Herald*. August 2, 2016.

Bayer, Kurt. "DNA Could Crack Open Kirsty Bentley Cold Case 20 Years After Ashburton Schoolgirl's Murder." *The New Zealand Herald*. December 30, 2018.

Bayer, Kurt. "Winz Double Killer Quizzed Over Kirsty Bentley Murder." *NewstalkZB*. May 30, 2018.

Baynes, Chris. "Men Arrested Over 1988 Murder of Teenage German Backpacker in Northern Ireland." *The Independent*. May 22, 2018.

Beach, Randall. "Jovin Murder Mystery Continues 20 Years Later." *New Haven Register*. December 2, 2018.

"Bedford Police Working on 1987 Cold Case Murder." *WKYC 3*. March 11, 2016.

Beever, Susie. "Advances in DNA Technology Close Net on Killer of Lindsay Jo Rimer." *Examiner Live*. November 3, 2017.

Bencks, Jarret; Jedra, Christina. "They Still Ask: Who Killed Deanna?" *The Boston Globe*. April 7, 2013.

Bennet, James. "His Life as a Murder Suspect." *The New York Times*. September 12, 1999.

Bennetto, Jason. "Police Say Killing of Devon Teenager Was Planned." *The Independent*. November 18, 1997.

Bennett, Will. "Police Question Ex-Girlfriend of Gun Victim." *The Independent*. December 13, 1994.

Bentley, Jill; Williams, Tony. *Kirsty: Her Mother Writes with Love*. New Zealand: Reed Books, 2001.

Bergman, Brian. "Murder in the Giant Mine." *Maclean's*. January 30, 1995.

Bergmann, Joy. "A Bitter Pill – Someone Killed Seven People by Putting Cyanide in Tylenol Capsules – When James Lewis Was Caught for Writing an Extortion Letter, Prosecutors Appeared To Stop Looking for the Killer – Almost 20 Years Later No One Has Been Convicted of the Murders." *Chicago Reader*. November 2, 2000.

Bernstein, Richard. "All of France is Asking: Who Killed Petit Gregory?" *The New York Times*. July 16, 1985.

Betz, Dean. "Cold Cases: Details on 28 Cold Murder Cases from 1952 to 1999." *Houston Chronicle*. May 30, 2011.

"The 'Beauty in the Bikini' Murder." *The True Crime Enthusiast*. July 18, 2017.

"Billy London Murder Reinvestigated." *AVN*. October 28, 2005.

Bindel, Julie. "The Real-Life Swedish Murder That Inspired Stieg Larsson." *The Daily Telegraph*. November 30, 2010.

Bindel, Julie. "'There Will Be No Peace For Me.'" *The Guardian*. October 10, 2006.

Bingham, Larry. "Nearly Three Years After Teen Girl's Body Found, Officials Nearly Have Her Identity." *The Monitor*. April 28, 1999.

Bircher, Morgan. "UNSOLVED: Wisconsin Cold Case Murder Victim May Have Arizona Ties, Authorities Say." *ABC 15*. May 17, 2018.

Bird, Steve. "Jill Dando Bubbly Excited and In Love Then She Was Shot on Doorstep." *The Times*. August 2, 2008.

Blaser, Aaron. "35-Year-Old Murder Case Has Possible Ties to Rockport and Aransas Pass." *KZTV10 CBS*. November 3, 2015.

Bleakley, Caroline. "Police Release Image of Jane Doe Found in 1980." *Las Vegas Now*. October 5, 2015.

"Body Found in SE Houston Field Confirmed to be Jessica Cain." *ABC 13*. May 20, 2016.

Boggan, Steve. "Hitman Theory After Oxford Lecturer Shot." *The Independent*. December 12, 1994.

Bohr, Nick. "New Image Released of Jane Doe Found in Racine in 1999." *WISN 12 News*. December 12, 2012.

Bolger, Timothy. "Unidentified Murder Victim Dubbed 'Peaches' Linked to Gilgo Beach Killings." *Long Island Press*. December 13, 2016.

"'Bolney Torso' Riddle Still Baffles police." *The Argus*. August 11, 2004.

Boneske, Kevin. "'John Doe' Hearing Held in 17-Year-Old Murder Case." *The Lakeland Times*. May 29, 2007.

Booker, Jarrod. "David Bain Trial: Reasons to Acquit." *The New Zealand Herald*. June 6, 2009.

Boseley, S. "Police Name Woman Murdered on Train." *The Guardian*. March 25, 1988.

"Boy's 1981 Death to be Probed by IPCC." *BBC News*. March 3, 2015.

Brace, Matthew. "Police Find No Motive for Petrol Murder." *The Independent*. December 26, 1994.

Bradley, Donald. "3 Decades On, Who Killed Skidmore Bully Still Secret." *Kansas City Star*. August 29, 2010.

Brant, Abbott. "20 Years Later: I-84 Killing Remains Unsolved." *Poughkeepsie Journal*. February 5, 2017.

Brennan, Charlie. "Boulder Police Chief Updates Jon-Benét Ramsey Case, 20 Years On." *Daily Camera*. September 1, 2016.

Brenzel, Kathryn. "Tests Reveal New Details About Princess Doe Before She Was Murdered." *The Express Times*. September 26, 2012.

Breslow, Josh. "The Redhead Murders." *18 News NBC*. January 24, 2013.

Broadus, Don. "Child's Body Found." *The Mississippi Press*. December 5, 1998.

Broadus, Don. "Officials Search for Missing Mother." *The Mississippi Press*. December 1982.

Broward, Charles. "Suspect in Former Dallas Cowboy's Death Arrested on Jacksonville Rape Charges; Other Ties Surround Suspect." *The Florida Times-Union*. December 16, 2011.

Brown, Raymond. "The Shocking Truth About the Murdered Schoolboy Whose Naked Body Was Left Strangled in a Ditch." *Cambridgeshire Live*. June 24, 2018.

Brunt, Martin. "Ex-Detective Held Over Axe Murder." *Sky News*. 22 April 22, 2008.

Buchanan, Erin. "BPSO Detectives Asking for the Public's Help in Tracking Down Carol Ann Cole's Killer." *3 KTBS News WorldNow*. April 14, 2015.

Buck, Debbie. "Johanna Young: Unsolved Death 1992." *True Crime Diva*. July 1, 2016.

Buck, Debbie. "Rachael Runyan: Still No Justice Almost 33 Years Later." *True Crime Diva*. March 24, 2015.

Buck, Debbie. "The 1991 Murder of Penny Bell." *True Crime Diva*. February 25, 2015.

"'Buckskin Girl' Case: DNA Breakthrough Leads to ID of 1981 Murder Victim." *Crimesider*. April 12, 2018.

"Bungled JonBenét Case Bursts a City's Majesty." *The New York Times*. December 5, 1997.

Burbank, Jeff. "Teen Found Murdered in 1994 is Pacifica Girl." *The Daily Journal*. December 6, 2013.

Burfitt, John. "The Wrong Woman: A Tragic Case of Mistaken Identity and Murder." *Who*. February 25, 2019.

Burger, Beth. "Holmes Beach Horror: 30 Years Later, Murders Still Unsolved." *Bradenton Herald*. August 1, 2010.

Burger, Beth. "Man's Blurry Photos Captured Killer, But Case Still Unsolved." *Bradenton Herald*. September 9, 2010.

Burke, Dana. "Kidnapper Convicted in Texas City Teen's 1986 Disappearance Denied Parole Again." *Chron*. October 3, 2017.

"Bush Seeks Extradition on Murder Suspect." *Amarillo Globe-News*. October 21, 1999.

Button, Victoria. "Police Keep File Open on Karmein." *The Age*. September 13, 1997.

Byers, Christine. "Research Unlocks Some Secrets About Decapitated Girl for St. Louis Detective." *St. Louis Post-Dispatch*. January 21, 2014.

Cambridge, Ellie. "Cold Case Mystery: Who Was Lindsay Jo Rimer, What Do We Know About Her Murder and Who Has Been Arrested?" *The Sun*. April 25, 2017.

Campbell, Duncan. "Police Re-Examine Murder Conviction." *The Guardian*. February 2, 1993.

Campbell, Duncan. "With Barry George Innocent, Who Did Kill Jill Dando?" *The Guardian*. August 1, 2008.

Campbell, Greg. "Bracelet May Hold Key to Hettrick Murder." *Greeley Tribune*. April 29, 2008.

Campbell, Greg. "Tim Masters Case - Discovery Process is 'A Complete and Utter Failure.'" *Fort Collins Now*. November 30, 2007.

"Canadian Cases Of Wrongful Conviction." *CityNews*. January 31, 2007.

"Car Accident in Hesse Turns Out to be Murder." *Teller Report*. July 19, 2018.

Carbonell, Rachel. "A Tragic Case of 'Mistaken Identity.'" *The World Today*. July 26, 2004.

Carloss, Tracy. "Amy Mihaljevic Case Gets National Exposure, Police Get New Leads." *News 5 Cleveland*. February 11, 2019.

Carter, Chelsea J. "In Memoriam: A Youth's Troubled Life, Tragic Death : Society: Thousands of New York's Homeless Teens Live with Violence and Despair. Ali Forney Was One of Them." *Los Angeles Times*. September 5, 1999.

Casale, Steven. "Dead Man's Code: The Mysterious Case of the Ricky McCormick Murder Notes." *The Lineup*. August 31, 2016.

"Case File: 113UFGA." *The Doe Network*. Retrieved May 13, 2019.

"Case File 662UMFL." *The Doe Network*. Retrieved May 13, 2019.

"Case Report - NamUs UP # 9787." *National Missing and Unidentified Persons System*. January 13, 2012.

Cassidy, Luke. "Gardaí Appeal in Raonaid Case." *The Irish Times*. September 4, 2009.

Catalanello, Rebecca. "Bossier Parish Detectives Order DNA Test in Cold Case Homicide of Young Woman." *The Times-Picayune*. February 18, 2015.

Catalanello, Rebecca. "Detectives Turn to New Bethany Home for Girls in Search of Leads in Woman's 1981 Death." *The Times-Picayune*. February 9, 2015.

Catalanello, Rebecca. "Homicide Detectives Refocus on the Man Who Found Body of 'Bossier Doe' 34 Years Ago." *The Times-Picayune*. March 27, 2015.

Catalano, Antony. "Brutal Abductor Breeds Fear with Cruelty." *The Age*. May 4, 1991.

"Catching Her Killer: Justice for Jane Doe - Part .2" *WKBT TV*. May 2, 2012.

Chan, Melissa. "JonBenet Ramsey: What to Know About the Beauty Queen's Murder 20 Years Later." *Time*. September 12, 2016.

"Charge Laid in 1981 Murder." *PG Public Library / PG Citizen*. February 6, 1988.

"Children and Baroness Ex-Wife Charged in Slaying of Recluse." *AP*. January 8, 1988.

Chiquillo, Julieta. "Blood, Fingernail Found at Home of Texas Man Link Him to 1988 Slayings of 2 Teens, Authorities Say." *Dallas News*. June 2017.

Chodak, Adam. "Masters Walks Free After 9 Years in Prison." *KUSA-TV*. January 22, 2008.

Choe, Jonathan. "Family Renews Calls for Tips in Unsolved 1993 Murder of 10-Year-Old Girl." *NBC Boston*. October 21, 2018.

Christensen, Aoife Ryan. "State 'Trying to Buy Silence' of Kerry Babies Case Victim Joanne Hayes." *Evoke.ie*. January 27, 2019.

Christensen, Sheila. "Inmate May Be a Suspect in '82 Slaying of Sunset Girl." *Deseret News*. October 14, 1989.

Christodoulou, Holly. "Cole Case Arrest: Police Arrest 68-Year-Old Man on Suspicion of Killing Schoolgirl Lindsay Jo Rimer 23 Years Ago." *The Sun*. April 25, 2017.

Chua-Eoan, Howard. "Crimes of the Century: The Murder of JonBenet Ramsey, 1996." *Time*. March 1, 2007.

Churchill, Laura. "The Dog Walker Stabbed Ten Times, Battered Around Head and Strangled to Death in Woods." *Bristol Live*. July 28, 2018.

"Clerk's Body Found in Field After Robbery." *The Orlando Sentinel*. September 21, 1989.

Clark, Amy. "Mr Cruel Tormented Melbourne for a Decade. 31 Years On, We Still Don't Know Who He Is." *Mama Mia*. April 14, 2019.

Clarke, Allan. "Turning Up the Heat on Cold Cases." *Medium*. December 11, 2017.

Clausen, Victoria. "Kirsty's Killer 'Familiar with the Area'; Inquiry Head Rules Out Early Resolution." *The Press*. January 23, 1999.

Cohen, Sharon. "'Ringmasters' Unlock Truth, Free Man Who Confessed to Murder." *Los Angeles Times*. March 31, 1996.

"Cold Case Files: A Former Dallas Cowboy Murdered." *D Magazine*. January 2016.

"Cold Case: Richard Aderson." *Unsolved Mysteries*. January 12, 2018.

"Cold Cases: Christine Jessop, Queensville, Ont. (1984)." *CBC Digital Archives*. Retrieved April 15, 2019.

"Cold Cases In Flagstaff & Coconino County." *Coconino County Sheriff Department*. Retrieved April 2, 2019.

Coles, Jonathan. "Brutal Murder of Weston-super-Mare Woman Helen Fleet Remains Unsolved Ahead of 32-Year Anniversary." *Somerset Live*. March 25, 2019.

Connaughton, Maddison. "Twenty-Five Years On, Here's Everything We Know About the Murder of Karmein Chan." *Vice*. April 13, 2016.

Connor, Neil. "After 13 Years in Jail, Chance of Appeal." *Birmingham Post*. April 21, 2001.

Conroy, J Oliver. "Tim Miller Can Find Almost Anyone. Can he Find His Daughter's Killer?" *The Guardian*. June 12, 2018.

Cook, Caroline. "Brave Mum Dies Without Finding Murdered Son Mark Tildesley." *Reading Post*. January 21, 2011.

Cook, Russell. "Officers Receive Tip Off Into Unsolved Murder of 82-Year-Old Doris Shelley at Her Home in Martlesham." *East Anglian Daily Times*. March 25, 2018.

Cooley, Patrick. "Bedford Police Reopen 1987 Cold-Case Murder." *Cleveland.com*. July 7, 2015.

Cooper, Glenda. "The Boy Who Was Left Out in the Cold." *The Independent*. January 10, 1997.

Corke, Jonathan. "Paedophile Sidney Cooke's Potential Links to Murder of Boy, 8, Ignored by Police." *Daily Mirror*. May 30, 2015.

Corona, Marcello. "Investigator Closer to Solving Keddie Murders." *Reno Gazette Journal*. April 13, 2016.

"Coroner: Kirsty Bentley Killed by Massive Blow to Head." *The New Zealand Herald*. July 16, 2016.

Corrigan, Naomi. "Ann Heron's Daughter Speaks, 20 Years On." *Teesside Live*. August 3, 2010.

Cramer, Maria. "New Lead in '93 Killing of Holly Piirainen, 10." *Boston Globe*. January 3, 2012.

Crimesider Staff. "Suspected Serial Killer Charged in 1997 Murders of 2 Texas Girls." *CBS News*. September 2, 2016.

Cromelin, Richard. "Singer-Poet Henry Rollins Fuels His Art With Rage." *Los Angeles Times*. April 2, 1992.

"Crown to Appeal Morin's Acquittal." *Ottawa Citizen*. March 6, 1986.

"'Crucial' Evidence to 1990 Oxfordshire Murder." *BBC News*. June 14, 2010.

Cullen, Phillip. "$100,000 Reward to Killer's Accomplices." *The Herald Sun*. September 17, 2001.

Culley, Jeremy. "30 Years On and Still No Justice for Murdered Leigh Schoolgirl Lisa Hession." *The Bolton News*. December 4, 2014.

Cullinane, Jonothan; Sturgeon, Kevin. "Did David Bain Do It? The Case For and Against." *Noted*. March 21, 2018.

"The Curious Case of the Alcàsser Girls." *Sword and Scale*. September 25, 2016.

Curry-Reyes, Traciy. "Reyna Marroquin, Howard Elkins: 'Grave Secrets'–Drum Barrel Murder Of Missing Pregnant Immigrant From El Salvador Found Mummified In Jericho, New York Home On ID." *TV Crime Sky*. November 13, 2017.

Curtis, Genevieve. "Investigators Still Searching for Identity of Teenager Murdered in Dona Ana County in 1985." *KFOX14*. May 10, 2017.

Curtis, Henry Pierson. "1 Man, 2 Differing Impressions - He's Suspect in Up To 15 Deaths." *The Orlando Sentinel*. March 20, 1994.

Cusack, Jim. "Did a Jealous Love Rival Kill Raonaid?" *Independent.ie*. July 24, 2019.

Cusack, Jim. "Raonaid's Friends Grieve for Promise Brutally Terminated." *The Irish Times*. September 8, 1999.

Dalrymple, James. "Murder Agony Haunts the Village of the Stars." *Sunday Times*. June 16, 1991.

Dalton, Anita. "The Strange Case of Tristan Bruebach and Manfred Seel." *Odd Things Considered*. February 8, 2017.

"Dana Bradley's Murder Investigation 'Active' After 25 Years: Police." *CBC News*. December 14, 2006.

"Dane County Detectives Continue To Investigate Priest's Killing." *WISC-TV*. March 5, 2008.

"Daniel Morgan Murder Case 'Corruption Link' with Lawrence Investigation." *BBC Wales*. March 7, 2014.

"David Bain Found Not Guilty." *3 News NZ*. June 5, 2009.

"David Bain Moving On With Life." *Newshub*. March 5, 2012.

"David Bain: Retired Judge to Head Compensation Claim." *The New Zealand Herald*. March 20, 2015.

"David Somerton Maintains Innocence in Dana Bradley Murder." *VOCM News*. May 27, 2016.

Davies, Nick. "Murder Among Children." *Options*. December 1, 1993.

Davis, Kristina. "Crowe Case Back in Courtroom." *San Diego Union Tribune*. October 25, 2013.

"Daughter's Killer Terrorizes Parents." *Statesman Journal*. August 20, 1984.

"Deadly Encounter, A Brutal Murder, Still Unsolved." *CBS News*. September 14, 1998.

"Dead Woman May Be Linked to 5-State Redhead Murders." *Observer-Reporter*. April 26, 1985.

Dean, Eddie. "The Murder Victim Next Door." *Washington City Paper*. July 30, 1999.

"Deanna Cremin Cold Case: Search for Killer Continues in Massachusetts Teen's 1995 Murder." *CBS News*. March 30, 2015.

"Debbie Linsley Murder: Reward Offer Over 1988 Train Death." *BBC News*. March 21, 2013.

"Debbie Linsley's Last Train Ride." *Considering Cold Cases*. September 14, 2017.

"Deborah Deann Poe." *The Charley Project*. October 7, 2015.

De Courcy, Anne. "I Never Realised I Was Number One Suspect in My Wife's Murder." *Evening Standard*. February 18, 1992.

DeForge, Jeanette. "25th Anniversary of Holly Piirainen's Killing Brings Call for Information." *MassLive*. August 2, 2018.

De Graaf, Peter. "België Smacht Naar de Waarheid Over X1; Gruwelijke Getuoigenissen." *De Volkskrant*. January 28, 1998.

DeLong, William. "The Story of the Unsolved Disappearance Behind the Amber Alert." *ATI*. May 21, 2018.

De Sturler, Alice. "Remembering the Frog Boys." *Defrosting Cold Cases*. March 1, 2017.

"Detectives Search for Leads in Death, Identity of 'Pogonip Jane' 16 Years After Her Body Was Found." *Santa Cruz Sentinel*. January 10, 2010.

De Vaal, Danny; Webb, Sam. "LOST INNOCENT: What Happened to Nikki Allan, When Did the Seven-Year-Old Disappear in Wear Garth and Who Was Arrested for Her Murder?" *The Sun*. October 6, 2017.

Dick, Sandra. "Scotland's Unsolved Murders: The 1990s Saw Deadly Games Played Out on Mean Streets Across the Country." *Scotland Now*. December 27, 2015.

Dissell, Rachel. "Retired FBI Agent Phil Torsney Returns to Tackle Unsolved Murder of Amy Mihaljevic." *The Plain Dealer*. November 4, 2013.

Di Stefano, Giovanni. "Will the 1984 Murder of Janice Weston Ever Be Resolved?" *OPC Global News & Media*. July 4, 2017.

Donelan, Jennifer. "Potomac River Rapist; 17 Years Later, Where the FBI Stands." *ABC 7 WJLA*. July 30, 2015.

Donnelly, Brian. "I Miss My Son Every Day, Says Mother of Murdered Scientist." *The Herald*. December 11, 2014.

Donnelly, Brian. "Reward of £20,000 as Mother Renews Plea Over Gun Murder of Gifted Scots Scientist." *The Herald*. December 10, 2014.

Dower, Erin. "Cremin Family Still Seeks Justice for Slain Daughter." *Somerville Journal*. March 29, 2006.

"DNA Evidence Quashes Murder Conviction." *Police News*. June 29, 2003.

"DNA Holds Key to 1988 Murder." *BBC News*. September 13, 2002.

"DNA in Doubt: New Analysis Challenges DA's Exoneration of Ramseys." *Daily Camera*. October 27, 2016.

"DNA May Lead to Killer." *North Wales Live*. April 20, 2013.

"DNA Profile Created in Body Probe." *BBC News*. March 14, 2012.

"DNA Techniques Could Finally Solve Mystery of Chester Massage Parlour Killer." *Cheshire Live*. July 23, 2013.

Dodd, Vikram; Laville, Sandra. "Scotland Yard Admits Daniel Morgan's Killers Shielded by Corruption." *The Guardian*. March 11, 2011.

Doerschner, Kristen. "Investigation Into Killing of Sarah Boehm Continues After 24 Years." *The Times*. July 16, 2018.

Donaghue, Erin. "25 Years Later, Push Continues to ID 'Valentine Doe.'" *CBS News*. February 12, 2016.

Donaghue, Erin. "Yale Murder Mystery: Witnesses Sought in 1998 Killing of Student." *CBS News*. December 4, 2014.

"Doris Shelley: 'Interesting' Lead in Martlesham 1993 Murder Case." *BBC News*. March 25, 2018.

"Doris Shelley Murder - 25th Anniversary Appeal." *Suffolk Constabulary*. February 9, 2018.

Doughty, Sophie. "Nikki Allan Murder: Northumbria Police Confirms Probe Latest One Year On From Arrest Breakthrough." *Chronicle Live*. April 17, 2019.

Downey, KC. "New Hampshire Unsolved Case File: Road Rage Killing of Richard Aderson." *WMUR 9*. June 21, 2018.

Drummond, Michael. "Why the 'Bolney Torso' Killing is Still Unsolved 27 Years Later." *West Sussex County Times*. October 19, 2018.

Duggan, Paul. "Digital Blitz Launched Against '90s D.C. Area Serial Rapist." *Washington Post*. December 15, 2011.

Duncanson, John; Pron, Nick. "Elusive Killers Leave Cold Trail for Police." *Toronto Star*. April 2, 1992.

Dupont, Gilbert. "Katrien De Cuyper a été Exhumée." *La Dernière Heure*. September 21, 2006.

Eady, Kera. "DPS Needs Help in San Angelo Double Murder." *CBS7*. February 8, 2016.

Eccles, Peter R. "New Wave Musician Killed; Family Creates Harvard Fund." *The Harvard Crimson*. March 18, 1983.

Edwards, Anna. "Could She Finally Be Named? Police Confident They Can Identify Jane Doe Murdered 14 Years Ago Using New Technology." *Mail Online*. October 17, 2013.

Edwards, Peter. "Christine Jessop Killing: 10 Things That Were Learned from the Case." *The Star*. October 2, 2014.

Eeckhaut, Mark; Neyt, Geert; Verhaeghe, Tonny. "Verdachte Gaf Katrien Laatste Lift." *Het Nieuwsblad*. August 11, 2006.

Elbow, Stephen. "To Catch a Cold." *The Capital Times*. September 1, 2009.

Elworthy, John. "Was Rikki Neave the Victim of a 'Bulger-Style' Killer? That's What His Mum, Acquitted of His Murder, Wants to Know." *Wisbech Standard*. October 27, 2014.

Evans, Heidi. "Remains Confirm Family's Fears." *Los Angeles Times*. August 17, 1984.

Evans, Peter. "TV Crime Watch Gets Results." *The Times*. June 15, 1985.

"Ex-Cop Links Yorkshire Ripper to Unsolved Moors Murder." *The Press*. November 25, 2013.

"Experts Dissect JonBenet Ramsey Ransom Note." *ABC News*. September 27, 1998.

Failla, Zak. "Homicide of Former School Administrator in Fishkill Remains a Mystery." *Southwest Dutchess Daily Voice*. February 10, 2017.

Farberov, Snejana. "Police Release New Sketch of Mysterious 'Cheerleader in the Trunk' 30 Years After Grisly Murder." *The Daily Mail*. June 4, 2012.

Farrell, Jenn. "Single Wound Killed Hettrick, Jury Told." *The Coloradoan*. March 20, 1999.

Fasol, Tara. "Brutal Jefferson County Murder Still Goes Unsolved." *The Southern Illinoisan*. January 12, 2008.

"Father of Julie Ward Relives the Discovery of Her Body Parts." *The Times*. April 26, 2004.

"Father Wants DNA in 1988 Murder Case." *BBC News*. September 6, 2018.

Fausto, Alma. "Who Was the Teenager Found Dead in Anaheim in 1987?" *The Orange County Register*. August 31, 2017.

"FBI Can't Crack the Code in This Murder Case — Can You?" *MSNBC*. March 30, 2011.

"Federal Judge Gives Tankleff, Suffolk Time to Settle Suit." *New York Newsday*. October 30, 2017.

"Feds Convinced Lewis Was Tylenol Killer." *WCVB-TV*. February 12, 2009.

Ferguson, Zoe. "Where Is John Mark Karr, The Man Who Falsely Confessed to JonBenet Ramsey's Murder, & What Is He Doing Now?" *Bustle*. March 26, 2015.

Field, Annemarie. "Ex-Detective Links Eastbourne Disappearances to Serial Killer." *Eastbourne Herald*. April 11, 2018.

Fifis, Fran. "Law Enforcement To Review Tylenol Murders." *CNN*. February 5, 2009.

Figueroa, Teri. "New Book Tells Tale of Crowe Case." *San Diego Union Tribune*. August 14, 2006.

Fiorina, Steve. "Retrial Jury Finds Richard Tuite Not Guilty in 1998 Slaying of Stephanie Crowe." *KGTV San Diego*. December 6, 2013.

Fischer, Courtney. "Man Seen at Jessica Cain Body Search Site Linked to Young Girls' Disappearances." *ABC 13*. February 26, 2016.

"Five States Join Probe of 'Redhead Murders.'" *Gadsden Times*. April 25, 1985.

Fletcher, Dan. "A Brief History of the Tylenol Poisonings." TIME. February 9, 2009.

Fogle, Asher. "Police Vow to Finally Solve Amber Hagerman's Murder, 20 Years Later." *Good Housekeeping*. January 13, 2016.

"Four Years After Killing of Priest, New Clues Few." *Milwaukee Journal Sentinel*. March 5, 2002.

Fox, Kara. "A Baby's Murder Opened a Dark Chapter in Ireland That Still Hasn't Been Closed." *CNN*. Retrieved April 11, 2019.

Foyen, Lars. "Baby's Testimony Convicts Doctors of Murder." *The Glasgow Herald*. March 9, 1988.

Foy, Ken. "Raonaid Prime Suspect - Garda Chief Reveals Who He Believes Killed Schoolgirl." *Herald.ie*. October 18, 2011.

Francis, Enjoli. "JonBenet Ramsey's Brother Breaks Silence 20 Years After Her Murder." *ABC News*. September 12, 2016.

Frank, Josh and Buckholtz, Charlie. *In Heaven Everything Is Fine: The Unsolved Life of Peter Ivers and the Lost History of New Wave Theatre*. Soft Skull, 2010.

"Fresh Appeal in Masseuse Murder." *North Wales Live*. April 20, 2013.

"Fresh Appeal to Solve 1994 Murder of Michael Meenaghan." *Heart*. December 10, 2014.

"Fresh Plea Over Barmaid's Murder." *BBC News*. November 22, 2007.

"Fresh Probe Into Kenya Murder Urged." *Metro*. December 6, 2006.

"The Frog Boys of South Korea." *Criminally Intrigued*. January 6, 2019.

Frost, Bill. "Convicted Paedophile Jailed for Raping and Killing Boy of 7." *The Times*. October 23, 1992.

Fuoco, Michael A. "Unsolved Killing of Beaver County Teen Still Haunts Detective." *Pittsburgh Post-Gazette*. November 1, 2014.

Galleck, Peggy. "Cleveland Heights Police Make New Push to Solve Two Murders from 1982." *Fox 8 Cleveland*. October 27, 2016.

Gallucci, Jaclyn. "Identifying Princess Doe: 30 Years After She Was Slain, New Technology May ID Her and The Killer." *Long Island Press*. August 2, 2012.

Gallucci, Jaclyn. "Long Island's Unidentified Murder Victims." *Long Island Press*. July 1, 2010.

Gallucci, Jaclyn. "Two Ocean Parkway Remains Still Await Identification." *Long Island Press*. May 11, 2011.

Gardner, Andy. "'Dogwalk Slayer' on the Loose: One Man Behind 'Cold Case' Murders, Says Ex-Cop." *Daily Star*. August 16, 2015.

Gardner, Bill. "Father Claims Scotland Yard Covered Up Son's Murder by Westminster Paedophiles." *The Telegraph*. November 18, 2014.

Garrison, Chad. "The Case That Haunts." *Riverfront Times*. December 1, 2004.

Gauen, Pat. "Baby Girl Born During Attack Was Murdered." *St. Louis Post-Dispatch*. November 22, 1987.

Gauen, Pat. "Gruesome Illinois Mystery Appears to End with Texas Execution." *St. Louis Post-Dispatch*. April 10, 2014.

Gauen, Pat. "Slaying of Family Remains Baffling, Horrific." *St. Louis Post-Dispatch*. November 16, 1997.

Gay, Edward. "David Bain Could Not Explain 111 'They're All Dead' Call, Court Told." *The New Zealand Herald*. March 17, 2009.

George, Justin. "Years After Murder, Hope Dims and Stigma Remains." *The Baltimore Sun*. October 10, 2014.

Germano, Beth. "Murder Of Holly Piirainen Remains Unsolved 25 Years Later." *CBS Boston*. August 3, 2018.

Gieseke, Winston. "Some Of Hollywood's Most Notorious Gay Murders Remain Unsolved." *Queerty*. November 28, 2014.

Gilchrist, Aaron. "Serial Rapists Killed Joyce Chiang: John Walsh." *NBC 4 Washington*. May 13, 2011.

Gilligan, Matt. "How Many Did He Kill? The Mystery of Convicted Killer Mark Riebe." *CrimeFeed*. July 17, 2018.

Gillis, Timothy. "Princess Doe Murder Case Revived with Fresh Leads." *The Portland Sun*. September 27, 2012.

Gleeson, Michael. *The Jaidyn Leskie Murder*. Australia: HarperCollins Publishers (Australia) Pty Ltd., 2007.

Glista, Kelly. "Texas Homicide Victim Identified As Missing New London Girl." *Hartford Currant*. January 10, 2014.

Goldfarb, Kara. "The Story of Ken McElroy -- The Vicious Bully Killed By His Town." *All That's Interesting*. June 11, 2018.

Goldfarb, Kara. "They Said She Was Eaten By Lions — But The Real Story Of Her Disappearance Is More Grim." *ATI*. July 11, 2018.

"Goldman Friend is Slain Resisting Robbery." *Deseret News*. September 12, 1995.

Gonzalez, David. "An American's Death Bares Guatemalan Blunders." *The New York Times*. June 18, 2002.

Gonzolez, Vicki. "Jane 'Arroyo Grande' Doe." *NBC 3 News*. August 16, 2015.

Goodwin, Phil. "Brother of Brutally Murdered Schoolgirl Kate Bushell Breaks His Silence to Help Catch Savage Killer." *Devon Live*. December 1, 2017.

Goudie, Chuck; Tressel, Christine. "Jaclyn Dowaliby Cold Case Reexamined 28 Years Later." *ABC Eyewitness News*. May 14, 2016.

Gouk, Annie. "Sister of Murdered Girl Makes Appeal 21 Years After Disappearance." *The Guardian*. April 12, 2016.

Green, Sue. "Mr. Cruel May Have Inside Information." *South China Morning Post*. April 14, 1993.

Green, Yantis. "30th Anniversary of the Unsolved Murders of Shane and Sally Remembered." *San Angelo Live*. July 4, 2018.

Green, Yantis. "Double Homicide Suspect in Cold Case Appointed an Attorney Wednesday." *San Angelo Live*. August 31, 2017.

Gregory, Peter; Baker, Richard; Arup, Tom. "DNA Blunder Sinks Kill Trial." *The Sydney Morning Herald*. August 6, 2008.

"Gregory Villemin: Three Held in 1984 French Child Murder Mystery." *BBC News*. June 14, 2017.

Grey, Orrin. "The Chilling, Unsolved Dardeen Family Murders." *The Lineup*. September 4, 2018.

Grierson, Jamie. "Man Arrested Over 1994 Murder of Rikki Neave." *The Guardian*. April 19, 2016.

Grimaldi, Jeremy. "Ontario Cold Case: Christine Jessop's Tale One of Tragedy, Little Redemption." *YorkRegion.com*. April 29, 2018.

Grimaldi, Jeremy. "Ontario Cold Case:Private Investigators Still Working on 'Solvable' Christine Jessop Murder." *YorkRegion.com*. June 19, 2018.

Gritt, Emma. "Murderer in the Family? An Unsolved Murder That Saw a Man Wrongly Jailed for 15 Years for Killing His Parents and Three Siblings is Now a Gripping New Podcast." *The Sun*. August 1, 2017.

Grollmus, Denise. "In 1983, a Young Girl Was Assaulted and Decapitated. Police Still Don't Know Who She Is." *True Crime Report*. November 4, 2009.

"The Gruesome End of Korea's 'Frog Boys.'" *Real Clear History*. March 26, 2018.

Gutierrez, Hector. "Juror Had Doubts But Believes Panel Was Right to Convict." *Rocky Mountain News*. January 23, 2008.

Haag, Den. "Klein, Willem." *Huygens ING*. November 12, 2013.

Haag, Matthew. "University Park Police May Have Break in 1993 Killing of Ex-Dallas Cowboy Colin Ridgway." *Dallas News*. December 2011.

Hall, Sarah. "Victims of a Serial Killer?" *The Guardian*. April 14, 2002.

Hall, Simon. "Kate Bushell 1997 Murder Case in Doubt After Forensic Errors." *BBC News*. August 30, 2014.

Handelman, Ben. "Racine Jane Doe Investigation Continues With New Leads." *Fox News*. October 25, 2013.

Hanneman, Joseph M. "Dead Suspect Cleared in Fr. Kunz 1998 Homicide." *The Catholic World Report*. March 5, 2019.

Harris, Brian. "A Decade Later, Guatemala and U.S. Dismiss a Missouri Reporter's Death Unsolved Murder." *St. Louis Post-Dispatch*. December 23, 2009.

Harrison, David. "Jaguar Murder: Bearded Man Sought." *The Observer*. June 16, 1991.

Harrison, George. "30 Year Mystery: Pregnant Marie Wilks Broke Down on a Motorway, Left the Kids in the Car to Phone for Help and was Murdered – So Who DID Kill Her?" *The Sun*. September 17, 2018.

Hayes, Christal. "Body Found 27 Years Ago was Transgender Woman, Authorities Say." *The Orlando Sentinel*. November 15, 2015.

Hayes, Christal. "Rarely Used Test Could Help ID Transgender Woman in 30-Year-Old Lake County Cold Case." *The Orlando Sentinel*. July 9, 2017.

Hayes, Joanne. *My Story*. Brandon Books, 1985.

"Headless 'Bolney Torso' Body Exhumed." *West Sussex County Times*. March 26, 2009.

Hearn, Dan. "New Evidence in 20-Year Taxi Driver Murder Mystery." *Oxford Mail*. June 14, 2010.

Heath, Sally. "Agony and Hope of the Waiting Family." *The Age*. April 11, 1992.

"Helen Fleet Murder Appeal Yields New Suspect Names." *BBC News*. April 4, 2017.

"Help Us Catch Lynne's Brutal Killer." *The Standard*. June 22, 2012.

Hendricks, Larry. "Cold Case Close-Up – File: Valentine Sally." *Arizona Daily Sun*. August 28, 2013.

Henley, Jon. "The Murder of Little Grégory: Unsolved Case That Haunted France May Soon Yield Secrets." *The Guardian*. August 28, 2017.

Herbert, Ian. "Murderer Questioned About Sex Attacks." *The Independent*. October 23, 2002.

Hevesi, Dennis. "Dennis Cole, 'Felony Squad' Actor, Is Dead at 69." *The New York Times*. November 23, 2009.

Hickman, Hayes. "'The Bible Belt Strangler': E. Tenn. Students Draft Serial Killer Profile in Unsolved Cases." *USA Today Network*. May 14, 2018.

Hickman, Hayes. "Cold Case: Redhead Murders Among Alarming Trend of Unsolved Highway Homicides." *Knoxville News Sentinel*. October 26, 2018.

Hicks, Tim. "'Nude in the Nettles' - Was It Sutcliffe?" *North Yorks Enquirer*. April 20, 2018.

Higgins, Jessie. "Police Hunt for Possible Serial Killer in 1980s 'Redhead Murders.'" *UPI*. October 9, 2018.

"Highway of Vanishing Women." *Daily Beast*. July 10, 2011.

Hoare, Callum. "Jill Dando Murder: What Woman Who Found BBC Star's Body Noticed That She'll NEVER Forget." *Express*. April 3, 2019.

Hockridge, Stephanie. "Brenda Gerow Update: 'Jane Doe' Identified After 34 Years of Mystery." *ABC 15*. September 29, 2015.

Holden, Wendy. "Mystery of Murdered Wife's Appointment." *Daily Telegraph*. June 10, 1991.

Holgate, Ben; Daley, Paul. "Mr Cruel Executed Karmein: Police." *The Sunday Age*. Aril 12, 1992.

Hollandsworth, Skip. "Is Robert Abel Getting Away With Murder?" *Texas Monthly*. October 1999.

"Holly Piirainen: New Details Emerge in 19-Year-Old Murder Case." *Fox 25 Boston*. November 19, 2012.

"Holly Piirainen Remembered 25 Years After Murder." *The Lake 940*. October 21, 2018.

"Hope for New Leads in Fife Murder." *The Herald*. September 22, 1998.

Horrock, Nicholas M. "Missing INS Lawyer Case Called Homicide." *UPI*. July 28, 2001.

Horsnell, Michael. "Freed Child Abuser Linked to Paedophile 'Catweazle.'" *The Times*. November 30, 1994.

Horswell, Cindy. "Detectives Hope 'Killing Fields' Film Help Solve 60 Murders." *Houston Chronicle*. October 20, 2011.

Houghton, Kimberly. "Missing Nashua Woman Identified as Arizona Cold-Case Murder Victim." *Union Leader*. September 30, 2015.

Houlihan, Liam. "Jaidyn Leskie's Mother Calls for Law Reform." *Sunday Herald Sun*. March 16, 2008.

"House Fire Victim Was Stabbed." *The Independent*. November 23, 1993.

Huff, Steve. "The Forgotten Redhead Murders: Coincidence or Serial Killer?" *Inside Hook*. January 3, 2018.

Huff, Steve. "Pima County Jane Doe: Her Name Was Brenda Gerow." *True Crime Wire*. September 30, 2015.

Hughes, Mark. "George Not Guilty: So Who Did Kill Jill Dando?" *The Independent*. August 2, 2008.

Hughes, Trevor. "Critical Information Left Out in Masters' Original Trial." *The Coloradoan*. January 3, 2008.

Hunt, Elissa. "The Circus Surrounding the Jaidyn Leskie Murder Trial Remains Etched in Victorians' Memories." *Herald Sun*. April 3, 2013.

"Inga Maria Hauser Murder: Police Get DNA Results." *BBC News*. May 1, 2018.

"Inga Maria Hauser Murder: Suspect Released After Questioning." *BBC News*. February 6, 2019.

Inglis, Tom. *Truth, Power and Lies: Irish Society and the Case of the Kerry Babies*. University College Dublin Press, 2003.

"Investigators Get Clues to a Car Accident Camouflaged Murder." *Teller Report*. July 26, 2018.

Iovannone, Jeffry J. "Justice for Venus Xtravaganza." *Medium*. July 12, 2018.

Irons, Meghan E. "18 Years Later, Still No Answers in Deanna Cremin's Death." *Boston Globe*. March 30, 2013.

Ison, Rebekah. "Colin Ridgway, The Tragic Tale of Australia's First NFL Player." *The Sydney Morning Herald*. October 17, 2014.

"It's Fifteen Years Since Raonaid Murray Was Murdered, Gardaí Issue Fresh Appeal." *TheJournal.ie*. September 4, 2014.

"It's One of Our Worst Unsolved Cases, So Why Have We Forgotten Margaret and Seana Tapp?" *Herald Sun*. April 22, 2018.

"'I Was the Last Person to See Ann Alive.'" The Northern Echo. February 23, 2008.

Jaglois, Jessica. "Identification Provides New Hope in 'Redhead Murders.'" *WKRN*. September 13, 2018.

"Jaidyn Dumped in Dam: Coroner." *The Sydney Morning Herald*. October 4, 2006.

Janisse, Kier-La. "In Heaven Everything is Fine: Murder and Martyrdom in the Lynchverse, from Peter Ivers to Laura Palmer." *Off Screen*. Volume 21, Issues 11-12. December 2017.

Jarrett, Tommy. "The Unsolved Yogurt Shop Murders: True Depths of Human Depravity." *Dark Viral Times*. November 20, 2018.

Jarvis, Robin. "5 Unidentified Murder Victims in South Carolina That Will Chill You To The Bone." *Only In Your State.* September 9, 2017.

Jedra, Christina. "A Look Back: The Case of Deanna Cremin." *Boston.com.* April 7, 2013.

"Jenkins County Jane Doe (1988)." *Unidentified Wiki.* Retrieved May 13, 2019.

"Jessie Earl Death: Parents Want Inquest Verdict Changed." *BBC News.* September 25, 2018.

"Jill Dando Murder: Brother Hopes Case is Solved." *BBC News.* April 1, 2019.

"Johanna Young 1992 Murder: Key to Case 'In Local Area.'" *BBC News.* December 22, 2017.

"Johanna Young 1992 Murder: Mother's Disappointment After Appeal." *BBC News.* February 17, 2018.

"John Doe 1988." *National Center for Missing and Exploited Children.* Retrieved May 13, 2019.

"Johnny Lee Wilson Loses High Court Vote for Trial; Supporters Vow Renewed Fight." *The Springfield News-Leader.* July 24, 1991.

Johnson, Bianca Cain. "Mystery Still Surrounds 1986 Aiken County Slaying of Jackie Council." *The Augusta Chronicle.* October 11, 2015.

Johnson, Bianca Cain. "Woman's Slaying in 1992 Thought To Be By Serial Killer." *The Augusta Chronicle.* August 21, 2016.

Johnson, Kirk; Frosch, Dan. "Colorado Hearings Re-examine '87 Murder Case." *The New York Times.* December 27, 2007.

Johnson, Krista. "Friends and Family Celebrate Birthday of Homicide Victim, Sally McNelly." *Go San Angelo.* March 26, 2018.

Johnson, Matt. "Authorities Seek Help in Grisly 1984 Murder in Vernon County." *Wisconsin State Journal*. May 5, 2012.

Johnson, Matt. "New Forensic Drawing Released of Vernon County's 1984 Jane Doe." *La Crosse Tribune*. December 16, 2015.

"JonBenet: DNA Rules Out Parents." *CBS News*. December 16, 2004.

"JonBenét Ramsey's Parents Cleared." *ABC News*. July 10, 2008.

Jones, David. "Second Bradford Man Arrested Over Lindsay Jo Rimer Murder." B*radford Telegraph and Argus*. April 25, 2017.

"Joseph Doucé Profile." *LGBTQ Religious Archives Network*. March 2007.

"Joyce Chiang 1999 Murder Mystery May Be Solved." *ABC 7 WJLA*. May 12, 2011.

"Judy Smith's Final Destination: A Bizarre Murder Mystery." *Strange Company*. January 28, 2019.

"Julie Ward: Father Wants DNA in 1988 Murder Case." *BBC News*. September 6, 2018.

Jüttner, Julia. "Kommissar Fey und das Rätsel vom Liederbach-Tunnel." *Spiegel Online*. March 24, 2018.

Kachor, Kate. "A Sister's Heartbreak Over the Unsolved Murder of Her Twin." *9 News*. October 31, 2016.

Kappal, Bhanuj. "Who Killed the 'Elvis of Punjab'?" *LiveMint*. May 27, 2018.

"Karen Hales Murder: 1993 Killing 'Deprived Baby of Grandmother.'" *BBC News*. November 21, 2018.

"Karen Hales Murder - 25th Anniversary Appeal Update." *Suffolk Constabulary*. December 18, 2018.

"Karen Hales Murder: 'Fresh Information' on 1993 Killing." *BBC News*. December 18, 2018.

Karmin, Hannah. "New Leads in a Cold Case." *Yale Alumni Magazine*. September / October 2008.

"Kate Bushell's 1997 Murder Remains Unsolved." *BBC News*. March 29, 2018.

Kava, Brad. ""Two Decade Old 'Pogonip Jane' Cold Case Solved by Santa Cruz Police." *Santa Cruz Patch*. December 4, 2013.

Kay, Lindell. "Police Investigate Killer's Possible Connection to Cold Case." *Jacksonville Daily News*. December 17, 2012.

Kay, Lindell. "Skeleton Remains Unidentified." *Jacksonville Daily News*. December 17, 2012.

Keeling, Neal. "In 1984 a Schoolgirl was Murdered, After 35 Years a Journalist it's the Case that Still Haunts Me." *Manchester Evening News*. November 26, 2017.

Keeling, Neal. "Lisa Hession was Murdered 30 Years Ago - Now One Town is Being Asked to Help Solve the Case." *Manchester Evening News*. February 24, 2018.

Keller, David. "The Keddie Murders: 20 Years Have Passed Since Four Lives Were Taken in a Brutal Slaying." *Westwood Pine Press*. April 25, 2001.

Keller, David H. "Multiple Murder Suspect Used to Manage Chester Airport." *Lassen County Times*. March 21, 1996.

Kelley, Laura. "Who Killed Venus? The Unsolved Murder of Venus Xtravaganza." *Rebel Circus*. August 18, 2017.

Kendall, Ben. "Rikki Neave Cold Case: Man Arrested Over Death of Schoolboy in 1994." *The Independent*. April 19, 2016.

"Ken McElroy Murderer, Rapist and Consummate Intimidator." *Trutv.com*. July 10, 1981.

Kennedy, J. Michael. "Hope Dims for a Quiet Woman Who Vanished." *Los Angeles Times*. June 14, 1980.

Kennedy, Maev. "Police Reinvestigate Julie Ward Murder in Kenya." *The Guardian*. April 13, 2010.

"Killer Calls, Mom Says." *The Orlando Sentinel*. August 20, 1984.

"Kim (10) and Ken (8) Remembered 25 Years After Their Disappearance." *VRT NWS*. January 5, 2019.

Kimble, Mark. "Jane Doe: 21 Years Here in a Grave Marked UNK." *Tucson Citizen*. April 11, 2002.

"Kingfish Boat Ramp Murders." *Manatee County Crime Stoppers*. August 1, 1980.

Kirby, Terry. "The Strange Case of Baroness de Stempel: How the Death of an Eccentric Architect Revealed a Web of Murder, Fraud and Intrigue." *The Independent*. August 4, 2007.

"Kirsty Bentley Killing: Russell John Tully Linked to Murder." *Newshub*. March 15, 2017.

Knight, Athelia. "Senate Aide Beaten to Death In His Northeast Apartment." *Washington Post*. June 2, 1981.

Knight, Jerry. "Tylenol's Maker Shows How to Respond to Crisis." *The Washington Post*. October 11, 1982.

Knox, Patrick. "COLD CASE: When Did Jessie Earl Disappear, Was Her Death Linked to Serial Killer Peter Tobin and What Has Mark Williams-Thomas Found?" *The Sun*. April 19, 2018.

Kole, William J. "Holland Discovery: Internet Child Porn Ring Brings Painful Fallout." *Kitsap Sun*. July 30, 1998.

Kolker, Ken. "Missing for 34 Years, But Not a 'Missing Person.'" *WoodTV 8*. April 24, 2015.

Koubaridis, Andrew. "Child Abducting Murderer Mr Cruel Could Still 'Be Alive.'" *News.com.au*. April 13, 2016.

Koubaridis, Andrew. "David Bain, Who Was Jailed Then Acquitted of the Murder of His Family, is Coming to Live in Australia." *News.com.au*. May 29, 2017.

Koubaridis, Andrew. "Murder of Teenager Kirsty Bentley Has Haunted New Zealand for 17 Years." *The Advertiser*. January 4, 2016.

Krause, Kevin. "Body Is Identified, Linked To West Boca." *Sun Sentinel*. September 30, 1999.

Krause, Kevin. "DNA Links Suicide to Killing." *Sun Sentinel*. January 22, 2000.

Kretschmer, Anna. "Who Killed Jill Dando? Shock Theory BBC Presenter Was Assassinated by IRA." *Express*. March 30, 2019.

Kreytak, Steven. "Still No DNA Match in Yogurt Shop Case." *Austin American-Statesman*. September 18, 2008.

Krueger, Paul. "Deputy Sickened by Michael Crowe's Interrogation." *NBC 7 San Diego*. April 27, 2012.

Krupski, Alli. "Police Cast Wide Net in Ramsey Investigation." *Daily Camera*. October 24, 1997.

Labbé-DeBose, Theola. "D.C. Police to Make Announcement in Cold-Case Death of Joyce Chiang." *The Washington Post*. May 12, 2011.

Lambert, Bruce. "Man's Appeal in Killings of Parents Takes a Twist." *The New York Times*. August 4, 2004.

Lambert, Bruce; Vitello, Paul; Schweber, Nate. "The Names Stay Linked: 'Bagel King' and Tankleff." *The New York Times*. January 20, 2008.

Larkin, Brent. "Still on the Hunt for Amy's Killer." *The Plain Dealer*. June 24, 2007.

Larson, Amy. "'Pogonip Jane' Murder Mystery Solved by Santa Cruz Police." *KSBW 8*. December 5, 2013.

Laville, Sandra. "'Sutton Bank Body' Exhumed as Part of Cold Cases Review." *The Guardian*. January 4, 2013.

Laville, Sandra; Halliday, Josh. "Paedophile Ring Allegations: Police are Failing Us, Murdered Boy's Father Says." *The Guardian*. November 19, 2014.

Le, Pauleen. "Catching Her Killer: New Possible Lead in Jane Doe Case." *News 8000*. May 3, 2013.

"Leskie Inquest Media Driven, Says Lawyer." *The Age*. September 6, 2005.

Leung, Rebecca. "The Confession: Brother Confesses to Girl's Murder. But Did He Do It?" *CBS News*. October 14, 2004.

Lewis, Frank. "Missing." *My City Paper*. July 17-24, 1997.

Lindwasser, Anna. "The Mysterious Case of Penny Doe, The Murder Victim Who Is Still Unidentified." *Ranker*. 2019.

Little, Jane Braxton. "New Evidence Revives Plumas County Quadruple Murder Case." *The Sacramento Bee*. May 7, 2016.

Lee, John. "Joanne Hayes May Take State to Court as Family Have Yet to Agree to Deal Over Kerry Babies Case." *Extra.ie*. February 3, 2019.

Lee, Miyoung. "BC's Infamous 'Highway of Tears.'" *CBC Digital Archives*. November 17, 2009.

Lee, Rick. "Cold Cases: Update on the Judy Smith Unsolved Murder." *York Daily Record*. September 14, 2016.

"Lindsay Rimer Death: New DNA Leads in 1994 Murder Case." *BBC News*. April 12, 2016.

"Lindsay Rimer Death: Second Man Arrested by Police." *BBC News*. April 25, 2017.

"Lindsay Rimer Death: Sister Speaks on Murder Anniversary." *BBC News*. April 9, 2015.

Lohr, David. "How Police Failures May Have Allowed A Cocaine Cowboy's Suspected Killer To Strike Again." *Huffington Post*. February 15, 2017.

Loncich, Julie. "Family of Murdered Teen Hopes New Cold Case Unit Will Provide Answers." *WCBV 5*. March 25, 2019.

Long, Calvin. "Cold Case of Eileen Jones Turns 29 Years Old." *WCJB 20 Gainesville*. January 13, 2019.

Longworth, R.C. "King Arthur, Sex, Murder Make for an Unusual Case." *Chicago Tribune*. August 3, 1989.

Lopez, Tony. "35 Years Later, New Clues May Solve Keddie Murder Mystery." *CBS Sacramento*. May 2, 2016.

Loreno, Darcie. "'End is Near': Authorities Send Message to 'Person of Interest' in 1987 Cold Case Murder." *Fox 8 Cleveland*. March 11, 2016.

Lotan, Gal Tziperman. "Murder of 12-Year-Old Lake County Girl Remains Unsolved 35 Years Later." *The Orlando Sentinel*. September 26, 2015.

Loy, Wesley. "Unsolved Slaying Still Haunts Town." *The Orlando Sentinel*. April 8, 1990.

Lucia. "Unresolved: The Redhead Murders, The Bible Belt Strangler, and the Inexact Art of Identifying Serial Murder." *The Ghost in My Machine*. August 27, 2018.

Lusher, Adam; Alderson, Andrew; Sawer, Patrick; Perry, Andrea. "In Margate, the Hunt to Ease a 27-Year Pain." *The Telegraph*. November 18, 2007.

Lusher, Adam. "Who Killed Jill Dando? The Main Theories Behind Murder of British TV's Golden Girl." *The Independent*. April 26, 2019.

"Lyn Bryant 1998 Murder Appeal Gets 100 Calls to Police." *BBC News*. October 17, 2018.

Lynne, Freddie. "The Thirty-Five-Year-Old Murder Case of Janice Weston Found Beside the A1 Has Been Reopened." *Cambridgeshire Live*. September 11, 2018.

Macey-Dare, Rupert. "True Crime - Guilty or Not Guilty - David Bain." *SSRN*. July 25, 2012.

Machelor, Patty. "Kalhauser Makes Deal for 20-Year Sentence." *Tucson Citizen*. March 11, 1999.

Machi, Sara. "Louisiana Woman Says Her Father Killed Bossier Doe Carol Ann Cole." *KTBS 3 WorldNow*. March 27, 2015.

MacGuill, Dan. "Gregory: The Smiling Boy Whose Murder Haunts France 33 Years On." *The Local*. July 12, 2017.

MacKinnon, Ian. "Murder Beside Motorway Struck Fear Into Women: Freed Man Tells Family 'To Go Back to the Police for Truth.'" *The Independent*. May 14, 1994.

MacLean, Harry N. *In Broad Daylight*. NY: Harper & Row, 1988.

Madden, Mike. "Joyce Chiang Murder Solved?" *NBC 4 Washington*. May 12, 2011.

Malkovich, Becky. "Interview with a Murderer." *The Southern Illinoisan*. May 16, 2010.

Malone, Kyle. "Monday Mystery - Disappearance of Judy Smith." *You're Listening Now*. August 18, 2014.

Maloney, Alison. "WHO KILLED JILL? Who Killed Jill Dando? Six Sinister Theories on Her Murder 20 Years Ago – From Serbian Mafia Bosses to a Paedo Ring." *The Sun*. April 25, 2019.

Maloney, J. J. "Caller Claims He Killed OC Woman." *Orange County Register*. June 13, 1980.

Maloney, J. J.; O'Connor, J. Patrick. "The Murder of Jon-Benét Ramsey." *Crimemagazine.com*. May 7, 1999.

"Man, 28, Charged in City Murder." *The Prince George Citizen*. February 10, 1986.

"Man Arrested Over Girl's 1991 Murder." *Expatica.com*. August 11, 2006.

"Man Held Over 1992 Johanna Murder." *The Northern Echo*. April 24, 2014.

"Marie Wilks Murder: Wrongly Convicted Eddie Browning Dies." *BBC News*. May 17, 2018.

Markel, Howard. "How the Tylenol Murders of 1982 Changed the Way We Consume Medication." *PBS NewsHour*. September 29, 2014.

Marlowe, Lara. "'L'affaire Grégory' Mystery May Have Reached its Dénouement." *The Irish Times*. June 16, 2017.

Martel, Frédéric. *The Pink and the Black: Homosexuals in France Since 1968*. Stanford University Press, 1999.

Martin, Claire; Simpson, Kevin. "Experts Incredulous Over JonBenét Confession." *DenverPost.com*. August 17, 2006.

Martinez, Edecio. "FBI Seeks Public's Help Cracking Cryptic Notes in 1999 Murder Victim's Pocket." *Crimesider*. March 30, 2011.

Martin, Florian. "26 Years After Her Disappearance, Relatives of Shelley Sikes Still Fighting to Keep Kidnappers Locked Up." *Chron*. February 8, 2012.

Martin-Hidalgo, Margarita. "One-Time Suspect in Tina Janose Murder Case Is Still Full of Hate." *The Ledger*. October 31, 2003.

"Martin Tankleff Awarded $10 Million Settlement in Suffolk." *New York Newsday*. April 19, 2018.

Martin, Yvonne. "I'm a Suspect, Says Kirsty's Big Brother." *The Dominion*. January 16, 1999.

"Martlesham: How the Reclusive Doris Shelley was Found Cowering in Corner by Her Concerned Neighbour." *Ipswich Star*. February 11, 2013.

Matt, Guillermo. "Henderson Slaying Victim Still Unidentified 35 Years Later." *Fox 5 Vegas*. October 5, 2015.

Matthews, Chris. "Lyn Bryant Murder Reconstruction Re-Released as Part of 20th Anniversary Campaign to Catch Killer." *Cornwall Live*. October 15, 2018.

Matthews, Natalie. "With New Imagery, Orange County Officials Hope Someone Will Recognize John, Jane Doe." *WRAL.com*. July 10, 2018.

May, Gerry. "Investigators Had Bossier Doe's Name When Mystery Began in 1981." *3 KTBS News WorldNow*. March 18, 2015.

Mazzolini, Chris. "Man Serving Time for Killing New Hanover Woman Indicted on Murder Charges in Tenn." *Star News Online*. August 7, 2009.

McCabe, Scott. "Police Now Say '99 Chiang Suicide Was a Homicide." *Washington Examiner*. May 12, 2011.

McCafferty, Nell. *A Woman to Blame: The Kerry Babies Case*. Cork: Attic Press, 2010.

McCaffrey, Mick. "Cold Case Unit Chases New Lead in Killing of Raonaid Murray." *Sunday Tribune*. December 14, 2008.

McCracken, Heather. "New Leads in Bentley Murder Case." *The New Zealand Herald*. April 11, 2010.

McDaniel, Matt. "Sheriff's Office Announces Developments in 26-Year-Old Double Homicide." *San Angelo Live*. July 2, 2014.

McDonell-Parry, Amelia. "3 Big Ways 'The Case of: JonBenét Ramsey' Got It Wrong." *Rolling Stone*. September 20, 2016.

McDonell-Parry, Amelia. "Pedophile Confesses to Killing JonBenet Ramsey in Letters to Friend." *Rolling Stone.* January 11, 2019.

McFadden, Robert. "Suicide Adds to Mystery Of Corpse Found in Barrel." *The New York Times.* September 13, 1999.

McKinley Jr, James C. "New Evidence Opens Old Wound in 1991 Slaying of 4 Girls." *The New York Times.* July 1, 2009.

McLaughlin, Eliott C. "DNA Points to New Killer in '99 Case." *CNN.* January 18, 2008.

McLaughlin, Tom. "Could There Have Been Two Serial Killers?" *NWF Daily News.* February 14, 2018.

McLeod, Ramon G. "Remains Are Identified; Mom Missing Since '80." *Orange County Register.* August 16, 1984.

McMahon, James. "The Inside Story of Britain's Most Notorious Cold Case Murder." *Vice.* November 15, 2018.

McMahon, James. "The Unsolved Murder of Jill Dando, Britain's 90s TV Sweetheart." *Vice.* April 26, 2019.

McNeish, James. *Mask of Sanity.* Auckland, NZ: David Ling Publishing. 1997.

McPadden, Mike. "Who Killed Jaclyn Dowaliby?" *The Lineup.* October 10, 2017.

McQuiston, John T. "Body in Barrel Is Believed to Be Woman Who Vanished in '69." *The New York Times.* September 14, 1999.

McRoberts, Flynn. "13-Year Vigil Of Fear Eases In Illinois Town." *Chicago Tribune.* March 13, 2000.

McSherry Breslin, Meg. "Reports Sought In Jonbenet's Sister's Death." *Chicago Tribune.* February 21, 1997.

McVeigh, Karen. "New Kenyan Government May Reopen Julie Ward Murder Case." *The Scotsman.* January 3, 2003.

McVeigh, Tracy. "Cinderella Case 'Killer' Could Be Freed." *The Guardian*. October 21, 2001.

Meagher, John. "Close to Home: The Long Hunt for Raonaid's Mystery Killer." *Independent.ie*. February 23, 2019.

Meeks, Ashley. "Dona Ana County Investigators Hope Sketch Helps Identify Victim." *Albuquerque Journal*. December 12, 2011.

Melanson, Alana. "Police Seek Woman's ID in Cold-Case Probe." *Lowell Sun*. December 6, 2014.

Merrifield, Ryan. "Marie Wilks Murder: 'Further Forensic Work Did Not Reveal Additional Evidence' Say Police." *Worcester News*. February 19, 2018.

Merti, Steve. "Missing B.C. Woman's Body Found." *Brandon Sun*. January 28, 1995.

Mervosh, Sarah; Ballor, Claire. "Portrait of a Serial Killer: He Went Undiscovered for 19 Years -- Then Led Authorities to the Bodies. Now, One Big Question Remains: Why?" *The Dallas Morning News*. May 3, 2016.

"Metropolitan Police Faces £4 Million Lawsuit Over How It Handled Daniel Morgan Murder Inquiry." *Croydon Advertiser*. October 20, 2014.

Meyer, Ed. "DNA Identifies 1994 Homicide Victim - Remains of Pennsylvania Girl, 14, Found in Portage." *Akron Beacon Journal*. June 4, 2003.

Michael, Neil. "DNA of One Tragic Woman's Family Could Hold the Key to the Kerry Babies Mystery." *Extra.ie*. March 1, 2019.

"Michelle Garvey Identified As Teen Found Slain In '82." *Huffington Post*. January 11, 2014.

Midgley, Dominic. "Will Jill Dando's Killer Be Named at Last?" *Express*. February 9, 2017.

Millard, Kevin. "Who Is 'Jane Doe'?" *WXOW 19 ABC*. May 3, 2012.

Miller, Vanessa. "Boulder Police Take Back Ramsey Case." *Colorado Daily*. February 2, 2009.

Milmo, Cahal. "Napper Questioned on Unsolved Murders." *The Independent*. December 20, 2008.

"Missing Mark: Police are Baffled." *Wokingham Times*. June 14, 1984.

"Missing Persons Ignored." *JoongAng Daily*. September 28, 2002.

Mitchell, Corey. *Murdered Innocents*. Pinnacle, 2016.

Moffeit, Miles. "Masters Sees Conviction Vacated, Awaits Retrial Hearing." *The Denver Post*. January 23, 2008.

"Mom of Slain Girl Found Dead in Vegas." *Post-Tribune*. October 2, 2001.

Monahan, Lisa; Stein, Deanne. "A Pattern of Killing by Suspected Serial Killer William Reece." *News 9*. October 19, 2018.

Moonan, Niall. "Thug Protecting Raonaid Murray's Killer Told to Hand Them Over to Gardai." *Irish Mirror*. September 4, 2015.

Mooney, John. "Raonaid Murray's Killer 'May Be a Woman.'" *The Times*. July 19, 2009.

Moore, Evan. "Prostitutes' Grim Lives End Violently on Highway." *Houston Chronicle*. March 21, 2004.

Moor, Keith. "A Cruel Time on Manhunt." *Herald Sun*. April 2, 2001.

Moor, Keith. "Babysitter Greg Domaszewicz Still Denies Guilt, But Says Jaidyn Leskie Would Be 18 Now Had He Not Left Him At Home Alone." *Herald Sun*. April 11, 2014.

Moor, Keith. "Mr Cruel: Unsolved Child Abduction and Murder Case." *The Courier Mail*. May 4, 2016.

Moor, Keith. "Sex Tape Clue in Double Murder of Margaret and Seana Tapp in Cold Case Files." *Herald Sun*. October 3, 2014.

Moran, Greg. "Stephanie Crowe's Parents Say DA Candidate Stephan 'Using My Dead Daughter to Promote Her Political Ambitions.'" *San Diego Union-Tribune*. June 16, 2017.

"More Testimony Expected in Yogurt Shop Murder Trial." *Lubbock Avalanche-Journal*. May 11, 2001.

Moriarty, Erin. "'The Killing Fields': Disappearance of Texas Girl Still Haunts 48 Hours Reporter." *CBS News*. July 5, 2012.

Morkis, Stefan. "Breakthrough Claimed in Sandy Drummond Murder Case." *The Courier*. June 24, 2016.

Morris, Steven. "Police Hope New DNA Evidence Can Solve 1998 Cornwall Murder." *The Guardian*. October 15, 2018.

Moura, Erica. "New Clue Found in Unsolved 1995 Slaying of Deanna Cremin." *The Boston Herald*. November 18, 2018.

Moylan, Tom. "Is 'Princess Doe' Really Diane Dye? Body Discovered In N.J. May Be Calif. Runaway." *The Morning Call*. January 31, 1985.

Mueller, Aaron. "Louisiana Police Credit Facebook in Helping ID Victim in 1981 Homicide as Carol Ann Cole, of Kalamazoo." *MLive*. March 6, 2015.

Muir, Hugh; Campbell, Duncan. "DNA May Solve Killing That Shamed Met." *The Guardian*. November 20, 2006.

Mullin, John. "Things Like This Don't Happen Here." *The Guardian*. April 3, 1993.

"Murdered Girl's Body Found." *Daytona Beach Morning Journal*. April 19, 1980.

"Murder in the Suburbs: Who Killed Karen Hale?" *Mysterious Murders*. December 12, 2015.

"Murder Mystery Could a Pair of Dunlop Volleys Lead to the Killer." *Herald Sun*. August 10, 2014.

"Murder of April Dawn Lacy." *Count Every Mystery*. September 19, 2018.

Murillo, Lupita. "New Technology Helping in '81 Cold Case." *KVOA News*. NBC. June 25, 2013.

Murtaugh, Peter; Lucey, Anne. "'We Are All Guilty.' Kerry Remembers the Babies Scandal." *The Irish Times*. January 20, 2018.

"My Partner's Murder Changed Me Forever." *East Anglian Daily Times*. February 24, 2010.

"Mysterious 'Dr. No' Sought in Ohio Truck Stop Prostitute Murder." *The Pittsburgh Press*. April 19, 1987.

"Mystery of Lost Child Lingers: Baby Jane Would Be 25." *The Sun Herald*. December 8, 2007.

Nakiska, Tempe. "The Legacy of Venus Xtravaganza." *Dazed*. November 20, 2013.

"Natalie Pearman 1992 Murder: 'Persons of Interest' Ruled Out." *BBC News*. January 28, 2018.

"Natalie Pearman Case: DNA Could Solve 1992 Murder." *BBC News*. November 20, 2012.

"Natalie Pearman Murder: Norfolk Police Renew Appeal." *BBC News*. November 20, 2017.

Naughton, Gareth. "Hope for 'Crisis of Conscience' in Student Murder." *Irish Examiner*. February 12, 2013.

Neff, Lisa. "Kingfish Killings Remain a Mystery." *The Islander*. July 29, 2009.

Nesbitt, Jim. "Serial Killer Likely Preying On Redheads." *The Orlando Sentinel*. April 21, 1985.

"New Appeal in Helen Fleet 1987 Murder Case." *BBC News*. March 28, 2017.

"New Arrests Over 1984 French Child Murder Mystery." *France 24*. June 16, 2017.

"New Clues in Bolney Headless Body Murder Mystery." *West Sussex Gazette*. October 11, 2011.

"New Clues in Headless Man Inquiry." *BBC News*. October 11, 2011.

"New Clues in Police Hunt for 'Mr Cruel.'" *Sydney Morning Herald*. December 14, 2010.

"New DNA Evidence 'Breakthrough' in Dana Bradley Murder Case." *CBC News*. May 27, 2016.

"New DNA Evidence Found in 1998 Lyn Bryant Murder Case." *BBC News*. October 15, 2018.

"New DNA Evidence Uncovered in Unsolved 1981 Murder of Dana Bradley." *The Globe and Mail*. May 26, 2016.

"New Evidence Emerges in Cold Case Disappearance and Murder." *ClickOrlando.com*. December 29, 2012.

"New Evidence in 'Cinderella Murder.'" *BBC News*. 3 July 3, 2003.

"New Evidence Surfaces Regarding Unsolved 1995 Somerville Deanna Cremin Murder Investigation May Have Been Stifled." *The Somerville News Weekly*. November 4, 2017.

"New Forensic Evidence May Help Solve 1993 Holly Piirainen Homicide Case, District Attorney Mark Mastroianni Says." *MassLive*. January 3, 2012.

"New Leads in 10-Year-Old Murder Hunt." *Manchester Evening News*. January 22, 2013.

"New Probe on Driver's 1990 Killing." *Mirror*. June 14, 2010.

"Nikki Allan Investigation: Hunt For Sunderland School Girl Killer Continues." *SR News*. May 3, 2018.

"Nikki Allan Murder: DNA Clue in Girl's 1992 Killing Inquiry." *BBC News*. October 6, 2017.

"Nikki Allan Murder: Man Arrested Over 1992 Death." *BBC News*. February 20, 2014.

Nimmo, Joe. "£20,000 Offered to Finally Solve the Murder of Michael Meenaghan in Oxford 20 Years Ago." *Oxford Mail*. December 10, 2014.

Noell, Mandy. "Who Murdered 14-Year-Old Sarah Boehm and 17-Year-Old Kathryn Menendez?" *WKBN 27*. November 16, 2018.

"No Justice for Dana." *The Telegram*. December 14, 2011.

"No Justice for JonBenet." *Newsweek*. October 24, 1999.

Norman, Michael. "2D Tainted Bottle of Tylenol Found by Investigators." *The New York Times*. February 14, 1986.

Nowlen, Chuck. "The Devil and Father Kunz." *Las Vegas Weekly*. April 12, 2001.

O'Connor, Matt. "Prosecutors Reveal Dowaliby Evidence." *Chicago Tribune*. February 17, 1989.

O'Donnell, Philippa. "New Suspect in Decades Old Mr Cruel investigation." *ABC Radio Melbourne*. December 14, 2010.

"Officials: Slain Priest Had Relationships With Women." *The Telegraph-Herald*. March 3, 2000.

O'Hanlon, Sinead. "The Mystery of Kirsty Bentley." *The Press*. January 9, 1999.

"Ohio Unsolved Homicides: Kathryn Menendez." *Norwalk Reflector*. October 2, 2013.

Olden, Mark. "Justice – But At What Cost?" *The Independent*. August 19, 2003.

Olsen, Lise. "Investigators Hope DNA Provides Answers in 30-Year-Old Murder." *Houston Chronicle*. November 27, 2011.

O'Neil, Helen. "Amateur Sleuths Restore Identity to the Dead." *Seatle Pi*. March 30, 2008.

O'Neill, Marnie. "Boston Nurse Vanished in Philadelphia, Found Dead in North Carolina." *News.com.au*. May 14, 2016.

"One Night of Savagery Triggers Years of Turmoil." *The Springfield News-Leader*. September 9, 1990.

Orrell, Harriet. "Answer to 25-Year Riddle of Schoolgirl Johanna Young's Murder Lies in Her Hometown of Watton, Say Police." *Watton & Swaffham Times*. December 23, 2017.

Orr, James. "Kenya Agrees to Reopen Julie Ward Death Case." *The Guardian*. October 11, 2009.

Oslin, Irv. "Ashland County's Murder Mystery: Author James Renner Explores Killing of Amy Mihaljevic." *Times-Gazette*. February 8, 2007.

Owen, Penny. "Parents Awaiting DNA Tests Before Believing Body is Daughter's." *NewsOK*. April 27, 1999.

"Oxford University Scientist Murder: Police Offer £20k Reward." *BBC News*. December 10, 2014.

Pack, Cynthia. "13-Year-Old Keddie Murders Still Plague Sheriff." *Feather River Bulletin*. September 14, 1994.

"Paedophile Gets Life for Killing Boy, 7, at Orgy: Homosexual Ring Abducted Children and Drugged Them for Group Sex." *The Independent*. October 23, 1992.

"Paedophile in Jail Rape Allegation." *The Herald*. January 7, 2002.

Parascandola, Rocco. "Exclusive: NYPD Takes Fresh Look at '90s Transgender Murders in Harlem." *New York Daily News*. April 6, 2016.

"Pardoned Man Wants 'To Pick Up My Life.'" *St. Louis Post-Dispatch*. September 30, 1995.

Paoletti, Gabe. "The Unsolved Mystery of the Redhead Serial Murders." *ATI*. October 26, 2018.

Parsons, Ben. "32-Year Wait for Answers Over Eastbourne Student's Death." *The Argus*. May 19, 2012.

"Pas de Traces de Ken et Kim." *Le Soir*. January 14, 1994.

"Patsy Ramsey, JonBenet's Mother, Dies." *CNN*. June 24, 2006.

Peebles, Frank. "Three-Generation Wipeout Still Under Investigation." *Prince George Citizen*. February 6, 2011.

Pelisek, Christine. "Washington D.C. Rapist: Why Police Think He Could Be Back." *Daily Beast*. June 12, 2011.

Pelling, Nick. "Ricky McCormick's Mysterious Notes." *Cipher Mysteries*. March 12, 2013.

Perkarsky, Michelle. "Authorities Try to Locate Body of Girl, Killed & Beheaded 30 Years Ago." *Fox4KC*. June 17, 2013.

Peters, Mike. "Donald Long: Is He the Hettrick Murderer?" *Greeley Tribune*. February 29, 2008.

Pflanz, Mike. "'Fresh Evidence' in Julie Ward Murder." *Daily Telegraph*. December 7, 2006.

Phillips, Sandra. "Stephanie Crowe's Brother Cries as He Recalls Her Murder." *Fox 5 San Diego*. November 14, 2013.

Philpin, John. *Shattered Justice: A Savage Murder and the Death of Three Families' Innocence*. Avon Books, 2006.

Pithers, Malcolm. "Uproar After Acquittal in Nikki Allen Murder Case: Not Guilty Verdict Ends Six-Week Trial in Which Judge Refused to Admit Alleged Confession on Interview Tape as Evidence." *The Independent*. November 22, 1993.

"Plea to Free Husband of Dead Solicitor." *The Times*. December 17, 1983.

"Plumas County Sheriff Seeks Pair in Keddie Triple Slaying." *Lassen County Times*. May 27, 1981.

"Police Appeal for Information 30 Years After Woman Stabbed to Death on Train." *Belfast Telegraph*. March 23, 2018.

"Police Appeal for Information in 34-Year-Old Cold Case Murder Investigation." *Global News*. November 10, 2017.

"Police Disband Penny Bell Murder Team." *Daily Telegraph*. July 2, 1992.

"Police Drop Some Potential Suspects in Ramsey Killing." *CNN.com*. January 21, 1997.

"Police Fear Boy is Dead." *The Times*. June 4, 1984.

"Police Find Girl, 6, Dead in Home." *The Denver Post*. December 27, 1996.

"Police Identify 1 Redhead Murder Victim." *Daily News*. June 27, 1985.

"Police Look for Key to Unsolved Murder." *Fife Today*. March 11, 2013.

"Police Officer Deal to Former Bikie Over Murder of Jane Thurgood-Dove." *The Daily Telegraph*. November 4, 2012.

"Police Plea Over Unsolved Murder of Nude in the Nettles." *The Daily Mirror*. August 24, 2011.

"Police Probe East Cleveland Girl's Death." *The Akron Beacon Journal*. December 17, 1982.

"Police Review 1993 Murder of Martlesham's Doris Shelley." *BBC News*. February 9, 2018.

Portlock, Sarah. "Vital Evidence in Murder Case." *Coventry Evening Telegraph*. May 24, 2002.

"Possible Break in Case of Federal Attorney Found Dead in Potomac River in 1999." *Fox News*. January 26, 2011.

"Potomac River Rapist Cold Case." *FBI*. December 15, 2011.

Potter, Tom. "Ipswich Mum's Brutal Death Has Haunted Family and Detectives for Last 25 Years." *East Anglian Daily Times*. November 21, 2018.

Powell, Laura; Brown, Mick; Gatenby, Alex. "Art Student Jessie Earl Disappeared 38 Years Ago... Has the Mystery of Her Murder Finally Been Solved?" *The Telegraph*. September 21, 2018.

Powers, Kathleen. "Family Still Seeks Justice, 13 Years After Deanna Cremin's Murder." *Somerville Journal*. March 26, 2008.

Probert, Sarah. "Police Follow Up New Leads in Hunt for 1994 Killers of Tracey Mertens." *Business Live*. May 30, 2013.

Pryce, Mike. "Could DNA Advances Finally Bring Justice for Worcester Mum Who Was Murdered on the Motorway?" *Worcester News*. February 19, 2018.

"Punk Rock Band's Road Crew Member Slain." *Los Angeles Times*. December 20, 1991.

"Purse from Unsolved Murder of Donna Awcock Returned to Family." *CTV News London*. January 11, 2017.

"Rachael Runyan Cold Case." *Criminally Intrigued*. August 4, 2017.

Ramnath, Nandini. "'Mehsampur' Movie (Sort Of) Resurrects Slain Punjabi Singer Amar Singh Chamkila." *Scroll. In*. November 15, 2016.

Rasmussen, Sarah. "Unsolved Mystery: Susan Poupart." *News Watch 12*. November 25, 2010.

Rayner, Jay. "Gone But Not Forgotten." *The Guardian*. February 16, 2003.

"'Redhead Murder' Victim in Campbell County Identified After 33 Years." *Knoxville News Sentinel*. September 6, 2018.

"'Redhead' Murders Probed." *The Galveston Daily News*. April 25, 1985.

Reed, Elizabeth. "Help Solve Akron Cold Case Slaying of Rachael Johnson." *24 News*. February 28, 2013.

Reed, Naomi. "Sandy Drummond Has Scotland Perplexed." *Enormous Crime*. August 9, 2017.

Reed, Sara. "Search for Hettrick's Killer Renewed." *The Coloradoan*. January 20, 2008.

"Remembering Jessica Cain, 20 Years After Her Disappearance." *ABC 13*. August 17, 2017.

"Retarded Man Set Free After 8 Years in Prison." *The New York Times*. October 1, 1995.

"Retired Drugs: Failed Blockbusters, Homicidal Tampering, Fatal Oversights." *Wired.com*. October 1, 2008.

"Reward in Mother Murder Mystery." *BBC News*. 6 September 2005.

"Reward Offered Over Norwich Natalie Pearman 1992 Murder." *BBC News*. December 14, 2011.

Ricapito, Maria. "Cold Case of the Week: The 1998 Murder of Yale Student Suzanne Jovin." *A&E*. April 26, 2017.

"Riddle of the Recluse Who Searched for Camelot But Found Only Death Instead." *Hereford Times*. August 27, 2004.

"Rikki Neave Death: No Charges Over Schoolboy Murder." *BBC News*. June 21, 2018.

"Rikki Neave Death: Portugal Extradition Set for 1994 Murder Suspect." *BBC News*. August 5, 2016.

"Rikki Neave Death: Suspect in 1994 Murder Arrested in Portugal." *BBC News*. August 2, 2016.

"Rikki Neave Murder Case: Man Arrested Over Boy's 1994 Death." *BBC News*. April 19, 2016.

"Rikki Neave: Sensational Trial Hears of Black Magic, Beatings and Drug-Dealing." *Peterborough Telegraph*. November 24, 2004.

Rimer, Geri. "I Don't Know What Happened to My Daughter." *The Guardian*. November 4, 2006.

Rintoul, Stuart. "Riddle of a Sad Little Death." *The Australian*. October 5, 2006.

Roberts, Anna. "New Clues in Bolney Torso Mystery." *The Argus*. October 11, 2011.

Roberts, Lesley. "Parents of Murdered Student Jessie Earl Hope End May Be In Sight After 28 Year Hunt for Her Killer." *Daily Record*. December 7, 2008.

Roberts, Michael. "Peggy Hettrick: New DNA Evidence in Murder That Led to Improper Tim Masters Conviction." *Westword*. September 20, 2010.

Robinson, Grant. "Potential Daughter of Redheaded Jane Doe Visits Town Where Body Was Found." *10 News NBC*. June 26, 2018.

Robinson, Marilyn. "Victim's Brother, 12, Questioned." *DenverPost.com*. May 26, 1997.

Rollins, Henry. "Henry Rollins: Joe Cole and American Gun Violence." *LA Weekly*. April 11, 2013.

Roos, Robin. "Murdered Children and Pedophile Networks in the Low Countries." *Cvlt Nation*. October 1, 2018.

Rose, Corey. "Unsolved: Woman's Identity Still a Mystery Decades After Body Found Near Campsite." *9News.com*. May 8, 2018.

Rosenbaum, Philip. "Teens' Bodies Found 800 Yards Apart in '94." *CNN*. May 17, 2010.

Rosenberg, Tina. "Editorial Observer; Helping Them Make It Through the Night." *The New York Times*. July 12, 1998.

Ross, Hannah. "Her Killer is Still Out There." *The Northern Star*. May 1, 2007.

Rule, Andrew; Silvester, John. "A Mother, Her Daughter and a Murder Case That Got Away from All." *The Age*. June 19, 2010.

Runnels, Jim. "Barefoot Girl Missing; Searchers Scour Area." *Sentinel Star*. April 10, 1980.

Sabato, Nick. "Murder of Susan Poupart Remains Unsolved." *Northwoods River News*. February 4, 2017.

Sabawi, Fares. "East Texas Sheriff Hoping to Identify Dead Woman." *Corpus Christi Caller-Times*. November 3, 2015.

"Sally McNelly & Shane Stewart: Is a Satanic Cult to Blame for the Murder of Two Texas Teens?" *Unsolved.com*. ABC Networks. January 13, 2017.

Saltzman, Jonathan. "Fatal Tampering Case Is Renewed." *Boston Globe*. February 5, 2009.

Sangiacomo, Michael. "Ohio Attorney General Seeks Info on 1991 Akron Murder." *Cleveland.com*. February 28, 2013.

"Santa Cruz 'Pogonip Jane' Cold Case Murder Takes Ironic Twist." *KCBA News*. December 5, 2013.

Santos, Nico. "ASU Group Works to Solve Wis. Cold Case." *ABC News 12 KPNX*. February 26, 2016.

Sauer, Mark. "Michael Crowe Found 'Factually Innocent' In Sister's Murder." *KPBS*. May 22, 2012.

Sauer, Mark; Wilkens, John. "Haunting Questions: The Stephanie Crowe Murder Case. Part 1: The Night She Was Killed." *San Diego Union Tribune*. May 11, 1999.

Sauer, Mark; Wilkens, John. "Haunting Questions: The Stephanie Crowe Murder Case. Part 3: The Knife." *San Diego Union Tribune.* May 13, 1999.

Sauer, Mark; Wilkens, John. "Haunting Questions: The Stephanie Crowe Murder Case. Part 4: More Arrests." *San Diego Union Tribune.* May 14, 1999.

Sauer, Mark; Wilkens, John. "Haunting Questions: The Stephanie Crowe Murder Case. Part 5: In Court." *San Diego Union Tribune.* May 15, 1999.

Sauer, Mark; Wilkens, John. "Haunting Questions: The Stephanie Crowe Murder Case. Part 6: The Bombshell." *San Diego Union Tribune.* May 16, 1999.

Savage, Richard. "Jill Dando's Last TV Show Goes On." *The Mirror.* September 4, 1999.

Schaefer, Heather. "Playing Cards May Solve Vilas Cold Case." *The Northwoods River News.* July 30, 2011.

Schena, Susan C. "Santa Cruz Police Crack 1994 Cold Case, ID Murdered Teen." *Mountain View Patch.* December 5, 2013.

Schiller, Rebecca. "Venus Xtravaganza's Nephew on Her Legacy: 'She Never Envisioned Herself Becoming a Transgender Martyr.'" *Billboard.* June 25, 2018.

Schluter, Kaitlin. "Senate Staffer's Death Remains a Mystery." *Washington Examiner.* March 22, 2010.

Schultz, Rob. "20 Years Later, Murder of Dane Priest Alfred Kunz Still Unsolved." *Wisconsin State Journal.* March 4, 2018.

Schwartz, Larry. "When Life is Murder." *The Sydney Morning Herald.* October 8, 2007.

Sclafani, Tony. "Josh Frank on Peter Ivers, Murder & 'New Wave Theatre.'" *The Washington Post.* September 9, 2008.

Scofield, Drew. "Amy Mihaljevic was Kidnapped in 1989, and Police are Still Searching for Her Killer." *News 5 Cleveland*. February 15, 2019.

"Search for Baby Jane's ID Continues." *The Clarion-Ledger*. December 20, 1982.

Sengupta, Kim. "Mother Draws Line Under Julie Ward's Murder." *The Independent*. September 18, 1999.

Shaffer, Cory. "Amy Mihaljevic Investigation Shifts to Mother's Acquaintances 25 Years Later." *Cleveland.com*. October 27, 2014.

Shapiro, Emily. "Jane Doe Murder Victim Finally Identified 3 Decades Later Thanks to Forensic Technology: Sheriff." *ABC News*. January 17, 2019.

Sharma, Amita; Sauer, Mark. "$7.25 Million Settlement Reached In Stephanie Crowe Murder Case." *KPBS*. October 22, 2011.

Shaw, Danny. "Sailor Awaits Murder Appeal Ruling." *BBC News*. July 2, 2003.

Shaw, Neil. "Murder of Devon Schoolgirl Kate Bushell, 14, Unsolved Despite Fresh Appeal." *Devon Live*. March 29, 2018.

Shaw, Neil. "Unsolved Murder of Exeter Girl Kate Bushell Could Be Linked to Other Cases, Says Retired Detective." *Devon Live*. August 17, 2017.

Sheil, Bill. "Renewed Push to Find Person Who Killed Amy Mihaljevic." *Fox 8 Cleveland*. February 8, 2019.

Shelton, Caitlyn. "1985 Tennessee Homicide Victim Identified as New Hampshire Missing 17-Year-Old." *WZTV*. November 14, 2018.

Sherwood, Sam. "Work and Income Double Murderer Interviewed Over Kirsty Bentley Cold Case." *Stuff.co.nz*. May 30, 2018.

"The Shirley Case: The Night a Club Pick-Up Used Babysitter as a Trick to Run Away." *The Birmingham Post*. July 4, 2003.

Shuttleworth, Kate. "Dunne: Bain Should Be Compensated." *The New Zealand Herald*. December 14, 2012.

Siciliano, Carl. "At Long Last, Progress on Homeless LBGT Youth." *Gay City News*. March 8, 2006.

Sickles, Jason. "Who Killed Amber Hagerman? Murder Case That Inspired Amber Alerts Remains Unsolved 20 Years Later." *Yahoo News*. January 13, 2016.

Silverman, Rosa. "Jill Dando's Brother: What I Think Really Happened to My Sister." *The Telegraph*. April 25, 2019.

Silvester, John. "16-Year Search for Justice for Murdered Mum Jane Thurgood-Dove." *The Age*. November 9, 2013.

Silvester, John. "Hitman's Planned Victim Felt Marked for Death." *The Age*. July 27, 2004.

Silvester, John. "'Mr Cruel' Filmed His Victims, Say Police." *The Age*. April 8, 2006.

Simon, Stephanie. "The Bundy Drive Irregulars : Second Anniversary of Slayings Finds Sleuths Still Sorting Through Evidence." *Los Angeles Times*. June 12, 1996.

"Simpson Team Seeks Access to Police File on Unsolved Slaying in Hollywood." *The Los Angeles Times*. September 1, 1994.

Singh, Arj. "Baroness Nuala O'Loan of Kirkinriola to Take Inquiry into Unsolved Murder of Private Investigator Daniel Morgan." *Western Daily Press*. July 5, 2014.

SisterScythe. "Susan Poupart, Unsolved Lac Du Flambeau Murder." *Justice for Native Women*. December 19, 2015.

Smith, Cameron. "Policeman Cleared of Murder." *The Herald Sun*. October 7, 2003.

Smith, Candace. "Cold Case Murder of Holly Piirainen, 10, Linked to Dead Man." *ABC News*. January 3, 2012.

Smith, Dave. "Holly Piirainen Case: David Pouliot Linked to Death of Missing Girl in 1993." *International Business Times*. January 3, 2012.

Smith, Greg. "Police: Body Found in 1982 in Texas is Missing New London Teen." *The Day*. January 11, 2014.

Smith, Jennifer. "Twenty Years After Her Murder, Somerville Teenager's Loved Ones Hope for New Leads." *Boston Globe*. March 29, 2015.

Smith, Rohan. "Clues Link Serial Killer to Mr Cruel." *The Morning Bulletin*. April 25, 2018.

Smith, Steven B. "Chapter 34 – Wim Klein." *The Great Mental Calculators: The Psychology, Methods, and Lives of Calculating Prodigies, Past and Present*. Columbia University Press, 1983.

Snow, Mary; Moller, David. "Triple Slaying in Keddie." *Feather River Bulletin*. April 15, 1981.

Solin, Jennifer. "JonBenét Ramsey Death: Everything We Know About The 1996 Murder Case." *International Business Times*. September 13, 2016.

"Solving the Unsolved: New Technology Could Tell Who Murdered Eileen Jones." *4 News Gainesville*. May 14, 2014.

"Son Says Father Could Be Mother-Daughter Tapp Killer." *Sky News Australia*. August 18, 2018.

Spencer, Susan. "Missing for 30 Years: Reyna Marroquin Left El Salvador For New York." *CBS News*. March 7, 2000.

Stark, Cody. "Sheriff's Office Reopens 1980 Murder Investigation." *The Item*. November 6, 2015.

"State Asks for Help in Solving 1991 Akron Slaying." *Akron Beacon Journal*. March 1, 2013.

"Statute Runs Out for Unsolved 'Frog Boys' Murder." *Chosun Daily*. March 24, 2006.

Steer, Jen. "21 Unsolved Murders and Disappearances in Northeast Ohio." *Fox 8 Cleveland*. February 17, 2017.

Steer, Jen; Wright, Matt. "FBI Looks for New Evidence in 1994 Unsolved Murders of Two Teen Girls." *Fox 8 Cleveland*. November 9, 2015.

Stephenson, Lauren. "Newswatch 12 Exclusive: Inside the Susan Poupart Cold Case Investigation." *News Watch 12*. May 21, 2014.

Steward, Michael. "Calls Lead to 'Fresh Information' in Unsolved Karen Hales Murder Case." *Ipswich Star*. December 18, 2018.

Stokes, Paul. "Man Held in Hunt for Wife's 1990 Murderer." *The Telegraph*. November 10, 2005.

"Store Clerk Found Dead With Bullet Wound." *Gainesville Sun*. September 21, 1989.

Storie, Marilyn. "Missing Teenager's Body Found." *The Prince George Citizen*. December 13, 1989.

"The Strange Death, and Unbreakable Code, of Ricky McCormick." *True Noir Stories*. September 14, 2016.

Suhr, Jim. "Unsolved 1987 Slaying of Illinois Family Haunting." *Associated Press*. April 12, 2014.

Sullivan, Mike. "Detective Held Over Axe Murder." *The Sun*. April 21, 2008.

Sulzberger, A.G. "Town Mute for 30 Years About a Bully's Killing." *The New York Times*. December 15, 2010.

Sung-Kyu, Kim. "Police Continue Excavation, Find Loaded Shell Near the Site." *Dong-A Ilbo*. September 27, 2002.

Sun-yoon, Hwang. "Bodies of 5 'Frog Boys,' Missing Since 1991, Found On Mountain." *JoongAng Daily*. September 27, 2002.

Sun-yoon, Hwang. "'Frog Boys' Baffle Investigators." *JoongAng Daily*. October 11, 2002.

Sun-yoon, Hwang. "'Frog Boys' Probably Murdered." *JoongAng Daily*. November 13, 2002.

Surmont, Eddy. "Ken et Kim Perdus en Plein Centre d'Anvers." *Le Soir*. January 8, 1994.

Surmont, Eddy. "Les Deux Enfants Anversois Ont Disparu Depuis Six Jours, Ken et Kim Sont-Ils en Fugue? On les Aurait Même vu au Cinéma." *Le Soir*. January 10, 1994.

Surmont, Eddy; Vantroyen, Jean-Claude. "Elle S'Accuse du Meurtre de Katrien de Cuyper: X1 Longuement Interrogée à Anvers." *Le Soir*. January 28, 1998.

"Susan Poupart Cold Case." *News Watch 9*. June 12, 2008.

"Suspect: JonBenét Ramsey's Death 'An Accident.'" *NBCNews.com*. August 17, 2006.

Sutcliffe, Robert. "Watch: Man Tells of Moment He Found Murdered Schoolgirl Lindsay Rimer's Body." *Examiner Live*. November 4, 2016.

Sutyak, Kara. "Cold Case: Information Wanted in Woman's Brutal Murder." *Fox 8 Cleveland*. February 28, 2013.

Swancer, Brent. "A Strange Code and the Baffling Death of Günther Stoll." *Mysterious Universe*. December 21, 2018.

Swaint, Jack. "Who Killed 13-Year-Old Barbara Ann Barnes?" *Who Killed_? Pittsburgh, PA*. Bloomington, IN: Rooftop Publishing, 2007.

Tagharobi, Sherene; Stickney, R. "Michael Crowe Speaks Before Testifying in Richard Tuite Trial." *NBC 7 San Diego*. November 14, 2013.

"Tankleff Case Heads for Trial." *Long Island Business News*. October 30, 2017.

"Taxi Murder: Daughters Still Hope for Justice." *Oxford Mail*. June 14, 2010.

Tench, Megan. "A Mother's Renewed Hope for Justice." *Boston Globe*. March 30, 2005.

Tendler, Stewart. "A1 Murder Victim Identified." *The Times*. September 15, 1983.

Tendler, Stewart. "Detectives Reopen A1 Murder Enquiry." *The Times*. October 29, 1991.

Tendler, Stewart; Ford, Richard. "Killer Paedophile Found Strangled in His Prison Cell." *The Times*. October 9, 1993.

Tendler, Stewart. "Police Seek Motive for Knife Murder of Businesswoman." *The Times*. June 8, 1991.

Tenuta, Marci Laehr. "Authorities Continue Working 12-Year-Old Homicide Case 'That Burns in All of Our Minds.'" *Journal Times*. August 8, 2011.

"The Theories: Why Was Jill Dando Shot Dead?" *The Independent*. August 1, 2008.

"Third City Murder Admitted." *The Prince George Citizen*. March 20, 1989.

Thomas, C. Lynette. "Sarah & Kathy, Linked." *Uncommon Knowledge*. September 7, 2010.

Thomas, Steve; Davis, Donald A. *JonBenet: Inside the Ramsey Murder Investigation*. Macmillan, 2011.

Thompson, Craig. "Mum of Murdered Sunderland Schoolgirl Nikki Allan Warned Over 'Abusive' Facebook Post." *Chronicle Live*. June 26, 2016.

Thompson, Craig. "Nikki Allan Murder: Could a 12-Year-Old Babysitter Hold the Key to Sunderland Schoolgirl's Death?" *Chronicle Live*. March 6, 2016.

Thompson, Emily. "Bitter Creek Betty & Sheridan County Jane Doe." *Morbidology*. July 6, 2018.

Thompson, Emily. "Who Killed Georgia Crews?" *Morbidology*. November 1, 2017.

Thompson, Emily. "Who Killed Penny Bell?" *Morbidology*. January 13, 2019.

Thompson, Sheryl. "Man Charged in Girl's Murder." *The Prince George Citizen*. August 12, 1986.

Thornlow, Brenda. "Deanna Cremin: The Tragic and Unsolved Murder." *Medium*. September 12, 2018.

Tippet, Gary. "Jaidyn Leskie, the Final, Tragic Chapter." *The Age*. June 13, 2002.

Tobin, Bruce. "Karmein Possibly Shot in Panic." *The Age*. April 13, 1992.

Tobin, Bruce. "Police Receive 400 Calls on Kidnap Drawings." *The Age*. January 28, 1993.

Tobin, Bruce. "Rumors Hurting Family, Says Kidnap Girl's Father." *The Age*. May 3, 1991.

Togneri, Chris. "Slain Jane Doe's Curious Case in Ohio Still Puzzles After 35 Years." *TribLIVE.com*. June 4, 2016.

"Tracey Mertens Death: Fresh Appeal Over Cheshire Graveyard Petrol Fire Murder." *BBC News*. December 23, 2016.

Tribunal of Inquiry into the "Kerry Babies" Case (October 1985). Report (PDF). Official publications. Pl.3514. Dublin: Stationery Office. Retrieved April 11, 2019.

"Tristan Brübach." *Unresolved*. March 28, 1998.

Tristan. "The Inokashira Park Dismemberment Incident." *Bizarre and Grotesque*. July 12, 2015.

Tritto, Christopher. "Code Dead: Do the Encrypted Writings of Ricky McCormick Hold the Key to His Mysterious Death?" *Riverfront Times*. June 14, 2012.

"Trucker Not a Suspect in 'Redhead Murders.'" *The Evening Times*. February 6, 1986.

Truelove, Sam. "Family of Bromley Woman Who Was Murdered 30 Years Ago Make Emotional Plea to Catch Her Killer." *Croydon Advertiser*. March 23, 2018.

Truesdell, Jeff. "A Daughter's 35-Year Fight For Justice: Sheila Sharp Longs to Know Who Murdered Her Family in Their Cabin." *People*. November 25, 2016.

"Tuite Found Guilty of Manslaughter." *San Diego Union-Tribune.* May 27, 2004.

Tunkieicz, Jenny. "Investigators Find Ties Between Jane Doe, Illinois Case." *Milwaukee Journal Sentinel.* July 21, 2000.

"TV Show Explores Murder of Lismore's Lois Roberts." *Echo Net Daily.* March 15, 2018.

Tweedie, Neil. "Calling All Codebreakers..." *Daily Telegraph.* April 7, 2011.

"Two Held Over 1988 Murder of German Backpacker Inga Hauser." *The Irish Times.* May 21, 2018.

Tye, Chris. "30 Years Later: New DNA Evidence Surfaces in Amy Mihaljevic Case." *WKYC 3.* February 12, 2019.

"Tylenol Figure Is Convicted." *The New York Times.* January 15, 1984.

Tyler, Jane. "Tracey Mertens Murder: The Christmas Crime That Shocked the Nation." *Birmingham Live.* December 22, 2014.

Udell, Erin. "29 Years Later: The Cold Case That Haunts Fort Collins." *The Coloradoan.* September 8, 2016.

Udell, Erin. "Murder in Fort Collins: Who Was Peggy Hettrick?" *The Coloradoan.* February 11, 2019.

Uittenbogaard, Marthijn. "The Joseph Doucé Murder Case Must Be Reopened." *Marthijn Uittenbogaard.* April 12, 2018.

Ujhelyi, Stephanie. "Alliance Cold Case Murder Victim's Mom Remembers." *The Alliance Review.* August 26, 2009.

"Ungeklärte Mordfälle: Mord an dem 13-jährigen Tristan Brübach." *BKA.de.* November 18, 2006.

"The Unsolved Murder of Janice Weston." *WolfieWiseGuy.* March 25, 2014.

"The Unsolved Murder of Lisa Hession." *WolfieWiseGuy*. December 11, 2014.

"The Unsolved Murder of Lynne Trenholm." *WolfieWiseGuy*. October 20, 2013.

"Unsolved Murder Police Criticised." *BBC News*. February 18, 2008.

"Unsolved Murder: Tracey Mertens, Killed After Being Set on Fire in Eaton." *Manchester Evening News*. January 21, 2013.

"Unsolved: The Murders of Kirsty Bentley and Jennifer Beard." *True Crime Reader*. April 1, 2012.

Vance, Andrea. "Collins Seeks Second Opinion on Bain." *The Press*. December 4, 2012.

'Valentine Jane Doe,' Murdered in Florida Keys, Remains Unidentified 25 Years Later." *True Crime Daily*. February 12, 2016.

Vallieu, Melody. "'Buckskin Girl' Identified." *Troy Daily News*. April 11, 2018.

Van Beynen, Martin. "David Bain's Prison Guard and Close Family Friend Speaks Out on the Murders." *Stuff*. July 23, 2017.

Van Olson, Cora. "Missing, Now Found: Michelle Garvey." *Crime Library*. January 13, 2014.

Vargas, Hermelinda. "Yogurt Shop Murder Conviction Overturned." *News 8 Austin*. May 26, 2006.

Vaughan, Kevin. "Key Questions Linger in Prominent Cold Case: The Killing of Peggy Hettrick." *The Denver Post*. September 21, 2018.

Vaughan, Kevin. "Lawyer: Innocent Man Paid Price for Larimer Prosecutors' Blunders." *CNN*. September 27, 2007.

Vernon, Hayden. "Hunting England's Notorious Murderer the 'Beast of Buckland.'" *Vice*. March 27, 2019.

"Victims Snared at Funfairs." *BBC News*. October 5, 1999.

Voight, Sandye. "Autopsy: Priest Died from Loss of Blood." *The Telegraph-Herald*. March 7, 1998.

Vongsarath, Chris. "Campbell Teachers Captivated by the Tragic Story of 'Cabin 28.'" *The Mercury News*. July 18, 2008.

Wahn, Aleida K. "Who Killed 12 Year Old Stephanie Crowe in The Dark of Night?" *Aleida K. Wahn*. December 13, 2013.

Wainwright, Martin. "Husband Arrested in 1990 Murder Investigation." *The Guardian*. November 10, 2005.

Walford, Jessica. "Murdered as She Rang for Help on a Motorway: The Mystery of Pregnant Marie Wilks' Horrific Death." *Wales Online*. September 23, 2018.

"Walker County Detectives Say They Won't Give Up On 37-Year-Old Murder Mystery." *KBTX-TV*. March 4, 2018.

Walters, Sharon. "Murder at the Mansion." *Shropshire Star*. September 14, 2007.

Waters, Robert A. "DNA Exoneration - Guy Paul Morin." *Kidnapping, Murder and Mayhem*. March 12, 2010.

Webber, Chris. "Ann Heron Murder: 'After All This Pain We Deserve Closure' - Daughter's Appeal in Room Mother was Found Dead." *The Northern Echo*. August 5, 2015.

Webber, Chris. "'I Met the Man Who Claimed to be Ann Heron's Murderer' Says Retired Shopworker." *The Northern Echo*. August 21, 2015.

Webber, Chris. "Peter Heron: 'Police Banged on My Door to Accuse Me of Murder - and My Life was Destroyed Yet Again.'" *The Northern Echo*. August 3, 2015.

Webb, Sam. "Lindsay Rimer Death: 'My Sister Was Murdered When I Was a Baby - There's Always a Void.'" *Mirror*. April 12, 2016.

Weber, David. "Victim Loved to Work with Kids." *The Boston Herald*. March 31, 1995.

Weber, David; Ford, Beverly. "'Everybody Loved Her' Somerville Shocked by Murder of Girl, 17." *The Boston Herald*. March 31, 1995.

"We'll Catch Lenny's Killer." *Oxford Mail*. June 13, 2000.

Wereschagin, Mike. "Mystery of Girl's Death Still Haunts Ohio Town." *Trib Live*. October 2, 2005.

Westerman, Toby. "New Hope in Case of Murdered Priest." *International News Analysis Today*. March 17, 2008.

Wheatstone, Richard; Kendall, Ben. "Rikki Neave Murder: Detectives Release Sketches of Two Boys Spotted Near Scene Where Boy Was Strangled." *Mirror*. November 17, 2015.

"Wheel Clue to Killer of Solicitor." *The Times*. September 17, 1983.

Whelan, Micheal. "The Shaw Creek Killer." *Unresolved*. June 6, 2018.

White, Grace. "Investigations: Who Killed Michelle?" *KHOU*. January 28, 2018.

White, Grace. "Missing Pieces: A Killer's Secret" *KHOU*. November 8, 2017.

White, Stephen. "Police Arrest Man Over Notorious 1992 Murder of Seven-Year-Old Girl Nikki Allan." *Mirror*. February 20, 2014.

"Who Killed Barbara?" *Prinnified.com*. May 13, 2012.

"Who Killed Karen Hales?" *The True Crime Enthusiast*. January 8, 2017.

"Who Killed These Girls? Cold Case: The Yogurt Shop Murders." *Kirkus Reviews*. September 28, 2016.

"Who Murdered Richard Aderson?" *Oh, How Peculiar!* February 19, 2017.

Wilkens, John; Sauer, Mark. "Haunting Questions: The Stephanie Crowe Murder Case. Part 2: The Arrest." *San Diego Union Tribune*. May 12, 1999.

Williams, Arthur. "Missing Since '89." *Prince George Free Press*. April 3, 2008.

Williams, Clarence. "Potomac River Rapist Linked to 1996 Attack in the District." *Washington Post*. June 14, 2012.

Williams, Rebecca. "Kate Bushell Murder: Police Renew Appeal to Find Girl's Killer." *Sky News*. November 6, 2017.

Wilshire, Ron. "Penny Doe Cold Case Makes No Cents." *Explore Clarion*. October 19, 2014.

Wilshire, Ron. "Police Explore Penny Doe Cold Case Connection with Missing Barbara Miller: DNA Could Provide Link." *Explore Clarion*. June 2, 2018.

Wilson, Jamie. "Unsolved: Woman Knifed in Jaguar." *The Guardian*. January 11, 2000.

Winsor, Morgan. "Body of 'Buckskin Girl' Found in Ohio in 1981 Identified as Arkansas Woman." *American Broadcasting Company*. April 12, 2018.

Wittmer, Carrie. "All the Theories About Who Really Killed JonBenét Ramsey." *Business Insider*. May 3, 2017.

"Woman Identified in 23-Year-Old Cold Case in Jacksonville." *WITN*. February 26, 2019.

Woolner, Ann. "FBI Wants Unabomber's DNA for 1982 Tylenol Poisoning Probe." *Bloomberg News*. May 19, 2011.

"Working to Bring Their Killers to Justice at Last." *Oxford Mail*. September 4, 2014.

Wu, June Q. "D.C. Police Renew Efforts to Find Man Who Killed Christine Mirzayan in 1998." *The Washington Post*. July 25, 2011.

Wynne, Kelly. "Inside 'The Alcàsser Murders': True Story Behind Netflix True Crime Series." *Newsweek*. June 13, 2019.

Yeatman, Dominic. "Murder Arrest After Christmas Killing in 1992." *Metro*. April 24, 2014.

"Yogurt Shop Murder Defendants To Be Released." *KVUE*. June 24, 2009.

Young, Audrey. "Bain Innocent and Deserves Payout, Judge Tells Cabinet." *The New Zealand Herald*. September 10, 2012.

Young, David. "Inga Maria Hauser: Pair Arrested Over 1988 Murder of German Backpacker." *The Irish News*. May 21, 2018.

Zagria. "Joseph Doucé (1945 – 1990), Pastor, Facilitator." *A Gender Variance Who's Who*. February 11, 2010.

Zouhali-Worrall, Malika. "Tankleff Murder Investigation Ends." *CNN Money*. July 2, 2008.

Index

A

E

I

J

P

R

T

U

Made in the USA
Columbia, SC
08 November 2022

70643815R00265